Microcomputer Handbook

Charles J. Sippl

VNR VAN NOSTRAND REINHOLD COMPANY
NEW YORK   CINCINNATI   ATLANTA   DALLAS   SAN FRANCISCO
LONDON   TORONTO   MELBOURNE

To our seven children—Andy, Brad, Christine, Diane, Chuck, Rog, and Tom—and to their mother, Margaret, who has kept her sanity through their college years and her husband's production of seven books—so far.

The author expresses appreciation to all the manufacturers and suppliers who forwarded photographs and other graphics for use in this book. Definitions are excerpted with permission from the book *Microcomputer Dictionary and Guide*, Matrix Publishers, Inc., Champaign, Illinois, 1976, 704 pp., by Charles J. Sippl and David A. Kidd.

Van Nostrand Reinhold Company Regional Offices:
New York Cincinnati Atlanta Dallas San Francisco

Van Nostrand Reinhold Company International Offices:
London Toronto Melbourne

Copyright © 1977 by Litton Educational Publishing, Inc.

Library of Congress Catalog Card Number: 78-9414
ISBN: 0-442-80324-9

Manufactured in the United States of America

Published by Van Nostrand Reinhold Company
135 West 50th Street, New York, N.Y. 10020

Published simultaneously in Canada by Van Nostrand Reinhold Ltd.

15 14 13 12 11 10 9 8 7 6 5 4 3 2

Library of Congress Cataloging in Publication Data
Sippl, Charles J.
    Microcomputer handbook.

    Includes indexes.
    1. Microcomputer. I. Title.
QA76.5.S554   1978   001.6'4'04   78-9414
ISBN 0-442-80324-9

Microcomputer Handbook

PETROCELLI/CHARTER COMPUTER SCIENCE SERIES

Ned Chapin, Ph.D., General Editor

Computers and Management for Business
DOUGLAS A. COLBERT

Management of Information Technology: Case Studies
ELIZABETH B. ADAMS, editor

Reliable Software Through Composite Design
GLENFORD J. MYERS

Strategic Planning of Management Information Systems
PAUL SIEGEL

Top-Down Structured Programming Techniques
CLEMENT L. McGOWAN and JOHN R. KELLY

Operating Systems Principles
STANLEY KURZBAN, THOMAS S. HEINES, and ANTHONY P. SAYERS

Hospital Computer Systems and Procedures, Vol. 1 Accounting Systems
RAYMON D. GARRETT

Flowcharts
NED CHAPIN

Operating Systems Survey
ANTHONY SAYERS, editor

Logical Design for Computers and Control
K. N. DODD

Flowcharting: An Introductory Text and Workbook
JOHN K. LENHER

Compiler Techniques
BARY W. POLLACK, editor

Documentation Manual
JULIA VAN DUYN

Computer Techniques in Biomedicine and Medicine
ENOCH HAGA, editor

Hospitals—A Systems Approach
RAYMON D. GARRETT

Management of EDP
M. M. WOFSEY

Introduction to Artificial Intelligence
PHILIP C. JACKSON

Information Management Systems: Data Base Primer
VIVIAN C. PROTHERO

CONTENTS

Preface   vii

Introduction   xiii

1. A New World of Microelectronic Control Systems   1

2. Standard Computers: Fundamental Operations and Capabilities   25

3. Minicomputers: Big Competition to Standard Systems   73

4. Microcomputers: Where They Are, What They Are Doing, and What Is Next   123

5. The Available Microsystem Products—Systems and Criteria   175

6. Microcomputer Kits, Development, and Testing Systems   223

7. Microcomputer Software: Why the New Systems Are Easier to Use—ROMs and RAMs   267

8. Microcomputer Applications: Distributed Intelligence in Business, Banks, and Factories   309

9. Microcomputer Applications Continued: Examples of the Wide Ranges of Microcomputer Utilization   355

Appendix A Microcomputer Product Analysis   379

Appendix B Analysis of Design and Testing Tools:
Software Support Systems   417

Definitions Index   435
Subject Index   441

PREFACE

One trade newspaper reported that microcomputers are the "bobby pins" of the future: "They'll be in your car, your office, your shop and your home . . . they'll wake you up, start your car, work your tools and warm the coffee in your office . . . and they'll perform these and hundreds of other functions and duties in the very near future because they're so easy to teach." [1] There is little doubt that the American public is getting used to high digital technology—especially in the form of electronic calculators, microprocessors in ovens, intelligent business machines, small computers, supermarket terminals, bank terminals, and the like. America is already wired with telephones. Soon the majority of these will be ten-key pad "transaction" types. Moreover, CATV lines are practically all being converted to have computer-controlled "front ends" for two-way TV. And the list goes on . . . to microcomputer-controlled "smart" instruments and tools, medical monitoring and testing devices, machine tool automation, traffic light control, optical character recognition, automatic remote banking, environmental control of buildings, process control, conveyor systems, and so on. Thus, for the third time in two decades, the computer industry itself has experienced the beginnings of another revolution, with processing control concepts and practices in markets several magnitudes larger and at costs an order of two magnitudes lower. "Consumer computers," the "computer on a chip," and "pocketfuls of memories" have become very meaningful phrases. Remote contact to distant libraries to permit the display on TV sets of practically any published material, computer-controlled heat pumps

[1] LeRoy H. Anderson, "Microcomputer Technology May Do Everyday Duties," *Comstar Concepts*, Volume 1, Number 2, Fall 1974, p. 1.

used with solar-energy converters for comfort control in temperate and sub-tropical climates, housed on roofs and walls—these are not things of the future. They are in the marketing process today, and more are coming.

Trade journals of the computer industry, the components industry, and the communications industry almost shout that the great MPU race is on. New companies are entering the field almost weekly, staking out claims in the media and in the financial community to sudden new technological advances, new systems or manufacturing approaches, and ever-increasing and broader applications. Many experts already maintain that the computer industry's future belongs to microcomputers, strongly attesting to coming LSI densities increasing by a factor of ten, one hundred, or more. And there are few doubters. And as these densities and the consequent greater numbers of functions and powers increase, then one or two LSI chips will be able to emulate or substitute for many of today's medium to large computers.

As fast as microcomputers substitute or take over the low-end minicomputer and its markets, the minis are eroding the domain of the medium- and large-scale systems. Today's standard high-end minicomputers, typically with a 32-bit word and a million bytes (characters) of directly addressable memory, cost far less at the present time than they did ten years ago. It is expected that history will repeat itself and that by 1985 units similar to the largest and most powerful CPUs marketed today will likely be available for $25,000 or less. Medium type computers of today, priced at about $250,000, could easily be equaled in power and versatility in the 1980s for as little as $2,500 in microcomputer form. Thus, at one end of the micro-computer revolution, the "standard" computer industry is using from ten to hundreds of microprocessors in the manufacture of their systems; and, at the other end, microcomputers are beginning to appear in the millions for use in calculators, watches, alarms, television sets, washing machines, dishwashers, refrigerators, automobiles, and innumerable inexpensive business machines.

Thus, the microprocessor/microcomputer "happening" is being hailed as a completely new industry where those who do not get in fast will be left far behind and perhaps totally out. Engineers, especially, cannot afford simply to sit back and watch an expanding parade of MPU products unfold before their eyes. Rockwell, RCA, Texas Instruments, Honeywell, and others have resorted to national television to announce the "speck" size of their powerhouse components. Manufacturers of thousands of products are asking their engineers to explain, "How does this new technology fit into our present and future products?" Practically none of them can afford to ignore the new micros. And at an early point they must make decisions—they can afford neither to ignore the devices nor to plunge in wildly. The pressure to include and feature microprocessors in products increases as each day passes. Mistakes are being made because of the terrible inexperience of most purchasers in this very young, aggressive industry, and standardization is still quite far away, making practically every new product very difficult to assess competitively. Information as to distinct advantages and disadvantages is at a premium, and the educational institutions, as has become quite usual, are far behind the real world. In consequence, "MPU road shows," seminars, conferences, in-house special training programs, and every type of "learning curve" effort are being introduced. These are generally quite down-to-earth, "hands-on" working demonstration efforts that succeed very well. But the phrase "present state of the art" seldom applies because of the exploding characteristics of the technology, the new versatile products, and the thousands of new "buzz" words that have already become part of the lexicon for everyday use.

Microcomputer costs are also difficult to judge, whether at the chip, card, or system level. Factors influencing the cost comparison relate to anticipated sales volume, sensitivity of anticipated sales volume to product development time, product fixed and variable costs, and exterior cost factors that influence total fixed and variable costs such as promotion and distribution. It will be noted that a few technicians in a laboratory can make thousands of tiny chips, which, for a few dollars each, reproduce or replace a roomful of expensive electronic equipment, making possible advances that are stunning, truly creative, but also very easily copied. The novelty of new logic technologies is a most serious consideration—and also a very perplexing one, each of the following requiring specific evaluation: MOS, CMOS, SOS, I^2L, ECL, TTL, and a dozen more.

Microcomputers are indeed "real" computers, the prefix *micro* relating to size and fabrication technique only, not to performance or versatility. The pioneer people in the new industry watched with amazement but understanding as collapsing component and unit prices in the midst of an inflation economy continued unabated. They watched and participated in the development of products so powerfully useful that they were economically marketable even when crudely designed and inefficiently used.

All of the giant semiconductor manufacturers are heavily committed. Tons of literature are being distributed by Texas Instruments, Inc., RCA, National Semiconductor, Intel Corp., Rockwell, Fairchild, Motorola, Signetics, and scores more of the leaders in America, France, Japan, England, West Germany, and a dozen other countries. And the minicomputer manufacturers, too, are now all reaching down and building their own micros. One popular microcomputer, the Intel 8080, is being manufactured by five different competing companies under license—all using the same instruction set and same software. One of the big progress inhibitors of computer proliferation has always been the high cost of software—applications and control programs. With this kind of competition, software is coming down fast; in fact, many of the most common types are totally free. The cost of memory has fallen almost equally as fast as that of microprocessors, often called CPUs (central processing units) or CPEs (central processing elements [slices]). Until 1975 there were approximately 150,000 operating computers in the world. It is expected that within two years ten times that many will be shipped each month and be in full processing and controlling operation by ordinary workers and citizens instead of by the former "super-elite," that is, the big system specialists.

It is estimated that more than 200,000 computer hobbyists now belong to some type of club, group, or formal association. Most are computer owners, and the majority are searching for low-cost terminals and more and more memory. As always, with new technologies, the language is difficult for most. But several dictionaries are now available, and product manuals and texts will soon flood the markets. Special seminars, conferences, conventions, exhibitions can be found all over the United States on any given week, sponsored by manufacturers, distributors, dealers, clubs, and so on. The pace of development, user-acceptance and price decreases has been so fast that no one denies it is a true revolution. Take, for example, the Denver Amateur Computer Society. In five months after a few people got together and after one article appeared in a daily newspaper, the "club" membership zoomed to 200 individuals at $12-a-year membership fees. The Southern California Computer Society, with over 9,000 members, sprang from nowhere, and growth continues unbounded. More than 200 such clubs exist in the United States, with members from all walks of life.

All sorts of new simplified languages are springing up besides the old reliable BASIC. Some of them are based on the sturdy, versatile IBM-developed PL/1. They are called PL/M (Intel Corp.), MPL (Motorola), SMPL (National Semiconductor, Inc.), PL/W, PL/Z, and so on. These languages are easy to learn, and the result of all this is that microprocessors are now spread into homes, into stores, on ships, and the like—all with programmable equipment that is "intelligent" and versatile and that uses very low power in operation. Microprograms are, more or less, general-purpose instructions sets, tailored to specific applications by the combining of these into macroprograms—the sets of instructions that do the entire specific job, often on a plug-in ROM (Read Only Memory) chip or board.

But microcomputers are certainly not causing minicomputers and standard computers to become "endangered species." On the contrary, the micros are becoming primary architectural units of these older standbys. Micros reduce the costs and complexities of standard systems and thereby make them also more popular, more easily utilized, and less expensive. So the computer engineer also is heavily impacted as he designs improvements into larger information-processing systems. It is thus very necessary that students, professionals, and processing-power users of all stripes learn computer capability "from the ground up," as it were. The text thus begins with the unraveling of the basic concepts of a standard computer and quickly moves into the capability ranges of minicomputers. With this background, then, the reader is introduced to microcomputer systems, software, development aids, and applications.

It is necessary that the reader acquaint himself or herself with many new concepts and also the new nomenclature of the devices that have sprung up all around. Most of the chapters thus have a short glossary of term definitions appended to them, which pertain to the subject matter so covered. With this tutorial aid used for "browsing" as well as for reference, much of the "system" explanation will become clearer and easier to master.

To adapt the microprocessor to an application, one must program the microprocessor to achieve all the objectives sought. However, unlike the previous control logic, which was "fixed," a change in objectives does not mean that the microprocessor must be broken down, redesigned, and rewired. The speed, economy, and versatility of changes, adaptable utilization, and expanded capabilities require only an alteration of the program or the addition of some low-cost input-output or memory chips—themselves often programmable. It is in this sense, primarily, that the microprocessor represents a revolution rather than a slowly developing evolution, with the revelation proved by the sudden radical change rather than a slow methodical growth in variety and power. In effect, then, the hardware remains unchanged whereas the control program, usually in ROM, is changed in minutes—and the instrument, appliance, toy, or device becomes "new" or more powerful. This is a most impressive advance in testing, measuring, controlling, interfacing, and so on, in electrical, automotive, business, computer, communication, and hundreds of other endeavors and enterprises.

Some officials believe that within the next five years inexpensive microprocessor-based terminals (like the ones millions of clerks, bankers, managers, and production and communication people are using) will be sold over the counter in retail stores, much as the pocket calculators are marketed today. And, indeed, reports of several hundred "computer stores" around the country attest to the popularity of microcomputers among hobbyists. Moreover, the trek of the small businessman, the professionals, and others to these stores for terminals and microprocessor devices of hundreds of types is not far off. Already, voice input commands to microprocessors are very popular; and if Stanford Research Institute can modify a standard Unimate industrial robot to be trained for a specific task by following verbal instructions, surely some of the ingenious computer hobbyists will build them in many varieties and for hundreds of other projects—and the low price alone will create a market for these and other "strange" but very pragmatic devices and automatically controlled contraptions. The magazine *Popular Mechanics* is filled practically monthly with gadgets that prove that "the home computer is here."

Charles J. Sippl

INTRODUCTION

THE "BIGGER IS BETTER" MYTH

Practically from the beginning, it seems, computer people held fast to the concept that the bigger the computer, the better. The more power it had and the more jobs it was able to process, the better it was for the developer, manufacturer, and owner. The example is given that no sooner did the United States develop a computer-controlled, radar-aimed antiaircraft gun than the power leaders with the money control wanted computer-controlled, multiple, individually recontrollable reentry vehicles with hydrogen-bomb warheads. And the multinational corporations acted similarly. After automation of payroll and inventory control, they immediately ordered data-processing systems capable of automatically developing and controlling complete financial models and follow-on operations.

Now, with the convenience of hindsight, it is easy to establish these "bigger is better" concepts as based on a logic that is clearly discernible as faulty. Nevertheless, these strivings by the early industry leaders and the supportive military and giant corporate industries and banks led to huge and unwieldy machines controlled as well as possible with nearly incomprehensible programs. Only a relatively very sparse elite could claim even partial mastery over the monstrous number crushers of old. The hardware, software, and research and development costs were horrendous and ludicrous as one looks back, wondering why the concepts and practices of distributed computing did not catch on sooner. Trying to compete with the champion of the "big systems," IBM, several industrial giants, losing the battles, fell out of the computer industry with great losses—RCA, General Electric, Raytheon, and others, with the most recent being Xerox and Singer.

But a change to minicomputers occurred. An effective rebellion by small businessmen, many educators, and laboratory and communications people, aided and abetted by a few "gutsy" small system manufacturers, took place in the late 1960s. At first, these were computers dedicated to specific purpose processing. They were crude and difficult to program—but they were cheap. There was not enough profit for IBM to bother with them. Thus, such companies as Digital Equipment Corp. (more than 50,000 sold through 1975), Data General Corp., General Automation Inc., Computer Automation Inc., and others grew like weeds. Users, in most cases, forced intelligent applications and lower costs.

And then it happened! A technological bombshell! The invention of the microcomputer. A Japanese manufacturer of small calculators ordered a custom "processing" chip—smart enough to perform arithmetic and other functions and still fit inside a hand-held case and also cheap enough to result in a total price sufficiently low to create a mass market for the complete unit. Intel Corporation, of Santa Clara, California, accepted and delivered the tiny, powerful, silicon-based semiconductor chip. But the metal-oxide-semiconductor, large-scale-integrated (MOS-LSI) chip in 1971 could do much more than simple calculator functions. Within a very short time that chip came to include not only the microprocessor, but also a control (programmable) memory (read-only memory—ROM). Incorporated also were 18 to 24 pins that acted as input-output connections, and an on-chip communications bus was developed that could be interfaced (matched) to devices for control and to other board-attached or exterior memories—low-cost, tiny random access memories (RAMs). The cost of these "processing powerhouses," these versatile chips dropped from a few hundred dollars each in quantities of a few thousand to $10 to $30 each even in quantities as low as 50.

It quickly became obvious that these microcomputers could be "stacked" and that multimicros could perform with as much power, capability, and efficiency as medium-sized computers costing up to $1 million. Then the floodgates opened. A total new technology was born. Within three years of the invention, hundreds of companies began manufacturing, fabricating, adapting, and redesigning these "chip computers" into thousands of low-cost, processing applications of a thousand varieties. Moreover, constant series of "little" technological explosions continue unabated today . . . with the limit unforecastable.

Quite soon, at least a million new computer users will find that "smaller is better." They are less likely to consider computer development for missiles than for new computer games, oven controllers, home alarms, and calculators. These can fit into wristwatches, pens, and "intelligent" terminals that can be connected to worldwide computer time-sharing systems for access to thousands of data bases in libraries, hospitals, laboratories, and so on. The microprocessor within the microcomputer becomes more powerful, smaller, and cheaper almost weekly. In effect, the semiconductor industry has shown that it is possible to price a processing product so low as to create an inordinate market demand for it. This demand and the miracles of mass microelectronics production have created a level of supply of processors undreamed of, as well as constant innovative exploration.

It is quite difficult even for experienced computer and communications people and electrical, mechanical, and other engineers to develop clear concepts and get the right "feel" for microprocessors. The microprocessor unit, often labeled MPU or μP, is the central processing unit that performs the arithmetic-logic activity or processing of the microcomputer. When control memory, usually in read-only memory (ROM), is added to the chip along with input-output pins and some interfacing circuitry, the basic units of a stored-program, communicating computer are present. For engineers, hobbyists, computer operators, electronics workers, and scores of other people, this tiny powerhouse becomes an exciting, challenging game and tool. Because it is so versatile and really not too complex, most people in the field quite quickly realize the impact it can have as a controller for hundreds of devices, appliances, processes, and services. But even for the experts, and there are very few at this stage, the dynamic nature of microcomputer developments, the new techniques developed, and the already large and steadily increasing markets are, in a word, astounding. Most of the electronics, computer, and communications community members today strongly agree that they have now a control machine whose capability and power exceed anything they previously had available to them.

In contrast to the processing mysteries engendered by the huge, nearly unmanageable computer monsters, this quite simplified system quickly demonstrates that the new world of microprocessor engineering and operational utility is conquerable individually and totally, albeit with some small educational strain and pain. Indeed, some 200,000 enthusiasts have already joined into educational groups, "swap" clubs, and formal associations to learn from each other and from the limited materials available how to put low-cost kits together. They learn how to program the units, test new components and devices, and prove to each other that controlling computers is not some mystic rite—that computer power is not some privilege or elitist control reserved for or accessible only to various high priests or barons of a computer fiefdom. Computer mastery takes only dedicated effort, not super brainpower or years of training or experience. The revolution—it is already too sudden, rapid, and widespread to be called an evolution—in hardware, software, design aids, test equipment, components, and applications is one that is like hundreds of thousands of breeder reactors. Considerably more progress comes out of the individual projects than the amount of effort put in. For those already "on board" or who have deeply delved into the realities of microprocessor control activities, the challenges continue to be more and more exciting as costs of microcomputer peripheral equipment continue to fall. This allows them to purchase visual display terminals, low-cost disk or cassette memories, new "pocketfuls" of RAMs and ROMs (tiny electronic memory chips), which can carry large programs and massive amounts of data and information. Moreover, amateurs, novices, and experts alike can measure their progress against an amazing variety of real-world applications that are now detailed in hundreds of information-loaded, special new microcomputer club newsletters and slick periodicals. Some of the traditional computer and communications journals regularly devote half or more of their issues to microcomputer design, capability, applications, and new components—much at the almost rabid insistence of the readers.

THE IMPACT OF LOW-COST MICROPOWER

In this introduction, everyday language can be used to demonstrate why these practically spontaneous scientific and pragmatic achievements have taken place so quickly. First, very low-cost, hand-held computing capability can be put to use practically anywhere a designer, manager, or executive wants it. Second, for any digital system, microprocessors and microcomputers can greatly reduce the size, complexity, and difficulty of application over older electronic devices. And, third, the design, prototype, and implementation of formerly rather expensive and complex products can be "turned around" in a drastically shorter time and, consequently, with very pleasing reduced costs and bother. These are perhaps the simple basic truths that have caused this explosion in new technology.

There are few data-processing or device control systems at or below the small and minicomputer level of complexity that are not being designed and implemented with microprocessors. The all-pervasive availability of plain, "cheap" computing power enables planners, designers, engineers, and system managers to incorporate decision-making capability into devices and system applications never before considered. Although microprocessors at first seem to be complex devices they are soon discovered to be readily understandable and individually controllable. Moreover, they are adapted quite simply to many different tasks. Microprocessors and the components that make them into computing and communicating units are mass-produced, but they can be customized instantly by programming. Although they are themselves low in cost, they also add value by providing less costly utility to products because they add such great extra power and versatility to the devices in which they are implanted or over which they exercise control. Indeed, teaching microprocessor electronics to college design engineers has proved to be a totally new experience for the great majority of professors.

The traditional logic (fixed) diagrams are gone; the "old-fashioned" (unprogrammable) test instruments are obsolete; teachers and engineers now work with compilers, assemblers, editors, and debugged software. Moreover, changes are made, *not* by redoing whole projects, but, instead, by simply changing or altering a pattern that is stored in a programmable read-only memory, a PROM. Few users or programmers are concerned with gates, flip-flops, and the like, as of old, but are now more inclined to devote most of their time to the evaluation of hardware, such as wide ranges of memory types and new, almost magic input-output devices (pens, scanners, and so on). Users are rapidly becoming very adept at doing their own programming with BASIC, a simple language now being implemented into a great many microcomputers and their counterparts, programmable calculators. This is a radical transition—the purchasing, managing, and evaluation duties are more and more being assumed by users, owners, and executives. These are duties formerly almost exclusively "owned" by computer systems analysts, programmers, and high-priced consultants. It is fortunate that developments are happening so quickly—fortunate for users. It is a bit unlucky, however, for the students who must read through and try and test the hundreds of new concepts, procedures, and equipment innovations—almost all described in a new, this time, "micro" computerese—just after they thought they had mastered the older nomenclature of "standard" computer systems and capabilities.

The low cost and the ease of entry into the development and fabrication of at least hundreds of types of microcomputer systems have enticed entrepreneurs around the world. Dominated by a score or more of American semiconductor companies, with Japanese, British, and other national companies supplying the raw microprocessor chip, the system innovators spring up by the dozens almost weekly. With only a few thousand dollars and a nucleus of "seasoned" microprocessor or applications specialists, a new company can become quite big in the highly sporadic, new segment-generating markets: calculators, watches, toys, appliances, instruments, terminals, communications devices, machine controllers, and an unending list of products that now contain the ubiquitous microprocessor chips. The "families" of microprocessors become smaller, cheaper, faster, and more powerful with each new announcement from Intel, RCA, National Semiconductor, Texas Instruments, Rockwell, Fairchild, Signetics, and other giant semiconductor manufacturers. The architecture and performance of chips and boards of microprocessors, memories, and input-output devices change with new manufacturing technologies, new logic types, and new quality testing innovations; and the users gain constantly as the competition gets rougher. This reinvigorates market activity, promotions, and wide distribution, resulting in even greater ranges of applications from cash registers to blood analyzers to communications devices. "Intelligent" terminals are causing a reverberating explosion in the communications industry also, owing to the miracle of the microprocessor.

The first microcomputer became commercially popular in 1973–1974. In 1975–1976 a second and third wave of system designs quickly supplanted the pioneer devices. Many users are already veterans. Single-chip microcomputers have become simple and cheap, at less than $10, in large quantities. Other 16-bit processing units are challenging the minicomputer capability and at much lower costs. Input-output power has been significantly enhanced by new sets of programmable I/O chips. On-chip controllers abound and sit on the same chip with the CPU, separately controlling program storage, RAM, I/O registers, and other "intelligent" communication chores. The MPU kits are real "fun" for a wide range of people who play with them in earnest—from people like accountants and Boy Scouts to math professors and high school freshmen. The typical kit contains the CPU chip, PROM chip, some RAM, I/O interface devices, and additional circuits to complete the computer—all set to go for, in some cases, less than $300, but usually from $500 to $800. To varying degrees, engineers and users must become programmers to save time and to get "personal." To much of the microcomputer industry and the multitude of users, the microprocessor has come to mean practically any processor chip that uses some form of large-scale integration (LSI) technology. This covers 4-bit, 8-bit, 12-bit and 16-bit devices as well as multichip 2- and 4-bit "slice" chips, which build into the larger chip systems. Some "stacked" or multimicrocomputer systems have been built into ultrafast 64-bit supercomputers, and much excited activity is taking place in this area. To study properly the characteristics and power of microcomputers, one must give consideration to the architecture and technology of specific chips, that is, the chips themselves as opposed to the product development hardware and the software support, including boards, boxes, peripherals, programs, and so on, and the end use or applications of the systems.

One major research firm stated that volume in 1974 was slightly under half a million chip sets, rising to 60 million in three years. The great majority of these devices are appearing in games, appliances, and communications and computer devices. The projections to 1980 foresee a world market of from $700 million to $1 billion. "The output of U.S. manufacturers of standard devices is expected to total slightly over 20 million units in 1980," is the opinion of one source.[1] It is most difficult to project the foreign market developments, but the projection continues, "The consumer market will see dramatic growth; however, the majority of the 1980

[1] Robert F. Wickham, "Microprocessors—This Looks Like the Year," *Northern California Electronic News*, Jan. 26, 1976, p. 7. Wickham is president of Vantage Research, Los Altos, California, the reporting firm.

usage in auto, appliances, and entertainment are expected to be custom devices, built specifically for a given product or group of products. Total growth rate of the market will average 48% per year between 1974 and 1980." [2]

[2] Ibid.

1

A New World of Microelectronic Control Systems

Is the world ready for 15 to 20 million microcomputers? This many will be sold throughout the world before 1980, 9 years after microcomputers first saw service. As a contrast to that forecast, consider the fact that about 150,000 standard minicomputers were in service at the end of 1975, 24 years since the first use of computers. The fundamental basis for this very sudden impetus of acceptability and utility of very small-sized computers relates almost entirely to two factors: (1) the plunging cost of microminiaturized digital control products and (2) the great pervasiveness of versatility and new ease of user mastery of operations. Examples of the almost ridiculously low prices of computing and control products are the $10 microprocessor "chips," which, when combined with some memory, control circuits, input-output devices, and a power supply become a total computer system—all for under $200. Examples of the versatility relate to the use of microcomputers as controllers in household appliances; electronic games; programmable calculators; and thousands of instruments, communications devices, industrial tools and machines, and a seemingly endless number of completely new products.

Electronics conferences, conventions, and seminars are no longer dominated by engineers and specialists. The heaviest participation is now by marketing managers, distributor personnel, equipment manufacturers, teachers and scientists, businessmen, and professionals representing a wide range of disciplines. Since the first applications of microcomputers in 1971, wide-ranging developments practically skyrocketed while product costs plunged almost as rapidly. These events occurred much more quickly than anyone expected, and a very distinct educational gap resulted. Many

1

leaders are quoted as firm believers that the now-automated mass production of microcomputers will result in a thousandfold decrease in the cost of logic and control, and history shows that the cost of circuitry has dropped 50 percent a year since the 1960 advent of commercially available integrated circuits. A general consensus seems to be that after 25 years of computer development, the industry has reached its infancy—with the development of the "computer-on-a-chip." These developments are certain to bring the computer revolution directly to the doorstep of the average person.

Because millions of people must now come to learn the hows and whys of computing for the first time, this handbook has been developed with the assumption that the majority of its readers are unaware of the operational characteristics of computers. Practically everyone is cognizant of some computer capabilities and applications, but most people have feared the complexity of huge electronic monsters and have avoided confrontations with even rudimentary analyses of computer components and design. Computers are now considerably simpler in construction, user control, and operational comprehension. Indeed, by late 1976, close to 50,000 microcomputer "kits" had already been sold to hobbyists, students, product designers, and scientists of many types of skills and achievement. Most engineering and computer classes are shifting emphasis from standard computers and even minicomputers to the new micropower systems represented by microprocessors and microcomputers—the microprocessor being the heart or central processing unit (CPU) of the microcomputer.

Each of the three basic types or classifications of computers then must come under close scrutiny by all computer users, control product designers, and tens of thousands of managers and businessmen who purchase these products. To understand fully the most prodigious, effusive, and economical of the three, the microcomputer, one must also understand the principal characteristics of the other two, the standard computer system and the minicomputer substitutes. Therefore, after a brief introduction to the new world of microelectronic control systems in this chapter, a discussion of the basics of standard computer systems will follow in the next chapter. This, in turn, is followed by a "compare and contrast" chapter relating the advantages and capabilities of minicomputers. Beginners and novices to the microcomputer world can thereby feel stronger in their fundamentals as they attempt to master the concepts, procedures, and the nomenclature of microminiaturized CPUs, memories, interfaces, buses, and other "chip" circuits. Although it is possible to learn by comparison and contrast how standard computers are being superseded in a great many instances by minicomputers, the differences in architecture and design of microcomputers are so significant that it would not do simply to understand some of the basic "differences only" between the two.

Many diverse groups of professionals are being driven into the computer world because of the low cost and, therefore, the economically justified use of microcomputers in offices, banks, supermarkets, factories, schools, laboratories, and so on; and it would not be sufficient for them to understand only one type of computer. For, despite the fact that microcomputer systems can generally perform practically all the same computing and control functions of standard computers and minicomputers, they are not all that capable for all purposes. The basic principles of computing per se must be mastered before one can compare and contrast and before intelligent analyses of differences and advantages can be fully perceived. New users cannot completely appreciate the miracle of microsystems—why and how they work so efficiently—until they comprehend the capabilities and operating characteristics of the microcomputer's predecessors. Furthermore, most computer teachers emphasize three other subclasses of computers: the "maxis" or very large supercomputers; the "intelligent" terminals, which contain either minicomputers or microcomputers; and programmable calculators, which are calculating powerhouses in their own right.

It is necessary to step slowly into the examination of these systems. A procedure that can be used is the presentation of a brief review of their *activities* to build a base—first, for the understanding of *what* they do—to be followed by an explanation of procedures as to *how* they complete these control and information manipulation tasks. The supercomputers are often the hubs of vast communications systems, and programmable calculators are unique instruments that require their own "full book" analysis. Neither of these two systems will be covered in this text. The "intelligent" terminal will be discussed throughout the book, however, especially in the last two chapters on applications. Some of the most momentous aspects of low-cost computers that relate very specifically to societal impact are the concerns that must be considered with regard to "multiminis," "stacked micros," and "grade-school" builders of computers from $200 microsystem kits.

EARLY COMPUTER DEVELOPMENT—THE
INEVITABILITY OF THE MICROCOMPUTER

A conventional computer generally consists of a basic set of electronic and electromechanical units (hardware): the equipment for the processor, to perform the actual computing, control, and processing; the equipment for the main storage, to hold data and instructions until called for and used by the processor: the input equipment, to read punched cards, interpret tapes, disks, badges, documents, and so on; and the output equipment, to present reports, analyses, charts, and so on, using printers, card punches, cathode-ray tubes (CRTs), and the like. The 1960s represented the period of gestation when the military engineers, space scientists, theoretical mathematicians, large industrialists, and computer company executives directed and supported bigger, faster, and more complex and expensive computer systems, sometimes without regard to price, user convenience, or best-use utility.

In the period of the 1970s, advances in the technology enabled the computer industry to meet more closely the needs of the actual users of computers, such as managers, students and teachers, factory foremen, doctors, bankers, and wide ranges of businessmen. The users complained of the high costs of equipment; the miseries and mysteries of too big, too powerful machines; and, worst of all, of woefully complex software. All these enigmas dominated users without letup—a computer tyranny. Also, the dictatorship of system analysts and the narrowness of programmers irritated practically everybody. But it was their mistakes, blunders, and the nonprogress of practical applications software that hurt the most. The user revolt in the late 1960s finally forced (1) low-cost, simply operated and controlled systems; (2) smaller and more accessible computers and terminals; and (3) more versatile, user-oriented devices and programs. Popular, low-cost, and convenient devices known today as minicomputers, microcomputers, "intelligent" terminals, and programmable calculators resulted from the revolt. The users by their "dollar votes" are now directing the progress and causing the fulfillment of the computer promise. The computer "professional" cliques and the academic and military dominance are disappearing, and this new era of computer cost-effectiveness is benefiting all.

The advent of the microprocessor is the beginning of a new computer revolution in our technological society. Literally thousands of companies worldwide have announced microprocessor developments. There has been an avalanche of discussions of them in practically all electronics, communications, and computer magazine articles, conventions, conferences, and worldwide traveling seminars. Constantly increasing numbers of products using them indicate the revolution is well under way. The advent of the microprocessor is also a beginning of a spontaneous revolution for "public use" of a new computer architecture.

The technology has given equipment designers new freedoms to create products heretofore impractical or uneconomical. For example, microprocessors coupled with simple keyboard input-output (I/O) devices, RAM (random access memory) units ("chips"), and ROM (read-only memory), control programs form microcomputers with great power and versatility quickly and at very low cost. The technology has also challenged millions of noncomputer technicians and engineers to define and develop new control systems. This suddenly increased number of new computer system developments and offerings by hundreds of new suppliers all but guarantees a continuous acceleration of applications discoveries and inventions. Microcomputers are mass-produced for a few hundred dollars. They already control many devices and fit "inside" thousands of products from sophisticated

4

bank and retail store terminals to electronic robots soon to be used in thousands of factories.

Microprocessors have very quickly reached a third stage of component evolution in just a few years, as is noted on pages ahead. Major design developments in practically every field of digital logic systems have occurred even though the microsystems are relatively very new. They are now the basic component and have the most far-reaching implications for future developments in the computer or practically any control systems area since the transistor. Microprocessors are the foundation upon which the architecture of future generations of most or all computing machines of every type will be based. The powerful control devices and systems that are available today are most adequate for achieving practically all objectives of control system innovators. They serve very well in an enormous number of very cost-effective pragmatic applications, and they are a financial success for practically all firms that produce and use them.

The distinction between a microprocessor and a microcomputer is basic and very clear. The word *micro,* which is the first part of both terms, quite simply indicates the very tiny physical size of the components involved. Large-scale integration (LSI) produces tiny (usually) silicon-based "chips" of components (transistors, diodes, and so on) and is now the basic state of the art of the semiconductor industry. The second part of each term defines the difference of the two "machines" most explicitly. The term *processor* indicates that section of a computing system that is dedicated to performing the basic system control for executing the operations and processing the data as specified by the user's program. Traditionally, this has been referred to as the central processing unit or CPU function. The term *computer includes* the processor and is used to indicate a complete data-processing system consisting of the three basic units: the processor chip itself and the main and auxiliary memories, ROMs (1024 to 16,384 bit read-only memories) and RAMs (up to 65k (thousand bit) random access memories), also on chips (cards) connected by buses to the input/output section. Thus the microprocessor is defined as the component constituting the control section of a microcomputer.

Microprocessors are often as small as 1/4 inch square and contain on a single integrated circuit "chip" all the elements of a central processor, including the processing (arithmetic) and control logic, the instructions for decoding, and main or operating memory. When they are combined with other memory and input/output circuitry, they become full microcomputers. These new "tiny machines" can be united on a single chip, or they can be constructed on two to four chips on a single, printed circuit board. Microprocessors sell for $20 to $30 and microcomputers for as little as $200 to $1,000, depending upon quantity ordered, sophistication of design, and amount or size of memory required. They are "mighty mites" of control intelligence.

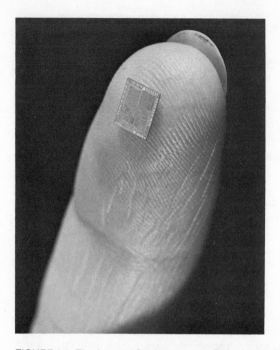

FIGURE 1.1. The famed "Computer-on-a-Chip," the miracle of microminiaturization. The microprocessor chip shown contains the logic, control memory, and other components to compute and remember, to switch and signal. With support circuits, they now control millions of devices. *Courtesy: Intel Corporation*

Microcomputers thus have many very significant advantages. They are very low-cost, highly reliable, and versatile devices that can fit practically anywhere and operate under "ruggedized" temperature and other tough environmental conditions. They are available in 4-, 8-, 12-, and 16-bit word lengths, as we shall note later, and can interface (match) most other computers or peripheral equipment. They can be as fast as most minicomputers—and faster than many "standard" computers. Some are available as kits, and some are easy to operate, alter, program, and replace "in the field." The biggest shake-up and surprise and one of revolutionary impact to the computer industry was their very rapid development and immediate acceptance "by the millions" as basic microsystems in their own right.

Microcomputers became the "heart" of hundreds of user-controlled information instruments now finding economic justification in offices, factories, schools, and (soon) homes practically everywhere. The most visible utilization of these "miracle microprocessors" is their use in programmable calculators. These desk units or hand-held powerhouses have become computers in their own right—combining within their own expandable systems most of the kinds of processing and peripheral capability of standard computer systems. And the tiny, speck-sized-chip microprocessors are used within point of sale "cashier" terminals, as automated "word processors" in offices; and as microcontrollers for scores of automation, communications, and appliance functions. Microcomputers and microprocessors, for example, are used expansively to test, measure, control, calculate, transform, and communicate. They are "buried" within and control hundreds of de-

FIGURE 1.2. The photo negatives represent two of the more than 300 steps involved in manufacturing tiny microcircuits used in electronic business machines. The square-shaped negative is photographically reduced to produce the smaller squares, which together form a negative of circular shape. Each of the little squares in the circle becomes a microcircuit, and each microcircuit contains the equivalent of hundreds of transistors. *Courtesy: NCR Corporation*

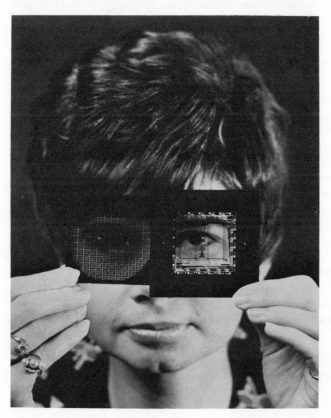

vices and terminals connected to counters and sensors, process and production machines, instruments and controllers, keyboards and readers, and hundreds of other information sources for control of both energy and "intelligence."

The scope of the new generation of microcomputerization activities has become so broad that it is difficult for anyone not deeply involved in active daily research in the entire field to follow even the main events of the massive ongoing changes presently occurring. The reasons for these rapid and very startling changes are many, varied, and basic. Fundamentally, computer power is now abundant, cheap, tiny, easy to use, and extremely versatile. This has occurred not only because of the cost/performance breakthroughs in both hardware and software (that is, meeting the requirements and capabilities desired by users), but also because of the drastic reduction in systems costs owing to the reduced time required to bring new products and services from the idea to the market stage. There is an expanding and eager market for demonstrable automated systems that prove significant dollar savings in energy, labor, and time. And microsystems are fulfilling these desires and demands.

Business and industrial user emphasis for computer services now is firmly centered on total system cost, straightforward performance, small size, and tested reliability. Formerly, these specific characteristics of computers were highly volatile, difficult to determine, and strongly influenced (dominated) by half a dozen major computer manufacturers—principally IBM, which traditionally controlled about 65 percent of all the markets.[1] Now many thousands of primary and supplementary computer equipment and service companies are in the field in the United States alone. Minicomputers and microcomputers have opened the floodgates—practically any company with the desire can become a "computer manufacturer." It is easy to buy, design, and adapt minicomputers and microcomputers into computerized, computer-controlled, or computer-contained products. And hundreds of electronic, automobile, machine-tool, communications, and business machine companies, and endless numbers of other "types" of companies are suddenly producing electronic products.

THE CONSEQUENCES OF LSI FOR MICROPROCESSORS

Several automated techniques are being used for large-scale integration (LSI). They have become mass-production processes of engineering excellence. The production-cost reduction magic is demonstrated by some

---

[1] As of mid-1974, IBM had obviously perfected microprocessor technology. They were a leading supplier of word processing and point-of-sale supermarket and bank terminals. But they had not yet brought out microprocessor products per se, nor had they entered the calculator markets. The rumors and expectations were abundant, however.

data from the electronics industry to the effect that it costs only slightly more to manufacture 10,000 microprocessors than it does to produce 1,000.

A popular ratio of computer costs is as follows: With relatively the same computing power, small standard computers can be sold for $20,000 to $150,000; minicomputers, for $2,000 to $50,000; and microcomputers, for $200 to $1,000. This is what the computer revolution is really all about. Until recently, the reasons for these price discrepancies were basically expensive software support, ensured maintainability, reliability, manufacturer reputation, and several other nonprice considerations.

Now when a department store manager, accountant, or production manager decides to purchase a terminal with a microcomputer or minicomputer in it to perform specific tasks or connect to a system, he really does not care if it uses bipolar or MOS logic or carries a big company brand name. He is fully assured of reliability with replacement warranties and he receives "free" software and training to program the unit himself, often using several of his current employees. He also receives a demonstration of equipment modularity, that is, that other high capability devices can be added to expand the system wherever and whenever needed or desired. And all of this is now offered at remarkably low costs.

Micro- and minicomputer customers are buying new efficiency, economy, extra services, "decentralized intelligence," tighter control of operations—and big savings in labor, time, and "normal" computer hardware and software costs. The systems they are purchasing and leasing are not large, expensive, complex masses of expanding software and support expenses. They seldom find it necessary to change completely their whole operation or hire expensive "strange-thinking" programmers or systems analysts. These are the real reasons for the explosive expansion of computer sales—competitive, dollar-saving efficiency gains—without traps, grief, disruption, or complexity. Managers and other people with similar jobs can operate, control, understand, and personally grow with these computer systems. Thus the "computerization era" has taken on a totally new and massive turn. The microcomputer is here, there, and everywhere. The competitive race has become a stampede. The impact on business, industry, medicine, education, and all of society is unpredictable, and sometimes is turning out to be surprising.

Microprocessors and microcomputers are having a quite startling effect on the computer industry itself. They are not following the growth pattern of the standard computers or even the minicomputer development. There certainly is no slowdown in evolution or innovation or acceptance in the marketplace. This is evident owing to the very sudden massive sales of 13 million calculators in 1973, 22 million in 1974, and an estimated 42 million in 1976.[2]

[2] Data announced by the respected New York research firm of Frost and Sullivan, Inc. (*Electronic Merchandising*, June 1974, p. 19).

The almost monthly announcements of lower costs, new sophisticated and increased capability, and simpler programmability make many of these "computing" units attractive as "systems" to the smallest business, factory, or professional office. The obvious and easy "trade-up" is from these instruments to microcomputer-based terminal systems. It is not difficult at all—almost painless—for managers, accountants, students and teachers, engineers and technicians, and countless others to work calculators and then to slip in "preprogrammed" and programmable strips, cards, or tape cassettes to make those calculators capable for solving complex problems. With the addition of some simple, low-cost input devices and the connection of $500 printers or $700 CRTs or plotters, many "regular" office or factory workers suddenly are operating, controlling, and even designing information systems.

The essence of these transitions is that the programmable calculators contain microprocessors. As more memory is added and input-output units are attached or connected, the managers, accountants, students, and the like become, in effect, "computer people"—using full computer power. The upgrading, the utilization of the embedded versatility, and the purchase of more and varied "firmware" (ready-made, pluggable programs) come about rapidly, naturally, and without the normal computer-fear syndrome. Compared with human skills, the new and "easy" 100,000-arithmetic-operations-per-second, "personalized" computer convinces all but the most stubborn diehard that the computer way is the best way. (The descriptions of the most popular models of microcomputers and their capabilities and procedures are developed fully in Chapters 4 through 8. Specific areas of these chapters develop (1) the costs, (2) manufacturing procedures, (3) versatility ranges, (4) operating procedures, (5) models available, (6) advantages over minis, (7) new microcomputer architecture, (8) key points in choosing a microcomputer, (9) microcomputer applications, (10) microcomputer programs, and various aspects of the future of micros.)

From the industry standpoint, whereas the typical development cycle—the time from product conception to full production—for regular computers is typically about five years and for minicomputers is about two years, for microcomputers, it is about five months. Standard computer designers had to make decisions about system performance, circuit types, memory hierarchy and modules, packing approaches, and so on four or five years ahead of production. When they chose to use existing technology in the design state, they knew the final product would be three to five years behind the then existing technology when that final product was marketed. If they decided to extrapolate or project ahead to the "possible" new technology, they probably made some very bad guesses and lost their positions as "rising young innovators." Last-minute redesign inefficiencies would certainly be "less optimal" and probably wrong. It would probably not be possible at all to change "locked-in" production and supply schedules. Five-month microcomputer design turnaround makes excellent use of latest technology, and last-minute changes are routine—almost "nonexpenses."

The quite sensational low prices of finished products almost insure the mass markets for production-cost reductions, and these products are programmably versatile. They are microminiaturized and do not require expensive, specially designed cabinetry, power supplies, and so on. Servicing problems are very often solved with simple plug-in replaceability. Microprocessors are even becoming "disposable," and other modular components are manufactured to be substitutable, insertable, or attachable by operators, salesmen, or regular employees. The fast trend toward "buildup" systems of stacked microcomputers or multimicros is also obvious.

Forecasts of "microcomputer-multiplied" applications are difficult. Competition in the industry by giant electronic components manufacturers and the very easy entry into computer entrepreneurships make "intelligent electronics" a wide open field. There have been sound predictions of microprocessors costing as little as from $2 to $5 within 20 years, with microprocessing rates up to 5 to 10 million instructions per second, and few experts will challenge them. Although the processors represent only 20 to 25 percent of microcomputer or system costs, extended main memory and auxiliary memory in the form of RAMs and ROMs [3] are also becoming cost-effective miracles, with prices 4K to 8K (thousand bit) at $12 to $30, with increasing capacity and continuing price decreases still ahead.

NEW EMPHASIS IN COMPUTER SCIENCE CLASSES IN HIGH SCHOOLS AND COLLEGES

Microcomputer kits are being mass-produced by the hundreds of thousands and are retailing in single units for about $300. Several companies were already pioneers in 1975. Microcomputers were making systems smarter, opening new markets, and preventing much energy waste. They control more and more traffic lights, mass-transit systems, reservation systems, and energy use in large buildings. Robotic factory systems, fast-food restaurants, test equipment, and even electronic screwdrivers and slot machines are among a thousand other machines, operations, appliances, and so on that contain or use them. The reasons are generally based on their ability to do things cheaper, better, faster. It is most interesting to take a note from a project at the University of Illinois in Urbana-Champaign: "Computers are playing an increasingly pervasive role in our society, to the extent that most students who are enrolled in schools today can expect to interact with computers in their daily work. Hence, it is important that every educated per-

[3] Random access memory (RAM) chips contain the "space" for the data and instructions that are input and held until called for by the processor. Read-only memory (ROMs) generally are plug-in control programs.

son should have some understanding of the principles on which computers operate, and some skill in their use."

In recognition of the increasing importance that a basic knowledge of computers has for an individual, the enrollment in introductory computer science courses has increased rapidly. At the University of Illinois, enrollment in 1974 was about 2,000 students per semester, and it was expected that this number would continue to increase until a substantial majority of all students at the university would take an introductory computer science course at some stage of their studies. Most of these courses now are beginning to have a new emphasis on microcomputer and minicomputer systems. Because microcomputers and minicomputers have become so cost-effective and because many community colleges have new heavy emphasis on an increased number of "how-to-do" courses or vocational areas, micros and minis have become popular purchases in these school systems. Students, therefore, have greater access to the instruments themselves and learn directly from use rather than from texts. Furthermore, low-cost micros and minis are turning up in many laboratories and research facilities and on teacher's desks as instructors' "aids."

Microcomputers are now available as programmable calculators, and "intelligent" terminals are beginning to completely "shake up" the entire computer industry, practically obsoleting many types of older equipment, processes, and procedures. All this began in 1971 in test phases and soon became commercially marketed with great success in 1974. These developments will change the ways mankind works, conducts business, educates, entertains, and adjusts to a whole new social environment. Programmable calculators are already in use in medical schools to teach students; minicomputers are similarly fundamental instructional units in other colleges such as the University of Texas, University of Indiana, and others—and intelligent terminals are in full operation at the University of California at San Francisco and elsewhere to instruct and test students in their classrooms. All are low-cost and easily operated by the students and teachers.

They are used without programming experience by many students or with half a dozen specially developed computer medical languages. Other medical schools are using time-shared computer services offered by scores of major companies with very large computers and national networks. Time sharing results in hundreds of simultaneous remote users of the same computer who share initial costs, programs, and special techniques. For example, as many as 40 individual hospitals are sharing one computer in a cooperative operation, and many more will do the same. One minicomputer system at the University of Southern California is so unique that its use is primarily as a human simulator, called "Sim One." It is a computer-controlled manikin that has been developed for instruction in anesthesiology skills. The manikin is under the instructor's control but responds to the student's actions by changes in respiration rate, temperature, blood pressure, and heart rate. Fasciculation, contraction, and dilation of the pupil of the eye and other physiological events can also be induced.

Will teachers become less important or necessary in the computerized educational system? There is no doubt whatever about this. Teacher ranks will shrink considerably, but basic responsibilities will also certainly change. Commensurately, many more adults will seek greater ranges and degrees of education. The teachers will be dealing with many new ways of presenting wide-ranging materials, topics, and depth. Obviously, teachers will "restructure" their roles, and these teaching procedures and techniques must "interface" or fit with new computer-oriented student minds. Practically all courses will become available as programmed for computer terminals. On the basis of rapid, broad-scope, or deeply detailed testing procedures and scores, teachers directed by computer output can easily recognize students who are progressing rapidly or slowly and give them advanced or remedial materials. This may make it no longer necessary or even possible to separate students in grades, and this might require the teacher to guide learning activities not on just one grade level but on all levels simultaneously. Present four-year college programs may no longer be standard. Instead, courses may become programs for continuous learning. In essence, the education of all people, regardless of age or occupation, may have to be continuous simply to help them stay abreast of "dialable" visual and audio information from huge data bases. Other courses will be designed simply to permit them challengingly to utilize their excess leisure time. Education will quite likely be continued in the home, using nothing more than computer terminals. Courses could be provided free—as National Educational Television courses are today—or a small tuition fee might be added to one's telephone bill. It is also possible that academic degrees of the past will undergo significant change. Many highly intelligent and motivated high school graduates might be considered at least as qualified for particular technical jobs as college graduates, or a two-year college student might be regarded as being equally as qualified by computer-measured competence ratios as many six-year college students. A student could serve as an apprentice on a job and find out if he or she is temperamentally suited for it before making the financial or "opportunity cost" commitment for a college program in that field.

COMPUTER APPLICATIONS IN TRANSPORTATION, MEDICINE, BUSINESS, AND INDUSTRY

The computer has become important in many fields other than education. Most of us are already aware of computer-controlled pressure sensors and electronic "imagers" that record and photograph vehicular traffic on city streets and transmit the information directly to computers. In many U.S. and foreign cities, computers control timing of stoplights singly and in networks to permit the most efficient flow of traffic. Some traffic engineers believe computer-controlled, automated highways could be constructed within the next five years. Some existing toll roads, they say, could be quite quickly and easily modified to include recessed electronic tracks that would transport cars at speeds of 80 or 90 miles an hour. Cars would attach to the track at an entrance ramp and then be automatically shuttled into the flow of traffic. To leave the track, the driver might pull a dashboard lever, causing the car to disconnect from the track. The car would then roll to an exit ramp or, in the case of emergency, to the side of the road. Operating automated individual vehicle control systems are in San Francisco and elsewhere in the United States. PRT, or personal rapid transit, systems are installed in the states of Texas, Washington, and in Canada, and France. And many more are on the drawing boards for cities around the world.

In medicine, among the many uses of computers, one of the most cost-effective is the simultaneous monitoring of many individuals' physical conditions. Small electronic sensor transducers are attached to different parts of the body's surface. Data are automatically and continuously transmitted to distant computers. These procedures are used in intensive care programs to monitor the physical conditions of patients. These signals are instantly transmitted as a basis for consultation by specialists anywhere in the world. On-scene doctors are alerted immediately when treatment is necessary. Doctors' office terminals are also connected to hospital computers so they can be alerted at any time. Paramedics or nurses can type in sets of symptoms and have the graphic information immediately displayed and transmitted to computers for detailed analysis and visual or audio retransmission anywhere in split seconds. The computers display on the specific doctor's terminal various types of successful comparative diagnosis, drug or physical therapy, or suggestions as to what the various symptoms mean as correlated with the individual's complete stored medical history, even indicating additional tests to be made, as well as probable results of the performance and evaluation of them. However, the physician is still responsible for diagnosis and treatment.

Entire personal medical histories are already carried on computer or microfiche readable "chips" that fit in the corner of a credit or ID card. These cards (given free to customers by some savings banks) eliminate the time-consuming and frequently error-filled chore of recording and retrieving patients' medical histories. When the doctor has finished examining or treating patients, information indicating the nature of the treatment or the findings of the examination are recorded in the computer and transferred to the patient's "history card," thus automatically updating it.

The "paper blizzard" we all witness daily is about to diminish in many areas. Under present methods, almost every purchase or financial transaction we make is accompanied by slips of paper—currency, checks, money orders, receipts, invoices, bills, ledgers, credit memos, and so on. Until recently, credit buying and the use of credit cards did not effectively reduce the paper work problems. Some "paper" problems are, however, being eliminated completely by fully utilizing "plastic money"—magnetic striped cards. Many types of financial dealings and accounting are being handled electronically by interacting nationwide networks of computers. Other sections of this book relate the current general public's acceptance of "money cards"! Many means of efficient computerized credit verification and control covering practically anyone's transactions instantly in all parts of the country are already approved and in use, and many more are being established worldwide. "Touchtone" telephones and other button units act as computer terminals in many businesses and some homes, permitting people to discover at any time the status of their bank balances and soon, one hopes, everything that appears on their credit records. Laws to this effect have been proposed.

Several nationwide complexes of computerized credit verification centers have been established by BankAmericard, Master Charge, American Express, and others. The primary purposes are to indicate who is and who is not a good credit risk and for what amount. Procedures for depositing employees' payroll checks, social security payments, and other governmental payments directly into banks are in operation in many states. Automatic bank payments of customer-approved bills are being directly debited or subtracted from their accounts. Other remote financial transaction systems are operating successfully in the United States, Japan, and Europe. Many mortgage and other time payments, utility bills, and so on are now handled this way. Remote cash dispensing machines have become very popular. Ultimately, direct bank payment of the majority of consumer and many business bills will become part of the "cashless" society, primarily because these systems reduce paperwork and labor costs very significantly. Most problems relate to banking laws and disemployment of bank and financial personnel—disemployment because the job functions no longer exist.

What about computer supervision of industrial processes? A professional society of 250 computer experts from 22 countries predicted that by the end of the twentieth century, all major industries will be managed by computers. The impact on the labor force will be tremendous. Studies show that most of today's factory, office, transportation, and communication workers may have to find new positions in the next ten to 20 years. This will also apply to low-level professional workers. Most of these people will necessarily be out of jobs. Will sufficient new employment opportunities open up in production fields and also in hundreds of thousands of service enterprises such as conservation, human engineering, health care, recreational activities, social planning, government, and management of enterprises? The answer is difficult. Job categories such as these will be replaced by many other new categories. Even today, the volume of technical, professional, social service, and managerial jobs is rapidly changing. More than one-half of the current career opportunities did not exist 20 years ago. But the large numbers of those workers to be disemployed and the smaller numbers of the new employed do not extrapolate or project in proper balance.*

COMPUTERS AND ELECTRONICS AS AIDS TO ENERGY CONSERVATION, DISCOVERY, AND PRODUCTION

One of the good and most valuable activities for computers and electronics is to play a significant role in making more efficient use of resources. They can also help to increase production and to aid in making new discoveries of energy resources. The development of computers and other electronic systems for consumer and commercial use applies in a great many cases to systems and products that can be efficiently controlled to use less energy. These are not "promises" about applications five to ten years away. Many were already developed in 1974 and early 1975, and the markets for these control devices are practically everywhere. The recent development and utilization of low-cost microprocessors permit room-by-room heating and lighting system controls for large buildings. This permits considerably lessened and more efficient use of power, gas, and/or oil than by present large-area thermostatic methods. Other test and analysis systems have already been placed in operation to develop new sources and aids in the manufacture of new energy from thermal, solar, and gasified coal sources. New oil refineries and natural gas facilities are almost totally controlled by computers for decreasing waste and speeding operations. Seismology has become a computerized science.

In the computers themselves, the use of semiconductor rather than core memory has cut power consumption by 50 percent in large mainframe computers, with proportionate decreases in smaller systems. In mass transit, computerized bus and train systems in use and others in development allow portal-to-portal transport. Reduced energy requirements by tighter controls add to the savings brought about by greatly increased consumer usage and thus by fewer individual cars guzzling gas. Microprocessors in local power stations monitor energy continually, not only making more efficient use of electricity, but also, by close control, systemizing and leveling operations and thus averting large-scale brownouts or blackouts.

Another example is the use of electronic fuel injection and ignition systems on 1977–1978 automobiles. Many of these micros are expected to

* See Sippl, Charles J. and Bullen, Bob, *Computers at Large* (Bobbs-Merrill Co., 1976) for a full discussion of this problem.

produce an average 40 percent saving on fuel consumption. On a recent fuel injection test, one manufacturer increased mileage from 4 to 16 miles per gallon in worst-case "stop and start" conditions.

In the home entertainment field, solid-state television and stereo systems are reported to consume 50 percent less power than tube versions, and some ROMs in appliances, electronic humidity sensors, sonic cleaning systems, and so on will automatically shut off individual clothes driers, ranges, furnaces, lights, and the like more effectively than those on timing bases. The same principles and computerized products can be used in larger buiildings, factories, and so on. These and many other types of computer applications are indeed very beneficial for society.

ELECTRONIC DATA-PROCESSING SYSTEMS ARE NOW BECOMING BASIC TO MOST BUSINESSES

New on-line systems provide for complete data-processing requirements— at a realistic cost—that can grow with a company of any size. Small businesses can easily find low-cost, modular, multiterminal systems that make it possible to record all of the important business and accounting records on inexpensive "floppy" disks and to process those data on-line where and when they are needed, using regular company personnel. Source data are entered through familiar accounting machine terminals or, if preferred, through quiet, high-speed, quick-check video display terminals. Few extra steps are required for data entry; office personnel simply follow their standard data-recording procedures in many cases.

Such systems produce practically every report, record, or document needed to manage general businesses: orders, invoices, payroll checks, vendor checks, inventory records, sales reports, and monthly and annual statements. All of these and others designed to suit specific needs are produced in several output forms, using different types and speeds of printers, hard copies of CRT displays, tape cassettes, and so on. Meanwhile, all of the records, in detail, are on file, available for immediate access on low-cost rotating magnetic disks. The data are there to use when needed; the program can direct the system to produce a complete payroll or report the status of a single customer's account. With the disk, accountants eliminate bulky trays of punched cards or reels of punched paper tape or the inconvenience of scheduling work loads to accommodate an outside service bureau. Even though costs are low, systems are complete, modular, and efficient. Both the hardware and the software can be selected to match specific needs. Managers can add terminals, disk storage, and printers as work loads grow. And a great variety of proved applications programs are designed to complement present office procedures. There are usually no learning curves with most basic systems. Fewer employees are needed, and they can perform their duties almost exactly as they have in the past, but faster and more efficiently with computer entry procedures. Many accountants prepare their own programs by taking advantage of the easy-to-learn Business BASIC language, COBOL, or FORTRAN. A wide range of small computers or minicomputers are now products of nationally recognized companies, dedicated to solving the small-to-medium-sized company's data-processing problems. The majority offer single-source responsibility for hardware, software, applications programming, and service.

SMALL, SIMPLE COMPUTERS
SYSTEMS: GENERAL OPERATIONS

Generally, in small systems, raw data for the computer can originate from any department in the company: purchasing, sales, production, accounting, and finance. The output of the system is useful to every department in most companies. The function of the computer system is to combine, merge, process, and produce the documents and reports that are essential to operating a company. The processing is done with the computer system, using information stored in a common data base. Most of the clerical labor involved in the processing is eliminated because business data are entered only once and then repeatedly used for different applications.

A customer invoice, for example, requires the use of information from several sources within the company. Sales, manufacturing, shipping, and accounting all have their inputs. These can be entered into the computer system at any time and in random fashion. As the final steps of data entry

FIGURE 1.3.

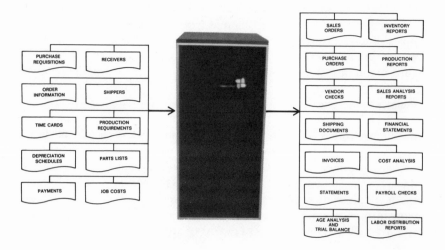

are in progress, the system automatically assembles the facts and produces the invoice. The same data are used in the preparation of inventory and sales-analysis records, accounts-receivable reports, and profit-and-loss statements.

ACCOUNTANTS AND BUSINESSMEN ARE BECOMING ALERT TO NEW LOW-COST SYSTEMS

Before 1971, the average company, wholesaler/distributor, and the like had few alternatives for controlling inventory or managing credit, receivables, payables, and sales. These alternatives included manual methods such as Cardex and ledger cards, semiautomatic methods such as magnetic ledger accounting machines, and more fully automated methods involving computer service bureaus. During 1971 the small business computer arrived on the scene in large numbers. Now small computers do these jobs (as they should be done) without strangling accountants with $2,000-per-month lease payments; a room full of expensive, complex hardware; and the costly programmers of a "standing room only" DP room. These new low-cost systems, which employ very efficient high-speed "floppy" disks, enable companies to get instant information on inventory status, customer order analysis, accounts receivable, payroll, and all the applications that are of immediate necessity. Comprehensive back-order reports, daily margin reports, and other management information reports are prepared in a few minutes. The new computer systems are available for as little as $500 per month lease/purchase. They provide firms with opportunities to cut costs drastically and increase information accuracy and availability.

Small computer systems also significantly increase the efficiency of the clerical functions involved in running a business. Onetime data entry is developed as each item of information generated by sales, purchasing, internal scheduling, accounting, and other business operations is entered into the terminal. After the source data are in the system files, they are available, on demand, as often as needed, for the processing and reporting tasks required to run the business profitably and efficiently. Personnel in warehouses may record, for example, that a particular shipment has been received from a supplier. This one data entry will then be automatically used by the system in updating inventory records, production-control records, the payment schedule to suppliers, and the monthly operating statement. There need be no shuffling of punched cards or spooling of magnetic or punched tape. This greatly reduces chances of error or loss of valuable data. The information, once entered, is immediately available (on-line). If there is any question, for example, as to whether the shipment has been received, an inquiry to the system will give an immediate answer.

By the use of on-line productivity, it is possible to combine even the original data entry process with normal document preparation and record-keeping functions. The terminal can be used, for example, to type sales orders or purchase requisitions. The hard copies produced by the machine can be used by the responsible departments while the information is electronically stored by the computer system for future processing and record keeping. In some instances, very low-cost typewriter terminals can also be used as output devices in the preparation of reports, checks, invoices, ledgers, and other documents. Video display terminals have the advantage of fast, quiet operation. A typical application would be in a manager's office, where the reports can be visual, copied, edited, charted, corrected, updated, and so on by the manager's own keyboard or light-pen entry—with immediate response. New low-cost data entry stations are full-capability terminal devices. They can be installed at any convenient location in all facilities or remotely, using ordinary telephone lines.

SMALL SYSTEM DATA BASES

Most computer systems use magnetic disk to store millions of characters of information concerning businesses. Because each record is immediately available to the system for inquiry or processing, all records needed for each task are, in effect, in one voluminous file—the disk. Usually, authorization to read and change data is controlled and limited by means of a "password," which must be typed before a user can access specific files. The low-cost disks are removable; and critial data can be copied onto spare disks, removed, and stored as insurance against accidental loss of data. Additional disk drives can be added to the minicomputer system. Any number of the removable disk cartridges can be used to store files for subsequent processing.

Disk storage provides significant advantages over both punched cards and punched or magnetic tape. Disks are less cumbersome, provide faster access, and are ideally suited for on-line, on-demand processing. Until recently, however, disk storage has been prohibitively expensive for small and medium-sized business systems. Mini or "floppy" disks have broken that barrier, extending the advantages of disk storage to small-scale data-processing systems. Prices are comparable with ordinary punched card and tape accounting systems.

APPLICATIONS PROGRAMMING SURVEYS

One of the most important procedures in tailoring a system to an existing set of business procedures is to survey and analyze each step of the data and document flow within the organization. After the data flow process and interactions between data paths and decision points (including exception cases) have been defined, the process of developing a system can begin. Applications specialists can work with company personnel to perform these detailed surveys and completely define the data flow model. Using this model, they can generate the appropriate procedures and software to perform the processing operations. During the development of the applications programs for the small computer system, complete documentation of the organizational data flow and decision-making elements is prepared, as well as complete documentation of the programs created to perform the processing work.

A system is only as effective as the people who use it. The training, installation, and cutover plan are designed to meet the needs of the user company. These can start as soon as the data flow model has been defined. This model develops a definition of the operator procedures required to perform such primary functions as entry of source data, verification and editing of data in files, interpretation of error messages, and the procedure for preparing reports and printed documents. When the applications program is ready to run, the key personnel can have hands-on training.

As the smaller companies become more experienced with regard to the capability of the system, managers desire to adjust their data-processing procedures to take greater advantage of the power of the system or to put it to work on tasks that were not considered in the original implementation. It is at this point that managers will realize the benefits of the programming capability built into most small computer systems.

A POWERFUL HIGH-LEVEL LANGUAGE

Generally, the control and monitoring programs that sequence input and output operations and manage the files also do all the housekeeping inside. Most small computer systems are modular and thus expandable. One of the primary features of most operating systems (OS) is the support of high-level programming languages such as Business BASIC, COBOL, and so on. Business BASIC, for example, includes special statements to schedule input/output operations, manipulate data in files, and format reports. The addition of these features transforms the easy-to-learn, easy-to-use BASIC language into a powerful programming tool for business applications.

On-line programming in Business BASIC

Business BASIC is terminal-oriented. The language is highly conversational and provides line-by-line checking of each input statement as it is generated. Applications software prepared for the minicomputer system by applications analysts is often written exclusively in Business BASIC; many others are in COBOL or FORTRAN. With only a few hours of training, most accountants and data-processing personnel can learn enough Business BASIC to write useful programs to extend the utility of the system. An example of a typical Business BASIC program designed to create invoices follows:

> When the small computer system runs the program, the computer "reads" from disk file "(5)" the item description indexed by part number P, its unit price U, and the stock quantity S (Line No. 101); then it "prints" the item description D and the unit price U in a dollar-and-cents form (Line No. 102); next it asks the operator to "input" the quantity shipped Q, and so on. Each line of instruction to the computer relates easily to everyday English; for example, to obtain the price extension E, the computer is instructed to multiply the unit price U times the quantity shipped Q (Line No. 104).

FIGURE 1.4. a. System configuration, b. The keyboard speaks for itself—in BASIC, c. Hard copy printout—in BASIC-oriented format

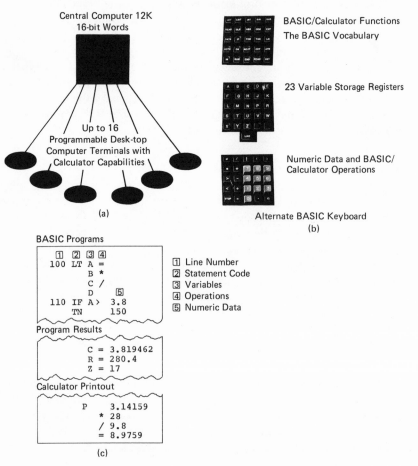

Central Computer 12K
16-bit Words

Up to 16
Programmable Desk-top
Computer Terminals with
Calculator Capabilities

(a)

BASIC/Calculator Functions

The BASIC Vocabulary

23 Variable Storage Registers

Numeric Data and BASIC/
Calculator Operations

Alternate BASIC Keyboard
(b)

BASIC Programs

```
    ① ② ③ ④
100 LT  A =
        B *
        C /
        D     ⑤
110 IF  A >  3.8
    TN       150
```

① Line Number
② Statement Code
③ Variables
④ Operations
⑤ Numeric Data

Program Results

```
        C = 3.819462
        R = 280.4
        Z = 17
```

Calculator Printout

```
    P     3.14159
    *  28
    /  9.8
    =  8.9759
```

(c)

An excellent example of simplicity, convenience, and low cost of terminal systems is Interplex System I [4] which uses the BASIC language for in-house time sharing: Interplex System I is a BASIC language, in-house, time-sharing system, which permits data-processing users in all disciplines to communicate with a multipurpose minicomputer. Using a desk-top data terminal, the user writes, assembles, debugs, and executes his own BASIC language programs. The Interplex system uses a terminal that combines the speed of electronic desk-top calculation with the ease of BASIC language programming. Moreover, the terminal functions as a sophisticated electronic calculator capable of performing a wide range of mathematical calculations.

Using Interplex System I practically eliminates all telephone line costs because the user communicates directly with the in-house computer. The system is easily expandable from four to 16 terminals. Unlike the fees for rented or leased facilities from outside companies, the fixed fee for Interplex System I allows unlimited use without additional cost. A unique feature of the system is a specially designed terminal. The language-oriented functional keyboard makes programming easier and minimizes operator error. A quite compact printer provides instantaneous hard copy. The system is designed to bring BASIC language programming within economic reach of everyone.

[4] Interplex Corp., 400 Totten Pond Road, Waltham, Mass. 02154.

2

Standard Computers: Fundamental Operations and Capabilities

Standard computers come in three sizes: small, midi, or maxi. This fact added to a wide variety of choices in costs and brands available gives scientists, managers, and engineers plenty of computer options. And low-cost minicomputers and microcomputers, as well as multicomputers, multiterminals, and new error-diagnosing and correcting networks, extend the options still further. But the choice of centralized or distributed systems using micros and minis has caused considerable difficulty in making decisions about equipment procurement, as we note in the pages ahead.

STANDARD COMPUTER SYSTEM OPERATIONS

In actual in-house operation, a programmer or systems analyst or the like contacts the system from a console, remote or attached terminal keyboard, and sometimes a control panel studded with lights and switches. The systems vary in type, complexity, capacity, speed, information retrieval and transmission, adaptability, and general or specific applications capabilities or purposes. All data-processing systems (the total group is most often simply called "computer"), regardless of size, type, or basic use, have certain fundamental concepts and operational principles. The data or information flow follows logical and functional lines.

Input devices

Data that are to be fed into a computer must first be converted to a form that an "input" machine can transmit. Many input units receive and convert information to numeric codes (see Figure 2.1). The CPU operates on, and ultimately receives, input consisting of only two basic symbols—a 0 or a 1. This is the internal binary mode. The term *binary* means that the computer components can receive and indicate only two possible states or conditions, and that is why they are so fast and basically uncomplicated. The ordinary light bulb operates in a binary mode; it is either on, producing light; or it is off, not producing light. Similarly, in a computer, the transistors, or circuits, are either conducting or not, in one direction or the other; input or storage conductors are magnetized or polarized one way or the other; voltage potentials are present or absent. All these conditions represent 0s or 1s. But the arrangement or coding, that is, the "positioning" of these two binary digits, or "bits," can form codes for numbers, letters, special symbols, alphabetic characters, and, in fact, complex sets of instructions. Thus a common method requires a keypunch clerk to punch holes in specific locations on a card (that is, $0110 = 6$) or paper tape; the presence or absence of holes in various positions represents the numbers or letters, that is, data and instructions, to the processor. Other forms of input can be magnetic tape or disks, magnetic ink (as on checks), or plain print or script (optically "read" and converted to binary—0s and 1s) in limited vocabularies. "Reading" (converting characters to binary numbers) by various types of optical scanners, some of which read 1,500 characters a second or 90,000 documents an hour, is done by translating visual electronic or magnetic pulses (or optic shapes) into electronic "signals." Some direct voice commands are now acceptable as input, as we have noted, and are converted to electronic impulses and to binary. Direct input can also be by telephone, teletype, or by "light pens" (stylus) pointed at the cathode-ray (TV-like) tube (CRT).

Memory or storage units

From the various input machines, including typewriter keyboards, data are moved to the storage (memory) areas now in the form of electronic pulses and to various numbered registers within the central processing unit (CPU). There or in special devices it is held or "remembered" and available for manipulation or conversion uses. The size of the main or auxiliary memory can be millions or billions of characters of data or instructions, including images or full ranges of complete tables; charts, diagrams, electronic voice patterns, and so on, and can be used over and over for retrieval or for solving specific problems. Communication equipment, speed-matching (interfaces) buffers or "multiplex" units usually are not contained within the processor. But billions of "bytes" (8-bit units that usually equal two nu-

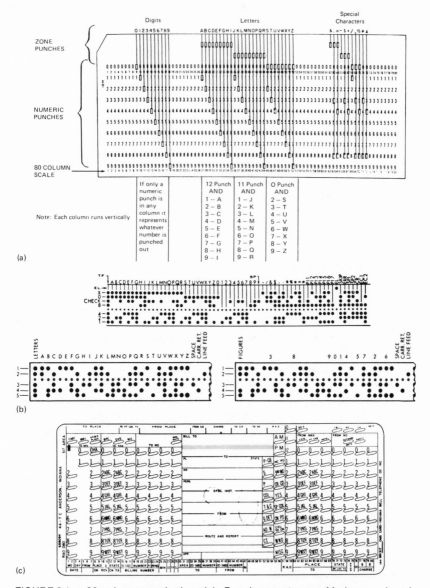

FIGURE 2.1. a. 80-column punched card, b. Punch paper tape, c. Mark-sensed card

merals or one character) of successive data can be held in disk, tape, drum, or cassette memory and then compared to be sure they are in proper order or for other control purposes. They are delivered when the computer "processor" (CPU) is ready and "polls" these devices every few thousandths (milliseconds) or millionths of a second (microseconds or μs) to accept whatever program or information input is present and needed.

Memory or storage devices or units can be connected to part of the computer system (OL or on-line), or they can be off-line in separate devices or units, and many units can be hooked in tandem. *Writing* means putting information into an internal CPU register; *reading* means taking information out of a register for use; *to erase* means to remove completely the information from the register; *to dump* means to remove or replace information with spaces or zeros or to copy or print all or part of the contents, that is, transfer from one storage device to another.

An intermediate memory storage (buffer) is a memory unit or area that is similar to an electronic scratch pad and is for holding working data temporarily. If it is a low-cost, "front-end" minicomputer, it can be programmed and expeditiously used for checking, scanning, or altering and for releasing "concentrated" information to the processor and then to a final output device.

Central processing unit

The arithmetic or logic unit (processor or CPU) is the functional unit that actually does the translation (to and from binary codes and compiler or high-level "languages") and other transformation or conversion work. Following the instructions as received by it (program inquiry or routine), the actual computing is the work of this "central" or basic unit. Data and instructions usually come from, and are returned to, storage and await further commands concerning output. The CPU controls the entire flow of data in and out of other (on-line) units. The "logical" operations include comparing two pieces of information; selecting which process to use if specific conditions are met (decision making); referring, shifting, complementing, rounding, diagnosing, or correcting errors (debugging), and so on. The CPU performs by using millions of electronic "flip-flops" per second, that is, changing 0s to 1s, as coded and instructed.

Output devices

Output devices "handle" data that can be "written" out from storage to output units, or they can be "read" into storage and then to output. The results of the processing are now converted to English (French, German, and so on) or decimals. They can be recorded in various ways: as a printed report (at up to a superfast 36,000 lines per minute) with from 60 to 150 characters per line; on a graphic (cathode-ray tube or plasma) display panel, in words, graphs, or drawings for viewing or altering; or as magnetic tape, paper tape, or cards for future input and processing or later conversion. Output can also be by phone, teletype, or audible and understandable sound in limited vocabularies, that is, New York Stock Exchange prices, credit reports, and the like.

Communications and control

The control section is used for those usual occasions when it is necessary to contact the computer other than to start or stop it. The console section may be used for input, but it is the slowest input, usually by typewriter. The control section often combines in one piece of equipment the internal memory, arithmetic, and inquiry sections. The control section thus directs, coordinates, and executes instructions in sequence and monitors the performance of the computer system. Operating systems (OS) are internal housekeeping or supervisory programs to direct the next cycle, terminal input, or inquiry after the preceding one is complete; or the OS can operate different cycles, programs, processes, or even other "slave" computers simultaneously (multiprocessing). The control section becomes extremely vital in case of component breakdown or when debugging (postmortem) routines are in operation. And, of course, the control section "handles" the input-output traffic,[1] the polling, time slicing, and all other types of communications. Many systems now use a separate low-cost minicomputer for these activities (or a specially programmed ROM-read-only memory or a low-cost microprocessor), saving the CPU of the main computer for "compute" operations only.

THE MANIPULATION OF INFORMATION

Information is power—financial power, production power, marketing power, and so on. When data have meaning to someone, they are information. We have noted that bit strings or instruction sequences are coded to connect information streams into action commands, problem solutions or other routines, procedures, and programs. The 8-bit strings (bytes) are often grouped into four bytes to represent 32-bit "words" or as two bytes into 16-bit "words." Human beings, usually programmers, put a great deal of intelligence into various codes. This human intelligence is then transferred to machine orders, specific demands and procedures, and interactive systems, which result in combinations of many short series of instructions being developed into long, complex programs. A simple and most common "evaluating" routine (benchmark) is designed to compare results of some arithmetic process. The program will cause a "jump" or branch to another process or program on the basis of comparison of a manipulation result; that is, is one answer "less than, equal to, or greater than the other" or many others? If one answer is, for example, less than a specific number (a temperature), the computer starts another routine that might order a machine

---

[1] IOCS, input-output control system, and DOS, disk-operating systems, are names for the rather complex internal operations software systems of routines for repetitive control. These large programs are also called executives, monitors, supervisors, and so forth.

(heater) turned on or an airplane to move to a specific higher altitude. Great ranges of arithmetic or calculated comparisons and consequent actions can be performed simply, very accurately, and extremely fast. Artists use bits as "light or dark spots" or shades of colors and easily organize them into pictures, musical notes, or reconstructed photos, as from the moon and Mars. Many of these codes cause other peripheral equipment to read in specific cards or tapes or to accept or reject communications, and so on. Results become balance sheets, neatly formated profit-and-loss statements, inventory control figures, or analysis charts in color or three dimensions. These are applications programs, dedicated for specific use.

Whereas most operating system or internal control programs were very complex and expensive, microminiaturized devices called PROMs (for programmable read-only memory) have severely reduced the cost and increased the versatility by making these "pluggable." Generally, once these fundamental control programs are in the computer, they remain so. Parts of the OS are read over and over to exercise various controls such as polling, new job entry, peripherals switching, and so on. Control programs are not written out or printed out (dumped) except to discover errors (to debug). ROMs are frequently used as hard-wired operating systems; they become "firmware"—software that is built-in but that is still variable because it is replaceable, pluggable. Once a software design and program have been devised, they can be easily and cheaply "burned" into a ROM. Dealers offer 24-hour service for ROMs, customized to user specifications. PROM programmers units are also available at low cost for in-house customer ROM development.

There are many kinds of memory, storage devices, and techniques. We have mentioned main memory within the CPU, the "scratch pad" or manipulation space for the data and programs used during runs. The size of this memory generally defines the capacity of the computer. It is usually described as a computer with a 32K (Kilo for 1024) "main memory," meaning a capacity of 32×1024 computer "words" of 8-, 16-, or 32-bit lengths. Applications programs, after being used, are returned to their storage location whereas ROMs remain within the computer to be used on immediate call from the CPU and are, in effect, part of it.

Random access memories (RAMs) are also now integrated circuit "chips." In contrast to ROMs, which are complete sequential programs, any bit or word can be accessed directly at random. They are now also very cheap and easy to produce and are beginning to compete with, and substitute for, tapes, disks, and other bulky electromechanical memory devices. They are pluggable, insertable—but data can be read in and out, changed—in contrast to "fixed" (in most cases) ROMs. "Intelligent" terminals make extensive use of ROMs and RAMs and single chip microprocessors, and many are "field-programmable"; that is, their versatility can be changed by adding new ROMs and RAMs by the users. These capabilities are the primary bases for the new very low costs of terminals, programmable calculators, minis and micros—and the real cause for the "computer explosion" that began in mass-production quantities in 1974.

THE ART OF FLOWCHARTING

Systems analysts develop flowcharts to speed up analysis and design. A diagram that shows the relation of one business operation to another is quickly and easily understood; a thick procedures manual is not. Flowcharts enable analysts and accountants to view the whole system at once, to pick out potential inefficiencies, and to make adjustments or improvements quickly. The instant overview is so desirable that continuous users must memorize most of the attributes of flowcharting.

The basic forms of flowcharting are the systems chart and the flow diagram. The systems chart outlines the entire system, all the paths that information takes and all the processes it undergoes. It always follows the same basic format:

Input: What information is coming in?

Process? What is done to the information?

Output: What is the final result?

A system may contain several two- and three-step operations. A data document goes to clerk A, who does something to it and sends it on. This output becomes the input to clerk B, and so on.

A flow diagram shows how information flows through a computer program and also the series of logical steps that the machine performs. It is the first step in translating management's procedures into machine instructions. The user easily sees the relation of one operation to another and sees it more clearly than he would in a written description. A flow diagram is a universal medium for communicating the program idea to persons who do not know computer language or who know a different one.

The examples in Figures 2.2 and 2.3 show how the symbols are used. These basics are all one really needs to describe a basic system, for example, input-output movement and processing. Other additional input-output symbols, when used, further classify and clarify the chart by pointing out the medium that stores information: punched card, tape, disk, or whatever. Effective users must gain wide practice in flowcharting. Each will need a plastic template of symbols. Drafting and office supply dealers carry them, and most computer manufacturers give them freely to potential customers. Users choose a system that they know completely. They go over the key steps in their minds, draw the appropriate symbol for each step, and keep asking, "What information comes in, and who gets it? Where does it go next?" and so on.

I. BASIC SYMBOLS	II. SPECIALIZED INPUT/OUTPUT SYMBOLS	III. SPECIALIZED PROCESSING SYMBOLS
INPUT/OUTPUT Any input or output operation, through any medium.	**PUNCHED CARD**	**PREDEFINED PROCESS** A subroutine or series of operations defined elsewhere.
	MAGNETIC TAPE	**DECISION** A point at which the program must determine which of a number of alternate paths must be taken.
PROCESS Any operation, or group of operations, that changes the value, form, or location of information.	**PUNCHED PAPER TAPE**	
	DOCUMENT	**PREPARATION** An instruction or routine that changes the program by modifying instructions, switches, or registers.
	MANUAL INPUT Usually by keyboard.	
ANNOTATION Provides additional notes or comments. Broken line shows symbol being explained.	**ON-LINE STORAGE** Magnetic disk or drum, magnetic cards or strips, or microfilm.	**MANUAL OPERATION** An off-line process.
		AUXILIARY OPERATION An offline operation done by equipment not directly connected to the central processor.
	MAGNETIC DRUM	**MERGE** Combining two or more sets of info into a single.
DIRECTION OF FLOW The direction of information flow is shown by lines drawn between figures. In charting, flow is left to right and from top to bottom. Use direction indicators whenever this pattern is broken.	**MAGNETIC DISK**	**EXTRACT** Taking one or more items from a set.
		SORT Arranging into a particular sequence.
	DISPLAY Any on-line device, such as CRT, console printer, plotter.	**COLLATE** Merging two or more sets of info items into two or more other sets.
		CONNECTOR Where lines of information come together.
	COMMUNICATIONS LINK Information is transmitted from point to point via a telecommunications link.	**TERMINAL** A terminal point in a flowchart: start, stop, delay, interrupt.

FIGURE 2.2.

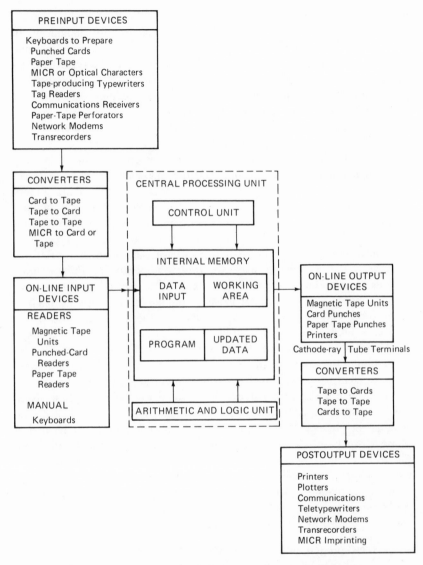

FIGURE 2.3. Configuration of a standard automatic data process system

PROGRAMMING PROCEDURES

Programming is still mistakenly considered a "black art" by many managers, and it will probably remain so for those too busy to learn something about it themselves. The most popular languages are FORTRAN, for general use; COBOL, for business operations; BASIC, APL, and PL/1 for terminals and telecommunications. The languages of the 1960s were the much more detailed and difficult mnemonic and internal assembly languages. In the late 1960s, the higher level (compiler) languages mentioned became very popular owing to the very significant reductions in most types of memory costs. These also permit less qualified technicians to enter the programming field. Management has also recently become very cost-conscious, especially about computer labor as well as hardware and software. They have also discovered that shortcuts, such as no documentation or standards control, have many unpleasant and costly side effects.

In the 1970s, especially the last half, there is great optimism for very widespread use of convenience and versatility of low-cost, rentable software packages. Thousands of inventor-owners are offering vast numbers of them to users. These packages do not represent unrealistic promises; they are simply functional products that are operational today at thousands of installations. The programming process at many commercial companies is frequently simplified as follows: here is a basic data-processing problem; write a program to solve it; make the program operational. Programming and maintenance of commercial systems are often viewed as a continuous and nonending requirement that exists for the life of the computer. If a program represents a standard requirement of the corporation—such as payroll or billing—its anticipated life is as long as that of the corporation.

Almost all programs pass through three phases: phase 1 is the implementation of the program; phase 2 is maintenance of the program to meet business changes; phase 3 is the possible conversion of the program to use other hardware. Figure 2.4 shows the detailed steps of each phase. Note that the testing and documentation requirements for phases 2 and 3 are the same as for phase 1. Programming disciplines and controls established in phase 1 can be carried over into phases 2 and 3. In parallel with these phases is the need for continual auditing of the program in order to ensure that it meets the installation's standards, that it operates efficiently, and that documentation is up-to-date.

Some very broad goals that the typical data-processing organization wants to achieve include the following:

1. Increase programming productivity and simplify problem solving.
2. Reduce hardware and maintenance costs.
3. Increase program reliability.
4. Protect data-processing assets, and minimize conversion requirements.

In order to achieve these generalized goals, one must attain the following specific goals:

1. Write fewer program steps to solve a problem.
2. Provide better debugging tools and simpler test data preparation.
3. Analyze programs for inefficient code.

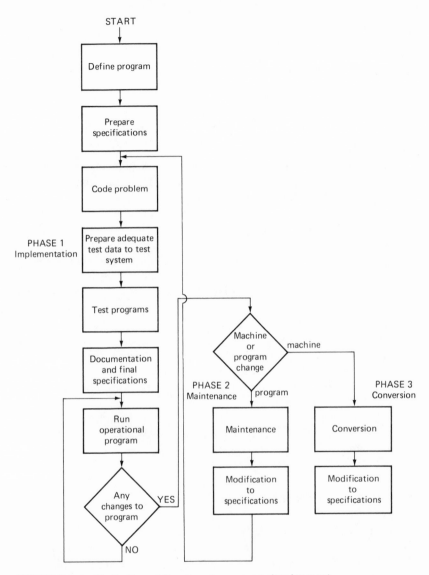

FIGURE 2.4. An illustration of the steps to program development

4. Establish systematic check-out methods.
5. Audit all program changes and enforce installation standards.

Documentation can be standardized and produced more easily with a program package that flowcharts a program, produces cross-referenced listings for ease in locating statements, and diagnoses errors in logical flow. Programs can be stored, maintained, and protected with a librarian system.

These "packages" store programs in compressed form to save space, maintain a history of program changes, monitor program activity, and use a password system for program security.

DEFINING THE OPERATIONS UNIVERSE

Computer operations generally include the following six "line" areas:

1. Data preparation—converting source documents into machine-processable units such as punched cards, optically read documents, and various forms and procedures of key-entered data.
2. Data control—organizing data into forms and system flows so that they get where they are supposed to in the proper format at the proper time.
3. Scheduling and staging—assembling all of the needed data in proper machine form for orderly computer processing if batch processing is used or developing and adhering to time frame schedules for on-line input.
4. Machine operations—managing input-output data as they are processed, including terminal or console control, use of other hardware devices, and proper machine handling for security and maintenance.
5. Output control—checking that the right data have been organized on files, on paper, and in proper format order for dissemination and use within the organization.
6. Work delivery—assuring that the output gets to the right department at the right time in an orderly sequence as visual reports, printouts, copies, signals of "exception" reports, or schedules and analyses.

GENERAL WORK FLOW PROCEDURES

Quite obviously, many variations exist in organization structures and functional activities of various companies. Such factors as size of organization, amount and type of data to be processed, and the relationship of the data to the needs of the organization determine the components of the structural makeup of the department as finally established. Personnel required for its operation are then sought and trained as operations personnel.

Usually, functional organization charts reflect the specific steps involved in processing information and data. They are based on sequences of three basic phases: (1) planning and analysis, (2) problem programming, and (3) operations, which include data collection, conversion, and processing. Often other DP personnel are located in units other than the data-processing department.

Phase 1: Problem planning, formulation, and system analysis

The primary phase is related to the overall planning, scheduling, and coordination of activities to achieve the desired results. By analyzing the data and the problem, one can determine the cost, machine capability, man- and machine-hours required, and whether processing can be performed electronically, mechanically, manually, or by a combination of such methods. Programmers frequently participate in a discussion of machine capabilities. The preparation of work-flow plans and procedures establishes the processing sequence. At this point, decisions are made pertaining to enlarging or altering the computer system to meet adequately the organization's processing needs. Budget estimates are prepared to justify the cost of processing operations and equipment. The problem that has been developed is then formulated more specifically and further refined. A mathematical or statistical analysis and statement of the problem is developed when required. Mathematical procedures are devised, and illustrative charts, tables, and diagrams are prepared.

Systems analysis and design

The systems analysis portion is concerned with the determination of the data-processing needs of an organization. Systems analysis is the fact-finding phase of system design and is a methodical systematic study of the administration and operation of the organization. In this phase every fact pertaining to the operation of the organization is collected, organized, and evaluated. The rigorous review of all the facts and findings developed in the systems analysis phase is translated into an ideal plan or design of a data-processing system. The design devises or determines the most efficient methods and techniques for implementation, including detailed process flowcharts or diagrams. The specific computer system requirements are worked out at this stage, usually in collaboration with high-level programmers.

Phase II: programming

Fundamental programming is designed to the ideas and language of human beings developed in the system analysis and the system design phase into the language of equipment. Such a language, which is a predetermined coding system, provides the equipment with the means for executing and controlling all the steps required in problem solution. Programming also involves analysis of equipment capabilities and limitations in order to break up the program into successive runs whenever required and to establish a machine configuration.

Phase III: operations

The operating stage is related to the actual data-processing machine operations that are involved in solving a problem and in obtaining the solution. In many installations all necessary data are transferred directly onto magnetic tape from punch cards or paper tape or are keyed directly to tape or to the computer from typewriter terminals. The various data tapes and program instructions are mounted in the pertinent tape units or stored on disks or disk packs. The system is then put into operation and carefully controlled during each step of the total process. Final results are recorded on printout forms, tapes, cards, microfilm, or cathode-ray tube (CRT) printouts, depending on the needs of the organization.

Some fundamental capabilities of most small computer systems

The memory protect/privileged instruction feature provides a "hardware protected" environment so that an executing program cannot destroy the operating system or another job.

Modular organization refers to executive functions common to several application environments that are included in the CPU nucleus, and executive or operating system functions unique to specific environments are embodied in subsystems as ROMS.

The *CPU nucleus* is partially memory-resident and partially disk-resident, with the disk-resident portions called into main memory as required, using dynamic allocation techniques. The nucleus provides for such functions as the following:

1. *Job management*—to provide the facilities for job submission, resource allocation, job initiation, execution management, and job termination. The number of active jobs is limited only by available resources.
2. *Task management*—for task creation, scheduling, synchronization, and termination. Multitasking is supported both across several programs and within a single program.
3. *Memory management*—for dynamic memory allocation and release.
4. *I/O management*—to provide I/O functions from programs to peripherals on a device-independent basis.
5. *File management*—to provide a device-independent interface from a program to data stored on disk. Generally three file types are supported:
   a. *Linked sequential file*, which has an access interface identical to that used for the various sequential devices (magnetic tape, line printer, card reader, and so on). Consistency between sequential device and disk is achieved with the linked sequential file.

b. *Relative record file*, which provides a low overhead direct disk access to a contiguous section where I/O transfers may be either blocked or unblocked.

c. *Indexed file*, which provides a directory-supported random access method based on a record identifier whose size is user-specified. File operations include record addition, insertion, modification, deletion, and retrieval, using either a random or sequential access method. A multiway balanced tree directory provides random access with extremely low disk access for search.

Operator communications provide an extensive command language that may be used from the system operator's console.

Subsystems are individually activated and deactivated by the systems operator as needed. When active, a subsystem (a programmed ROM) operates in privileged mode and is essentially part of the operating system. Main memory is allocated to the subsystem only when it is active so that a user who is not interested in a particular operating environment does not pay a penalty for the ability to support the environment.

VARIOUS TYPES OF EQUIPMENT
RELATED TO SMALL COMPUTERS

Batch input reader is used to effect direct assignment of a sequential input device to a sequence of serially executed programs.

Batch input spooler is used to effect spooled input from a sequential input device to a sequence of programs that may execute in parallel.

Batch output spooler is used to effect spooled output to a sequential output device.

Interactive terminal processing provides for interactive communications between the system and local or remote terminals. Features include an interface to support multi-user interactive applications programs, interactive file editing, remote job entry, and job status retrieval.

Real-time processing provides for multitasking on a priority scheduling basis. The processor may be switched from task to task by an I/O request, a supervisor call, a device interrupt, or at the end of a task. It provides a roll-out/roll-in feature to ensure real/time response to high priority requests.

Peripherals software includes multiple type disk drives, multiple disk cartridge drives, magnetic tape drives, silent ASR or KSR data terminals, card readers, line printers, alphanumeric CRT terminals, paper tape readers and/or punches, communications interfaces, hardware vectored interrupts, and up to 64K word main memory.

Computer standard software includes loaders, I/O support packages, assemblers, linkage editors, source editors, debug aids, and so on.

The Wang 2200S Basic vocabulary
Hard-wired for convenience, it contains the
following functions, statements, and commands:

Functions

EXP	#PI()	INT
LOG	SGN	STR
SQR	ARCSIN	LEN
ABS	ARCOS	HEX
SIN	ARCTAN	VAL
COS	RND	NUM
TAN		

The Wang System 2200S automatically shifts in and out of
floating point arithmetic when needed and provides
13-digit accuracy throughout its 10^{-99} to 10^{+99} range.
Trigonometric arguments can be calculated in radians,
degrees, or gradians.

Statements

COM	HEXPRINT	PRINT
CONVERT	IF END THEN	PRINTUSING
DATA	IF THEN	READ
DEFFN	%(IMAGE)	REM
DEFFN'	INPUT	RESTORE
DIM	KEYIN	RETURN
END	LET	RETURN CLEAR
FOR	LOAD	SELECT
GOSUB	NEXT	STOP
GOSUB'	ON (GOSUB,	TRACE
GOTO	GOTO)	

Commands

BACKSPACE	LIST
CLEAR	RENUMBER
CONTINUE	RESET
HALT/STEP	RUN
LINE ERASE	STATEMENT NUMBER

Commands in EDIT mode

INSERT	ERASE
DELETE	RECALL

FIGURE 2.5. The new and popular trend—BASIC language keyboards on ''smart''
terminals and stand-alone terminal-computers. Note the BASIC language commands on keys for direct input. *Courtesy: Wang Laboratories, Inc.*

Computer hardware is designed to take advantage of the hardware features of microcomputers. Other characteristics include hardware multiply/divide, memory parity, memory protect, privileged instructions, power fail interrupt, ROM bootstrap loader, removable control panel with keylock, hardware breakpoint and program sense switches, DMA interface port, bus ports, and so on.

Typical system components are described as follows:

1. Direct data entry facility enables information to be typed directly into the system without the need for punched cards or paper tape. Eight to 16 (or more) stations can generally be employed according to work loads.
2. Visual display units enable access to up-to-the-minute information on orders, stock, credit, and so on in seconds. Multiples of eight stations can usually be employed, sited locally or remotely. They can also be used for updating and entering data. Printers or copiers can be added to produce the necessary documents.
3. Telephone data terminal facilities enable the system to be used as groups of intelligent satellite terminals to a parent or remote system or to data banks of other systems.
4. Central processors employ integrated circuitry and microprogramming for reliability and flexibility. MOS semiconductor main arteries are available in sizes of 16,384 to 32,768 words or more in 4,096-word increments and have cycle (instruction execution) times of about 1,000 nanoseconds for each word.
5. Fixed/exchangeable disk memories have minimum storage capacity of 10 million characters, expandable to 30 million or more characters by adding extra units.

FIGURE 2.6. Basic configuration of a small computer system

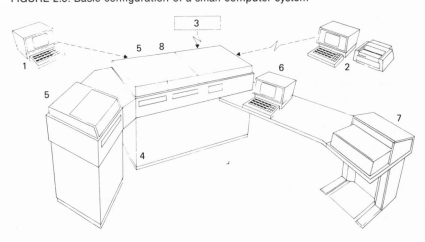

6. Operator's consoles give swift, silent, visual communication between computer and operator.
7. Line printers operate at 150 or 300 or more lines a minute with 132 print positions, and faster, nonimpact ones are available.
8. Card readers operate at 300 cards a minute or faster.
9. Basic software generally includes two levels of disk-based operating systems together with RPG2, COBOL, BASIC APL, and FORTRAN and a comprehensive set of utility programs.
10. Applications software generally includes packages for PERT (project evaluation and review technique), file inquiry, payroll, and other financial projects. Other packages are used for on-line order entry, inventory control, and many other types of processing. These are often written in RPG so that the user can tailor them and add his own special requirements.
11. Included with most basic systems is (a) the facility to run a single batch program together with input and output spooling and inquiries via the operator's console or (b) executive facilities for key-to-disk direct data entry with eight or more keyboards, each with a video screen.

SMALL COMPUTERS FOR SMALL BUSINESS

Just a few years ago small and medium-sized businesses had an idea of computers as always being too tricky to handle. Too much grief needed to get a system into action—and keep it working? Too complicated to assess whether it would be doing the job properly or not? They may well have been right. First-time users have had a lot to cope with. Till now. Now many firms have designed systems specially for the smaller company. And so, for many people, their first computer has fewer technicalities on the inside and simple controls on the outside. Thus practically anybody's staff can easily learn to operate or program it. Compact pieces of equipment now look good and fit easily into offices without disturbance or fuss.[2] Generalized small systems include the following:

1. Generous minimum-storage capacity—to hold files for immediate access.
2. Direct data entry facility—eliminating the need for punched cards or paper tape.
3. Local or remote visual display units—to help staff members do their jobs more efficiently.
4. Multiprogramming—more than one job running at the same time to get the most out of the computer.

[2] According to International Data Corp., of Newtonville, Mass., by 1977 small business computers will compose fully half the total number of general-purpose computers installed. Another finding of the study: 25 percent of all U.S. businesses with 100–249 employees now perform in-house processing.

1. MAGNETIC TAPE SYSTEM

High performance magnetic tape systems usually are designed for plug-to-plug compatible use with all IBM System|360 and System 370 tape drive systems. Most have single density (1600 bits per inch—bpi) nine-track or dual density (800/1600 bpi) and seven-track features, including a controller to permit off-line service of individual tape units without disturbing the system.

2. "FLOPPY DISK" DRIVE

A typical low-cost disk drive for computer system use is one by Cal Comp's Century Data Systems Division, the Model 110 "floppy disk" drive. This is a random access, removable media memory device with storage capacity of more than 1.4 megabits of data. It provides track-to-track access time of 6 msec. (1,000ths of a second) and transfers data at 33.8 Kbits (thousand bits) per second. The recording medium is a flexible mylar, oxide-coated disk, permanently jacketed in an 8.0 inch square plastic envelope. The CDS 110 provides the system designer with a reliable, flexible, and inexpensive method of transferring digital data at high speed. Available with read/write capability, it is suited for use as a data retrieval and storage device for data entry, terminal communications or auxiliary storage, or as an integral part of a peripheral controller or mainframe to provide control program load, diagnostic program storage, memory backup storage, and control command storage.

5. ALPHANUMERIC COMPUTER OUTPUT MICROFILM (COM) SYSTEMS

COM printing speed, high quality, ease of operation, and superior reliability are now available in low-cost COM systems. These can replace impact printers or add COM printing capability in basic configurations. Each configuration may be equipped with either a 16-mm. or a 105-mm. microfiche camera. The microfiche camera will also transport 16-mm. film. Typical throughput speeds of 10,000 to 15,000 lines per minute are achieved with 132 characters per line and a maximum of 66 lines per page. Actual throughput speed depends on data input rate and tape blocking.

4. DRUM PLOTTER

Large-scale plotters are often designed specifically for plotting operations where speed, and high volume are of prime importance. They have a throughput capacity of up to 10 inches (25 cm.) per second, making them especially well suited to applications such as contour mapping, PERT and CPM charting, and graphing and verification plotting for circuit and cartographic artwork and for dynamic overlay graphs of company financial data such as department or division comparison sales, projections of budgets, promotions, etc. They produce exceptionally smooth lines and are valuable electronic scaling devices. A built-in cutting bar allows the operator to cut quickly and easily remove completed plots.

3. DISK STORAGE FACILITY

A standard disk storage facility is usually designed to provide users with large-capacity, high-performance, on-line line data storage capabilities for medium or large-scale computers. Most offer up to 800 million bytes of on-line data storage with data transfer rates up to 806,000 bytes per second (dual 1,612,000 digits per second). A typical system consists of a disk storage controller integrated with up to eight spindles of storage. Rotational position sensing (RPS) allows the channel and storage control of the facility to be released during rotational delay, thereby making them available for other operations during this period, which serves to increase total system throughput.

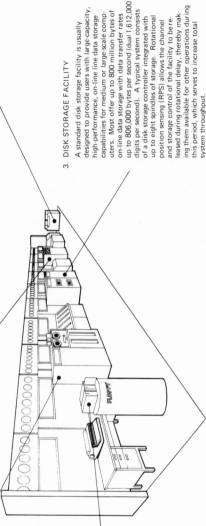

FIGURE 2.7. Basic configuration of a medium-sized computer system

5. Operator's video console—for swift, simple operation.
6. Simple programming languages—to get problems solved faster.
7. Satellite operation—to give small computers access to the facilities of a bigger computer system.
8. Integrated circuitry and microprogramming techniques also usually employed—to give reliability and flexibility to the systems.

BASIC PROGRAMMING CONCEPTS

The beginning programmer must start with the most fundamental of all concepts; that is, the computer is a mute and dumb electronic machine; it is totally useless unless it has intelligent, step-by-step, very specific guidance. That guidance, direction, or set of instructions is called a program. There are generally five basic components that are fundamental to the development of a program. A program is itself a system, and each system must have design. Therefore, the first step is system design, which is, in effect, a detailed systems chart or block diagram that analyzes the processing desired. The programmer requires this design, and the computer demands, owing to its specific construction, a chained group of procedures necessary to achieve the objective of the specific application.

Step two concerns the planning of the program. This relates to the detailed logic of the procedure and the exact steps for the computer processing required. The flowchart is the basic instrument to be developed and followed. Step two includes the very important documentation. This refers to the specific annotations or explanations that accompany the systems flowcharts and block diagrams. It specifically relates to the preparation and assembly of documents that describe a program and its operating characteristics.

Step three is the actual coding. This is the writing of the "run" computer instructions. The programmer usually has a choice of several languages that he may choose and that are dependent upon the type of application and the model and size of the computer. For example, most business programs will be written in COBOL. Many scientific and problem type programs will be developed in FORTRAN. Those who are more terminal-oriented will probably use BASIC, especially if their system is designed for time sharing. Other specialists will use LIST processing languages, such as LISP, or production control languages, such as APT III.

Step four is a compilation of the program for direct computer use. This relates to the translation of the programming instructions from the specific language selected into the actual machine language for the run.

Step five is error detection and correction, more commonly referred to as diagnostics and debugging. This function relates to the various procedures and tests designed within the computer instructions and hardware for the elimination of errors in procedure, logic, coding, and transmission. Basically, the above can be broken into three general topics: (1) system and programming design and planning, (2) specific explanations of processing instructions, and (3) analysis of techniques for program modification and input/output instructions.

Computer instructions designate the elementary steps for execution or operation of programs. They are in sequences and designed to specify what shall be done under each and all potential circumstances that might arise during the processing stage. Most languages have capabilities for altering instructions as the program is run. Fundamentally, the computer is instructed to read a message from a card, terminal, tape, and the like and store the contents in memory. The next basic step is to move the contents from one memory location to another and to input/output the results the instruction seeks. Therefore, the program is, in effect, the specification of the execution of a number of individual, rigidly defined steps or operations. If the program offers or seeks alternatives, different program paths must be directed for each of these conditions or alternatives, based upon a "choice" test that these instructions include. Perhaps the best example of this "resultant branching" after a decision has been made is the "if" statement in FORTRAN, such as: if X is less than Y, branch to instruction A; if X is equal to Y, branch to instruction B; if X is greater than Y, branch to instruction C. This is, in effect, an instruction modification feature, and the instructions provide for each possible eventuality.

In the preparation of the instructions, the programmer designs a processing system to record, collect, sort, process, or disseminate the desired information. He has predetermined the format of the input, reports, files, media, and output. He has also specified the individual computer runs and the segmentation and flow of procedures. He is fully cognizant of the detail provided in the source documents, the various pieces of equipment that will be handling the information being processed, the type of computer files to be maintained, and the design of the report or output to be produced.

Coding is the actual writing of computer instructions in the selected language that will be translated into machine language. If the programmer is using various assembly languages or symbolic codes, he must follow those very rigid rules with respect to punctuation, semantics, format, and so on. The conversion of the language selected or the symbolic coding to machine language instructions is done in the compilation process. Generally, "assembling" a program refers to those symbolic languages, such as AUTOCODER, SPS, and so on. The term *compile* refers to the translation of programs written in such procedure- or problem-oriented languages as FORTRAN, COBOL, ALGOL, and so on. In either case, the assembly or compilation is carried out by an internal program either built in or automatically called by the computer. The result is that a machine language is developed to perform steps represented by the original programmer's prepared instructions but in the binary form that the computer can accept and manipulate.

The programmer can avoid various errors or mistakes ("bugs") by thoroughly reviewing the program at his desk before he releases it for assembly or compilation. Most compilers (internally stored translator programs) print out diagnostic messages when errors are discovered. The programmer might do some preventive error control by first running tests or segments of the program for comparison with preplanned results. If diagnostic messages are printed out, there are many procedures available to trace the error and correct it. One is a memory dump (printout), which allows the programmer to inspect the instructions and data at various points in the program. The programmer might also refer to his documentation to see that all documents, notes, and specifics associated with the program and the run follow the manuals of operating instructions of the equipment being used. Such manuals usually contain systems flowcharts, record layouts, files reports, decision tables, symbolic coding, sample test data, and change records. The programmer quite likely has used various tools as he developed his program, which include the flowcharts and decision tables mentioned earlier. Many systems analysts and programmers also use layout charts, grid charts, and sample programs to help organize their thinking and visualize the tasks that the program is designed to complete. The layout charts are usually preprinted forms supplied by the manufacturer for card layouts, tape and disk layouts, printer layouts, and so on. Name of fields, types of characters, location of decimal points, formating, space allocation, and so on are his primary guides. Grid charts are basically tabular procedures for summarizing the connections and relationships between translating segments or sets of data. A close analysis of these help eliminate redundancy in data, formating, and reports. The system flowchart shows the flow of data through all parts of the data-processing system. The program flowchart shows the sequencing of the coded program steps, and both contain information and procedures for converting the source media to output media. A decision table describes the logic of a computer program and can be used as a substitute for, or supplement to, the program flowchart. It is especially useful if the program has a complex set of conditions that require testing before action is to be taken or determined. The order in which conditions must be tested is made clear with this handy device.

The actual instructing of a computer involves writing the sequence of instructions, the execution of which will produce the planned result. These instructions are stored in identifiable locations within internal memory. Such identification can be a physical location or, in virtual memory, can be addressed by content or "string." An instruction is usually called upon by specifying either directly or indirectly its location or address. Data words and instruction words are significantly different from each other, and, obviously, the data word cannot be translated into an operating command. Each computer has its own repertoire of instructions distinctly and uniquely based on the circuitry of that machine. Instructions for one computer will not usually work on another unless an emulation program has been prepared and is used.

The basic type of computer instruction contains at least two segments—the operation code and the operand. The operation code is the actual specification of what is to be performed. The operand is the specification of what is to be *used* to form the operation. The particular *operation* code, therefore, determines how the *operand* code is to be interpreted. The operand can be a location of an instruction, an addressable register, a memory address, a unit of the computer configuration such as a tape unit, printer, and so on; or it may be a literal number used by the program. The basic construction with actual data specified by the operand is known as an *immediate instruction*.

Most instruction formats are single-address or two-address. Three things must be specifically noted to complete an arithmetic operation—either the circuitry or the sequence of instructions, that is, the addresses of the factors to be used and the address for storing the result. To add two numbers and store the result require the three instructions if only one operand is specified by each instruction. For example, (1) place one number in an accumulative register, (2) add a second number to the number in that register, and (3) store the contents of the accumulator register in a specific memory location. The two-address system usually specifies the location of both factors for the arithmetic with storage of the result at the address of one of the factors (which causes erasure) or a specified unit of memory. If both numbers are to be preserved, one of them must be moved to another location before the add instruction is given. After an instruction is executed, the next instruction must be located. This can be accomplished by sequential location or specific location. In the first case, instructions follow one after another unless a branching instruction breaks the sequence.

Writing sequences of computer instructions as designed on the flowchart is known as coding, and coding can take place at different levels. There are many types of coding, such as machine language codes or procedure- or problem-oriented codes or still others. The levels are (1) machine language, (2) symbolic language, (3) symbolic with macro instructions, and (4) higher-order language (problem- or procedure-oriented). The general form for all instructions at all levels except (4) is operation code plus operand. The computer can only proceed with the absolute or machine-level coding. All other codes must be converted into that form.

The procedure then suggests that higher-order or "English" type languages must be translated into assembly languages and then into binary language. The translating programs that accomplish this are called compilers. A distinct compiler must be available for higher-order languages. Consequently, when a computer is purchased or leased, the user must specify which compiler he requires, either built-in hardware or available on tapes or placed on disks. The most popular higher-order languages are FORTRAN, COBOL, BASIC, ALGOL, and so on. Therefore, users will buy a machine with a FORTRAN compiler and/or a COBOL compiler, and so forth. The compilers create machine language programs from the much easier-to-use languages as substitutes for symbolic or machine coding.

Users can learn the BASIC language in a few hours and FORTRAN and COBOL in a few weeks. Developing reasonable proficiency in a machine coding may take many months or even years for some machines. The trend, therefore, is for most programming to be developed in higher-level languages and run through compilers for direct machine use. Machine programs may be, in some cases, significantly more efficient in running time with machine language if particular segments are run extremely repetitiously. For example, inventory programs or special accounting programs will take longer to run through a compiler for translation to binary than if they were programmed in assembly or direct binary. Compilers, however, have become so efficient that running-time losses are relatively insignificant. In summary of the preceding, the reader should differentiate quite distinctly between the programming sequence. The assembly programming is the software aid that translates the symbolic language program. When the symbolic language is the one the programmer uses, it is the "source program." The source program can also be FORTRAN or COBOL if the programmer writes in any of these higher-level languages.

The machine language program is always the object program, that is, the final program that the computer will accept. The programming steps following this sequence are these: (1) The assembly program is read into the computer in order to control translated procedure. It is manufacturer-supplied and considered part of the total hardware-software package. (2) The source program that is written by the programmer in the symbolic language of the particular machine is recorded on the input media, such as tapes, cards, and so on. (3) During the assembly operation, the source program is treated as data, and the CPU accepts one instruction at a time as controlled by the assembly program. (4) The assembly programmer's system is thus the program translator of the source program written by the programmer into machine language or object program. This is the output of the assembly run. The source program then is in place and ready to begin execution of the problem when it is entered. (5) After the assembly run, that program is stored and kept on hand for other runs. The object program is now ready and read into the CPU as the first step in the production run. (6) The problem data is then run from a medium on which it was recorded and held in storage until the appropriate time.

Programming aids

Until 1969 most manufacturers provided a considerable amount of software, or programming aids, and whole ranges of program support systems at no cost to users. In 1969, IBM "unbundled" the hardware from the software. The big firm decided to price hardware and software separately. Several competitors followed suit. Now computer users must pay for programming aids, special program systems, and applications programs separately from the hardware. Many computer manufacturers have not followed suit and still provide these pieces of software at no cost. Software of every type, including compilers, can also be obtained from independent programming and software firms and from most of the many user associations that promote an exchange of programs for users who have purchased the same machines. Programming aids include, besides symbolic assembly programs and compilers, other systems such as utility programs, report program generators, library routines, special conversion routines, and hundreds of special applications programs.

1. Utility programs are usually concerned with performing "service" or "housekeeping" routines or functions. They are also concerned with operating and testing characteristics of types of software. They most often control machine functions or machine-produced conditions. Usually, they have very little relation to the actual processing of data. Examples include loading programs in memory, dumping programs from memory (output contents to tapes or printout contents in hard copy), tracing operations by printing out specific steps, duplicating magnetic tapes, or performing various sort programs.
2. Report program generators are programs that permit the computer to write other programs automatically according to specifications of particular problems. These routines or program segments are most often referred to as RPG, report program generator. They produce complete programs in the desired format of various reports. They usually can specify considerable detail as to desired headings, styles, and data positions on output sheets. RPG is very popular and extremely convenient. In effect, it is a program that generates or writes another program.
3. Library routines are ordered sets or collections of standard and proved routines that solve common computational or information retrieval problems. Library routines most often include wide ranges and specific types of mathematical and statistical routines. The most common example is the routine for calculating the square root of a number. When such a routine is spliced directly into a main program, it is often called an "open subroutine." If it is "attached" to a main program but remains separate, it is called a "closed routine." In effect, it is a checked-out or proved routine that may be incorporated into a larger routine, or a pro-

gram is maintained in the library with others to be used as an aid to programming.

4. Conversion or translating routines, when customers change from one computer to another, are usually written by the manufacturer and provided at no cost to assist in changing their older programs so that they will operate with little difficulty on the new machine. This is, in effect, rewriting old programs for a new computer. Such activities involve the simulation of one computer by another, but this is inefficient. Most often, hardware manufacturers have stored program routines called "emulators." These interpret instructions for the old computer and execute the corresponding set of instructions on the new computer. Quite often, they are an extra option.

5. Applications programs are usually business, scientific, accounting, and other programs that have been developed and used successfully by computer companies, computer user firms, and academic institutions, and so on. They are complete programs that solve problems common to many users. They are usually "ready to go" and require a set of data prepared according to the specifications. Some specific examples are sales analysis, inventory control, general ledger accounting, linear programming, PERT or project evaluation and review techniques, and so on.

In summary, therefore, the essential elements of programming concern program planning, usually with flowcharts; coding, assembly, or compilation; and diagnostics and debugging. All of these include the proper and accurate documentation. The tools available to complete these functions are types of system and flowcharts, block diagrams, layouts, grid charts, decision tables, and so on. The documentation must be thorough and intersubjective, that is, understandable to others, including other programmers, system analysts, or many management and supervisory people.

The basic form of a computer instruction includes an operation code plus an operand. Depending upon the instruction format, more than one operand may be specified. The types of coding include (1) absolute machine language coding, (2) symbolic coding, (3) macrocoding (that is, symbolic coding with macroinstructions), or (4) problem- or procedure-oriented full languages, such as FORTRAN, COBOL, BASIC, and so on.

Computer "words"

As mentioned earlier, the ultimate goal in the design of a scientific computer is the maximum internal processing speed, primarily arithmetic. Electronic computers of this type usually have what is called a fixed-word-length memory. Just as it was necessary to deal with groups of columns or "fields" of information in punched cards, it is necessary to work with groups of characters within the computer memory. These are called "words."

A computer word may be defined as an ordered set of characters that are treated as a unit in processing. In "fixed-word-length" computers, information is handled in units, or cells, containing a predetermined number of bit positions. As previously mentioned, each bit, which is represented in the machine by some device or medium capable of being magnetized in one direction of polarity or the other, may be likened to the "on" or "off" conditions of a light bulb. By various combinations of these "on" or "off" devices, corresponding to the logical rules of a number system known as binary notation (two state), decimal numbers and codes are represented. The maximum length of the decimal number that may be contained in a single word depends on the number of bit positions in the word. That number of bits is fixed by the manufacturer and varies with different computers. Numbers exceeding the length of a word are split among two or more words.

Because all numbers in the word are accessed simultaneously (most computers), they may be added to other words in parallel, rather than the usual serial (right to left) fashion. The ability to perform binary arithmetic with long strings of bits operating in parallel allows for faster internal processing of large numbers.

FOR SENSING, COMMUNICATION, CONTROL— A MODERN CENTRAL PROCESSOR [3]

In the minicomputer system described (see footnote 3), the central processor is a 16-bit word, high-performance machine. It has a 775-nanosecond-per-word cycle time and high I/O throughput facilities. The CPU is a solid-state processor organized on a single-address, TWOs complement basis.

Its standard features include and are explained as follows:

Control panel for displaying and controlling registers and states in the processor.

Keylock for control panel to prevent unauthorized use.

Operator's halt register to facilitate debugging.

16.6-ms. real-time clock.

Power failure interrupt.

Automatic restart after power failure.

Trace interrupts to facilitate program debugging.

Stack overflow/underflow interrupt.

The processor has a repertoire of 78 standard instructions plus added instructions and addressing techniques. With the standard instruction set and

[3] The minicomputer system described is the Honeywell System 700 with the basic Type 716 central processor.

high-speed memory, the CPU can effectively handle data manipulation, control, arithmetic, byte processing, and input/output operations. Its standard processing capabilities and instruction set can be expanded by optional features.

High-speed arithmetic package. The high-speed arithmetic package includes hardware multiply/divide and floating-point operations, a virtual necessity for applications requiring control equations and extensive or problem-solving capabilities.

Main memory parity. Main memory parity provides parity checks and additional instructions.

Real-time clock and watchdog timer. The real-time clock and watchdog timer serves to protect the system from illegal program loops and includes additional instructions and two timers that can be used together or independently.

Data multiplex control adapter. The purpose of the data multiplex control adapter is to achieve compatibility with Series 16 peripheral devices and controls.

Read-only memory (ROM). Read-only memory is for nonvolatile storage of programs. It never needs reloading and facilitates unattended operation and downtime loading.

Additional main memory in 4K-word increments

Memory and input/output options can be intermixed on the processor's I/O bus. The I/O bus is implemented as a printed-circuit backplane with signals for both the memory and I/O options.

The central processor is housed in a rack-mountable drawer, which is approximately 10.5 inches by 17 inches wide by 22 inches deep and can be mounted in a standard, 19-inch-wide cabinet. The circuits are packaged on eleven 9.9-inch by 10.2-inch boards. Eight additional card slots are available in the processor drawer for either device control units or memory. Additional card slots are also available in expansion drawers. The central processor comprises three major components: (1) the processing unit, (2) the input/output system, and (3) main memory and read-only memory.

The processing unit is the computing and control center. Design features include:

1. An extensive instruction set with many instructions requiring only one memory cycle for execution. (See Table 2.1.)
2. Simple, easy-to-understand operation procedures.
3. Built-in power failure protection and auto restart.
4. Real-time clock (16.6 ms.).

In the processing unit are the registers that store, compute, and transfer data under program control. The major registers available to the program-

TABLE 2.1. Typical instruction repertoire with execution timings

OP code	Mnemonic	Description	Type	Execution time (ns.)	Notes
01	JMP, JMPQ	Unconditional Jump	MR	775	1
02	LDA, LDAQ	Load A-Register	MR	1550	1
02	DLD, DLDQ	Double-Precision Load	MR	2325	1,2,3
03	ANA, ANAQ	AND Memory with A-Register	MR	1550	1
04	STA, STAQ	Store A-Register	MR	1550	1
04	DST, DSTQ	Double-Precision Store	MR	2325	1,2,3
05	ERA, ERAQ	EXCLUSIVE OR Memory with A-Register	MR	1550	1
06	ADD, ADDQ	Add	MR	1550	1
000015	XFX	Index from X-Register	G	775	
000017	XFS	Index from S-Register	G	775	
000021	RMP	Reset Memory Parity Error	G	775	2
000041	SCA	Shift Count to A-Register	G	775	2
000043	INK	Input Keys	G	775	
000101	NRM	Normalize	G	$775 + 350N$	2
00201	IAB	Interchange A- and B-Registers	G	775	
000401	ENB	Enable Interrupts	G	775	
001001	INH	Inhibit Interrupts	G	775	
001401	ERM	Enter Restrict Mode	G	775	2
004005	POPA (LDA5)	Pop Stack Top to A-Register	SMR	2325	
140024	CHS	Complement Sign	G	775	
140040	CRA	Clear A-Register	G	775	
140100	SSP	Set Sign Plus	G	775	
140200	RCB	Reset C-Bit	G	775	
140320	CSA	Copy Sign and Set Sign Plus	G	775	

Type Abbreviations
MR = memory reference
I/O = input/output
G = generic
SMR = specially defined memory reference
SH = Shift

mer include two arithmetic registers, one program counter and two index registers, one of which can be used as a hardware stack register.

Programs are executed sequentially, with the contents of the program counter (P-register) incrementing by one upon the execution of each instruction. Certain instructs (SKIPS, COMPARE, I/O) conditionally increment the program counter by an additional one or two, thereby causing a skip. Others (JUMP, JUMP-STORE) unconditionally load the program counter with a new effective address, thereby causing a branch in the program.

The processor features a repertoire of instructions that, with tremendous flexibility and power, can handle all arithmetic, logical, control, and input/output functions necessary for control and communication processing. Also included in the processors are instructions dealing with peripherals and communications interrupts and for handling data in 5- to 8-level codes.

Processor operation

The processor is operator-oriented. With the computer operator in mind, the design engineers developed the system to display extensive control information but allowed for flexibility to satisfy user requirements. The standard control panel on the front of the processor contains binary displays in octal representation and runs status displays and all operator controls. By pressing the appropriate select switch, the operator can display registers contents and memory information as well as internal counters and flip-flop status. Registers can be cleared and/or altered from the panel, and the contents of memory locations can be displayed or changed. (Memory locations 1-17 contain program load instructions and can be loaded manually only.)

Other control panel functions include selection of the operation mode (memory access, single instruction, continuous runs), four sense switches for control of programs, and a power failure interrupt inhibit switch. The control panel also provides an operator's halt register to aid program debugging.

In addition to a control panel, a teletypewriter keyboard unit with (or without) a paper tape reader and punch is available for the System 700 Processor. When used in conjunction with software check-out functions, this I/O device becomes the primary control for breakpointing programs, changing memory contents, displaying memory, and performing related functions. It can also be used off-line for preparation, duplication, or listing of program tapes.

Control registers

There are five processing control registers. These registers (see Table 2.2) normally contain the addresses of instructions and data being processed during a program run. For example, the address register (Y-register) contains the location in memory to which information is being transferred or from which it is being retrieved. The operation in which the value of this location is established is called "effective address formation." Figure 2.8 illustrates this typical control unit function. In the illustration, an instruction stored in memory is loaded in the memory register (M-register). After the address portion of this instruction is added to the portion of the program

TABLE 2.2. Summary of processing registers

Register	Function	Mnemonic
	Control registers	
Program Counter	15-bit register containing the location of the next instruction to be executed	P
Memory Register	16-bit register used to transfer information to and from memory	M
Address Register	15-bit register containing the location in memory to or from which information is being transferred	Y
Index Register	16-bit register used in address modification	X
Stack or Index Register	16-bit stack top pointer or alternative index register	S
	Arithmetic registers	
Primary Arithmetic Register	16-bit register in which all arithmetic and logical bit manipulation occurs	A
Secondary Arithmetic Register	16-bit register used in conjunction with A when arithmetic operands exceed one word in length	B
Overflow or Carry Bit	1-bit register used to indicate an overflow or carry condition	C
Adder	Logic gating, which performs all arithmetic operations	

counter (*P*-register) that designates the memory sector, the result is stored in the *Y*-register as the instruction is executed.

The stack register provides the hardware for reading and writing lists. On the central processor, this register is a push-pop stack; that is, it is a last-in/first-out stack. The stack register is used to form message or priority queues. For interruptible software, the stack can be used to store the contents of registers so that the interrupted program can be restored.

On the processor console, control registers can be displayed at the operator's control console. For instance, the operator can interrogate the program counter to determine the exact location at which a program has halted. A register is addressed from the control panel by pressing the appropriate push buttons; the contents will appear in an "on" or "off" status on the 16 control panel indicators that represent a memory location. The

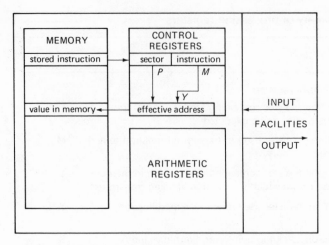

FIGURE 2.8. Typical System 700 control register activity

index register (X-register), if indexed addressing is specified, is utilized in address formation and modification.

Arithmetic registers

Arithmetic and logical operations are performed in the adder and in a series of arithmetic registers (Table 2.2). Including a primary arithmetic register (A-register), a secondary arithmetic register (B-register), and an overflow indicator (C-bit), the arithmetic registers give the processors the great computing flexibility so important to process and bit manipulation application.

Figure 2.9 illustrates a typical arithmetic function—an add operation. Before this operation begins, the control registers have established the "effective address" in memory, and the nature of the operation to be performed has been stored. Acting under these established facts, the control directs the addition operation. If the programmer desires to return the sum to a location in memory, another instruction is required.

The functioning of the other arithmetic registers, the B-register for the C-bit, depends on the nature of the instructions being executed. The arithmetic registers are accessible from the control console as well as by programmed instruction. An operator can change their contents.

Both the control and the arithmetic registers function under the control of a clocking system that enables the processor rapidly to select, interpret, and execute all instructions in a stored program. This clocking system also coordinates the various activities of receiving data from input devices and transferring data to output devices.

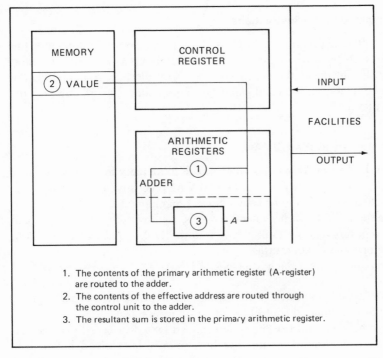

1. The contents of the primary arithmetic register (A-register) are routed to the adder.
2. The contents of the effective address are routed through the control unit to the adder.
3. The resultant sum is stored in the primary arithmetic register.

FIGURE 2.9. Typical arithmetic function

Input/Output system

The input/output system regulates the flow of data, instructions, and control information between main memory and peripheral device controls. As in most computer systems, it works in conjunction with the system software, main memory, and peripheral controls to allocate central processor time to input/output operations, to identify peripheral controls that will use that time for data transfers, and to use a priority system for accesses to memory.

But unlike many other systems, the I/O system uses a new distributed priority network that takes the burden off the central processor's I/O logic for the control of peripheral data transfers. The controls for the peripheral devices now perform many control tasks that would otherwise require central processor time and resources.

An added feature of the new I/O system design is the use of a star configuration rather than the conventional "daisy chain" for the location of peripheral devices, thus giving added flexibility for the arrangement of the computer room. The input/output system supports three classes of I/O operations: programmed input/output via instructions, direct memory access, and distributed priority interrupt.

Programmed I/O via instructions

Functions of programmed I/O are (1) outputting control information to a device (such as "read a tape record"), (2) setting up a DMA data transfer, (3) transferring data if the device characteristics allow programmed I/O (for example, teletypewriters and paper tape equipment), and (4) checking the status of a device.

Direct memory access (DMA)

The DMA provides an alternative path to memory for high-speed data transfers. I/O transfers that use the DMA are processed on a cycle-stealing basis and proceed automatically after a programmed I/O instruction has been issued. Up to 32 peripheral controls, each with its own address and range registers, can be multiplexed into the DMA to allow simultaneous and independent data transfers.

Here are some of the advantages of DMA:

1. Overlapped operations in that while one I/O data transfer takes place, another peripheral control is setting up for a transfer.
2. Peripheral control priority is determined by a distributed priority network and position on the I/O bus; priority is resolved before data transfer takes place—no wait.
3. Fast response to peripheral device requests for access to memory because DMA has highest priority break request.
4. Byte or word transfers.
5. Parity checking for DMA transfers on the I/O bus (one parity bit per byte).

Priority interrupts

A priority interrupt causes a jump from the current program to another program at the end of an instruction execution. The distributed priority network allows the programmer to specify that lower priority interrupts be inhibited without inhibiting higher priority interrupts. Thus higher priority interrupts can be serviced more quickly. In addition, the normal priority of the distributed priority network can be overridden by the programmer.

The new distributed priority network is particularly efficient in the processing of priority interrupts. It eliminates the need for the programmer to code instructions that cause polling of peripheral devices to determine the source of an interrupt. With the new design, a peripheral control sends to the central processor the address of its controlling program's starting location. Thus, with the peripheral controls handling this identification function, the central processor is free for other activities. Up to 32 peripheral controls can be attached to the distributed priority network; the physical location of the peripheral control on the I/O bus determines the interrupt priority.

Main memory

In the central processor, main memory consists of a memory controller and up to eight 4K-word magnetic-core storage modules. Storage capacities range from 8K to 32K words. The cycle time required to read and restore the contents of a memory location is 775 nanoseconds. Both program instructions and the data to be manipulated by the program reside in memory during a program operation. As a key to programming, every word is identified by a unique numeric address.

Access to main memory

Priority access memory is important to the real-time power of the system process. The various functions of the input/output and processing logic are executed in a priority sequence when two or more functions request access to main memory simultaneously. The priorities are

1. Direct memory access.
2. Data multiplex control break.
3. Real-time clock increment.
4. Power failure interrupt/watchdog timer.
5. Trace interrupt.
6. Stack overflow/underflow interrupt.
7. 316/516 compatible interrupts.
8. Standard 7161 I/O bus interrupts.
9. Program execution.

Breaks

Certain operations may occur between instructions without affecting the contents of the program counter. When the operations are complete, the program resumes. These actions are called "breaks" and include the operation of transferring data via DMA or DMC and incrementing the real-time clock.

It may be noted that the program being executed and other operations are always computing and vying for access to memory. Only one function at any given time can have access to memory, and that is either the program, interrupts, the real-time clock, or the DMA or DMC.[4]

[4] DMC transfer operation is available with the optional DMC adapter.

Interrupts

A multilevel interrupt facility provides simple but efficient supervision of processing involving combinations of input/output and computing. This facility allows branching as necessary between a main program and servicing routines for all input/output devices and for internal central processor conditions. It eliminates the need for programmed tests to detect the completion of input-output operations. A flexible interrupt capability has important applications in the field of data communications and other real-time areas, but it is equally applicable to the supervision of operations as universal as reading and punching cards or reading and writing magnetic tape.

Interrupts in the system are classified in two groups: controlled and privileged. The source of a controlled interrupt is a peripheral device control in the I/O system (that is, 316/516-compatible interrupts or standard I/O bus interrupts). Privileged interrupts are caused by internal conditions in the central processor (for example, stack overflow/underflow, trace, power failure, or real-time clock).

Controlled interrupts are enabled and disabled by the ENB and INH instructions, respectively. Because privileged interrupts must inform the system about critical conditions within the central processor, such as power failure, they have a higher priority than controlled interrupts and are not affected by ENB and INH instructions.

A controlled program interrupt occurs whenever a peripheral device has computed an input/output operation. For example, an interrupt occurs at the end of data transmission in a tape read or write operation. Likewise, the receipt of a character from a remote station by a communication control may be signaled by a program interrupt. Interrupts from a particular peripheral control can be allowed or inhibited by a privileged program as necessary.

A program interrupt is accomplished by (1) automatic storage of the interrupted program's location and (2) automatic identification of the interrupt by branching to a routine whose address was previously loaded by program into a dedicated memory location. This routine can then service the device that caused the interrupt.

Data storage formats in main memory

The basic addressable unit of storage in main memory is the 16-bit word. This is also the basic unit of information transferred between main memory and the central processor's A-register. Essentially, there are two types of words—data and instruction—each of which can be further categorized. As shown in Figure 2.10, the contents of a 16-bit word can be interpreted in *any* of the following ways:

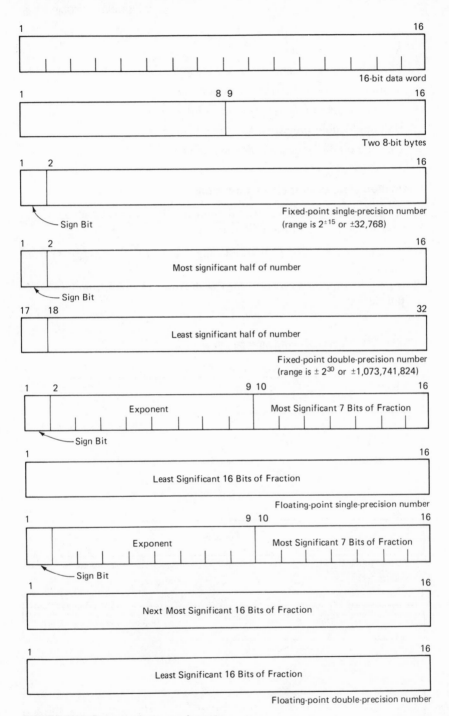

FIGURE 2.10. Data word storage formats

A 16-bit piece of data.

Two 8-bit bytes of data.

A single-precision, fixed-point number.

Half of a single-precision, floating-point number.

Half of a double-precision, fixed-point number.

Part of a double-precision, floating-point number.

Instruction storage formats in main memory

As shown in Figure 2.11, the contents of a 16-bit instruction word can be interpreted as any of the following types of instructions:

1. A memory reference instruction—for storing or retrieving data from memory.
2. An input/output instruction—for transferring data to or from input/output devices.

FIGURE 2.11. Instruction word storage formats

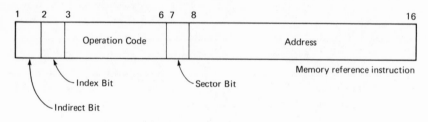

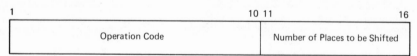

3. A shift instruction—for movement of data in the A- and B-registers.
4. A generic instruction—for any type of operation not mentioned above.

Addressing

For addressing purposes, memory is divided into 512-word sectors. The processor can directly address 1,024 word locations: the base sector (the first 512 locations of main memory) and the currently executing sector (the memory area to which the program counter currently points). All of main memory can be addressed indirectly or through the use of an index register. Two additional addressing modes are standard: general register and stack. The address bits of a memory reference instruction determine the addressing mode.

Indirect addressing. For all instructions that permit indirect addressing, the chain can continue indefinitely; that is, it is multilevel. An indirect address can be either pre- or postindexed. When indirect addressing is required, the effective address is assumed to be in the location specified by the address portion of the instruction and the selected sector address. However, if this location also calls for indirect addressing, an additional memory cycle is initiated. Indirect addressing adds 775 nanoseconds per level to the instruction execution time.

Indexed addressing. When the index bit of an instruction is set, the contents of the index register are added to the direct address of the instruction to produce an effective address. If indexing is specified in the instruction word, it occurs before any indirect addressing; if specified in an indirect address, it occurs after indirect addressing. Most important, no additional cycles are required for instruction execution when indexing.

Extended addressing. With extended addressing, the indirect address format includes 15 address bits in order to access more than 16K words of memory; indexing is specified in the instruction and is applied after indirect addressing.

General register and stack register addressing. For programming flexibility, two additional addressing modes are standard: register and stack. These modes allow the programmer to address registers as if they were memory locations.

Read-only memory

Like main memory, ROM has a storage format of 16-bit words, and its cycle time is 775 nanoseconds. Addressing overlay, a ROM feature, ensures that with the addition of the ROM no addressing capabilities or main memory storage are sacrificed. It allows read access to ROM via the same addressing circuitry used for accessing main memory.

A 2,048-word ROM is included with each of the system remote concentrators. ROM is optional for other system configurations. On the remote concentrators, ROM facilitates unattended operation by allowing downline bootstrap loading of the processor by the main (host) computer. It also provides for transmission of status information to the host. ROM is programmed ("wired") by the manufacturer and cannot be field-modified. When a remote message concentrator is configured at the factory, ROM is programmed according to a standard loader. For all other models, ROM is wired according to customer-designed programs.

OPTIONAL PROCESSING CAPABILITIES

Parity for main memory

With main memory parity, two additional bits are provided for each word in main memory. Parity is generated on all memory write cycles and checked on readout. Detection of a parity error causes a parity-error indicator to be set. The indicator can be tested under program control. Setting of the indicator can also cause a program interrupt. Special features provide parity for the first 4K words of main memory; other features provide parity for an additional 4K words of memory.

When parity is installed, the following instructions are added to the standard instruction set:

TABLE 2.3. Additional instructions for parity

OP code	Description	Execution time
SMK '20	Set Mask (A-register bit 15 controls parity)	2300 ns.
SPS	Skip on Parity Error	775 ns.
SPN	Skip on No Parity Error	775 ns.
RMP	Reset Memory Parity Indicator	775 ns.

Space is reserved in the mainframe for this feature.

High-speed arithmetic package

Another feature, the high-speed arithmetic package, provides hardware multiply, divide, and normalize and hardware double-precision capability, as well as base sector relocation. Ten instructions are added to the standard instruction repertoire with this feature. Space for this feature is reserved in the mainframe.

Capabilities

Extended arithmetic capability. Single-word multiply and divide memory-reference instructions are indexable and indirectly addressable.

Enhanced floating-point operations. Normalize and shift count to A instructions facilitate automatic formating of mantissa and exponent.

Hardware-implemented double-precision operations. Add, subtract, load, and store of double-word (32-bit) operands.

Faster arithmetic library subroutines. For example, the square root is six times faster; arc tangent, seven times; sine, sixteen times.

Instructions provided with feature 2010

Mnemonic	Function
MPY	Multiply
DIV	Divide
NRM	Normalize
SCA	Shift count to A
DBL	Enter double-precision mode
SGL	Enter single-precision mode
DAD	Double add
DSB	Double subtract
DLD	Double load
DST	Double store

Base sector relocation

Included with the high-speed arithmetic package is base sector relocation. It allows the base sector for the currently operating program to be relocated from physical sector 0 to any sector. An additional register, the J-register, identifies the physical sector currently assigned as the base sector.

Real-time clock and watchdog timer

The real time clock/watchdog timer consists of two independent clocks—one controlled by the line frequency; the other controlled by crystal. Both clocks may be used independently or simultaneously and are always under program control. The time interval is detected through automatic interrupt generation.

The watchdog timer provides a means of detecting system failure by generating an interrupt upon time-out. It can also activate an external alarm.

65

CONCLUSION

Small decentralized computer systems usually produce better results than large systems because the latter force users to conform too rigidly to "total" systems. Budgets for computers must allow for intelligence as well as for capital equipment. There is always a tendency in computer systems to "solve the wrong problem." This can easily happen when the computer system is designed for the computer center personnel and not for the appropriate user of the services. Another danger or oft-committed sin is to give too much emphasis to machine optimization and efficient utilization for the processing of large quantities of data and voluminous reports, but far too little preplanning or emphasis to manager optimization or efficient utilization. It is almost always advantageous to bring the corporate manager and his staff into direct contact with the computer system through the use of various types of computer terminals, especially visual types. The improvement of the corporate-computer interface ("fit") is well worth all efforts to this end. The computer provides teaching capabilities and potentials that are largely untapped in the corporate environment. The computer can be a very effective instrument for management and technical and professional training at all levels, and this activity should increase exponentially in this decade. Manufacturers have seen the "handwriting on the wall" and have very recently changed their marketing strategies from selling hardware and software to selling "computer services" and backing them up with careful "service" maintenance. The new user-orientation of such services has fostered a development among computer people of not merely "doing a thing right," but also of doing "the right thing" and doing that "right thing" right. Computer professionals have greatly toned down their former sins of intellectual arrogance. They are now more humble and demure and make stringent attempts to know and understand the user's problem better than he does and always to maintain a sense of their own fallibility. All computer people should get into the unrelenting habit of talking about *what* services they perform personally, *what* they themselves do to improve system performance, and *what* the computer does along these lines instead of "how" the computer does it.

FURTHER DEFINING THE WORLD
OF STANDARD COMPUTERS

The special language pertaining to data-processing systems, operations, and equipment can be perplexing owing to its combination of traditional scientific terminology with modern proprietary product definitions. Actually, students and user/managers need to know very little about the technical aspects of the inner workings or microelectronic pulse transfers of computer equipment. They should, however, understand the capabilities, capacities, and applications as well as the procedures used to develop solutions to problems that relate to computer system operations. A few of the most basic terms and concepts relating to standard computers are explained in the following pages.

Background processing. The procedure of background processing more clearly relates to the specific work that is usually of lower priority and is handled by the computer system when higher priority immediate entry and real-time responses are not requested or occurring. Batch processing usually concerns such items as inventory control, payroll, and various computer housekeeping procedures. These can be interrupted by higher priority programs or on orders from executives or managers at computer terminals, that is, as developed by programmed inquiries from other units. Such background programs are usually not time-dependent, time-sensitive, or related to immediate requirements as are management information system segments.

Batch processing. Batch processing is a basic term and concept that usually refers to processing in which similar input data items or problem segments are developed as groups or "batches" for manipulating as a whole in single machine runs, usually with the same program for each week or month. This sequential processing procedure thereby uses an accumulation of data as contrasted to on-line processing, during which each unit of data or information is processed immediately at the time of presentation or terminal entry to the computer system.

Compatibility. Compatibility is a term closely associated with both hardware and the software aspects of EDP. If the routines or programs developed for one member of a computer "family" can be processed on any other member of the family, it is said that this equipment has a high degree of compatibility. Compatibility is considered an upward capability in that computer X can feed into computer Y, which, in turn, can feed into computer Z. When equipment is compatible, the central processing units of each generally use the same operation codes. Consequently, the programs contain similar instructions. When similar central processing units have the same or equivalent word sizes, amounts, and types of memory, and so on, the equipment can often be considered compatible. Another point to keep in mind is that some manufacturers make equipment that is compatible with that of others as well as their own "family" of units. Industry compatibility usually means IBM compatibility, for IBM is the de facto standard in the computer industry. Thus the phrase *plug-to-plug compatible* with IBM equipment is frequently used.

Flexibility. Flexibility is a term that pertains to hardware and describes the computer's capability to handle almost any job—business, scientific, real-time, or communications—regardless of the nature or size of the application. Flexibility is also used to describe processing capabilities that can grow in speed, size, and power to meet most needs. This is called "system flexibility." Another type of flexibility is "functional flexibility." This means that the computer can handle the changing functions of an application or business by accommodating a wide range of equipment easily and quickly. What is meant by a wide range of equipment is basically peripheral devices. These could include disks, drums, printers, and communication terminals. These peripheral devices can be removed or new ones added without reengineering the basic equipment. A system is understood to be flexible if the user can mold it to meet his particular needs. Flexibility and modularity are very closely allied terms.

Microprogramming. The concept of microprogramming was conceived as early as the 1950s by the British engineer M. V. Wilkes. But the large-scale commercial implementation of this concept was not begun until the introduction of the IBM 360 series of computers. Today most minicomputers and major computing systems can be microprogrammed. Microinstructions are usually stored in a read-only memory (ROM or ROS). These instructions take over many of the control functions (for example, gating, branching) hitherto performed by hardware. They are semipermanent (that is, not easily altered) and act as an intermediate language between assembler languages and higher-level languages. One of the major impacts of microprogramming is that new machines are now able to be more easily "customized," using machine or assembly language microprograms of repetitious routines. Higher language programs in FORTRAN, COBOL, and the like usually take longer to be accepted, interpreted, compiled, and executed. The two most outstanding advantages of microprogramming to accountants and managers are emulation and performance improvement. One computer can be microprogrammed to emulate almost any other machine. The advantage here is obvious and tremendous. Suppose a user has a large repertoire of assembler-written IBM computer programs. These programs may be used directly on a Burroughs, Honeywell (and the like) machine operating in IBM emulator mode, thus avoiding costly code conversion. Today there are microprogrammed machines that can emulate most of the major third-generation computers. Microprogramming improves performance in both mathematical and nonmathematical operations, the most dramatic improvement being in nonmathematical operations. These improvements have had a great impact on optimum algorithm design and have also promoted a wider application of nonmathematical programs, for example, pattern recognition, information retrieval, and file operations. Microprogramming is still in an early stage of development. Many people are not familiar with its concepts, but its impact will certainly continue to grow in the future.

Modularity. Most EDP systems change and grow. Modularity enables a user to start modestly, hooking on new units, memory units, terminals, and so on, as his or her work load increases, almost as a railroad hooks on boxcars as its freight load increases. True modularity also permits software growth, the addition of routines and subroutines to programs already in storage.

Modular programming. A module is a piece of programming that is designed to accomplish a single task, such as the formating of an error message. The module is, in effect, a miniature program, for it contains all the data descriptions and instructions necessary to perform the task. Modular programming—the breaking up of a large program into small, self-contained modules—offers several advantages to both designers and users of computer systems. A modular program is more likely to meet the needs of the user because careful preparation and planning are needed in the program design stage. As the modules are implemented, they can be exhaustively tested, separately and together, thus ensuring that the modules do indeed conform to the user's requirements. In use, a modular program is easily adaptable because it is necessary to revise only the particular modules involved in the processing that requires later modification. For the designer, modular programs offer the advantage of reusability; that is, they can be lifted from existing programs and used again, thus saving the cost and time involved in coding and testing.

Multiprocessing. Multiprocessing is a concept that usually refers to the computer's ability to interrupt running programs to handle specific real-time (instantaneous) inquiries and to perform direct signaling between multiple computers for better hardware/software control of complex data handling operations. In some systems, the number and types of programs sharing the processors are limited only by the amount of available memory and devices.

On-line systems. Some immediate information demands are sought by managers with programs that are most often contained in operating systems (OS) or in main programs in a multiprogrammed computer system. Before he or she evaluates the accounting records, it is fundamental that the manager ascertain whether or not the computerized information system has been designed to process data correctly and to do so completely. On-line systems are those in which peripheral equipment is directly connected to the central processing unit (CPU) thereby to compute, process, or transmit data and information immediately rather than hold for later manipulation, as in batch processing.

Program documentation. Program documentation is the phase of processing or implementation of computerized systems during which preparations are developed concerning operations information such as a thorough description of a system in use, a particular computer language being implemented, or various programs that are utilized, together with their objectives and detailed flowcharts. Program operations manuals are of critical importance to accountants and managers, for they provide the very necessary detail for system design, as well as the description of the nature of the business activities that are computerized. Alert managers are now developing sufficient sophisticated knowledge of EDP terminology to enable them to review the information system in use and to determine the proper test of the system so that they can certify as to the quality, accuracy, and adequacy of the client's financial reports and statement.

Real-time computing. Real-time operations refer to those particular system operations in which the data inputs to the system are given directly from measuring or acquisition devices, and computer output results are thereby obtained by terminals or printers during the progress of the continuing event. Such data concern the types of transactions usually developed from ultrafast retrieval random-access files. The technique does not require aggregation or segregation of the information to be processed, as did batch processing procedures, and it differs from on-line procedures by the fact that real-time means immediate response, not merely immediate entry of information. Management can receive better information with greater speed by using an on-line, real-time (OLRT) system and, therefore, make better, more immediately accurate and informed decisions on this specific immediacy basis.

Simultaneity. Simultaneity is a concept that generally refers to a specific number of input-output trunks that, when connected to the processor, provide simultaneous on-line operation of such low-speed devices as card readers or communications devices, usually modems, couplers, terminals, and so on, or any combination of these. The simultaneous functions of the single system could include reading from tape, printing a report, writing electronically on tape, and reading punched cards. Simultaneity is closely allied with the time-sharing concept.

Time sharing. These popular systems are ones in which business processing is developed through "conversational" access to computer systems that are remote and oftentimes quite distant from the terminals. Such almost personalized terminals are used as both input and output devices, even for entering and debugging programs and developing specific nonprogrammed inquiries. This multiterminal, simultaneous process provides for convenient means and low-cost operating procedures for smaller enterprises to implement thereby their computerized business activities quite effectively without requiring an on-site computer. Such time-sharing systems can accommodate many different business departments or separate company entities in what seems to be simultaneous activity and all from one computer at a headquarters center or a time-selling computer service company. Various types of time-sharing services relate to (1) *hardware sharing,* in which each remote user firm provides its own programs; (2) *program sharing,* in which each firm's needs are similar and thereby differ only in their own produced data required for the individual company processing; and (3) *data sharing* (information utility), in which various firms' specific requirements relate only to inquiries to that specific data base and, therefore, the computer mainframe (hardware) *and* the programs or software are shared. Time sharing or, more correctly, facilities sharing, concerns the use of a device, program, or data base by up to 300 or even 1,000, customers and all sharing facilities during the same overall time interval. This is accomplished by the ultrafast interspersing (time slicing) of customer demands with a single computer system. A multiple-checking, password-coding system develops absolute security of data and software (programs) through the use of highly specialized systems' capabilities developed by the time-shared service or facilities management (FM) company that specializes, owns, or operates such facilities.

Time-sharing attributes. Time sharing divorces the mechanics of the computer system from the techniques of problem solving. In doing so, it eliminates the steadily increasing crew of technicians around the computer and returns its control to the ultimate user. It achieves this by the following capabilities:

1. *Multiprogramming.* Several independent, but possibly related, programs or routines reside or operate within a single computer system.
2. *Real-time processing.* Programs can be executed that satisfy a particular operational response time that could range down to nanoseconds and produce answers in time to control continuously the reporting process.
3. *Remote processing.* Users can communicate with remotely located computer systems through input-output devices via conventional communications facilities.
4. *Interactive or on-line processing.* A computer system serves a human user or device through direct communication. For users, this often includes conversational interaction.
5. *Multiple access.* Several on-line communication channels provide access to common computer systems.

Fortunately, time-sharing and teleprocessing are becoming very popular and are being accepted by wide ranges of computer users. More than 350 such commercial systems are operating successfully about the country. Some are single-area oriented. Many of them are very large national networks, with GE the largest. Alert managers should be devoted to a full analysis of this commendable attribute of modern computing, which is already available in more than 500 distinct segments of commercial activities, including airline reservations, education, agricultural extension services, banking, welfare services, credit reporting, and so on. This computing activity is expected to grow to considerably more than $2 billion in income per year well before 1977, suggesting a growth rate of about 40 percent per year. Teleprocessing is very successful in reducing costs. Within the Washington, D.C., area alone, 45 time-sharing computer services could be employed by local telephone dialing in 1975. The National Crime Information Center in the Capitol is interconnected to over 3,000 law enforcement agencies in 49 states and handles more than 50,000 inquiries per day from these agencies.

Virtual memory and virtual machines. Nearly every serious programmer complains about his or her computer memory capacity, no matter how large it may be. In order to run large programs, various ad hoc techniques of segmentation and overlay schemes have been in use for years. Virtual memory denotes a formalized, efficient, and sophisticated algorithm that gives the user virtually unlimited memory. This is accomplished by paging and disk-core swapping, but it is transparent to the user. The concept of virtual memory is not new, but it has been commercially implemented only recently. Its advantages to scientific and engineering applications are obvious. Similar to virtual memory is virtual machine, whereby one machine can be commanded to behave like another machine, even with a specified operating system. Today virtual memory and virtual machines are mostly implemented by software and simulation. Wider use of emulation by microprogramming and associative memory will undoubtedly reduce the cost and improve the performance of such systems in the future. Instead of an entire program being held in main storage throughout its execution, only those parts actually needed by the computer are brought in at any given time. The rest is kept on magnetic disk files, ready for immediate use. Virtual storage thereby lifts many of the restrictions previously imposed by the physical size of main storage. It gives an apparent main storage capability that is vastly greater than the computer's real storage.

3

Minicomputers: Big Competition to Standard Systems

The accelerated development of mincomputer systems in business is giving rise to new opportunities and a completely new approach to management of computers by users. The chief impact of the use of microcomputers, minicomputers, and programmable calculators in business for a wide range of tasks will be to "bring computer management back to the people who do the work." Yesterday, when large central processors were shared by many departments, divisions, or companies, the people who wanted the work done were not the ones controlling or operating the computer system. When something went wrong, the "computer" was blamed, and users and operators spent their time and energies writing memos testifying that it was not their fault. Moreover, managers could not understand or would not control their own operations—directly or indirectly.

Now small organizational groups of users operate their own computer; the people who want the work done now can use their own energies to find ways to solve problems when they arise instead of going through several layers of computer people—and waiting. Where microcomputer or minicomputer systems are concerned, Grosch's first law (which can be formulated thus: "Throughput capacity of the computer increases as the square of the price") is no longer operative. Computer power and capacity do not increase significantly as either becomes more expansive. Both features too often are overpurchased and lie unused.

Because of its relatively low cost, the need to have a minicomputer system in operation most of the time is far less pressing than it would be for a large, costly computer system. Microcomputers could be used as little as one and a half hours a day, and they would still be more cost-effective than a fully used typewriter. Quite generally, if an organization or departmental group larger than ten people requires computers for any legitimate purpose, it is better for the enterprise that these people have exclusive use of their own computer provided that the computer is big enough to do the job properly. It need only be loaded to at least 10 percent of its capacity 10 percent of the time to return its cost. The minicomputer even as a single "intelligent" terminal now makes that use-ratio applicable practically anywhere in business.

Today computers dedicated to hundreds of single specific applications can be feasible even to simple repetitive operations, and this is ideal. Standardized software is either free or cheap to rent, and it is available from practically anywhere in the world by computer in hours or even minutes by long distance facsimile or transmitted paper-tape. Even "custom" software can be inexpensive on a minicomputer or a programmable calculator (that is, PROMs). It is no longer logical to state that if minicomputers are to attain their potential, standardized software products are indispensable. Software can be cheaply, quickly, and easily "emulated," that is, created to match practically any machine or language.

Instead of being a threat because of their growing use, minicomputers in business are a boon to service bureaus and those time-sharing companies that serve the large market for business data processing for small organizations. The more computer-wise more people become, the more customers service companies develop. Certainly, the trend is for smaller companies to

FIGURE 3.1. Prototype of low-cost TV display terminal built with microcomputers
Courtesy: Intel Corporation

FIGURE 3.2. The Datapoint 3600 for use in a Datashare network. Up to 16 of these units (or other TTY compatible terminals) may access simultaneously the computing and storage capability of the central Datapoint 5500 processor and associated peripherals. *Courtesy: Datapoint Corporation*

turn to their own minicomputer systems rather than to outside services. Moreover, big companies that need big computers for data base storage and operations are developing their own in-house, time-shared management information systems through mini or micro front-end communications processors. But millions of "computer amateurs" are using minis and micros for the first time, and their needs and desires expand quickly. Many move to service companies rather than purchase more equipment or sophistication, looking ahead instead to new technical development and coming lower prices in the minicomputer and microcomputer fields.

It seems obvious that an emerging concept that is spreading worldwide is the use of microcomputers and minicomputers with emulation hardware and software to make many special-purpose computers general-purpose ones. Giving impetus to this development is the recent dramatic lowering of the cost and ease of use of emulation hardware. The large investment by many users in existing software thus makes them some profits by exchanges. As an illustration, one specific software segment of a popular communications system, using emulation and its 16-bit minicomputer, runs without reprogramming, $3 million worth of software written in the machine language of a much more expensive 32-bit computer. The cost to do this is minimal. If it is government-developed or in the public domain, it is free.

Another implication for the future is the use of minicomputer systems as machines that will emulate special languages, such as APL, RPG II, or other special-use types. The cheap minicomputer has the capacity to run, without reprogramming, vast libraries of existing business applications software now running on IBM System 360/370 computers. The future for minicomputers as business systems is a big one, as they are being used today with readily available standard software application products and low-cost, customized programs. These are now commonly available on ROMs and RAMs, tape cassettes, and so on.

MINICOMPUTERS AND THEIR ENVIRONMENTS

Many minicomputers are powerhouses in their own right and are often more versatile than bigger, more costly systems. The prefix *mini* generally applies not to computing power, but rather to smallness as regards physical size. In terms of computing power, minicomputers are easily and rapidly expanding into the domains of the medium and large computers. In the past few years, minicomputers, coupled with microcomputers, have advanced so rapidly in power and versatility that today the whole industry is in a state of "obsolescent shock." A number of computers priced today as medium-scale systems offer no more computing power than do most modern minicomputers available at a fraction of their costs. The rapid downward cost movement of minis has reached a point where large new groups of users with specific problems are willing to pay the current price for a "solution tool," which is often a mini system, because it is the cheapest way.

When a procurement engineer or data-processing manager sees prices drop very rapidly, he seldom scrutinizes alternatives the way he would if prices were rising. Minicomputer prices have declined very rapidly in the past few years but not uniformly so. Some writers have suggested that, at some point in time and in the not too distant future, the cost of computers will drop to a point so that even the very small user, say, with a hot dog stand, will find that the cost-effectiveness is low enough to incorporate a mini into his business. Whereas minis generally are priced in the $15,000 to $25,000 range, some are in the area of $5,000 to $10,000, and a few mini manufacturers have offered their products from $2,000 to below $1,000 in quantities of 100 or more. These are *not* microcomputers, which are described in the following chapters.

There are significant factors that contribute to the total "system" costs or the total expense of an installation. Some of them are (1) the cost of the necessary hardware; (2) the cost of system software; (3) the cost of coding and correcting applications programs; and (4) the cost of adequate maintenance, service, and personnel training. Other options usually include a CPU console panel on the front of the mini; a power-fail, preferably with automatic restart; direct memory access (DMA); a bootstrap loader (software entry procedure system) often on a ROM; and other ROMs to execute repetitious programs faster. Most competitively priced computers will require from 150 percent to 300 percent more memory than those purchased or leased originally. This has become steadily and very economically available in RAMs. Many companies provide system software "free, with the deal" or at very low cost.

Minicomputers often become "front ends" or preprocessors for much larger systems. They help to make these larger systems more efficient and accurate and easier to control. They also substantially substitute for much "human participation" in the operation of computer systems and networks. We have already discussed standard computers, with emphasis on small systems, and the comparisons and contrasts will clarify various perceptions as we proceed in the pages ahead. As more models become available and as the emphasis continues toward user-oriented design, we will discover that minis are not very complex, as many standard systems are. Great progress is being made in the use of minis to diagnose illnesses and to correct, interpret, and recommend special studies for students using computer-aided instruction (CAI). Minisystems usually make fewer mistakes, are less complex, have fewer components, and are more easily intermixed than are standard systems. Digital Equipment Corporation, the largest manufacturer of minis, had installed more than 50,000 of them by mid-1976. In less than 20 years it grew to become number 207 in *Fortune*'s top 500 industrial companies and to become number 5 in earnings per share growth of 41.27 percent over the ten-year period from 1964–1974.

Much of the success of minis relates to the wide availability of dedicated or proprietary software. Some savings are due to the fact that they shorten the time taken to create, adapt, and debug many user applications programs. They provide much of the routine or "housekeeping" software commonly used by most applications. By making effective use of new microminiaturized add-on memory, users reduce the cost of the total system. Many customers ultimately develop multimini systems. This is also due to the new availability of "firmware," for example, software locked in ROMs.

MINICOMPUTERS—WHAT THEY LOOK LIKE AND WHY THEY ARE SO EASY TO USE

Probably the prime advantage of the minicomputer is that it can be operated by the same employees who previously manually handled the payroll, order processing, invoicing, and accounts receivable or by the shop foreman who was always worried when his managers threatened computer control of his machines or by managers who become fascinated at the range of capabilities that they themselves can develop with simple computer languages they learn in a week. Some computer manufacturers prepare programs and documentation in a week. Some computer manufacturers prepare programs and documentation in a loose-leaf binder of written instructions in clear, step-by-step detail as to how to execute each routine. Many systems are clearly demonstrated to each employee on a "show-and-tell" basis. When there is a malfunction caused by faulty part or incorrect procedure, the error or fault can quite often be corrected over the telephone, a distinct advantage of the mini. Other difficulties are often ironed out quickly during three-times-a-week, checkup visits by vendor maintenance men. Some employees attend one-week training courses on the operations of minis at their plants or offices. And the simplicity of minis offers a lot of straight trial-by-error education. Although the mystique of the "big" computer still carries with it a whiff of prestige, most users of minis become very dependent on minis and even new operations become "old hat" for most. Minis are not merely crutches; they have caused new waves of thinking wherever they are used. Moreover, chemists, accountants, factory foremen, middle managers, and so on can do the programming (in BASIC, FORTRAN, and the like) instead of requiring the employment of expensive, hard-to-control systems analysts and lead programmers. Minicomputers are so small they can be placed anywhere—on countertops, on lab shelves, check-out stands, and so on. The "bare bones" minis are modular. They can be expanded and upgraded at very low cost into really very large systems.

All this has caused a very strong impact on society, and its reverberations will soon be felt. Simplicity, low cost, ruggedness, ease of operation, big system capability, shrinking compactness, increasing speeds, and expanding memory capacity—these are fundamental characteristics of minis. And now, *enter the multimini*. A trend that is spreading very rapidly—and that is scaring some computer leaders—is the homemade combinations of many minis into one very powerful computer. A case in point: One of the most interesting computer architectures seen to date has been assembled by a Carnegie-Mellon University professor and a team of students. Called the Multi-Mini-Processor (MMP), it consists of 16 Digital Equipment Corp. PDP minicomputers, each with its own memory, tied to access any other mini's memory. The units can be set up to work on various portions of one job, operate in small groups, or be set up to work independently on 16 separate jobs. One of the first tasks the MMP will face is the real-time (immediate response) speech understanding problem. Another case: several mini companies are offering mini "kits" priced at less than $400. One such kit consists of 11 printed circuit boards offered to individual users complete with racks for assembly, much like high fidelity tuners. These become full computers with excellent capability CPUs, input-output controllers and memories; and they can be tailored in many varieties of systems handling printers, displays, and communications devices. The "home-built" computers can even be remotely accessed and operated with low-cost, battery-portable terminals costing about $100. Moreover, the college and high school kids love them, and they can be built up into multipurpose multiminis easily. One computer expert sees some real danger from these very powerful computers in the hands of amateurs and novices. Stacks of interconnected multiminis can develop power equal to that of huge $2.5 million systems, and people fully knowledgeable of devious computer uses begin to wonder and worry, but they see little that could or should be done about it.

Digital Equipment Corp., of Maynard, Mass., has put its popular PDP-8 on a single board, using semiconductor technology. Now called the 12-bit PDP-8A, it has a cycle time of 1.5 μsec. (microseconds) and is fully compatible with most PDP-8 family hardware, operating systems, and high-level programming languages like BASIC, FORTRAN IV, and FOCAL. The Omnibus™ backplane makes it easy to interface the PDP-8A directly to more than 60 PDP-8 options and peripherals. The seven most-requested options available are on two option boards: serial-line interface, 12-bit parallel I/O, front panel control, and real-time clock on one board; power-fail/start, memory extension, and bootstrap loader on the other. Memory can be expanded from 1K to 32K in either ROM, RAM, PROM, or ROM/RAM—mixed or matched. The parts were available in 1974 (CPU and 1K RAM) in kit form for under $600 in quantity purchases.

The inventiveness that can spring from uncluttered young minds should certainly not be stifled in any way. After all, if a minicomputer can run a Burger King fast-food restaurant, why not keep trying any and every type of application?

Minicomputers, especially those built by Hewlett-Packard and Digital Equipment Corp. (which offer large discounts to schools), are appearing in thousands of classrooms. "There are fifth and sixth graders writing sophisticated programs at the Burnsville Elementary School District in Minneapolis," says an H-P executive. "Generally the minis are used by the very bright kids who often are bored with school, and they become very proficient with minis by the time they enter high school. On the other hand, we have six systems in the Los Angeles schools for remedial work—for drill and practice. It's the same equipment in Minneapolis and Los Angeles, but the users are nearly opposite." Minis are appearing practically everywhere. Officers play war games with them at the Armed Forces Staff College in Norfolk, Virginia. Prisoners train on them for "a better life" when they are released. They are used in chess tournaments around the world. Hollywood "special effects men" used them in the films *2001* and *The Andromeda Strain* and for many cartoons and special effects. They operate driverless taxis in England.

THE DATAPOINT 2200—A TYPICAL
MINICOMPUTER SYSTEM

The heart of the Datapoint System is the Datapoint 2200. The size of an office typewriter, it provides a computer and memory, a keyboard and CRT display, and a dual cassette tape deck. It is available in both high- and low-speed memory versions with a memory size between 2K (kilobytes—thousands of bytes) and 16K bytes. (See Figure 3.3.)

The addition of either the Datapoint 2200 cartridge disk or industry compatible magnetic tape units provides the capability for creating and maintaining large data files at remote locations. The files may then be used to provide "hard" validation of source data entries and, additionally, processed to provide local job and essential source documents control reports that would otherwise be obtainable only from the central computing facility. DATABUS, the 2200 high-level language, is ideally suited for quickly programming local job control applications. The complete complement of Datapoint 2200 communications adapters, with extensive supporting software for commonly used disciplines, allows the remote station to communicate only those data required by the main CPU facility to be transferred.

Systems involving monitoring or acquisition of data, such as in the electrical and processing industries, are being configured with a small computer. The computer can accept data from a variety of devices, convert it to the desired format, and record it on tape. Besides the recording function, the program may check incoming data for reasonability and signal an audio alarm if the data have gone out-of-bounds. Both the screen and the printer may be used for logging, trending, and status update. The parallel interface offers electrical flexibility and will provide a straightforward connection to a wide variety of instrumentation. For instances requiring more than one instrument, the Datapoint 2200 will accommodate up to 14 parallel interfaces. Thus the Datapoint 2200 and many other competitive models are being used as preprocessors, instrumentation interfaces, transmitting devices, and data reporting and accounting devices and for scores of other applications. Moreover, the costs to manufacture them keep dropping.

The Datapoint 2200—the type of
mini most of us will use

It has become commonplace to view minicomputers stripped of their peripherals. Some of these minis may be best characterized as follows:

1. They are general-purpose, fully programmable computers.
2. Most have expandable modular memories.
3. Some have built-in power supplies.

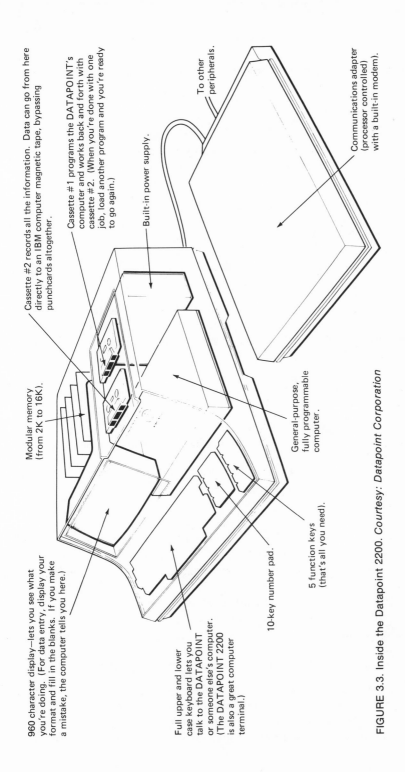

960 character display—lets you see what you're doing. (For data entry, display your format and fill in the blanks. If you make a mistake, the computer tells you here.)

Modular memory (from 2K to 16K).

Cassette #2 records all the information. Data can go from here directly to an IBM computer magnetic tape, bypassing punchcards altogether.

Cassette #1 programs the DATAPOINT's computer and works back and forth with cassette #2. (When you're done with one job, load another program and you're ready to go again.)

Built-in power supply.

Communications adapter (processor controlled) with a built-in modem).

To other peripherals.

General-purpose, fully programmable computer.

5 function keys (that's all you need).

10-key number pad.

Full upper and lower case keyboard lets you talk to the DATAPOINT or someone else's computer. (The DATAPOINT 2200 is also a great computer terminal.)

FIGURE 3.3. Inside the Datapoint 2200. *Courtesy: Datapoint Corporation*

81

The basic "mini-dress," without which the mini will not perform as a user terminal, consists of

1. An input device, usually a keyboard.
2. An output device, often a TV-like display.

Other "mini-apparel"—built-in or easily attached peripheral devices that permit the mini to perform better—might include

1. Data cassettes, to input more data or to record results.
2. Program cassettes to store instructions or for input when desired.
3. A number "pad" or typewriterlike keyboard.
4. Function keys, to select special performances contained within programs.
5. A communications adapter, to allow the mini to communicate with other peripherals or with other computers.

All of these are clearly shown in Figure 3.3, featuring the Datapoint 2200, a mini manufactured by Datapoint, Inc. (formerly the Computer Terminal Corporation), of San Antonio, Texas. Other typical peripherals, not shown, can include

1. Serial printers for "moderate-speed" (30 characters-per-second printing.
2. Line printers for "high-volume" (135 lines-per-minute) printing.
3. Magnetic tape input or output (7-track or 9-track).
4. Magnetic disk input or output (2.5 million characters per cartridge).

Software for the Datapoint 2200, again quite typical, includes

1. A high-level language like English, called "DATABUS," available in six versions.
2. Software packages called "communicators," which allow the mini to "talk back and forth" with a variety of other remote terminals and computers.
3. An assembly language—the program coding of the mini's basic logical operations.
4. A debugging language—to assist in finding errors.
5. An editor—to assist in making changes to programs.
6. Utility routines—to perform commonly useful functions such as sorting, listing, or fixing files.
7. Operating systems—in three versions, to control operations.

Many businessmen, industrialists, college deans, doctors, and so on have formerly been reluctant to purchase or lease computers owing to high costs of software and the complexity of much of it. Competition has encouraged manufacturers to provide wide ranges of programs to new users at

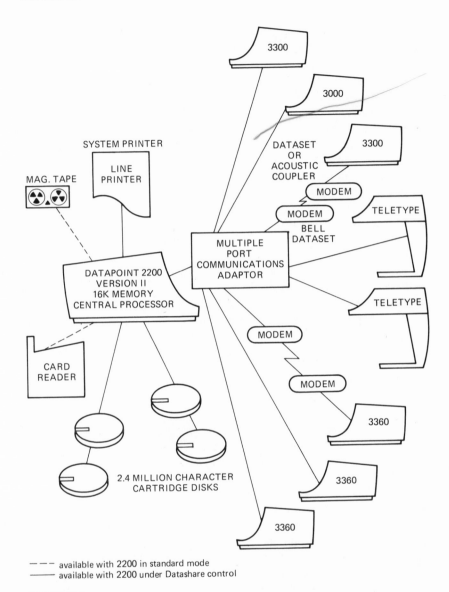

FIGURE 3.4.

no cost or for very small costs. Offered with the Datapoint 2200 (see Figure 3.4) are abstracts and documentation of many of the programs offered. The programs themselves are usually available on magnetic and paper tapes or cards. They include special languages, report generators, communication systems, loaders, emulators, and scores of other routines and subroutines.

Datapoint recently announced two new software "packages" available to customers: ACRONIM, a text editor for file management and interactive (man-machine "conversation") applications, and DISP, a special indexed-sequential file management system, which provides for random-access of records stored on disks.

Of considerable significance also is the availability of Datapoint's software system that controls up to eight remote terminals to access simultaneously the main computer (see Figure 3.4). Datashare permits a substantial reduction in costs associated with remote data entry, transmission, and processing from remote terminals. The terminals can be connected to the main computer with direct wire or by phone lines at any location, even across the country. Datapoint's DATABUS English-statement programming language is very well suited to perform administrative functions, including inventory control, production scheduling, sales order entry, and so forth.

With Datashare, data for varied applications, edited and formated according to rigid constraints, can be entered from various locations, centrally processed; and appropriate reports can be sent instantly. Datashare includes a Datapoint 2200, which integrates a fully programmable general purpose computer in the standard typewriter-sized unit, from one to four disk files, each capable of storing from 2.4 million characters in replaceable cartridges and a high-speed printer.

When Datashare is running, the line printer can be shared on a first-come, first-served basis by all remote stations. The line printer itself is not in a remote station but is colocated with the 2200 and disk. Communications interface with user terminals is achieved through a multiple port communications adapter. For "off-line" use (not controlled by Datashare), the central 2200 configuration can utilize 7- and 9-channel magnetic tape units, a card reader, and other peripherals as well as the disk units and high-speed line printer.

In accessing the central 2200, each remote user is provided its full 16K of memory for his or her programs through virtual memory techniques. The net effect of this technique is that even though he or she may be utilizing on-site a relatively simple video display terminal, the user enjoys almost all the computing power he or she would have with his or her own 2200. The 3300 input-output terminals can be connected for cross-city or cross-country purposes. The larger Datashare 5500 system with Model 3600 terminals is shown in Figure 3.5. The convenience, low cost, and simplicity of this system typifies the use of minis as time-sharing systems. Outside the United States, Datapoint is marketed worldwide by TRW Systems Inc. under license. Close competitors of the Datapoint products are Hewlett-Packard Inc.; General Automation, Inc.; Wang Laboratories, Inc., Data General Inc., among others, and Digital Equipment Corp.

16-USER-TERMINAL DATASHARE SYSTEM
FOR BUSINESS DATA PROCESSING

"The system is based on Datashare III, an expanded version of the original Datashare software package; the new 64K Datapoint 5500 Advanced Business Processor, which can provide computer power to as many as 16 user terminals; and the new Datastation 3600 user terminal with its new terminal printer. The initial and widely used Datashare is based on the Datapoint 2200 processor with which the new system is compatible. Deliveries of the new Datashare system are now being made. The Datashare system incorporating the 5500 processor represents a significant cost breakthrough for either the smaller company seeking an affordable total business processing capability for all the company's operations or for the larger company that wants to provide an independent processing capability for field offices as well as an efficient data communications link to a central computer facility. The Datashare concept is not unique in the field of business computing. Many systems put the power of a computer in the hands of the people who need it. Instead of the traditional one-at-a-time job-processing technique, Datashare allows up to 16 separate users to run individual application programs that can access common or private data files.

More processor power, peripherals added

"Datashare, with the greater computer power of the 5500 processor, offers an expanded variety of peripheral units. The 5500, like the Datapoint 2200 processor, is a highly compact unit, little larger than a typewriter; but it offers a powerful internal computer and up to 64K central memory. It has an 80 character × 12 line video display, standard typewriter keyboard, and dual internal cassette tapes. Peripherals that can be attached to the 5500 include up to eight 24-million character mass storage disk drives or, alternatively, up to four 2.4 million character cartridge disk units, a 300 LPM drum printer, a 120 LPM belt printer, a 30 CPS servo printer, 7- and 9-channel magnetic 800 and 1600 BPI tape drives, and a variety of communications interfaces. Users may access the system through the Datastation 3600 user terminal, a low-cost 'nonintelligent' video terminal unit designed specifically for use as a satellite work station in a Datashare configuration. These terminals have large, easy-to-read, glarefree displays and can be equipped with an impact printer if hard copy is desired. The Datapoint Datastation 3600 offers a large (24 line × 80 character) screen display, standard typewriter and ten key numeric keyboard, and upper and lower case display capability. The 3600 can offer users located at the user terminals (connected over standard telephone lines or via local twisted pair wires) the essential capability of the Datapoint central processor and com-

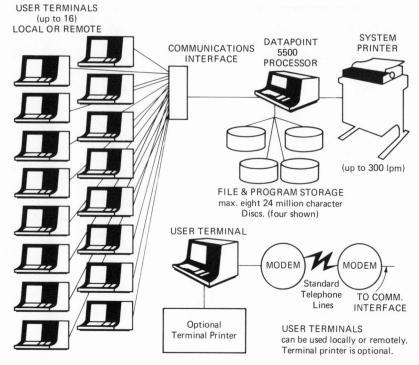

USER TERMINALS
(up to 16)
LOCAL OR REMOTE

COMMUNICATIONS
INTERFACE

DATAPOINT
5500
PROCESSOR

SYSTEM
PRINTER

(up to 300 lpm)

FILE & PROGRAM STORAGE
max. eight 24 million character
Discs. (four shown)

USER TERMINAL

MODEM   MODEM

Standard
Telephone
Lines

TO COMM.
INTERFACE

Optional
Terminal Printer

USER TERMINALS
can be used locally or remotely.
Terminal printer is optional.

FIGURE 3.5. Datashare 5500 system drawing. *Courtesy: Datapoint Corporation*

plete on-line access to appropriate disk files. The Datastation user terminals can be optionally equipped with a printer. Datashare III, the latest version of the master control program, allows access to the CPU by up to 16 remote or local work stations—using any mix of Datapoint 3600s, 1100s, 3360s, or other teletype-compatible user terminals. It provides true indexed sequential file-handling capability, enabling users at remote work stations to add to, merge, delete, append, sort, and otherwise extract useful information and analyses from files maintained on the disk storage media associated with the central processor.

"Primary applications for Datashare include all standard business data entry and data-processing functions, including order entry, general ledger, accounts payable and receivable, and inventory control and payroll. For processing jobs that require access to large mainframe computers, the Datashare-controlled network of remote work stations and disk and tape storage units also serves as an optimum means of pooling and then transmitting data to a central computer over standard telephone connections. Among the advantages is its dual functioning: on the one hand, as an integrated and independent total business data-processing capability, and, on the other, as a part of a larger computer/communications network.

"Operators of the Datapoint 3600 units (or other video display terminals under Datashare control) are assisted with data entry tasks or processing by the ready selection they can make of different work formats to display on the screen. Some companies will have over 100 of these different operator formats programmed into a Datashare system. The user, by making a simple keyboard selection, can flash the appropriate display on the screen, which makes it significantly easier to enter correct input data or select a processing program. In addition, programmed error checks, which prevent entry of erroneous data according to predetermined guide lines, greatly reduce the incidence of error and make for a more productive work force.

"Another key advantage of Datashare is its functional modularity, so that any business can readily acquire, expand, and construct the configuration best suited to their work load. A user, for example, can upgrade from a 2200 central processor to a 5500 and enjoy full software compatibility. He or she can, in the same fashion, add any needed peripheral units without having to alter or reprogram the existing system. Additionally, the new Da-

FIGURE 3.6. A Datashare system integrating Datapoint 5500 advanced business processor, two mass storage (24 million characters) disk units, a 330 LPM printer, and two Datapoint 3600 terminals (for system monitoring) in the user's home office *Courtesy: Datapoint Corporation*

tashare can also accommodate intelligent terminals such as the Diskette 1100. Remote work stations associated with a Datashare installation can be located in the same building or office complex and connected by common twisted-pair wires—which would be typical of the small and medium-sized business or the field office of a large company—or they may be connected via standard telephone connections—which capability would likely be used by the larger decentralized organization. In either case, the remote user in a Datashare network enjoys all the capability of the host processor, be it 5500 or 2200, and its peripherals." (Courtesy: Datapoint Corporation)

THE PROBLEMS OF LARGE COMPUTER SYSTEMS

Large computers have historically been structurally complicated, physically awkward, and difficult to program, operate, and maintain. Moreover, they have almost always been mysterious. Because they have the capability to control many processes and procedures and, therefore, also scores of types of input, storage, and output devices, they require very complex, hard-wired interior logic componentry. The software then must mesh or interface with a maze of electronics. Together the programs and components must be designed to effect proper control of all parts of many types of systems and equipment. Because the electronics is basically fixed, the software has become the source of some terrible problems. Most of the control or operating system (OS) programs are very difficult to design, implement, debug, change, or replace. To be cost-effective, the very expensive, large computers must obey many masters: accountants, communications managers, engineers, scientists, systems analysts, executives, and so on. The factory design engineers cannot put their machines in jeopardy by allowing programmers or other technicians to tamper with either the designed and built-in logic or their very sensitive internal control routines and programmed operations techniques. Most of these are tightly, even unalterably, "prepackaged." Large computer users must, therefore, be subservient to the demanding machine logic and these complex operating systems. They, the users, must give in; they must change their irregular procedures and operations—their input documents, schedules, organization, and so on—to fit the complex "computer way." It has also become difficult and very costly in big systems to change even the simpler "applications" programs, and it is practically impossible to "adjust" internal control programs or hard-wired logic.

Most of the difficulty, complexity, and plain grief for programmers, systems analysts, operators, and, certainly, users relates to this dictatorship of operating systems. The operating systems (OS) are also called executives, monitors, interpreters, and many unmentionable names. In essence, these are collections of read-only or wired-in operations, control routines, housekeeping subroutines and special control programs such as sort-merge procedures, system (program) loaders, input-output control programs, data conversion and communication interpreters, supervisory control programs, language compilers and assemblers, diagnostic and debugging routines, and scores of others. Few of these are output except when "dumped" for maintenance, examination, patching, and so forth. Some of them have special names, such as DOS (for disk operating system), IOCS (for input-output control system), CICS (for customer information control system), and so on. Then there are specialized versions of these, such as RTOS (real-time operating system), DOS/entry, DOS standard, CICS/VS (for virtual storage), and AOS (for advanced operating system). To complicate further the internal control processes of large systems, there are many manufacturer "releases" or updates (with corrections and "patches") of these, such as Release 26.2 of OS, Class C. Just as the OS version of CICS is a control system for management of large teleprocessing networks, other specific control systems are available for data bases, management information systems (MIS), computer-aided instruction (CAI), and so on. A recent announcement illustrates the pervasiveness of constant changes: ". . . major additions have been made to the operating and executive software routines . . . other new software products, as well as changed features and new enhancements . . . the "8B" release [concerns] new benefits of B4 multiprogramming, Stage III COBOL compilers, a new FORTRAN E system, and other supplementary automatic operations systems . . . ," and computer people cringe almost in despair.

All of this represents high costs of many types: the steep initial charge of $2 to $5 million for the system; the heavy expense of large salaries for expert and experienced personnel; the high costs of "matching" peripheral equipment; the purchase, lease, or rental of other software; the money lost through conversion time, downtime, learning time, repair and maintenance time, and so on. Moreover, big systems must be specially housed in controlled environments, away from extremes of temperature, humidity, electrical disturbances, magnetic fluctuations, and the like. Also, the reliability factors of peripheral or communications equipment, if weak, can jeopardize major parts or all of the full system. And, unfortunately, the direction of the industry, until recently, was controlled by IBM and the "dwarfs." [1] It was primed by billions of government dollars on "cost-plus" aerospace and defense contracts and "masterminded" by a small clique of military, scientific, and academic elite. The very wasteful, almost all-consuming drive for bigger and bigger—even huge, almost unworkable—systems continued. Only since the mid-1970s has this been slowed. Statements from knowledgeable business and educational leaders began to be heard, such as: "Within five years today's large computers and their un-

[1] Univac, Control Data Corp., NCR, Burroughs, Honeywell.

wieldy operating systems will be the dinosaurs of the computer world." Commander Grace Murray Hopper, one of the nation's most astute computer experts, in a speech to the American Management Association entitled "Systems of Computers: The Dispersal of Computer Power," stated, "Computer systems will be replaced by systems of [mini] computers." She called for the ultimate end to complexity and chaos, for the breaking up of massive files, and for getting rid of operating systems, data base management systems, and management information systems that are [excessively] adding to computer overhead. She cited one Navy program that is 80 percent overhead. For managements who still want to think they have a big computer, she suggested, "a big gray wall and flashing lights."

Other speakers making the strong case for distributed computing and increased use of minis in distributed networks stated that "networks have become easier and cheaper to put together and adequate facilities exist today." Still others pointed out that the "rate of change in small computer technology is so great that if you wait for it to stabilize, you'll wait for a long time." Commander Hopper said that minis someday will be available for as little as $500 apiece and that she would like to see them "treated like typewriters." That "someday" that she predicted in her 1972 speech arrived the next year, 1973, when $990-priced minis were met with $600-priced competitors from a major mini supplier (see Figure 3.1). And this was followed by micros at $395 and by some below $100 each. The consensus of the speakers seemed to urge replacement of operating systems with minis to remove complexity and to keep overhead from feeding on itself. The question was asked, "Why should we have a main processor going through tons and tons of code just to see what caused an interrupt?" [2] In early 1974, Xerox announced two multiprocessor-equipped, standard computers, the models 550 and 560, as replacements for earlier models; the larger system consists of 22 interlinked processors, with very low total system prices from $280,000 for the smaller of these two large capability systems.

THE USER REVOLT—THE DEMAND FOR BUSINESS COMPUTERS THAT WORKED SIMPLY

Unfortunately, the big system manufacturers dragged themselves behind the leadership and under the IBM "high price" product umbrella. They all continued making medium-sized systems with all the faults of the giants, and small systems, too, retained the complexity and problems. Most of these "small" systems sold for prices well in excess of $100,000. But, in 1968, the mini emerged from the single-function "black box" process control computers that had small memories and very little adaptive software.

[2] AMA Conference, "Distributed Computing," *Datamation*, November 1972, pp. 133–134.

Most of the users themselves programmed these machines in binary codes and with individual, step-by-step, machine language statements. This was costly, time-consuming, and often difficult because each brand of machine was virtually unique. But it required much less memory, and at that time memory was still quite expensive.

Very soon bigger, cheaper, and faster memories became available, and users quickly switched to English-type, high-level, problem-oriented languages, such as FORTRAN, BASIC, and now APL. Owing to new processes of microminiaturization of components, memory prices fell by 20 percent to 30 percent a year; and in 1972, by 50 percent. Minicomputers that formerly sold for $10,000 were offered for the same price, but with twice as much memory and far greater versatility. The ease of programming in higher-level languages often cut the programming times by two-thirds and more. This nice advantage for low-cost systems also practically eliminated the need for high-priced systems analysts and programmers. Users could rely on their graduate engineers, chemists, and even business administration people to write FORTRAN and BASIC programs. Now even high school graduates can write programs in these languages. And most minisystems have 16K (16,384), 16-bit (two-character or four-numeral) "words" on single 12×15 or 15×15 inch printed circuit memory boards.

Also, processor costs were cut drastically. By using more complex and very tiny circuitry, arithmetic-logic CPUs had cut the system costs, programming limitations, and machine size to make them saleable to even the smallest business, factory, office, school, or hospital. Indeed, the processor has now become the smallest cost of the entire computer system. Worldwide, the total of installed minicomputers began to grow by 75 percent (1972), and, according to *Modern Data* magazine, the total in use at the end of 1973 grew to nearly 100,000. Product obsolescence and user demands for pragmatic, user-controlled systems finally tumbled the high-and-mighty million dollar computers, and now all the big manufacturers are beginning to offer serious competition with their minis to the "little giant" manufacturers that grew rapidly and big in the fertile pasture of production for simple and straightforward "cheap" business and industrial automation computer systems.

Now minis are all around us—in applications ranging from the control of airborne rockets to optical character recognition, word-processing systems, automatic test and design systems, and cash-dispensing and point of sale systems. They are the primary base for an almost total revolution in communications, as they serve as data concentrators, message switchers, CATV "head-end" controllers, and so on. They provide the "intelligence" to intelligent terminals, they can support practically all types of peripheral equipment, and they are also easily maintained. Sales now are more than double those of all "standard" systems combined. The minicomputer is now a major part of the computer industry and deserves much broader treatment in educational institutions. All types of students should be informed and educated about their current use, capabilities, and future potential. There soon will be very few businesses that will not use these systems for order entry, billing, accounts receivable, sales analysis, inventory control, management problem solving, and other types of automation. Managers can easily measure completely tangible benefits, and they can control the costs and people who operate them. This is still not possible with most standard systems.

THE FUNDAMENTAL ADVANTAGES AND DIFFERENCES
OF MINICOMPUTERS VERSUS STANDARD SYSTEMS

Quite generally, large computer systems have traditionally established the following advantages: (1) They can be programmed in high-level languages owing to very large, even massive (million-word or "byte" [8-bit]) internal memories. (2) They are fully software- and service-supported by major, well-known companies. (3) They can provide graphic answers to many types of problems and systems. (4) They provide efficient centralization of decision making. (5) They can be multiprogrammed and time-shared, and they simultaneously perform repetitive processing and supervisory real-time control.

However, time and technologies have changed—radically and swiftly. As the large systems grew even larger, more powerful, more expensive, and more complex, the minicomputers evolved into immensely capable machines, and they were being offered at constantly reduced sizes. Now they can handle practically any process control, data processing, or decision-making task and at a fraction of the cost of a large computer. Furthermore, systems of multiple-minis have proved to be faster and more efficient, with far fewer drawbacks than major systems in wide ranges of test problems and capabilities and at small fractions of both programming and operating costs. For example, in one environmental simulation test, a 16K minicomputer took 52.8 seconds to run the test program as opposed to 20.3 seconds for the large computer with 262K of memory. The large computer performed the job faster, but, based on its hourly cost of $500 compared to the minicomputer's $1.63, the large computer cost 82 times as much as the minicomputer to run the simulation. Minicomputer systems with full lines of peripheral equipment—disk storage, magnetic tape gear, card readers, line printers, teleprinters, and so on—can control and monitor processes, take corrective actions, accumulate historical data, act on those data for process optimization, issue management reports, run self-diagnostics, and so on. And such systems sell at prices well under $30,000. Small "standard" systems costing twice that much have less than half that capability on the average.

Ten specific advantages of minicomputers over standard systems

The comparisons to be made will relate to the use of multiple minis—each unit with a cost of less than $5,000—and six or fewer were combined in order to demonstrate the same capabilities as practically any standard small or medium-sized system having far greater costs and complexities.

1. Large "total" projects are often not well defined and require several types of processing. Many functions are more easily computerized than others, and many total systems must be implemented in segments. Buying a standard system almost always results in "overkill," that is, buying more power, more equipment, and programming than necessary. If a manufacturing plant is using machine tools under computer control, minis permit managers to automate the least complex or the most critical operations first. They then gain valuable experience for developing later on other ongoing or more complex systems. Each "island" of automation operates, and all can be tied together, by using one or more supervisory or central control minicomputers. The same advantages apply for offices, businesses, hospitals, schools, and so on. As is usually the case, accounting functions are the easiest and the most critical for the new user to automate. Then come inventory control, management analysis, and so on. Such local use and distributed intelligence have many personnel advantages as well as those of lower costs, fewer "gambles," and less disruption.

2. The benefits of ease of installation, programming development, and time-phased, lower costs are many and varied. When building an information distribution system, the designer can purchase, install, and program one computer at a time. This is easy on the budget, the regular operating staffs, the management decision-makers, and the planners. The conversion is painless because all operations need not be shut down for full system implementation, as is the case with practically all standard systems. Conversions, forms, traffic, scheduling are easier.

3. Minicomputers work well with systems that have high incoming data rates or widely distributed information sources. Many laboratory, process control, and widely dispersed information-gathering processes feed data to computers at extremely high rates. Multiple minis can assure that no information is lost or significantly delayed. Multiple minis monitor, control, and quickly handle data from experiments, instruments, or field sources while these are active; and they correlate, analyze, or report the data very quickly after the event has occurred. The cases could relate to weather, to nuclear or chemical experiments or processes, or to point of sale terminals at many counters and from many stores or other cashier points. For extremely rapid communications handling, multiple minis are ideal. Large computers would probably "batch" this information for later handling whereas minis could handle it in real-time (immediate response).

4. Systems that require uninterrupted operations and redundancy safety fit minicomputer capabilities well. Multiple minis can be most economically configured to provide backup or redundancy systems practically, in effect, to prevent equipment failure or downtime. By their design and programming simplicity, they are also much less prone to error, failure, or malfunction than larger or conventional systems. When it is necessary to shut down owing to expansion, maintenance, or failure, a low-cost, redundant computer can be used to take over the processes temporarily while the other satellite minis continue their operations. With large centralized computers, downtime, for whatever cause, can be very disturbing, even disastrous. Redundancy machines would, in most cases, be cost-prohibitive for many standards.

5. Minicomputers perform operations that require extremely close monitoring—experiments, closed-circuit TV, and so on. Multiple minis can be placed very near, or become a part of, the actual operations they control or service. This saves considerable cabling costs and communications equipment costs and provides more frequent sampling for corrective and adaptive response, and such multiple systems do not require special cooling or other expensive environmental adaptions. Six minicomputers for Chicago's convention center, McCormick Place-on-the-Lake, using closed-circuit TV, monitor vehicle traffic into, through, and out of the building; count people; control lighting densities; monitor outside weather; automatically lock or unlock doors; and perform other security chores—all difficult for conventional systems.

6. Minicomputers permit ease and simplicity of design and system configuration. In standard systems, the design of multiterminal systems, the location of bulky equipment, the planning for human factors and safety considerations are all tough problems. Multiple mini systems can be built by using various multitier adaptable processes. Most can be placed in spaces out-of-the-way because they are often contained on very small 1- to 2-foot square circuit boards, or they can be added to peripheral units, attached to other office or factory machinery, and so on. Progressive installations permit getting one computer "on the air," then another, and so forth. For example, the data acquisition and control minis could be installed first; then others for testing, correcting, logging, reporting, and the like. Additional memory is simple to use as expansion becomes necessary. Choices for other processors include many with special performance characteristics, special connecting units designed to be added, for new services or backup. There are generally five ways computers can be interconnected: (a) by using an input-output bus (path or connection), (b) by using a multiprocessor communications adapter, (c) by sharing memory, (d) through a satellite/central computer system configuration, and (e) by using a grid network. (See Figure 3.7.) Very low costs for design, installation, or accommodation are involved.

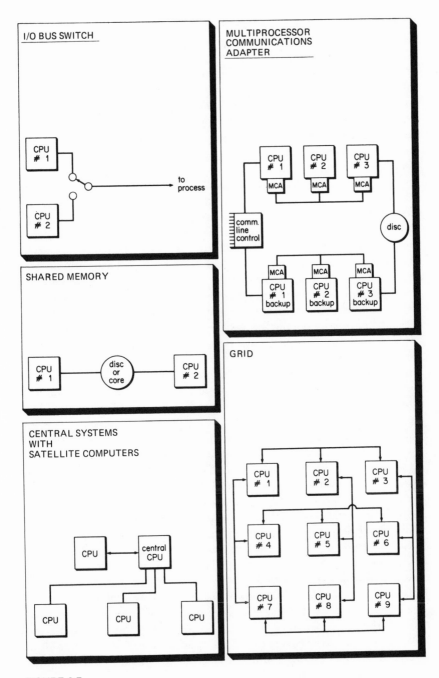

FIGURE 3.7.

7. Multiple mini systems permit very low-cost, simple multiprocessing. When larger systems require the collection of massive amounts of data and the main processor is also needed for real-time inquiry-response operations, very complex equipment, software, and new logic components are often required, with considerable increase in costs and problems. Multiple minis operating in a multiprocessing mode quickly collect and compile the data while simultaneously monitoring continuous processes. Adding second and third machines that manipulate the data, analyze, and report it, leaving the first machine dedicated to gathering information, eliminates the many complex operating system problems developed by standard systems.

8. Multiprocessor multiple mini systems save time and costs when expanding installations. Practically every computer user goes through the procedures of expanding his system many times. This is usually very costly, irritating to all, and often a traumatic experience to those closely involved. With multiple minis, this need hardly concern many people or budgets at all. Hardware can be added quite simply as described above. Additions to main memory can be quite simple for minis, and installations of new peripheral equipment introduce few problems. In standard systems, generally, significant difficulties are encountered with this and also with the necessity for reprogramming—especially the operating systems. Often this, in effect, requires a complete redesign of the system, writing the new actual programs needed, debugging them, and creating final documentation. A great deal of this can be avoided with multiple minis by either duplicating the system or using a second computer to handle new tasks while the first continues doing the previous job. This keeps the operation in process while the reprogramming is done, and this is usually not possible with standard systems. Programming the second mini takes less time and cost than programming a larger machine to do both the old tasks and the new ones.

9. Multiple mini systems cost significantly less in overhead than standard systems. Several of the key points listed earlier illustrate maximization of capabilities with low-cost multiple minis. The processors, peripherals, and software are all less costly by several factors than those of standard systems. Overhead or implementation time is also much less because the software is easier to write. Lower cost and fewer programmers are needed, and seldom are systems analysts needed except for short period consulting. Fewer people are needed to install, program, and debug the system because it is broken into well-defined segments. After the multiprocessor system is installed, it can be altered and reprogrammed faster and more easily than standards. Service and maintenance are much simpler, often completed with phone calls to the factory or service stations around the country. Thus, overhead—people or other problems—is greatly reduced, saving time, money, and mental anguish.

10. The simplification of communication capabilities is more easily accomplished with multiple mini systems. Perhaps more important than any

of the advantages listed above is the ease of adaptability of multiple minis to data communications environment. Standard systems are very difficult to adapt to distributed intelligence. Minis, however, are practically made to order to add and control terminals. Multiprocessor communications adapters (MCAs) and modems are offered by practically all mini manufacturers because most of them are heavily in the data communications equipment business. MCAs are most effective when large amounts of data must be transferred among computers through direct memory access facilities and when large amounts of data must be transferred among many computers. One MCA can handle up to 15 or more computers, each with the ability to communicate with any of the others in the network. Also, minis can easily share mass memory or bulk storage devices, and the only differences between disk and main memories are speed and capacity. Main memories can be accessed more rapidly than disk, but the disk can hold much more data economically. Shared memory configurations are much less complex to implement, especially if supporting hardware, such as dual port disk adapters, and software that operates under existing standard operating systems, are available. Moreover, widespread use is being developed with groups of satellite computers tied to larger central computers through communications links. This is especially so in business computing operations, where each remote mini or "intelligent" terminal has come with data-processing (preprocessing) capability of its own. A satellite mini transfers data to the central computer for tasks outside its capability, or it answers inquiries for data from the central computer. In a grid configuration, where any two machines can back up a third computer that has failed, many very critical applications can be nicely handled. The additional hardware and software cost for a multiprocessor grid is relatively small compared to the possible penalties of severe monetary or safety loss owing to failures.

Conclusion

Four multiple minis are monitoring 38,000 alarm points in an Asian country's communication network. The fifth one in this configuration is the system executive. The system detects outages immediately and reroutes messages. A Navy system uses eight minis to drive 40 navigation and communication training stations. Four drive the training stations, and two act as system executives, but instructors can let all 40 stations simulate one problem or let half simulate one and the other half another. The cost of this system was substantially less than if a standard system were required. To summarize, it is clear that many system functions can be split among several computers to gain reliability, to facilitate simultaneous data communication and processing, to make programming easy, to use same data bases economically, and to maximize the value of each controlled application. Wise managers and engineers are now very carefully checking mul-

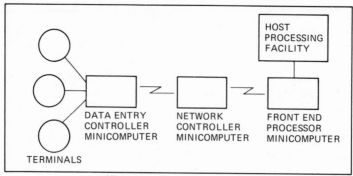

Minicomputers in Network Support

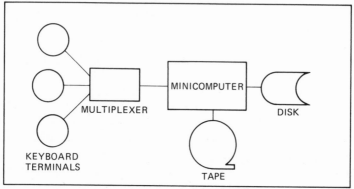

Shared Processor Data Entry System

FIGURE 3.8. Minicomputer flexibility provides local data capture, operator simplicity

tiple minis as substitutes for expensive, wasteful standards in many, many cases.

Minis in large information-processing networks can be classified as having three distinct functions: (1) front-end processors that interface the main center to the communications network, (2) network controllers that are used within the communications network to direct the flow of data (as in a message switcher), and (3) data entry controllers that perform I/O functions for each terminus of the network. The minicomputer used as a data entry controller implements the desired terminal functionally through applications-specific software within a cost-effective, high performance hardware configuration. Data entry tasks are off-loaded from the host processor, and data are validated and edited prior to submission to the host for higher-level batch processing. Where applicable, portions of the transaction-processing tasks may also be included in the terminal functionally. Key-to-disk systems are shared-processor configurations. This permits "machine-oriented" data capture; that is, the system has a high degree of control over the operator, who is required to make very few decisions. The operator keys data in the most convenient order, and the system restructures the data to meet the user's file requirements.

SOME EXAMPLES OF MINICOMPUTER SYSTEMS FOR
VERY SMALL BUSINESSES AND FACTORIES

Some of the major manufacturers have recently entered the mini business, but they are not yet down to the $5,000 and below class. Nevertheless, the NCR 299, like the IBM Model 5100 are good examples. The NCR 299 is a low-cost, multipurpose accounting computer with a unique optical-scanning programming capability, the first of a new generation of systems by NCR designed to be used by businesses with fewer than 150 employees. The basic system sells for about $7,000. NCR expects to sell about 50,000 of them by 1978. Their claim is that the system's simple programming and operation make it the most easily installed computer around. It is built around a powerful mini with extensive microprogramming contained in compact read-only memories (ROMs), providing very fast access time for computations and internal operations. User programs are internally stored in separate read-write core memories. They are used for many purposes, such as billing, payroll, general ledger, processing purchase orders, and so on, including decision-type budgetary accounting, job costing, and estimating. One of the 299's key features is the simple assembly of programs, using the customer's forms, and a simple (included) optical scanner that "reads" the presence or absence of reflected light from pencil or pen marks on a program assembly card. The scanning unit enters the information into the computer's memory, and the system performs various operations according to these programmed instructions, as developed by the customer as assisted by the NCR salesman, and in less than a day.

A unique characteristic of the NCR computer is the comprehensive library of standard accounting application programs and their very low cost. A basic 46-step program, such as one for accounts receivable, costs about $100; a 63-step program for payroll, for example, $150; or special programs developed at the customer's site, at $4.50 per step. A salesman fills out these customized programs on the form with basic one- and two-word answers to questions regarding functions or operations desired, marking the appropriate rectangles; the program is ready in minutes. Changing a program takes a maximum of 90 seconds. The machine has "lead through" lights to guide operators entering data, show operators their errors, and indicate what the processor is doing. Programming and training are handled by salesmen, eliminating complicated installation procedures involving systems analysts and instructors. Operators can be trained in hours; a machine delivered in the morning will, in many cases, be productive before the end of the business day. The turnover of unhappy personnel problem of many businesses is virtually eliminated with these simple systems. More than 5,000 were scheduled for installation in 1975, with sales expected to increase rapidly from NCR's large customer base worldwide.

THE EFFECT OF NEW MINIS AND PROGRAMMING
SIMPLICITY ON PROFESSIONAL PROGRAMMERS

Despite what some "experts" still predict and many educators still stalwartly hope, the "facts of life" that follow strongly suggest that the need for programmers will steadily diminish. Approximately one million people were at work in the computer industry, exclusive of manufacturing personnel, in 1974. Increases were steady in the ranks of marketeers, salesmen, service or maintenance people, and designers in components areas; but the ranks of programmers were thinning, with only the best and most experienced holding tight. Some of the reasons for this are enumerated and analyzed as follows.

1. The equipment manufacturers, as with the case of the NCR 299 discussed earlier, are very purposefully designing hardware specifically to eliminate the need for professional programmers. An IBM vice-president recently stated, "We must increase the hardware percentage of the data-processing dollar." It seems that the manufacturers would like to capture those funds that are going to programmers by building in and charging for these capabilities in the hardware price. Businessmen are demanding a reduction in the "human" costs (and errors) in computer systems, and some of IBMs "Gray Sheets" (information brought out at the antitrust trials of IBM) clearly show they (programmers) are designed for elimination in most systems.

2. In most surveys, conclusions are that there is an oversupply of "regular" programmers, that is, "coders," compiler writers, operations programmers, and so on. There will be a continuing need for applications design programmers, "inventors," and so forth. But other than the truly creative types, there is little hope for any needed increase to the present supply. Gaining experience will be extremely difficult for the thousands of amateurs being turned out by the colleges and trade schools. Packaged programs are becoming plentiful, flexible, efficient, and very low-cost. Thousands are available from colleges, software trade houses, suppliers and manufacturers, the government, computer user groups, and simply from the "public domain."

3. The ease of learning and the simplicity of use of high-level languages such as BASIC, APL, FORTRAN, and others, as well as the thousands and

thousands of students, managers, professionals, and so on who have mastered these capabilities, have almost universally reduced the need for professional programmers in most areas.

4. The small number of changes in languages during the past six years has developed a large reservoir of very skilled, experienced, and highly dedicated professional programmers. They have become very productive and efficient with practically all types of equipment, experiences, and systems. They have a great many productive years ahead of them and provide competition most novices cannot hope to overcome.

5. The ratio of programming cost to the amount of computing has dropped drastically. Many large networks of interconnected systems with intricate software capabilities for connecting many thousands of people make programming skill exchanges very easy and fast. GE's time-sharing network offers to act as an agent for thousands of instantaneous "trading posts" for people who want to sell, buy, or rent each others' programs; and IBM now has a system for trading and exchanging user-developed programs among its millions of customers. Although there is much more programming going on owing to the great number of increasing sales of systems, programs and programming are available very cheaply, quickly, and conveniently almost everywhere—except for the very topflight capabilities.

6. In the past, while the initial installation phases of computer systems had everyone "reinventing the wheel," while program exchanges were not known, and when most all users were first discovering how to run computers, programmers were needed practically everywhere. But the construction of original systems, like the railroads, is over, and these "workers" are not much in demand anymore; the need is only for true innovators.

7. It is expected that quite soon voice input to computers will be in vogue. It is also expected that huge data banks of program abstracts will be able to be searched by using a simple definition of the problem to be solved with a consequent automatic issue of the appropriate program and with an attached "fee" billing similar to a royalty for a song or use of copyright material. The Advanced Research Projects Agency (ARPA) of the Department of Defense has funded research in these areas under the heading of "automatic programming" at several universities, including MIT's Project MAC Automatic Programming Division.

8. Minicomputer and microcomputer manufacturers as well as electronic parts distributors have all developed significant investments in preprogrammed "cards," chips, tapes, strips, ROMs, and many other devices; and they have thus practically stolen the programmers' trade and made highly salable products of it. If it concerns money for this skill or function that could go into their pockets or those of programmers, it is obvious which effort will be selected. They are already spending millions of dollars promoting what formerly was the primary function of the programmer.

Conclusion

Many in the industry wonder, considering these facts, how current programmers will be able to compete. They also wonder how the annual entrants continually rushing into the field will become gainfully employed in their trade. Will even the present-day installations consider keeping most of the programmers they now have? Is there some new role for which programmers can be equipped to prevent a terrible calamity of a continuing massive oversupply of programmers? Why are college people still rather mindlessly turning out thousands of programmers into a world of automatically programmed computers? Similar problems will soon exist, it seems, for secretaries displaced by word-processing computer systems; for engineers and teachers who might become disemployed by computer-aided design and computer-aided instruction systems; for bank and grocery cashiers and clerks, by point of sale systems; and for accountants, middle managers, and scores of other people in other precarious areas where computer automation and system developments are beginning to dominate.

The largest manufacturer of minicomputers, Digital Equipment Corporation, of Maynard, Mass., makes minis with cost ranges from $500 to $250,000. In mid-1974 its market studies showed that the very low-cost minis were in a market segment that was growing between 30 percent and 50 percent per year. It very quickly brought out two low-priced mini systems that sold from $1,760 to $2,240 (PDP-8M). The company offered a combination of programmable units with read-only memory (PROM), as well as read/write memory. They are excellent machines for repetitive manufacturing operations, control applications, data collection, and instrument monitoring. The user has a chance to fix or change his or her control programs with the PROMs and still have read/write memory for active data. The control programs can be changed, as required, by erasing the PROMs with an ultraviolet lamp and/or reprogramming them with a "blaster" available from the company. The PROM memories are otherwise nondestructible and are available as add-on units in increments of 1,024 words each, including 256 words of read/write memory. A picture of DEC's PROM is shown in Figure 3.9.

MINICOMPUTERS: APPLICATIONS PROGRESS— WITH SMART TERMINALS

The material in the forepart of this text relating to minicomputers has stressed the very exceptional impact these low-cost units have had on the total society and economy. The implications of this "driving force" in the communications industry during the mid and late 1970s are developed very

FIGURE 3.9. The PROM memory, available in 1K and 2K, uses a new technique that allows read/write locations throughout the memory as the program requires. Ultraviolet light erases the PROM, which can then be reprogrammed by using a programmer (blaster) available from Digital. *Courtesy: Digital Equipment Corporation*

briefly here. Terminal-oriented computer systems (TOCS) currently have their most fulfilling acceptability in seven quite distinct capability areas: They are used

1. As front-end preprocessors, generally to handle various input/output data and information as controlled by internal housekeeping programs called "operating systems," and they thus prepare the "system" for the "compute" or manipulative processing.
2. As controllers for remote terminals in groups or as individual standalone "intelligent" all-purpose types.
3. As interface units for "matching" complicated data base entry speeds and codes to the central processing unit from various types of input units, and they then act as response "simplifiers," translating, formating, and "presenting" the output to the user audibly, visually, or in scores of types of hard copy.
4. As communications concentrators to affect a significant operating simplicity and cost reduction capability for larger telecommunications sys-

103

tems. Minicomputers clear out the "junk" in most messages, such as leading and trailing zeroes, end and start of word marks, codes, and signals, and so on, and then present the "main" computer with "fast and pure" data and information.

5. For unique and very specific user applications (decentralized divisions or profit centers) over a wide range and great variety of utilization aspects, that is, programs and information distinctly designed, amended, and addended to react to problems and tasks of special company units, professions, industrial or processing procedures and reports, and so forth.

6. As processors for point of sales (POS) or transaction processing, store-and-forward message switching systems, and other tasks resulting from or required by check-out or sales counter terminals in supermarkets, department stores, and so on.

7. As the controlling unit replacing formerly hard-wired (built-in), single-purpose, numerically controlled (automated) production and process machines. The minicomputer is the firm foundation of "computer numerical" control (CNC), which is now called "soft automation" and stands for a total revolution in the mighty process control industries, that is, minicomputer "programs" can instantly change the functions, speeds, purposes, and so on of many machines.

Many prestigious authorities suggest that several hundred thousand minis will be needed for automated laboratories, educational institutions, medical instrumentation and controls, and point of sale supermarket and department store check-out counter systems in the years ahead. All of this is based upon the already proved cost-effectiveness of the "mighty giants," which allow management segments of large commercial and institutional enterprises to establish decentralized independence but to still be under the ultimate control of the total system "executive team," which handles final feedback and reporting. Systemized (off-the-shelf) programming, the use of new simple access languages, and the speed and clarity of visual/audio response reports are just a few of the advantages that are basic to "terminal-oriented" computer systems.

The "smart tube"—some details

Very recently, microprocessors became the key elements in formerly expensive graphic terminal designs and special units. One of the reasons why former users delayed putting scores of terminals on minicomputers was that they would just run out of computer "driving" power. Most minis did not have enough power to support 20 or 30 terminals. But a great percentage of the total computer activity is local to terminals. An appropriately designed microprocessor located within the terminal does a lot to remove the overhead on the CPU. This allows users to put many more terminals on a conventional minicomputer CPU, and "plug-in" processors and ROMs build up great extra power for the enclosed minis. The analogy is that of having many small, programmable engineering calculators incorporated into the terminal. The processors and ROMs do much to remove much of the load on the CPU while being used for time-sharing systems, especially when mathematical calculations are being done.

Very low-cost tape cassettes, generally the Phillips type, are popular add-on offerings of intelligent terminal makers. Other peripherals available include low-cost floppy disks, for storage; autodialing modems, for remote batch jobs; and even plotters and card readers and so on. Other features included are often really needed, such as special characters, intensity control for forms work and editing, useful cursor commands, and both upper- and lowercase letters. All intelligent terminals allow users to keep considerable text in memory. The amount of text or software that a terminal can store is largely a function of expandable memory size. Processors can compress data, and good ones require very few instructions to do most user programs. Semiconductors, ROMs, and RAMs, used in terminal memories, cost little more per bit than magnetic tape but are tiny and mighty efficient.

Keyboards have one moving part per key, and each can trigger many programs contained on connected ROMs. The keyboards are generally read by a scanning technique. The processor polls each key, electronically debouncing and testing for multiple depressions. Contrast and clarity are a property of the display system, and if the terminal is to be used with high ambient lights, users may want a dark faceplate. Extra-large or extra-small tube faces are available for systems that will sit in special cabinets. Most intelligent terminals use large-scale integration for the heart of their processors because production economies make them much cheaper. Images and programs are stored in the same memory, which is usually expandable up to the large capacities that minicomputers now offer. One byte of memory is used for each character position on the screen in some terminals, and terminal processors now avoid filling up memory with blanks.

Broad ranges of peripheral devices are currently available for most intelligent terminals. Input-output interfaces permit add-ons of whatever type users choose to purchase or lease. Intelligent terminals offer several data rates and will generally let users choose either the ASCII (American standard code for information interchange) or EBCDIC (IBM's code) for communications, although nearly all terminals use ASCII codes for their own data storage and programming languages. This sector of the industry is young but growing rapidly, and the products offered will improve greatly during the next few years.

Intelligent terminals can become unique,
even speaking Japanese, Hebrew, Arabic

One company [3] has introduced a serial, nonimpact CRT hard copy device that prints at speeds up to 240 char./sec. on "electrosensitive" paper. The unit can print in Japanese, Hebrew, or Arabic script by means of a $200 option, which adds another ROM and a printing font selectable by code. The printer is compatible with CRT units using ASCII. The basic unit prints lines of 80 characters in 7 × 9 dot matrix at 120 char./sec., with the 240 char./sec. speed optional. Some versions of the printer can serve as I/O devices to minicomputers to thus make the terminals intelligent in many languages.

An example of low-cost, highly
adaptable, unique terminals

The Digi-Log Microterm [4] is a modular microprocessor-controlled terminal designed to meet the growing demand for a low-cost data communications terminal that can be easily tailored to a customer's specifications. It is fully programmable and, therefore, adaptable to a variety of applications in many disciplines. The concept consists of a bus-oriented microprocessor and a family of circuit modules capable of being configured to provide solutions to almost any conceivable data communication application from a low-speed alphanumeric CRT terminal to a high-speed multi-terminal communications controller. The family of modules is continually growing and may be retrofitted at any time as applications change. The basic configuration is a microprocessor data controller and a firmware program.

Any number of additional modules may be added, including input-output channels, display-drivers, printer buffers, memory storage, keyboards, or interfaces to peripheral devices, such as disk controllers or paper or magnetic tape controllers. Virtually any host computer system can be accommodated. The dual bus structure includes an 8-bit data bus and a 14-bit memory address bus allowing for 16K of addressable memory. If additional memory is required, the unique I/O port selection method enables any single address to select an entire peripheral memory controller. Multiprocessing is possible by the addition of microprocessor modules.

These terminals permit the configuration of a terminal that fits unique requirements. It is no longer necessary to design systems around the limitations of existing computer terminals. Most systems eventually change or probably should. The design provides for easy changes because many of its

[3] Scope Data, Inc., Orlando, Florida.
[4] System Series 3300 from Digi-Log Systems, Inc., Horsham, Pennsylvania 19044.

FIGURE 3.10. The Digi-Log Model 33 Interactive Data Terminal
Courtesy: Digi-Log Systems, Inc.

capabilities are a function of internal microprogramming. Changing these capabilities involves nothing more than programming new read-only memories (ROMs) and plugging them into the terminal. System downtime due to changes can, therefore, be reduced to almost zero—just the time required to plug in new ROMs and test the system. The low-cost terminal is designed for large users of computer terminals and is priced accordingly, with manufacturing economies coming from the modular designs being passed on to the user. These units are some of the lowest-cost microprocessor terminals on the market. Because microprogramming is used to provide many of Microterm's capabilities, most of the time-consuming development cycles usually associated with circuit manufacturing are eliminated. This means that systems can be up and running sooner after changes or expansion.

Turnkey data-processing systems

As noted earlier, mini, micro, and terminal-oriented small business computers are changing the face of the data-processing industry. This new generation of easy-to-program and easy-to-use machines is bringing automation to thousands of offices that could not consider it before. Buying that first computer is no longer a tough decision for an executive even if he has no data-processing background. Furthermore, many service organizations are dedicated to computer time sharing and have hundreds of thousands of business customers.

Many executives will follow the turnkey approach and shop for a preprogrammed computer. The computer itself is only part of an information system. No matter how efficient the hardware is, it takes a professionally designed system and well-written software working with—and through—the computer to make the total system perform the tasks that management wants done. When buying this total system, users should insist that the vendor have a capable professional staff who can thoroughly analyze the business and its problems and can translate this information into a computer-based system that solves these problems. Moreover, they must work closely with the user as a part of a concerted team effort that combines the user's knowledge of his business with their knowledge of hardware and systems.

There is more emphasis than ever on the availability of preprogrammed software packages. Nothing is more costly in business than to go without information. The small businesses have the same need as the large ones—they want to act, not react after it is too late. And to act, they need complete management information, both operational and financial, and they should not have to do their own programming. Suppliers must provide not only equipment, but also complete business management system libraries with application programs that are results-oriented. The day of the do-it-yourself program "kit" is over. Selection of programs from these libraries provides the user with packages that fit specific businesses exactly. These can be implemented as soon as the computer is installed. Moreover, their cost is only a fraction of the expense that the user would incur in designing his own system.

The new hardware is more sophisticated and more reliable than ever before. Today's data-processing dollar buys more than ever. Prices are way down, and capability and versatility are way up. The small computer user receives the greatest benefit from this trend because today's small systems have the speed and capability that were attributed to medium-scale systems a few years ago. Because of the push to squeeze maximum capability into a smaller machine, the small systems come closer to state-of-the-art technology than some of the larger systems. Well-trained management personnel will give the user a big edge in doing his data processing efficiently and independently and in getting the maximum performance from the hardware. More than 1,000 American companies manufacture and sell mini, micro, and terminal-oriented computer systems and peripherals.

FIGURE 3.11. The tiny microelectronic "chip" balanced on the head of a common pin contains as much circuitry as several hundred transistor radios. Microcircuits like this are used in the new, electronic, point of sale terminals being produced for the nation's department stores and supermarkets. *Courtesy: NCR Corporation*

FURTHER DEFINING THE WORLD OF COMPUTERS

Accumulator (AC). The accumulator is a 4-, 8-, 12- or 16-bit register that functions as a holding register for arithmetic, logical, and input-output operations. Data words may be fetched from memory to the AC or from the AC into memory. Arithmetic and logical operations involve two operands,

Definitions are excerpted with permission from the book *Microcomputer Dictionary and Guide,* Matrix Publishers, Inc., Champaign, Illinois, 1976, 704 pp., by Charles J. Sippl and David A. Kidd.

one held in the AC, the other fetched from memory. The result of an operation is retained in the AC. The AC may be cleared, complemented, tested, incremented, or rotated under program control. The AC also serves as an input-output register. Programmed data transfers pass through the AC.

Address. 1. A character or group of characters that identifies a register, a particular part of storage, or some other data source or destination. 2. To refer to a device or an item of data by its address.

Assembler. The essential capability of an assembler is to translate symbolically represented instructions into their binary equivalents. A well-designed computer is reflected in a versatile, efficient assembly language instruction set. It is a computer program that operates on symbolic input data to produce from such data machine instructions by carrying out such functions as translation of symbolic operation codes into computer operating instructions, assigning locations in storage for successive instructions, or computation of absolute addresses from symbolic notation.

Asynchronous (or nonsynchronous) computer. 1. One in which operations are not all timed by a master clock. The signal to start an operation is provided by the completion of the previous operation. 2. Having a variable time interval between successive bits, characters, or events. In data transmission, this is usually limited to a variable time interval between characters and is often known as start-stop transmission.

Automatic interrupt. 1. Interruption caused by program instruction as contained in some executive routine; interruption not caused by programmer but due to engineering of devices. 2. An automatic program-controlled interrupt system that causes a hardware jump to a predetermined location. There are at least five types of interrupts. (1) input/output, (2) programmer error, (3) machine error, (4) supervisor call, and (5) external (for example, timer turned to negative value, alert button on console, external lines from another processor). There is further subdivision under the five types. Unwanted interrupts, such as an anticipated overflow, can be masked out.

Automatic loader. A loader program implemented in a special ROM (read-only memory) that allows loading of binary paper tapes or the first record or sector of a mass storage device. The program is equivalent to a bootstrap loader plus a binary loader. When an automatic loader is installed, it is seldom necessary to key in a bootstrap program to load the binary loader.

Auxiliary processor. A specialized processor such as an array processor, fast fourier transform (FFT) processor, or input/output processors (IOP) generally used to increase processing speed through concurrent operation.

Background processing interrupt. Work that has a low priority and is handled by the computer when higher priority or real-time entries are not occurring. Batch processing such as inventory control, payroll, housekeeping, and so on is often treated as background processing but can be interrupted on orders from terminals or inquiries from other units.

BCD, binary coded decimal. A type of positional value code in which each decimal digit is binary coded into 4-bit "words." The decimal number 12, for example, would become 0001 0010 in BCD, as based on and sometimes called the 8421 code.

Bidirectional bus. The standard bus is a simple, fast, easy-to-use interface between various standard modules. Modules connected to this common bidirectional bus structure receive the same interface signal lines. A typical system application in which the processor module, memory modules, and peripheral device interface modules are connected to the bus can be briefly stated as follows: Bus data and control can be bidirectional open-collector lines that are asserted low. The bus can be comprised of data/address lines, control/synchronization signal lines, and system function lines.

Bootstrap. 1. A technique or device designed to bring itself into a desired state by means of its own action, for example, a machine routine whose first few instructions are sufficient to bring the rest of itself into the computer from an input device. 2. To use a bootstrap. 3. That part of a computer program used to establish another version of the computer program.

Branch. 1. Concerns the capability and procedure of a microprocessor program instruction designed to modify the function or program sequence. The actual modification is an immediate change in direction, meaning, or substance of intent of the programmer. 2. To depart from the normal sequence of executing instructions in a computer. Synonymous with *jump.* 3. A sequence of instructions that is executed as a result of a decision instruction.

Buffer storage device. 1. A storage device in which data are assembled temporarily during data transfers. It is used to compensate for a difference in the rate of flow of information or the time occurrence of events when transferring information from one device to another. 2. A portion of main storage used for an input or output area.

Bug patches. As bugs are uncovered in a program, patches can be inserted and documented in order to fix the mistakes. When a number of patches have been made, they should be incorporated into the source program, and the program should be reassembled. This ensures a well-documented program.

Bus. 1. As applied to computer technology, one or more conductors used as a path over which information is transmitted. 2. A circuit over which data or power is transmitted. Often one that acts as a common connection among a number of locations. (Synonymous with *trunk*.)

Byte manipulation. Refers to an ability to manipulate, as individual instructions, groups of bits such as characters. A byte is considered to be eight bits in most cases and forms either one character or two numerals.

Channel. 1. That portion of a computer's storage medium that is also accessible to a given reading station. 2. That part of a communication system that connects the message source with the message sink. In information theory in the sense of shannon the channel can be characterized by the set of conditional probabilities of occurrence of all the messages possibly received at the message sink when a given message emanates from the message source.

Checking, automatic. Refers to the numerous internal checks that continually monitor the accuracy of the system and guard against incipient malfunction. Typical are the parity and inadmissible-character check, automatic readback of magnetic tape and magnetic cards as the information is being recorded. The electronic tests that precede each use of magnetic tape or magnetic cards to ensure that the operator has not inadvertently set switches improperly.

Circuit, integrated (IC). Refers to one of several logic circuits, gates, flip-flops that are etched on single crystals, ceramics, or other semiconductor materials and designed to use geometric etching and conductive ink or chemical deposition techniques all within a hermetically sealed chip. Some chips with many resistors and transistors are extremely tiny; others are, in effect, "sandwiches" of individual chips.

Circuit, printed. Refers to resistors, capacitors, diodes, transistors, and other circuit elements that are mounted on cards and interconnected by conductor deposits. These special cards are treated with light-sensitive emulsion and exposed. The light thus fixes the areas to be retained, and an acid bath eats away those portions that are designed to be destroyed. The base is usually a copper-clad card.

Communications control device. Data devices that can be attached directly to the system channel via a control unit designed to perform character assembly and transmission control. The control unit may be either the data-adapter unit or the transmission control.

Computer circuits. Circuits used in the construction of digital computers are the following: storage circuits, triggering circuits, gating circuits, inverting circuits, and timing circuits. In addition, there may be other circuits used in smaller quantities, such as power amplifiers for driving heavier loads, indicators, output devices, and amplifiers for receiving signals from external devices, as well as oscillators for obtaining the clock frequency.

Computer run. 1. Refers to the processing of a batch of transactions while under the control of one or more programs and against all the files that are affected to produce the required output. 2. Performance of one routine or several routines automatically linked so that they form an operating unit, during which manual manipulations are not required of the computer operator.

Conditional jump. An instruction to a computer that will cause the proper one or two (or more) addresses to be used in obtaining the next instruction, depending on some property of one or more numerical expressions or other conditions. Also referred to as conditional transfer of control.

Controller. 1. An element or group of elements that take data proportional to the difference between input and output of a device or system and convert this data into power used to restore agreement between input and output. 2. A module or specific device that operates automatically to regulate a controlled variable or system.

Control panel. 1. A panel that has a systematic arrangement of terminals used with removable wires to direct the operation of a computer or punch-card equipment. The panel is used on punch-card machines to carry out functions that are under control of the user. On computers it is used primarily to control input and output functions.

Control read-only memory (CROM). In one specific system, all actions of the CPU module are directed by a microprogram stored in a CROM. The microinstructions are very basic and control the actions of the CPU at a very detailed level. Moreover, they have a short execution time; this makes it practical to use a number of these microprogram-level instructions (macroinstructions) used by the programmer.

Control sequence. Refers to the normal order of selection of instructions for execution. In some computers, one of the addresses in each instruction specifies the control sequence. In most other computers, the sequence is consecutive except where a transfer occurs.

Conversational language. Refers to various languages that utilize a near-English character set that facilitates communication between the computer and the user. For example, BASIC is one of the more commonly used conversational languages.

Core memory. 1. A computer memory device containing magnetic cores. 2. A programmable random access memory consisting of many ferromagnetic toroids strung on wires in matrix arrays. Each toroid acts as an electromagnet to store a binary digit.

Counter. 1. A circuit designed to count input pulses. Also called an *accumulator,* a device capable of changing from one to the next of a sequence of distinguishable states upon receipt of each discrete input signal. 2. A device or location that can be set to an initial number and increased or decreased by an arbitrary number by stimuli applied one at a time.

CRT storage. 1. Often relates to the electrostatic storage characteristics of cathode-ray tubes in which the electron beam is used to sense the data. 2. The storage of data on a dielectric surface, such as the screen of a cathode-ray tube, in the form of the presence or absence of spots bearing electrostatic charges; these spots can persist for a short time after the removal of the electrostatic charging force. 3. A storage device used as in the foregoing description.

Cycle shift. Refers to the removal of digits of a number or characters from a word from one end of the number or word and their insertion, in the same sequence, at the other end.

Direct memory access (DMA). 1. Direct memory access, sometimes called *data break,* is the preferred form of data transfer for use with high-speed storage devices such as magnetic disk or tape units. The DMA mechanism transfers data directly between memory and peripheral devices. The CPU is involved only in setting up the transfer; the transfers take place with no processor intervention on a "cycle-stealing" basis. The DMA transfer rate is limited only by the bandwidth of the memory and the data transfer characteristics of the device. The device generates a DMA request when it is ready to transfer data. 2. High-speed data transfer operation in which an I/O channel transfers information directly to or from the memory. Also called *data break* or *cycle stealing.*

Direct memory access (DMA) control requirements. The corollary characteristics of the DMA controller required to optimize I/O control consists of the following: (1) multichannel capability, (2) priority resolution logic, (3) block transfer repeat capability. Implied characteristics for each channel include address registers, the automatic address pointer updating with each transfer, and the counting of the number of characters transferred as well as an indication of block transfer completion.

Dumping. Many techniques are designed to provide a periodic "write out" of a complete program and its data, that is, the contents of the working storage area, to a backup storage or memory unit. A dumping program usually incorporates restart procedures to enable the program thereby to be resumed at the last dump point in the event of interruption due, for example, to a machine failure or some other job interruption. A periodic dump, therefore, avoids having to start from the original beginning if some unforeseen event causes erasure.

Duplexed system. A system with two distinct and separate sets of facilities, each of which is capable of assuming the system function while the other assumes a standby status. Usually, both sets are identical in nature.

Executive control system. Primary control of the executive system is by control information fed to the system by one or more input devices that may be either on-line or at various remote sites. This control information is similar in nature to present control-card operations but allows additional flexibility and standardization.

Executive programs. In systems where the write-edit-assemble-execute sequence is in any way predictable, users can have the computer schedule, load, and execute each system software module. The program that provides this service is called the *executive*. The *executive* (also called the *supervisor* or *monitor*) is a program (or set of programs) that coordinates and controls the running of other programs on the computer.

Feedback control action. That designed control action in which a measured variable is compared to its desired value to produce an actuating error signal, which is acted upon in such a way to develop a reduction in the magnitude of the error.

Feedback control loop. A closed transmission path that includes an active transducer and consists of a forward path, a feedback path, and one or more mixing points arranged to maintain a prescribed relationship between the loop input and output signals.

Fetch instruction. Refers to a basic instruction or procedure to locate and return instructions that are entered in the instruction register. Generally, the next or some later step in the program will cause the microprocessor to execute that segment of the program related to the fetched instructions.

FIFO stack operation. The FIFO operates in the following manner: after the application of power, reset both address counters to the empty state. Reset need not be used again in normal memory operation. In some systems, data is presented on the A through D inputs.

Firmware. 1. A term usually related to microprogramming and those specific software instructions that have been more or less permanently burned into a ROM control block. 2. An extension to a computer's basic command (instruction) repertoire to create microprograms for a user-oriented instruction set. This extension to the basic instruction set is done in read-only memory and not in software. The read-only memory converts the extended instructions to the basic instructions of the computer.

Floppy disk systems. A typical floppy disk provides random access program/data storage. Hard-sector formated, some disks hold over 300,000 data bytes. Because many floppy controllers have all of their intelligence in microcode, some microcontrollers offer features not practical in designs implemented with hard-wired logic. The host-computer driver need only issue a small sequence of commands to write or read data from the disk.

Foreground. 1. In multiprogramming, refers to the environment in which high-priority programs are executed. 2. Under time-sharing option (TSO) the environment in which programs are swapped in and out of main storage to allow CPU time to be shared among terminal users. All command processor programs execute in the foreground. Contrast with background.

Handshaking. 1. A descriptive term often used interchangeably with buffering or interfacing, implying a direct connection or matching of specific units or programs. Some computer terminal programs are called "handshaking" if they greet and assist the new terminal operator to interface with or use the procedures or programs of the system. Other handshaking relates to direct package-to-package connections as regards circuits, programs, or procedures. 2. Exchange of predetermined signals when a connection is established between two data set devices.

Hangup. 1. A condition in which the central processor of a computer is attempting to perform an illegal or forbidden operation or in which it is continually repeating the same routine. 2. An unplanned computer stop or delay in problem solution, for example, caused by the inability to escape from a loop.

Hardware priority interrupts. 1. Some hardware priority interrupts provide automatic handling, or recognition of an external event that requires immediate attention; identification of which event, among many, actually occurred; resolution of priority when several events occur simultaneously; and automatic vectoring of each interrupt to unique memory locations.

HASP. 1. An extension to the System/360 Operating System that provides supplementary job management, data management, and task management functions such as control of job flow, ordering of tasks, and spooling. 2. Acronym for Houston Automatic Spooling Operation. An IBM computer configuration for its 360 and 370 computer series. Several companies have provided their own remote job-entry system to fit the IBM equipment.

HELP program. HELP is a program and a system of files that provide assistance to the engineer or programmer in the use of software and hardware. Also provides up-to-date information on improvements and new de-

116

velopments to a specific microcomputer family of components and software.

Hertz. 1. A unit of frequency equal to one cycle per second (now also used in the United States). 2. A hertzian wave is the wave used in radio communication; it is produced by an alternating current at the sending station and received by the aerial of the receiving set.

Hexadecimal. Refers to whole numbers in positional notation with 16 as the base. Hexadecimal uses 0 through 16, with the first ten represented by 0 through 9 and the last six digits represented by A, B, C, D, E, and F.

Housekeeping operation. A general term for the operation that must be performed for a machine run usually before actual processing begins. Examples of housekeeping operations are establishing controlling marks, setting up auxiliary storage units, reading in the first record for processing, initializing, setup verification operations, and file identification.

Index register. 1. A basic register, the index register contains the addresses of information subject to modification by the control block without affecting the instruction in memory. The IR information is available for loading onto the stack pointer when needed. 2. A register designed to modify the operand address in an instruction or base address by addition or subtraction, yielding a new effective address.

Initial program loading (IPL). An initiation process that brings a program or operating system into a computer with the data records that participate in the process—or with the console button that initiates it. A routine such as the above is established in memory, making it possible to load and execute any other desired program . . . a first record loading the second, and so on. Similar to *bootstrap*.

Input-output bus. Input-output bus provides scores of parallel lines for data, command, device address, status, and control information. This eliminates the timing problems, created when data and address lines are time-shared. It makes interfacing easier, faster, and less expensive. Memory and input-output interfaces connect directly to the main bus. Each operates at its own pace. Under direct memory access (DMA), this means that transfers can be made directly between external devices and memory without affecting the central processor, if desired.

Interface. 1. Refers to instruments, devices or a concept of a common boundary or matching of adjacent components, circuits, equipment, or system elements. An interface enables devices to yield and/or acquire information from one device or program to another. Although the terms *adapter, handshake, buffer* have similar meaning, *interface* is more distinctly a connection to complete an operation. 2. A common boundary—

for example, physical connection between two systems or two devices. 3. Specifications of the interconnection between two systems or units.

Job control language—JCL. 1. The JCL for modern operating systems may be quite complex, and there are probably nearly as many user-prepared jobs that fail to execute owing to JCL errors as failures due to compiler language errors. 2. A programming language specifically used to code job control statements.

Load and go. A computer operation and compiling technique in which pseudolanguage is converted directly to machine language, and the program is then run without the creation of an output machine language.

Loop. Basically a self-contained series of instructions in which the last instruction can modify and repeat itself until a terminal condition is reached. The productive instructions in the loop generally manipulate the operands, whereas bookkeeping instructions modify the productive instructions and keep count of the number of repetitions.

LSI circuitry. Integrated circuits allow users to construct complex electronic components with reduced cost and size. Today, integrated electronics technology has advanced to MSI and LSI (medium- and large-scale integration), which allows hundreds of logic gates to be built in one tiny chip, reducing the cost and the space occupied by the components but increasing the testing problem due to the limited number of pins accessible for probing.

Macroinstruction. 1. An instruction consisting of a sequence of microinstructions that are inserted into the object routine for performing a specific operation. 2. The more powerful instructions that combine several operations in one instruction.

Major cycle. 1. That part of a memory device that can provide serial access to storage positions, the time interval between successive appearances of a given storage position. 2. The maximum access time of a recirculating serial storage element, the time for one rotation, that is, of a magnetic drum or of pulses in an acoustic delay line. A whole number of minor cycles.

Memory-device access times. Typical access times have been reported as follows:

TTL RAM	60 ns
MOS RAM	300 ns
Core	500 ns
Bubbles (Fast Auxiliary Config.)	3 ms
Head/Track Disk/Drum	8 ms

Moving Head Disk	50 ms
Floppy Disk	100 ms
Bubbles (Endless Loop Config.)	1 s
Cassettes	10 s
Tapes	10 s

Memory fill. Refers to the placing of patterns of characters in the memory registers not in use in a particular problem to stop the computer if the program, through error, seeks instructions taken from forbidden registers.

Memory map list. In some systems a memory map is provided at compile time on an optional basis. The memory map is a listing of all variable names, array names, and constants used by the program, with their relative address assignments. The listing will include all subroutines called and last location when called.

Memory protect. Memory protect is available for use in many processors. It protects the integrity of operating systems against accidental modifications. Memory protect sets up a fence that divides memory space into two segments, separating the operating system from user programs. If any part of a user program seeks to modify system space, the system interrupts and takes control. This is a necessity for many real-time environments and other highly interactive systems.

Memory, scratch pad. Refers to the central, high-priority, small, immediate access memory area of the CPU, with a significantly faster access time than the larger main store. This is normally used by the hardware and/or operating system for storing microcodes, most frequently used operands, groups of object program instructions, or registers.

Memory sharing, cache. A typical unit is an intelligent disk storage system designed to relieve host CPUs of the processing load normally associated with data base access. An example: A field expandable disk controller, containing interacting microprocessors sharing cache memories, takes over the tasks involved in handling all data access work, including indexing, searching, buffering, deblocking, storage management, and error recovery functions.

Memory, virtual (pointer). Virtual memory systems are designed for storage efficiency. Some computers are structured so that parts of programs and data may be scattered through main memory and auxiliary storage. Various pointers or sets of pointers automatically keep track of the location of these program portions. The user of computers so designed may be unaware of this scattering procedure and most often operates computing procedures as though he were using normal memory.

119

Monitor system, time-sharing. A time-sharing monitor system is a collection of programs remaining permanently in memory to provide overall coordination and control of the total operating system. It performs several functions. First, it permits several users' programs to be loaded simultaneously into main memory. The monitor makes use of the time-sharing hardware to prevent one user's program from interfering with other users' programs. Each program is run for a certain length of time; then the monitor switches control to another program in a rotating sequence. Switching is frequent enough so that all programs appear to run simultaneously.

Multiprocessing. Refers to various computer configurations consisting of more than one independently initiable processor, each having access to a common, jointly addressable memory. 2. Processing several programs or program segments concurrently on a time-share basis. Each processor is active on only one program at any one time.

Multiprogramming executive. Refers to a microsystem building block that provides the operating environment of concurrent execution of more than one program. It contains such services as priority scheduler, memory allocation, and deallocation.

Multitasking. Refers to procedures in which several separate but interrelated tasks operate under a single program identity; differs from multiprogramming in that common routines and data space as well as disk files may be used. May or may not involve multiprocessing.

Modem, communications. A MODulator/DEModulator connects the communications multiplexer from the remote outlet to the interface device in the computer center. On the transmission end, the modulator converts the signals or pulses to the right codes and readies them for transmission over a communication line in alternating current. On the receiving end a demodulator reconverts the signals to direct current for communication to the computer via the computer interface device. The computer operates on direct current.

OEM—original equipment manufacturer. The OEM has a well-defined problem. He needs a computer powerful enough to answer his product's requirements, with enough performance margin to accommodate the growth he expects in the future. Initial cost is important to him, for any savings are translated directly into profit. And because maintenance costs come right out of that same profit, he demands unfailing reliability. Besides these requirements, the OEM has other needs—unique to him—which further separate him from the end user. He needs to get his product to the marketplace fast, to establish his position before the competition can react. This means he wants to shorten his development cycle. He needs working hardware and software so he can get going on his prototype.

Oersted. Unit of field strength in e.m.u. system such that 2 oersteds are field produced at the center of a circular conductor, 1 cm. in radius, carrying 1 abampere (10 amperes). In the MKSA system

$$1 \text{ oersted} = 1,000 \text{ ampere-turns/meter}.$$

Parity check. A computer checking method in which the total number of binary 1's (or 0's) is always even or always odd. Either an even-parity or odd-parity check can be made.

Protocol. A protocol is essentially a set of conventions between communicating processes on the format and content of messages to be exchanged. To make implementation and usage more convenient, in sophisticated networks higher level protocols may use lower level protocols in a layered fashion.

Queued telecommunications access method (QTAM). A method used to transfer data between main storage and remote terminals. Application programs use GET and PUT macroinstructions to request the transfer of data, which is performed by a message control program. The message control program synchronizes the transfer, thus eliminating delays for input/output operations. Abbreviated QTAM.

Queuing list. Refers to a list frequently used for scheduling actions in real time on a time-priority basis. Appends are made following the ending item. The beginning item is always the removed item.

Real-time executive. Real-time executives usually are multitasking executive systems that handle all aspects of priority scheduling, timing, interrupt servicing, input-output control, intertask communications, and all necessary queuing functions.

Real-time executive systems (RTE). RTE multiprogramming, foreground-background systems, with priority scheduling, interrupt handling, and program load and go capabilities are offered with some systems. Disk and main memory resident versions and a dynamically mapped disk resident version are offered by some suppliers.

Recursion. 1. The continued repeating of the same operation or group of operations. 2. Any procedure *A,* which, while being executed, either calls itself or calls a procedure, *B,* which, in turn, calls procedure *A.*

Remote batch, off-line. Refers to various off-line remote batches or procedures that can involve the preparation of punched cards or magnetic tapes from source documents, then the transmission of data to produce duplicate punched cards or magnetic tapes at the computer site. In an on-line system, data is fed directly into the host computer through some form of communications adapter.

Satellite computer. 1. One used to relieve a central processing device of relatively simple but time-consuming operations, such as compiling, editing, and controlling input and output devices. 2. A processor connected locally or remotely to a larger central processor and performing certain processing tasks—sometimes independent of the central processor, sometimes subordinate to the central processor.

Semiconductor. A material with an electrical conductivity between that of a metal and an insulator. Its electrical conductivity, which is generally very sensitive to the presence of impurities and some structural faults, will increase as the temperature does. This is in contrast with a metal, in which conductivity decreases as its temperature rises.

"Smart" terminal capabilities. Besides editing, smart terminals often offer selectable baud rates by allowing transmission from below 110 bauds up to 19.2 kbaud. Many terminals have buffer memory, so that blocks of data may be transmitted synchronously as well as asynchronously. Once memory is added, many terminals also offer a feature known as "scrolling." Scroll memory is available to store the information that appears on the screen. The scrolling control can move the entire display either up or down one line at a time, saving the line that disappears at the top or bottom in the scroll memory. Then, if you scroll in the opposite direction, the lines will reappear on the screen.

Visual terminal types. There are several alternative technologies to CRT terminals, including plasma panel displays, magneto-optic displays, and injection electroluminescence light-emitting diode (LED) displays. In displays having a very small number of characters, plasma panel and LED techniques are being used. From a longer-range standpoint, the LED technology is perhaps the most promising because of its compatibility with other semiconductor LSI technologies.

VTAM (vortex telecommunications method). A special data communications software package that organizes and simplifies data-communications programming to serve remote work stations for a host computer.

Word length. Longer word lengths increase efficiency and accuracy, but add complexity and cost. Most common is 16 bit, but 8, 12, 18, and 24 bits are widely used, and 32 bits is used occasionally. Word length limits the number of memory locations that can be directly accessed using single-word addresses. For greater precision and memory access, multiple-word operands and instructions are convenient features, although they increase execution times and architectural complexity. Word lengths and formats should be compatible with peripherals to avoid complex and expensive interfacing requirements.

4

Microcomputers: Where They Are, What They Are Doing, and What Is Next

Most introductory computer texts devote more than 80 percent of their pages to the analysis of standard computer systems with only small space allocated to minicomputers, and only minor attention is given to microcomputers and programmable calculators. This is unfortunate, and such books do not serve the readers well. Minis, micros, and programmable calculators already outnumber the standard computers by factors of more than ten to one. Many experts feel strongly that large and very large computer systems, as we knew them yesterday and years ago, might well become extinct. The very pragmatic-minded new generation of students has a very strong desire to examine and analyze the new microminiaturized rather than the old "standard" technology, which is quite rapidly being obsoleted. Beyond this fact, it is also clear that very few students will actually become closely involved with large or very large (maxi) systems. To most, the study of large systems actually becomes only an academic exercise of futility. There is little need to grind out the concepts of older theories, projects, procedures, and practices. Most are no longer acceptable to the majority of computer users. Today, the mass use and the direct control of modern, small systems is by hardheaded, efficiency-minded, dollar-pinching business managers instead of mathematics-oriented "numerical analysts."

Students are now confronting minicomputers and microcomputers and programmable calculators in their classrooms, libraries, and laboratories and as "intelligent terminals" in their dormitories. They are also using regular and programmable calculators in their homes, or they wear them on their wrists (see Figure 4.5), or they use them as coin-operated vending machines on many campuses. A substantial number of managers now regard them as essential tools in most of the activities of business, the trades, and the professions. The emphasis in this text is, therefore, shifted from the traditional topics of binary numbers, switching theory, key punches and card systems, old-fashioned coding, esoteric languages, operating systems, and other large or so-called standard systems and design. Discussion of obsolete equipment, techniques, or procedures wastes time and space. Many of these topics are mentioned and defined only as a basis of comparison for the new systems of microprocessors, including supporting ROMs, RAMs, PROMs, and extensive capabilities of other new microsystems and devices, principally terminal units and their appendages, which are becoming so popular.

We will discuss in some detail the results of mass production of many micro components and the resultant reduction in costs. Very low prices greatly increase the marketability and versatility of microcomputers. Equally as important in the popularization of microprocessors and multiple microcomputer systems was the computer user revolt against high-priced, very complicated, and difficult-to-use standard computer systems in the large, medium, and even small classifications. Businessmen, especially, want to control their computer systems personally and intelligently. Many want to develop and design their own accounting, management, and production control systems instead of having all of these operations dominated by the computer equipment designers—and by systems analysts and programmers, whom they can neither understand nor trust to integrate business procedures with computer capabilities successfully.

In earlier chapters the reader was introduced to a wide range of computer activities, which practically engulf the lives of ordinary citizens. The author has also briefly touched on some of the problem areas that are being brought out into the open and "up front." The attempt is to explain to the reader "where he is going." Why? Because readers must constantly be alerted to the problems and be cognizant of the difficulty of the solutions to keep them "down-to-earth." There are too many unexplained marvels in the sometimes dreamworld of computer capability and too few problem analyses. Among the problems that still remain are unsatisfactory control of computer services, inadequate software management and measurement standards, the unresolved difficulties for wide sharing of computer resources, the dissipation of costly manpower skills due to the lack of user-oriented education, and a poorly defined marketplace for the sale and trade of computer products. There are some guidelines: small, decentralized computer systems usually produce better results because large systems often force the varying needs of many users to conform to the rigid format of unwieldy "total" information systems. Budgets for computer systems should allow at least as much time and money as are used for hardware, people operations, and interface education and not belittle user "intelligence." A planned growth period through man-machine experimentation and for the "cooperative" resolution of the problems listed above is vitally needed.

MICROCOMPUTERS—WHY THEY HAVE
COME ON SO STRONG SO FAST

Although the essential point of this section is *not* to explain how these new microcomputers work internally, some technical details are necessary to demonstrate and illustrate why a sudden, massive change—a major revolution in computer design and capability—is now occurring. It is quite necessary that we know the fundamentals of microcomputer equipment and their functions to understand fully the totally new and surging microcomputer impact. Most experts now agree that the underlying basis for the "computer explosion" on citizens personally and on society generally is the microcomputer, its low cost, and application simplicity. Several units are pictured and described on the following pages. They are programmable digital computers (or calculators) that have capabilities similar and equal to the minis and standard systems discussed earlier. But many of these micro powerhouses can fit in the palm of your hand or be attached to or become a part of a thousand devices.

The ramifications of the expandable capability of these microcomputers (new entries into the market are turning into a "flood") are called "earthshaking" by people within the industry. The reasons: Many of these processors and computers cost less than $100; they are being mass-produced as "standards" in size, capability, and so on and in custom versions as well. Many have become "computers within computers"; others are available as "kits." Most are modular and functionally additive, and they are capable of being parts of very powerful "multimicros." The great majority of calculator consumers that have built up a 20-million to 40-million annual electronic calculator market will "trade up" to better models. A rising percentage of these are programmable units. A microprocessor or microcomputer is the basic operating component of these types.

The message very rapidly became clear. The computer industry is in the throes of its third major technological advance. This time, the new units permit the application of computer control by anyone, including grade school hobbyists, at costs at least several orders of magnitude lower and also by markets several magnitudes larger than in the early 1970s.

SOME BASIC DEFINITIONS

The confusion in definition between the terms *microprocessor* and *microcomputer* also spills over into the term *microprogramming*. The act of programming a microcomputer is not to be confused with microprogramming per se. *Microprogramming* is the activity related to writing microcoded (primitive or most basic) instructions for any type or size of microprogrammable computer, which can be, but need not necessarily be, a microcomputer. The *microprocessor*, as noted, is the central processing unit or arithmetic-logic unit (CPU/ALU) of a system. It usually consists of one or several electronic circuit packages in large-scale integration (LSI). The definition excludes consideration of storage and input-output capabilities because, in some cases, the CPU is designed to communicate with a bus, and storage and I/O facilities are completely foreign.

A *microcomputer* is the microminiaturized computer system containing the microprocessor, storage and input-output facilities, and driving and interface circuitry. It is principally a collection or assemblage of matched or attached chips, which are generally mounted on printed circuit cards for insertion into standardized racks or enclosures. The sale prices of microprocessors are at the $20, $30, and $50 levels and have reduced the cost of system electronics typically in many applications by 80 percent for the electronic logic. The use of microcomputers expands the application base of electronics by putting simple programming techniques at the disposal of engineers, enabling them to put "sophisticated" control electronics inside their already sophisticated instrumentation and control technology. Furthermore, good software support for microcomputer customers can reduce that software development time by a factor of ten, thereby having a dramatic effect on customer costs. Low-cost, hard-wired, field-programmable ROMs, RAMs, cassettes, and so on have quickly changed basic concepts for most computer users as to what programs are.

SOME BRIEF DEFINITIONS OF TERMS
USED IN CHAPTERS AHEAD

Bipolar. The most popular fundamental kind of IC, formed from layers of silicon with different electrical characteristics.

Chip. A small piece of silicon impregnated with impurities in a pattern to form transistors, diodes, and resistors. Electrical paths are formed on it by depositing thin layers of aluminum or gold.

CMOS. Complementary MOS refers to a combination of P-channel and N-channel transistors that results in a device as fast as NMOS devices but consuming less power.

DIP. Chips are enclosed in dual in-line packages, which take their names from the double, parallel rows of leads that connect them to the circuit board. DIPs are sometimes also called "bugs."

Hybrids. Circuits fabricated by interconnecting smaller circuits of different technologies mounted on a single substrate.

IC. Integrated circuit, a complex electronic circuit fabricated on a single piece of material, usually a silicon chip.

LSI. Large-scale integration refers to a component density of more than 100 per chip.

MOS. Metal oxide semiconductor, a term referring to the layers of material, and indirectly to a fundamental process for fabricating ICs. MOS circuits achieve some of the highest component densities.

MSI. Medium-scale integration is a measure of the number of circuit components, like transistors, formed on a single chip. Presently, chips with 50 to 100 components are considered to be MSI.

NMOS. N-channel MOS circuits use currents made up of negative charges and produce devices at least twice as fast as PMOS.

PLA. A programmable logic array is an alternative to ROM that uses a standard logic network programmed to perform a specific function. PLAs are implemented in either MOS or bipolar circuits.

PMOS. P-channel MOS refers to the oldest type of MOS circuits, where the electrical current is a flow of positive charges.

PROM. Programmable read-only memory is any type that is not recorded during its fabrication but that requires a physical operation to program it. Some PROMs can be erased and reprogrammed through special processes.

RAM. Random-access memory is any type with both "read" and "write" capability.

ROM. Read-only memory is any type that cannot be rewritten; ROM requires a masking operation during production to permanently record program or data patterns in it. (Erasure is possible by using ultraviolet rays, that is, electronically alterable ROMs—EAROMs.)

SOS. Silicon on sapphire refers to the layers of material and, indirectly, to the process of fabrication of devices that achieve bipolar speeds through MOS technology by insulating the circuit components from each other.

TTL (or T²L). Transistor-transistor logic, a kind of bipolar circuit logic, which takes its name from the way the basic transistor components that are interconnected.

MORE ON MICROCOMPUTERS

An article in the November 1973 issue of *Fortune* magazine stated, "With auxiliary electronics, a $300 microcomputer no larger than a file folder packs into its tiny space the capacity of a refrigerator-sized computer of 1960 vintage, which rented for $30,000 a year. Smaller versions of the microcomputer sell for as little as $20; the larger ones cost about $1,000." [1] The thrust of this mass media article was considered to be startling and unbelievable. The "show me" proof is now happening.

To further alert, indeed, to stimulate the business and financial communities to this major but little publicized upheaval, a second major article appeared in *Fortune* in November 1975, entitled "Here Comes the Second Computer Revolution." [2] Announcing that the initial "ho-hum" reaction to the introduction of the microcomputer in 1972 has very suddenly changed to a microcomputer "craze," the article emphasized that the micro will affect us all very quickly in most aspects of our "work and play." What is most significant to its readers, however, is the impact of microsystems on corporate productivity and profits—and the shape of the computer industry. Using as examples the application of microcomputers to scales, microwave ovens, gas pumps, traffic devices, scientific instruments, and so on, *Fortune* editors sought to stress that the microcomputer is one of "those rare innovations" that simultaneously cuts manufacturing costs and adds to the value and capabilities of the product and is a very important and quite specific antidote for inflation and lagging productivity. The comments relating to the changing "shape" of the computer industry itself were significant, tending to confirm our statements about the demise of the computer behemoths and the revolutionary turn demonstrating user demand and power to change computers from being exclusive prestige products of the military, giant industries, and academia to being new power for small business, factories, and "average" people.

For 25 years (step one), standard computers dominated. The minis of (step two) the early seventies were successful and stimulated users to demand still smaller, cheaper, easier-to-use computers. Now, at step three, the highly advanced technology of microminiaturization has produced "sandwiches" of microsystem "chip" power of thousands of components by integrating them into ultrathin layers. Very soon, full capability processors were developed on single "chips." When memory chips were added to printed circuit (PC) boards with these single processor chips, I/O ports made them full microcomputer systems. The strongly automated production procedures of this popular large-scale integrated (LSI) technology re-

---

[1] Gene Bylinsky, "How Intel Won Its Bet on Memory Chips," *Fortune*, November 1973, pp. 142–147.

[2] "Here Comes the Second Computer Revolution," *Fortune*, November 1975, pp. 134–138.

sulted in severe component manufacturer competition, crashing costs, and a whole new world of computer and application innovation. Thus, at step three, we find that the development of still cheaper, smaller, and more efficient (micro) computers is now at an expanding rate of manufacturing and sales that is astonishing. The "micro" is much more than another sudden stepdown to tiny, more versatile computers. It is a generation of unique computer structures with greater user capability and more quick expandability magic than any other.

The entire microcomputer "system" is physically not much more than a handful of packaged integrated semiconductor circuits, altogether priced at just a few hundred dollars, which includes abundant memory for most applications. But product designers are using this power and great range of capabilities in thousands of truly inventive ways. The first of these micropower products began to hit the mass market in late 1973 as "programmable" calculators, automotive control systems, supermarket check-out and bank terminals, and scores of other totally new products. Potential applications are practically unlimited. It became quickly and clearly evident that microcomputers could be used in thousands of applications not previously even remotely considered for "regular" computer use. One manufacturer of these tiny "systems" (Intel Corp., Santa Clara, California) had more than 12,000 inquiries in 1973, its first year of production. Many other firms—some of the largest in the electronics field—are being overwhelmed by a flood of "computer-on-a-chip" business—deliveries backed six months or more in 1974.

The basic concepts: what is a microcomputer?

A microcomputer consists of five basic and fundamental electronic elements: (1) a central processing unit (CPU)—a "processor," (2) single or multiple read-only memories (ROM) for preassembled control program storage, (3) one or more random access memories (RAM) for data and/or program storage, (4) an expandable universal input-output (I/O) bus (that is, a connection, path, or circuit for peripheral equipment), and (5) a computer clock. This is a generalized definition of a standard microcomputer. Many single-circuit micros are quite similar to dedicated or specific-purpose minis. Using different design techniques, various firms develop units that behave much like multipurpose minis. They use storage and peripheral devices with addressing capabilities via wide, parallel buses; BASIC and other compilers; displays and keyboard input; and so forth.

Most micros are using MOS-LSI (metal oxide semiconductor-large scale integration) technology or SOS (silicon on sapphire-LSI) wafers. There are several production processes. One can be briefly described as follows: Each "chip" is a thin piece of silicon with schematics designed in a pattern that interconnects diodes, transistors, resistors, and other electronic components. Electrical paths among the components are also formed in the silicon or deposited over that material in thin layers of aluminum or gold. When these are completed, tiny wires are attached to the chip. It is then put into a ceramic or plastic case equipped with contacts, and it is ready for testing and use in an assembly. The circuits used in microminiature computers and processors are quite complicated. Each chip must be tested in simulation, often on a medium- or large-scale computer. Actual circuits are about the size of this *o*.

Most microprocessors are purchased to be used by OEMs (original equipment manufacturers) as system or dedicated computers. The majority of sales are thus for devices that are incorporated into other products. The end customer may or may not be aware of the computer's existence. Network system computers can be minis or standard computers or "stacked micros." However, the microcomputer has in three and one-half years made a wide breach and heavy impact in the marketplace, where earlier "standard" computer systems for production control, testing, measurement, and distributed information processing made only small dents . . . over more than twenty years of use.

The first microcomputers covered most of the spectrum of word-length sizes. The most popular were 4- and 8-bit units, although some operate on 16-bit or larger words. Others are 12-bit types, to take advantage of many machine minicomputer programs already written, debugged, tested, and widely used in many markets. Practically all of the microprocessors can take advantage of almost any kind of storage technology—ROM, RAM, disk, core, shift register, cassette, printed circuit card, and so on. Interface logic is usually cheap and easy, consisting of a few to ten or more IC packages. Although only a few of the major IC manufacturers originally brought out development micros, in mid-1974 most of the largest component giants had brought them out or were thought to have them ready to come out. Even those few that had production up at that stage were shipping all they could build. Some were shipping more than 10,000 per month in mid-1974, and several of the largest component suppliers were doubling their MOS capacity and microsystem marketing staffs. Some of the early suppliers were Intel Corp., National Semiconductor, Western Digital, Inc., Teledyne Corp., General Automation, American Microsystems, Inc., Fairchild, RCA, Motorola, Intersil, Rockwell International, Burroughs Corp., Signetics, Inc., and so on, as well as Toishiba, Nippon Electric, and others in Japan. Others that came into the market in 1975 were Texas Instruments, Solid State Scientific, Harris, Siliconix, Mostek, TRW, Pro-Log, Com-Star, Control Logic, Plessey, Inc. and so on—an unending list.

Many microprocessors are designed with specific types of application considerations. The Fairchild PPS-25, Intel MCS-4, and the Rockwell PPS-4 all had sophisticated calculator features, especially in their organization of RAM. Many others have minicomputerlike structures. Although microcomputers in strict technical behavior are symbol manipulators whereas calculators are often restricted to specific sets of "number" symbols, the classifications are now very blurred, and many calculator manufacturers with products on the market being announced and promoted as calculators do indeed have the versatility, power, and capabilities of computers. Rockwell and Intel devices and many others use 8- and 16-bit instructions. Fairchild and Intersil use 12-bit instructions. An early Rockwell unit had as many as 16,384 bytes of instructions, and all ranges of competing capacities, capabilities, and interfaces now swirl in the markets. In the following chapter a wide-ranging discussion is developed relating to comparison and contrasts of the early popular brands and models of competing microsystem products. The highly explosive field opened quickly and widely, with many electronics giants expending hundreds of millions of dollars to establish strong market shares in a new industry that showed early a practically unlimited growth potential—and "International Bull Moose" (IBM) was not bothering them. Things look very healthy.

Single chip "intelligence" for thousands of new devices

Single-chip microprocessors have opened up whole new worlds of computing and controlling applications. They have, in effect, freed system and device designers from the constraints of the former hard-wired device control and computer logic. Microprocessors are achieving new highs in performance, radically reduced cost, and expanding versatility of computer control—in operations, procedures, and other innovations formerly far beyond the reach of users. The rush with which microprocessors and microcomputers have been appearing and accepted created quite severe shortages of MOS circuits in early 1974. The semiconductor industry became quite frantic to expand and to control various percentages of what it viewed as an almost inexhaustible domestic and foreign market. Although the history of development of the types and specialities of the first micros is interesting, the complexity of their history is somewhat beyond the purposes of fulfillment designed for this book. We shall, therefore, concern ourselves only with current products and developments.

Because the move to micros was so sudden and because so many major companies jumped so quickly into production, definitions that could be firmly developed and agreed upon have not yet been established. Therefore, in this text we shall use several of them as developed by the industry itself and by the expert observers in the various applications areas. The microprocessor is generally the central component or the CPU of the microcomputer. It requires the addition of memory devices for its control program, plus input/output circuits to operate peripheral equipment. The microcomputer is most often defined as consisting of the micro CPU,

RAMs, ROMs, clock generator, direct-memory-access controller, and an assortment of general-purpose input/output parts or devices. Some microprocessors are controlled by microprograms; some are not. Quite specifically, the microprocessor is the control and processing portion of a tiny microcomputer, usually built with LSI-MOS circuitry and on one chip. Some microprocessors handle both arithmetic and logic data in a bit-parallel fashion under the control of a program. They are distinguishable from minis and standards because of their tiny size, low power requirements, very low cost, and their unique programmability characteristics. Single-chip bipolar and CMOS-on-sapphire processors—and other versions—compete with NMOS types and most of these closely approach the capabilities of minis—and even exceed many older standard "small" computer capabilities—at about one-twentieth of the cost.

Because these tiny but powerful microcomputers have now appeared all over the calculator and computer markets, great interest in them has been quickly developed by practically all computer users, purchasers, students, hobbyists, and so on. It is really not too difficult to understand them—or, in fact, to build these microcomputers. A Montana State University senior in electrical engineering built one. His story goes like this. "I set out to build a small computer for use in fixed applications, but one that could be reprogrammed without having to go through the process of programming a ROM (a read-only memory)," the student designer stated. The basic building block in his particular microcomputer set was a complete CPU on an LSI gold chip. He cleverly put the system together so that the software could be changed at any time by using a random access memory (RAM) type of read unit. It could interface the CPU chip so that any type of auxiliary memory could be incorporated with the unit. The system can also be interfaced with tape readers or practically any other kind of exterior peripheral quite simply, according to the student.

These micros are now so cheap, versatile, and easy to use that they are widely available in terminals, calculators, and as controllers of thousands of devices, processes, and applications. Our society can no more accurately gauge the vast potential and great impact of this new "microcomputer era" than one could have imagined the significance of the steam engine or the electric motor in the past. Many compare this period of history to that of the beginning Automobile Era. Although still in its infancy, the new microcomputer "technology imporatus" has already profoundly altered the ways in which we work, think, live, entertain, educate, play, and communicate with one another. Now, today, the microcomputer alone, tiny as it is, ranks as a distinct giant in its own right and among those revolutionary inventions that have abruptly altered the course of human history.

The emergence of microprocessing permitted final instrumentation companies (original equipment manufacturers—OEMs) to take a "computer on a chip," design it into a specialized system, and sell it to a particular market without asking the end user to program or learn Boolean algebra. Microcomputers quickly began to invade the still unsaturated business, industrial, and professional markets where specialized computer power is required on a local basis. This capability typically can involve and solve the preparation of multiple, complex input for further centralized processing by large existing systems much as was the case with minicomputers. The difference, however, is that the micros now provide local service to a much larger population. "Smart" instrumentation in control devices or terminals also presents a special growth area for the microcomputer. Every safety director, business executive, medical doctor, and so on, on the continent, bound in his practice or operations by clearly defined safety provisions, regulated reporting, and difficult accounting procedures, becomes a prime potential customer.

In many quarters, computer professionals suggest that the advent of the microcomputer has turned the daydreams of science fiction writers into many practical realities. To demonstrate its power, chapters 8 and 9 are devoted to explanations of wide ranges of applications. Many technical achievements that are being announced would otherwise be unfeasible without these tiny powerhouses. Reading what others have done with them inspires countless new ideas for increasing varieties of new uses of microsystems. For today's engineer—whether a designer of computers, a user of them, or both—practically everything is now new in computer power. Design concepts and applications have changed—very radically in some cases. Not only hardware—software, too, is affected. Microcomputer chips quickly began to fill the gap between simple calculator chips and minicomputers. These MOS/LSI programmable chips can be designed to perform not only arithmetic functions, but practically all data-processing functions as well. They have also begun to replace dedicated (special-purpose) minicomputers rapidly in thousands of applications and have opened new markets never anticipated before these developments.

Perhaps the most dramatic change brought about by microcomputers is in the new computer architecture, stemming from the influence of low-cost semiconductor logic and memories and the insertion of microprocessors within other computers. The semiconductor industry rushed to develop ever-larger, more powerful systems still on a single chip. The microcomputers used as fully capable machines themselves now provide a totally new architecture for all computers. Most people will seldom be able to recognize computers—except perhaps as terminals—and will be cognizant only of their effects. In effect, the microcomputer will relegate the computing system to the level of a minor subsystem component of communications or information networks. Thus, when users integrate microcomputers into control systems, they become "slaves" of larger systems—almost like transistors or integrated circuit components—in terms of both cost and usage. And this "preprocessing function" further provides revolutionary changes in the whole range of greatly expanded computer network markets. The microcomputer has already moved strongly into the minicomputer areas (see further on), and now it is quickly moving into the small and medium computer field, replacing a large number of these simply because many of their applications can be more cheaply performed by microsystems.

The microprocessor is the heart of a microcomputer

The primary control section of the microcomputer system, as noted earlier, is the microprocessor, which is designed as CPU. Whereas the other basic sections (ROM, clock, RAM, I/O) are well defined and fairly standardized, the CPU is characterized by wide variations among available units. It contains the following functions: microinstruction decode and control, registers, arithmetic unit, and control. These functions are grouped in different ways on LSI chips by different manufacturers and are referred to by different names. The partitioning and the complexity of these chips are what give the microprocessor its salient architectural characteristics and capabilities, such as instruction set, word length, speed, memory capacity, and so on. Some microprocessors are on a single chip whereas others are distributed on more than one chip. Single-chip units are generally less expensive but also less flexible. Multiple-chip designs make use of more silicon area and, therefore, can generally offer more functions. In fact, from the overall system cost standpoint, a careful analysis may show that the somewhat higher cost of the multichip system may be offset by the savings in additional peripheral circuitry, which may be needed with single CPU units.

FIGURE 4.1. Typical microcomputer block diagram

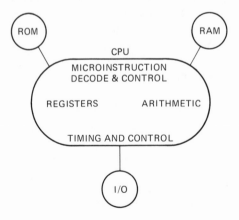

There are at least four major classifications of systems that can be designed using microprocessors: calculators, controllers, data processors, and general-purpose computers. Controllers and calculators are the most likely candidates for single-chip CPUs. Data processors and general-purpose machines require more flexibility and are, therefore, better served by a multichip system.

Most microcomputers employ ROM chips to hold the final version of the control program and RAM chips as data or scratch pad memory. Mask-programmed ROMs are used in high-volume applications once the programs are debugged and frozen. PROMs (electrically programmable ROMs) are used in lower volume situations or where there are several versions of the programs. Erasable, reusable PROMs are often used in the final stages of testing and for many final system program memories. However, it is most convenient if the program can be stored in RAM during initial testing, when many changes are likely to be made. Easy interchangeability of RAM and PROM is an important consideration, for this feature can make testing much easier.

MICROCOMPUTERS AND MICROPROCESSORS DEVELOP INTO SYSTEMS

We have already pointed out that new advances in these technologies have made it possible to put an entire CPU on a single piece of silicon about three millimeters on a side and to sell the unit for under a hundred dollars. The effects within the industry have been traumatic, a word that we may also use to describe the drastic impact these devices will have on society. The "single chip" processors, when incorporated with the other devices mentioned earlier, form a complete, full-capability microcomputer. Most micros lie deep within other products and are sometimes practically invisible to users. Options include special memories and broad ranges of very low-cost peripheral devices. Micros use one or many control circuits and are supported by many switches, connectors, clocks, alarms, indicators, and so on. A one-board microcomputer, the LSI-12/16, produced by General Automation, Inc., of Anaheim, California, is displayed, with its supporting components labeled. It is also shown in its enclosure and with its power supplies, controllers, and channels in Figure 4.3. Other micros, ROMs, RAMs, programmable ROMs (PROMs), and PROM programmers are discussed on the following pages. One microcomputer uses over 14,000 MOS transistors on a single chip. Some units use more; others, less.

A single four-bit microprocessor for dedicated controllers can replace a rackful of minicomputer TTL chips. It saves design time and production costs. And there are only simple redesign jobs for options and changes. That is because the logic is stored in reprogrammable ROMs. Many micros

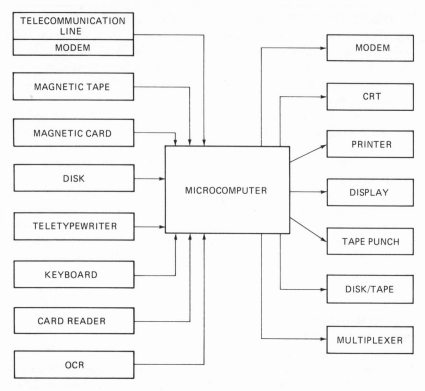

FIGURE 4.2. Many types of peripheral devices can be connected to microcomputers. Interfaces depend upon word lengths, buses, and so on.

are available in one, two, and three card systems. Additional interface cards for special requirements are often off-the-shelf delivery. They are cost-effective microcomputers and make economic sense.

An example of microcomputer system capabilities

Because many students, teachers, managers, and professionals are most anxious to become very well versed in microcomputer technology and capabilities, this chapter includes some of the detail that is ordinarily omitted in an introductory text. It is somewhat technical and relates directly to some of the essential internal structures and operations of micro systems. Even the basic electronic complexities cannot be completely presented here, and most readers will find manuals on manufacturers' device operations will be required to grasp the full scope of the detail required for thoroughness.

The following pages offer some company-provided specifications of General Automation's LSI-12/16, such as the input-output operations; memory types, including ROM, RAM, and PROM; and software systems offered at the time the microcomputer first became available commercially. Other enhancements, programs, and special capabilities have been added to this and other models since the introduction. Products of several competing companies with accompanying operating and design notes are pictured and analyzed in brief scope in the next chapter to illustrate some of the breadth and scope of capabilities of the now very large microcomputer industry. The many applications capabilities are explained and pictured on pages later in the text. Parts of these chapters also offer very brief discussions of the current and potential societal impact of these quite marvelous instruments of expanding power and versatility. But the wider range of pragmatic consumer utility examples are detailed in chapters 8 and 9.

Most microcomputer families feature extremely high-speed and flexible input/output systems. Data move between the computer and peripheral devices under program control. A program may poll devices to determine if they are ready to be serviced, or the devices may be allowed to request and interrupt when they require service. The I/O bus for many systems provides a standard, easily understood, slot-independent mechanism for interfacing peripheral hardware at a greatly reduced cost vis-à-vis standard computers and minicomputers.

FIGURE 4.3. I/O system

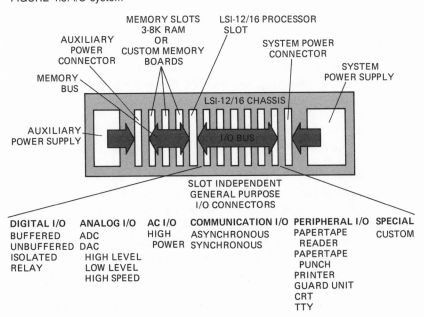

This compatibility with the members of practically all microprocessor logic families provides a large line of I/O devices:

Process—Digital I/O, Analog/Digital Input, Digital/Analog Output, Relay I/O.

Communications—Asynchronous I/O current loop or RS232, Synchronous RS232, Asynchronous multiplexors for current loop or RS232.

Peripherals—CRT, cassettes, cartridges, floppy disks, printers.

The two classes of operations that take place on the standard I/O bus—programmed I/O, and program interrupts—are discussed in the pages that follow.

Programmed I/O operations. The programmed I/O allows data to be input or output from the B register. A programmed I/O operation occurs in response to the execution of an I/O instruction by the central processor. The I/O instruction specifies the peripheral to which it refers generally by means of a 16-bit device select address. Each device interfaced has a unique select address and a selection network to recognize that select address when it appears on the I/O bus. When an I/O instruction is executed, only the device whose select address is specified will respond to the instructions. The I/O instruction provides several classes of operations: data input, data output, control, test, and so on. An I/O instruction addresses any one of up to 64 or more peripheral devices. Often, one device is internal to the processor for detecting interrupting addresses. The remaining select addresses may be assigned to peripheral controllers as needed.

Interrupts. An important requirement for computers in real-time applications is that the processor must always be in control. Thus, whenever a device external to the processor requires the services of the processor, it is accomplished at the processor's convenience rather than the device's. Normally, this means that interrupts must be disabled when the processor is performing tasks where interruptions are not allowed, thus enabling interrupts from external devices when the processor's task is completed and at the processor's convenience.

The maximum period of time that the interrupt is disabled is called "worst case interrupt response time"; it is the longest period of time that a device will have to wait in order to have an interrupt processed by the computer. When the interrupt does occur, the processor must save all registers and status bits as part of the interrupt routing, so that when the interrupt servicing is complete, the processor returns to continue the interrupted routing. Many systems solve this problem by opening a "window" when interrupts are enabled; at all other times, interrupts will be disabled. These windows are placed throughout the program in accordance with the system's response requirements. Enabling of interrupts can also be accomplished in such a manner that the requirement of saving registers is eliminated. This type of approach in the many interrupt systems improves processing efficiencies, saves memory, and provides greater system flexibility while allowing the processor to maintain control of its process or device at all times.

The external equipment interrupts are serviced over the interrupt request lines of the parallel I/O system. The interrupt request line can service numerous external devices where the service priorities are established under program control and using the hardware serial priority chain. When an interrupt is acknowledged, the address of the highest priority interrupting device is transferred, in some systems, to the B register by performing a "read device zero," and thus the time-consuming search for the interrupting device is eliminated.

Read-only memory (ROM and PROM)

ROM. For large volume applications programs that are well debugged, the use of ROM memory is the most practical and economical way to package internal control. Well-designed ROMs also provide greater protection for proprietary software products. Most standard configurations provide the use of ROM memory in sizes from 1K to 32K, in increments of 1K or 4K. Special ROMs (or ROM board sections) of much larger size can be designed, using the standard or custom memory board sizes. These special ROMs will operate in the memory expansion slots provided in "cages" or other system enclosures.

PROM. PROM memories can be used economically in lower volume applications for program protection and for proprietary software. PROMs are more expensive per bit than ROMs but cost less to program because for some types there is no semiconductor mask to design. PROM configuration can vary from 1K to 16K in 1K increments in the standard or custom systems.

Pure procedure programming. For ROM to be of true value to the user, it must not impact programming efficiency as well as provide fail-safe programs. To achieve this, the computer must provide a variety of features to allow the efficient use of ROM from a programming point of view. Pure procedure I/O instructions, multiple general-purpose registers, base relative addressing, and an instruction set that can be executed from both ROM and RAM memory are import elements. "Pure procedure" defines a procedure in which no instruction can modify the coding or the contents of memory within any program that operates from ROM. Many systems have been carefully organized to incorporate most or all of these features, permitting full and effective use of ROM. Special design points that optimize the use of ROM with the typical systems include:

1. Various I/O instruction formats that provide for pure procedure programming by allowing the device addresses and control functions to be

loaded in a data table stored in RAM while the I/O instruction itself is in the executing instruction stream (ROM program).

2. Base relative addressing that allows ROM programs to address all of selected memory. Programs stored in ROM may operate on separate data tables stored in ROM or RAM that are addressed through the index registers. This internal feature is especially valuable in controlling a number of process steps with a single machine.

3. General-purpose registers that provide rapid access storage for programs executed in ROM. Thus the amount of time-consuming memory access needed during program execution is greatly reduced. This permits systems to be capable of performing arithmetic and logic operations between registers in a single command without reference to memory.

4. Entire instruction sets that operate in both ROM and RAM memory, thus reducing program developing and debugging time. Requirements for specialized programs are minimized for each hardware configuration. This facilitates transfer of programs from RAM to ROM. Any location in memory can be addressed.

5. Completely interchangeable memory modules that provide expansion and relocation flexibility, allowing memory configurations to fit specific applications.

6. Power-fail/auto-restart interrupt vectors that allow ROM to be used to always provide a loader program, enabling the computer to automatically reload the main program after a power failure.

The ROM patch. Quickly becoming a standard feature is the ROM patch that allows field corrections or changes to programs already committed to ROM. This is accomplished by installation of several pluggable PROMs. This type of innovation for many systems allows programs to be committed to ROM and ordered in quantity with minimal concern for future changes or corrections. The ROM patch logic is often found on piggyback boards, which consists of RAMs and PROMs. One almost standard PROM contains up to 32 address values representing up to 32 addresses within the ROM where a patch is required. Thus, when an address equal to one of the areas in ROM to be patched is given to the address register, one PROM outputs address data and control information to another PROM, allowing the next instruction to be taken from that PROM. By this means, minor program changes, constants, and program parameters can be implemented in spite of the use of ROM main memory.

RAM. A typical 4096-bit dynamic N-channel MOS RAM comes in a standard 16-pin ceramic package. The ordinary RAM features 350-ns access time and single-transistor cell design and typically offers read and write cycles of 500 ns. All inputs and outputs, including clocks, are generally directly TTL-compatible, and voltage pins are located on package corners to simplify board layout.

MICROCOMPUTERS COMPARED TO MINICOMPUTERS—THE VALUES

The first questions that come to mind are, Are microcomputers as fast as minis? Can memories be expanded to meet more applications specifications? Although some MOS micros are distinctly slower than most minis, the LSI-12/16 unit, on its 7¾-by-10-inch PC board, had a basic 12-bit instruction execution cycle time of 2.64 microseconds, and this compared favorably with most minicomputers. It came with random access semiconductor read-only or programmable read-only memory (PROM) in capacities of 1K to 32K. It also had features that included direct addressing of up to 4K memory locations, literal and indirect addressing, 8- and 12-bit arithmetic, single and double word instructions, and 16-bit parallel I/O. Again, these features compare very favorably with most minis and are even better than many older standard computer systems costing ten to fifteen times as much.

Is MOS technology reliable? What about "fail-safe" features?

MOS technology has now been used in thousands of applications and has become the basic component for use by many of the largest computer manufacturers. MOS technology has been used by the aerospace industry and by the military for many years and with complete satisfaction and success. The switching speeds, tight circuit density, and very low power consumption place it a few steps ahead of TTL. The use of semiconductor memory makes these units compatible with most equipment now on the market, increases the reliability over core memory by a factor of four, it is claimed, and provides for a significant reduction in cost. Semiconductor memory has a destruct or volatility problem, but this is overcome with most micro designs. Auxiliary battery pack backup systems immediately activate upon loss of main power and retain the contents of memory for up to 15 hours, depending upon the battery and memory size. In addition to the battery backup, the LSI 12/16 and a number of others protect their systems from costly consequences of power transients, power interruptions, component failure, or programming bugs. Some of the "fail-safe" procedures include operations monitor alarms, system safe lines, system reset lines, power fail detection, and automatic restart, and so on. Many of these are combined to provide the capability of reloading memory from any peripheral device or communication line without manual intervention.

141

Do microcomputers have full minicomputer organization, performance, and building blocks?

The LSI-12/16, like many others, can be expanded from 1,024 to 32,768 words of 8-bit memory, with 12-bit parallel addressing and allows direct addressing of 4,096 words without paging. It also provides eight 12-bit hardware registers, including an accumulator and three index/accumulator registers; 52 basic commands; a processor-controlled priority interrupt system; and a teletype printer interface. Standard control function facilities include a relative time clock, external priority interrupt, 16-bit parallel I/O bus, integral console, and a ROM-based console function program. It can execute stored programs in excess of 190,000 instructions per second and execute real-time programs efficiently. The system can also be interfaced to many standard, off-the-shelf peripheral units that provide modularity and versatility. Most have functional plug-in designs. Other nonstandard interfaces can be accommodated with custom-designed boards for maximum economy. All of these features suggest that even this low-cost micro can stand its own ground with all but the more expensive minis, and the 16-bit model can just about match any of them.

Do microcomputers use memory efficiently and make full use of ROMs? What about ROM errors?

Many microcomputer systems take advantage of piggyback ROMs to permit 32K of ROM to be connected directly on processor boards and also use pure procedure coding. Both augmented instructions and I/O instructions thus allow convenient list-processing commands and I/O commands in single byte instruction formats with addresses taken from associated lists. The LSI-12/16 has a unique built-in ROM patch capability that, in effect, allows specifically identified ROM addresses to be detected and rerouted to a PROM patch memory. This permits the heretofore impossible program correction by patching of a program in ROM. Because typically over 60 percent of the cost of a microcomputer is in memory, architectural design must use memory efficiently. A "shared byte" technique allows a two-byte instruction to be effectively stored in a single byte of memory. This can represent a typical 25 percent to 30 percent program memory saving. Also, auxiliary memory devices are no problem for most micros, especially when ROMs can be easily added.

Do microcomputers have sufficient programming aids, software adaptability, high-level language compilers?

Because micros are relatively new on the computer scene, they do lack many important standardized programming aids. It is true that many of them have considerable emulation capability, and some, like the LSI-12/16, provide complete cross program generation systems. Operating under a disk-based operating system, this cross program generation facility provides a complete assembly, editing, debugging, and memory load building capability. Also this model and others like it offer device-independent real-time executives, various series of I/O drivers to assist further in implementing real-time applications. A conversational assembly system is also provided for assembling programs on an LSI-12/16 with 4K or more of memory. It is also interesting to note here that programmable calculators are built around microprocessors, ROM and RAM units, and most of these have practically endless versatility in standard programs on cards, chips, strips, tapes, and so on. Also many of these contain ROM chips with BASIC compilers, and, quite likely, others will have FORTRAN capability. Although micros have a good deal of catching up to do, there is little doubt that they will soon compare favorably with minis in this area also.

What about the reliability of the quality or product, maintenance, and vendor services?

Some of the largest companies in the world are producers of micros: Rockwell International, National Semiconductor, Fairchild, Texas Instruments, Motorola, Intel Corp., RCA, and others. Rockwell International, for example, has sold more than 1 million minicomputer systems for many thousands of solutions to a wide variety of applications in many of the top companies throughout the world. All these firms guarantee high performance and long-life reliability. Design, manufacturing, and testing procedures are very carefully monitored, with constant "worst case" criteria. Practically all micros are built by using mass production techniques with wirefree integrated circuits. All components and subsystems are subject to 100 percent testing and inspection, and complete systems are successfully operated in environmental test chambers and receive prolonged burn-in prior to shipment. All designs have also been working, even unattended, around the clock in critical real-time industrial applications. As regards maintainability, most are constructed for on-site repair and replacement. Generally, each element-processor, memory, and so on is independently tested and is not dependent upon any other element. Practically all micro firms maintain strong national or worldwide networks of sales and service centers.

Microcomputer configurations

Initially, the rather standard forms of microprocessors were (1) MOS/LSI chip sets; (2) a single PC card with processor and memory; (3) a card cage system containing a CPU card, memory cards, direct memory access, channel cards, I/O bus, bit interface cards, a clock, switches, alarms, and connectors for attaching a portable control panel; and (4) all items in (3) plus power supplies, indicator, I/O cables, and the system enclosure (metal box).

Chip sets are suitable for large quantity requirements for OEM buyers. They must meet loading restrictions and supply the required clock wave forms for building their own products and, as these constraints are indicated in the specifications, for the MOS chip. A PC card approach, on the other hand, provides a low-cost CPU that can be incorporated into existing hardware, eliminating most of the problems of interfacing. It is an excellent method to get a new product under way quickly and can give way to lower cost, specially designed or expanded chip sets at a later time, if quantities are sufficiently high.

A card cage system is suitable primarily for breadboarding and prototyping. It comes complete with power busing and a breadboarding card, on which the user may construct his own interface logic. The fully contained stand-alone and enclosed micro can be its own individual powerhouse or rack-mounted in tandem as a part of stacked—or multimicro—systems.

INTEL STANDARD SYSTEMS AND OPTIONAL MODULES [3]

The Intellec 8 standard system includes the following modules:

Central processor module

Input/output module

PROM memory module

Two RAM memory modules

PROM programmer module

Chassis with mother board

Power supplies

Control and display panel

Finished cabinet

Standard software—system monitor, resident assembler, text editor

[3] We use the description of Intel Corp. (Santa Clara, Calif.) products here for some important reasons. M. E. Hoff, Jr., of Intel, is generally considered to be the "inventor" of the microcomputer in 1969, although the order to produce it was from a Japanese customer. Intel is the acknowledged leader on record because it has the most products that are considered "standard" and are "second sourced," that is, copied and produced (with and without permission) by other suppliers. For example, the Intel 8080 microcomputer is being produced and sold by at least six other manufacturers, including the giant Texas Instruments, Inc. Its software is almost universally copied, including PL/M. It is truly a standard and pace setter, as well as a top sales leader.

The "Bare Bones" Intellec standard system includes the following modules:

Central processor module

Input/output module

PROM memory module

RAM memory module

Chassis (rack mountable with mother board)

Standard software—system monitor, resident assembler, text editor

Optional modules available for the Intellec 8 and Bare Bones are

Additional I/O or output modules

Additional RAM memory modules

Universal prototype module

Module extender

Drawer slides and extenders for rack mounting

Typical Intel software

Standard. All peripheral interface to Intellec 8 standard software is via TTY, model ASR33. The standard software includes a system monitor, resident assembler, and text editor.

A. System Monitor
1. Contained in five 1702A PROMs located on the PROM memory module.
2. Program assigned to support 1280 bytes of memory.
3. Lower 15K of memory may then be used for either program or data storage.
4. Intellec 8 modular computer systems have a control program called a "resident monitor" in PROM so that no "bootstrap" operation need ever be performed. The monitor functions are as follows:
   a. Load RAM memory from paper tape, either in BNPF format or hexadecimal format.
   b. Display the contents of RAM memory on a printer.
   c. Modify individual bytes of RAM memory, move blocks of RAM memory, and fill blocks of RAM memory with constant data.
   d. Write contents of RAM memory to paper tape in either BNPF or hexadecimal format.
B. Resident Assembler
1. Translates the mnemonic code to binary machine code.
2. Loaded into system RAM memory via paper tape.

145

3. A requirement of 8K of memory storage for both the resident assembler and the symbol table.
4. This three-pass assembler generates a program tape that is reloaded via the monitor.

C. Text Editor
1. Loaded to system via paper tape.
2. Edits the source program during program development.

Development support: PL/M compiler, assembler and simulator. In addition to the standard software available with the Intellec 8, Intel offers a PL/M compiler, cross assembler, and simulator written in FORTRAN IV and designed to run on a large-scale computer. These routines may be procured directly from Intel, or, alternatively, designers may contact nationwide computer time-sharing services.

PL/M compiler. PL/M is a high-level, procedure-oriented systems language for programming the Intel MCS-8 microcomputer. The language contains the features of a high-level language, without sacrificing the efficiencies of assembly language. A significant advantage of this language is that PL/M programs can be compiled for either the Intel 8008, 8080 or future Intel 8-bit processors.

Assembler. The MCS-8 assembler generates object codes from symbolic assembly language instructions. It is designed to operate on a large-scale computer with input by paper tape, directly from a terminal keyboard or system file.

Simulator. The MCS-8 simulator, called Interp/8, provides a software simulation of the Intel 8008 CPU, along with execution monitoring commands to aid program development for the MCS-8.

PL/M compiler—a high level systems language and other microprogramming aids

It is relatively easy to program the Intel microcomputers using PL/M, a high-level language concept developed to meet the special needs of microcomputer systems programming. Programmers can utilize a true high-level language to program microcomputers efficiently. PL/M is an assembly language replacement that can fully command the CPUs and future processors to produce efficient run-time object code. PL/M was designed to provide additional developmental software support for the Intel microcomputer systems, permitting the programmer to concentrate more on his problem and less on the actual task of programming than is possible with assembly language.

Programming time and costs are drastically reduced; and training, documentation, and program maintenance are simplified. User application programs and standard systems programs may be transferred to future computer systems that support PL/M with little or no reprogramming. These are advantages of high-level language programming that have been proved in the large computer field and are now available to the microcomputer user. PL/M is derived from IBM's PL/1, a very extensive and sophisticated language that has promise of becoming the most widely known and used language in the future. PL/M is a subset of PL/1, with emphasis on those features that accurately reflect the nature of systems programming requirements.

As an example of comparative programming effort between PL/M and assembly language, a program to compute prime numbers was written twice, first in PL/M and then in assembly language. The PL/M version was written in fifteen minutes, compiled correctly on the second try (and "end" was omitted the first time) and ran correctly the first time. The program was then coded in Intel MCS-8 assembly language. Coding took four hours; program entry and editing, another two hours. Debug took an hour to find an incorrect register designation, the kind of problem completely eliminated by coding in PL/M. Results of this one short test show a 28 to 1 reduction in coding time. This ratio may be somewhat high; overall ratio in a mix of programs is more on the order of 10 to 1.

PL/M is regarded as an efficient language. The main reason for this saving in time is the fact that PL/M allows the programmer to define his problem in terms natural to him, not in the computer's terms. Consider the following sample program, which selects the larger of two numbers. In PL/M, the programmer might write: If $A > B$, then $C = A$; else $C = B$; Meaning: "If variable A is greater than variable B, then assign A to variable C; otherwise, assign B to C." A corresponding program in assembly language is twelve separate machine instructions and conveys little of original intent of the program. Because of the ease and conciseness with which programs can be written and the errorfree translation into machine language achieved by the compiler, the time to program a given system is reduced substantially over that for assembly language.

Debug and check-out time of a PL/M program is also much less than that of an assembly language program, partly because of the inherent clarity of PL/M, but also because writing a program in PL/M encourages good programming techniques. Furthermore, the structure of the PL/M language enables the PL/M compiler to detect error conditions that would slip by an assembler. The PL/M compiler is written in standard FORTRAN IV and will execute on most large machines with little alteration.

Cross assembler software packages are used with micros. The cross assembler translates a symbolic representation of the instructions and data into a form that can be loaded and executed by the microcomputer. The cross assembler is defined as an assembler executing on a machine other than the one used, which generates code for the desired unit. Initial development time can be significantly reduced by taking advantage of a large-scale computer's processing, editing, and high speed peripheral capability. Programs are written in assembly language using mnemonic symbols both for instruction and for special assembler operations. Symbolic addresses can be used in the source program; however, the assembled program will use absolute address. The assembler, designed to operate interactively from a terminal, is written in standard FORTRAN IV and can be modified to run on most large-scale machines.

Simulator software packages are also used. The various simulators are computer programs written in the FORTRAN IV language and are often called interpreters. These programs provide software simulation of the Intel micros, for example, along with execution monitoring commands to aid program development. The Intel Interp/8 accepts machine code produced by the 8008 assembler, along with execution commands from a time-sharing terminal, card reader, or disk file. The execution commands allow manipulation of the simulated MCS-8 memory and the 8008 CPU registers. In addition, operand and instruction breakpoints may be set to stop execution at crucial points in the program. Tracing features are also available, which allow the CPU operation to be monitored. Interp/8 also accepts symbol tables from either the PL/M compiler or MCS-8 cross assembler to allow debugging, tracing and braking, and displaying of program using symbolic names. The PL/M compiler, MCS-8 assembler, and MCS-8 simulator software packages may be procured from Intel on magnetic tape or, alternatively, from nationwide computer time-sharing services.

ARE MICROCOMPUTERS THE NEW FOURTH GENERATION OF SYSTEMS?

Many experts feel that the fourth generation of computer systems will be classified as "microcomputer communication and control systems." This is most plausible for four basic reasons. First, the fundamental nature of computing is data handling (data communications) and data control. Secondly, practically all the operations of third generation computing equipment are being designed or integrated into multimicroprocessor-controlled, total system networks, and with widespread specialized work function stations (decentralization). Thirdly, large-scale integration in several new component technologies is now being fully employed to reduce the size and cost of most peripheral equipment as well as operating systems and other programming (firmware). The attempts to substitute RAMs for magnetic disks, "chips" for modems, microsystem-controlled lasers for superfast entry and memory devices, and so on, all lead to "communications-oriented" control systems. Fourth, the development problems of large data management systems and/or complex operating systems have resulted primarily from a lack of understanding of the nature of applications to which microcomputers could be applied. Most of the data flowing in and out of computers in the past was quite unnecessary. Condensed and refined data collection has now become the standard rather than the exception in this microcomputerized generation. Low-cost microprocessors, RAMS and ROMs, and new technology mass memory have reduced or eliminated most repetitive entry of data.

The new generation of reports on "exception" (from expectations or plans) bases rather than "output it all" procedures are techniques very suitable to ROM system designs. Through the use of "front-end" processors, data reduction techniques, and so on, main processor time need no longer be consumed by expensive, complex operating systems, such as input-output control systems (IOCS) and others. Internal scheduling, accounting, housekeeping, error detection, job handling, polling, and so on can be completed by using programs contained in ROMs, leaving the more versatile CPUs to be used for faster job execution and control of decentralized terminals. These efficient procedures are no longer difficult problems for either hardware or software. There are now significant opportunities and potentials for great microprocessor developments in practically every phase of the computer operation field. And the concomitant need for new organization, direction, and coordination of communications between management-employee decentralized design is most apparent, and development efforts are now being so directed.

The rush to microminiaturization is on

The wonders of large-scale integration have been turned into great varieties of useful and practical applications. This new great technology is now readily available around the world. A great deal of foreign interest is focused on the American "CPU on a chip"—the LSI microprocessor—and hundreds of countries are importing it for applications in the form of micro-control devices from scores of microcomputer manufacturers. All computer customers, current and potential, have more than casual interest in microcomputers, and the odds are very good that many segments of the U.S. population soon will be using them. Microcomputers in various forms and at reasonable prices are being used in practical "everyday" activities as well as in exotic applications. And they are available as prepackaged systems, ready-to-use, for those who wish to avoid the time and expense of starting with "raw" ICs; but "build-'em-yourself" kits (see further on) have also become popular.

Microprocessors come in great variety—4-bit parallel processors, 8-bit parallel processors, 4-bit multichip models, and so on, which can be paralleled to form processors with wide data paths and so forth plus many serial processors. Some (for example, 4-bit parallel and serial processors) are very good at decimal arithmetic, with complex keyboards and numeric displays.

Such modules are well applied in point of sale terminals, electronic cash registers, programmable calculators, and a thousand similar devices. Others are good at processing logical and discrete data and characters that are best for even wider ranges of the application spectrum—general processing and control, machine tools, instrumentation, communication systems, and so on.

As promised two decades ago, breakthroughs in modern electronic technology have now created a new partnership between man and electronic machines in which the machines become an extension of man's brain, amplifying his capabilities and increasing his productivity. In the past, as previously noted, computers have been very large, complex, expensive machines. Because of their high cost and complicated systems, the largest machines tended to be used only for mass data processing in science, "big" industry, and government. Advances in microelectronic and component technology have now made possible low-priced "intelligent" terminals to connect and "associate" with human participants and have made it possible to package information for economical, rapid communication over large distances. Because sophisticated information-processing electronic circuits can now be placed on a single chip the size of a match head, versatility and reliability have been increased and enhanced. The net effect is that the computer has now become a very inexpensive component of communications systems. For example, one company, TRW, Inc., in 1973 had already installed dozens of transaction-oriented communications systems with more than 40,000 terminals in department stores and financial institutions. These systems perform a variety of functions from credit authorization to inventory control. Another TRW system handles thousands of credit inquiries daily, providing a nationwide network for credit grantors. TRW also operates "Validata," a computer network that allows airline terminals, hotels, car rental agencies, and others to check for stolen tickets, bad checks, and credit card validity. Microprocessors provide this "intelligence."

Microcomputer systems are now being used to help run railroads in England, Canada, and South Africa; to control parts and accounting in automobile dealerships in 14 European countries; and to process insurance claims for national insurance networks in Sweden and Germany. In Japan, several banks and department stores are using microcomputer-based systems. Whereas the electronic systems of the past were largely independent of human beings once they were programmed and operating, the new systems, on the other hand, enable human beings to communicate directly with the heart of the systems through remote terminals. This means they can inquire, oversee, and evaluate, as well as obtain needed information. The equipment thus makes it possible for tellers, store clerks, stockbrokers, accountants, and others to access and contribute to a large-scale information system. The new partnership between man and electronic equipment not only provides better service for customers, but it also lowers costs and increases productivity.

The United States is in a unique position to capitalize on this electronic revolution. It has more of the most advanced technology, the largest manufacturing capability, and an abundance of people skilled in using electronics creatively to meet business and professional needs. It is also a society that distributes its technology to many people rather than a few (for example, TV and hand-held calculators). Unit costs are reduced accordingly, bringing electronics into everyone's life. Taking advantage of new electronic technology in the service industries will give America a worldwide competitive advantage by reducing the costs and increasing the productivity and efficiency of such services. This, as well as the fact that the United States has become a major exporter of such technology, has helped the country with its balance of payments.

Who uses micros most?

All kinds of people are successfully using microcomputers: mechanical engineers, managers, architects, accountants, physicists, and so on. In general, anyone with enough intelligence to formulate step-by-step procedures accurately and with the time to study a little digital logic, or, with engineers, a little assembly language computer programming, can learn to use microcomputers. Users who are staffing a complex project that will use microcomputers look for electrical engineers with some minicomputer programming experience and/or minicomputer programmers with a knowledge of digital logic. "Big systems" programmers do not usually display enough mental flexibility to learn to "think small."

Most practical microcomputer applications call for small development teams, generally an engineer-programmer and one or two technicians or junior engineers (who should also have minicomputer experience). Most initially write programs in assembly language. Memory formerly was at a premium in many OEM (original equipment manufacturers) and end-user systems, and the first available compilers for microcomputers were somewhat inefficient in terms of object code, memory requirements, and speed. Now these compilers are available on microcomputers and mini time-sharing systems, and they contribute only slightly to development costs. And memory costs are only 1 percent of what they were ten years ago. But because most microcomputer applications call for relatively small programs (200 to 2,000 instructions), use of a high-level language provides only marginal savings in coding time in some systems but great convenience in others. Heavy memory and running time programs benefit by using BASIC and FORTRAN.

Microcomputers make very decent text processors, so that good source program text editors and assemblers are available. Because more microcomputer utility software is oriented toward using ASR33s (teletypes) or similar devices, most current users stick with assemblers that permit "free form" syntax and simulate tabulation—assemblers that force users to keep instructions and operands in particular columns. Some of these can be very hard to use. Software routines for fixed-point multiplication and division are available, as are many floating-point packages. Routines for standard functions are coming along and will quickly become very common. Manufacturers of prepackaged microcomputers are more than willing to give users lots of help with design, production planning, and manufacturing. For annual volume that is small-to-moderate (fewer than 500 systems) or for many models with a need for some customizing, it is economical to use a prepackaged microcomputer. If users need to get their product on the market quickly, using a prepackaged microcomputer can save from two to six months in lead time, depending upon the complexity of the system. Prepackaged microcomputer systems that support text editing, program assembly, testing and programming of read-only memories are available for less than $2,000. A useful system with processor, ASR interface, console, utility software and 1K of RAM memory can be had for less than $1,000, already wired, powered, and in an enclosure with plenty of room for expansion and tie-in to the user's own hardware.

Microcomputers as an idea whose time has come have been proved in situations that called for a computer but were held off because even a minicomputer was too costly. Exciting developments in microcomputers are fast. Many more powerful processors with even further cost reductions, as well as new LSI versions of current minicomputers with new interface chips, are all available from the leading microprocessor manufacturers. Moreover, prepackaged microcomputers with more peripheral interfaces are popular, as noted on pages ahead. All things considered, working with microcomputers is interesting and often exciting, even fun.

Microcomputer power boosts "intelligent factory" markets

Microcomputers were initially applied to programmable machine control, artificial intelligence,[4] process control, NC tape editing, medical instrumentation, word processing, transducer linearization, computation of ship loading, communication system control, automatic test station control,

[4] In scientific parlance, artificial intelligence is rather hard to define, but it roughly corresponds to the utilization of a set of techniques that enable computers to perform tasks that, if performed by human beings, would be called intelligent, nonrote activity. These techniques have included list processing, heuristic search, means-ends analysis, and theorem proving. With the repeated use of these techniques, it is only natural that they have been incorporated as facilities in special languages for AI. These languages are very complex and beyond this text.

and so on. The list expands daily. Microcomputer applications exceed the imagination of most people, and they are turning up in many places without being particularly noticed. They are hidden within or attached to devices. In the simplest terms, they can be applied to any information-processing, storage, or control problem as long as speed requirements are not too severe. In many applications where a minicomputer might have been used if it were cheap enough, a microcomputer can be applied very economically. The advantages of having it easy to "bury" it in an OEM product and thereby hide the product's true inner nature add to the low power drain of the microprocessor as being both economical and patriotic in an era of energy shortages. However, the "raw" integrated circuit is often useless until it is interfaced with other logic, peripheral devices, and a memory to hold programs and data. Interfacing a microprocessor has now become a simple task and is no longer a considerable impediment to some applications. To help remove this impediment entirely, several manufacturers offer prepackaged microcomputers with standard interfaces for memories, peripherals, and control devices. Users can assemble their own custom-tailored microcomputers from these prepackaged models, which come in the form of loaded printed circuit boards with various packaging accessories.

The expected major cost justification breakthrough is now occurring in factory automation because controls, which are rapidly declining in price, now account for a higher percentage of the value of machine tools. Minis

FIGURE 4.4. Selected factory automation markets. *Courtesy: Quantum Sciences, Inc., New York, N.Y.*

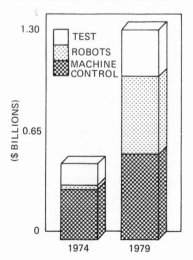

and micros now at very low costs also have increased monitoring, adaptive control, and pattern recognition capabilities. They will become the crux of the integrated, intelligent factory, which will feature several hierarchies of computers. Mastering new technologies will be critical to success in the factory automation competitive environment, which has now begun featuring near devastating cost-price battles.

Foreign competition is forcing U.S. companies to automate swiftly. Other governments (of Japan, West Germany, Sweden) sponsor and encourage far more research and development in factory automation than the United States. The result is that West Germany is ahead of the United States in the production of machine tools, and Japan produces four times the number of robots than the United States does. It is predicted that robot shipments will increase 16 times in the next decade as intelligence and pattern recognition are mastered, and increasing numbers of them are placed on assembly lines.

The clear perspective on factory automation is that the U.S. productivity rate will increase very measurably because adaptive control is now economically and technically feasible. The energy crisis and foreign competition threaten, and many types of automation and levels of control will be developed with nationalist and patriotic zeal, especially in Europe and some parts of Asia—and in the United States.

Technology trends indicate strength toward intelligent factories; the role of minicomputers and microcomputers will be to simplify data collection, expand the use of computer aided design, and so forth. Computer-aided manufacturing will center specifically on (1) machine control (N/C, CNC, DNC),[5] (2) machine monitoring, (3) mechanical testing and adjustment, (4) electronic testing, (5) communications, (6) facilities monitoring, (7) materials handling, (8) adaptive control, (9) robots, and (10) test equipment (including product, mechanical, electronic, and electrical pattern recognition, and new software. Simulation and modeling will also be a basic part of the new competitive environment, forcing strong trends toward systems "intelligence."

The economics of the new technology

Most of us realize that the direction of our world is most often guided by basic economics—the prices and supplies of goods and services. A brief explanation of this concept as it pertains to computers follows. The microcomputer is irreversibly moving forward on thousands of individual marketing plans. A key factor in this move is the spiraling downward cost of microcomputer systems. As the systems get cheaper, they reach a point where one

---

[5] Numerical control (punched tapes), computer numerical control (remote), and direct numerical control—microprocessor attached.

group of users after another with a specific problem is willing to pay the current price for a solution tool, the microcomputer. For example, in 1963 a fairly comprehensive ("naked" or "bare bones") minicomputer system cost around $27,000. In 1973 this cost dropped to around $2,000 for an equivalent system, and the equivalent micro was $700 in 1974. This drop in hardware costs turns out to be a fairly constant 35 percent per year, which seems to be a good estimate for the next few years at least. Following this downward slope, at some point the price of a micro system is going to be attractive enough to almost any given group of users.

Although prices of passive components like capacitors, connectors, transformers, wire, and cable are rising precipitously, semiconductors defy the inflation spiral and continue their steady downward trend in prices in spite of (or because of) increased demand. This is because the behavior of semiconductor prices is controlled by improvements in technological processes and not so much by labor and material costs. As yields increase, prices decline; and as new markets become involved, new products are generated, thus keeping the price decline cycle going at a strong pace.

Intel Corporation invites a comparison—the high cost of developing standard debugged, documented programs emphasizes microcomputer software value. The following example illustrates well the huge savings available to those who take full advantage of the software aids available from most major suppliers.

A cost-performance calculation

Assume a per-day cost for each programmer in your company, including salary and overhead share, to be $160.00. Assume that each of your programmers, using Assembly Language, writes 10 instructions daily, each fully debugged and documented. As each instruction occupies 16 bits of memory, you are paying $16 per instruction, or $1.00/bit. The same programmers, without Assembly Language, can write only 2 such instructions (in machine language) each on a daily basis, increasing your program costs by a factor of 5, to $5.00/bit. Using Intel's PL/M [or National Semiconductor's PL/M "Plus," for example], however, each of your programmers can write the equivalent of 100 fully debugged and documented instructions every day. This, of course, reduced your costs to $.10/bit.[6]

With Intel's and some other major suppliers' software developmental aids, including the PL/M language, programming costs decrease by a factor of ten! The exact value of the figures shown here may vary somewhat, but the ratios are indicative. Intel and most other manufacturers provide support to purchasers of their systems that can indeed open new markets for their products, reduce their costs, and expand their sales.

[6] From Intel Corp. promotional literature.

Manufacturers provide users' libraries for
control, applications, other programs

"User libraries" happily provide numerous programs for microcomputer purchasers. More new users' libraries are regularly announced by the major microcomputer systems manufacturers community. One library contains programs for the Intel 4-bit "computer-on-a-chip," the 4004, and a second library features the 8008, and so on. Motorola offers them for its M6800, and so forth. The libraries contain well-documented programs, using standardized documentation, and each library is bound into a manual. Library members receive updated, new programs quarterly. Membership in any of the libraries is available to those who have contributed a program or paid a membership fee. As the main purpose of the users' library is to provide all MCS users access to applications programs written by other users, new contributions make the library useful to everybody. To contribute a program, a user of an Intel (or other sponsoring company) product must prepare a microcomputer user's library submittal form. This form requires that a program must be adequately documented—a requirement that is rigorously enforced. The libraries contain a variety of microcomputer programs, or subroutines. Highlighted are cross assembler and simulator packages, which users may run on other computers.

Documentation for each of the programs included in the manuals includes the program name and function, required hardware and software, details of the user-program interface, and a listing of the program. All manuals are generally documented in the same way. The microcomputer users' libraries consist of many numbers of well-documented programs. For example, principal features of the Intel 8008 library are complete floating point arithmetic and I/O packages. These packages contain all necessary routines, for example, for add, subtract, multiply, divide, and negate; conversion to and from ASCII and conversion to and from fixed-point and hundreds more. All users are encouraged to take part in the various microcomputer users' libraries for the benefit of others facing similar problems and for their own benefit in generating new programs. These libraries provide users with opportunity to use all or part of a program that comes close to solving their development effort, thus reducing their costs.

Microcomputers are extremely cost-effective
for straightforward automation

The previous minimum memory of 4K and above for most minicomputers was "overkill" for many dedicated applications, that is, simple repetitive control or processing. Many customers really required less memory, which was expensive in both hardware and software costs. They had always desired to "fix" the program in read-only memory to keep these headaches from occurring. Using microcomputers and low-cost PROMs, these users can now avoid more expensive and cumbersome minicomputers and take advantage of many varieties of computer control possibilities without paying for additional computer flexibility they do not need.

Many minicomputer instruction sets are very memory inefficient. Microcomputers permit a large number of applications to be covered in 1K and 2K of memory. Typical applications that are made to order for low-cost PROMs include repetitive manufacturing operations and control applications for processing materials, chemicals, and so on, data collection, instrument monitoring and measurement, and many more. Programming the PROM is easy. Practically all of them use techniques that allow read/write locations to be spread throughout the 1K (or more) memory as the program requires. The program can be changed by erasing the PROM using an ultraviolet (UV) lamp and then reprogrammed by using a programmer (blaster) available from many component distributors and other sources.

Thus for procedures or systems that might be necessarily reprogrammed at a later date or redesigned for more production, faster rates, or different materials, the microcomputer systems are ideal. For engineer designers and production managers, the procedures make it possible to "get out there first." Microcomputer versatility and changeability facilitate easy, low-cost changes without the waste of high-priced talent or equipment change.

Microprocessors—users ask: where, which, when?

Microprocessor products were being sold in big-volume purchases in 1975 and 1976. Engineering and market planning managers at companies that manufacture terminals, process and traffic control systems, medical instrumentation, and the new electronic games are developing strategies on how to meet their microprocessor needs. Most companies have turned to the traditional semiconductor (integrated circuit—IC) suppliers such as Intel, National Semiconductor, Rockwell, Fairchild, Motorola, and others, which offered their own versions of microprocessor chips as well as microprocessing boards that include the chip, associated memories, and other peripheral parts. Many OEM users leaned toward use of chips (without racks, panels, boards, and so on) because it meant more value added and profit for them.

Digital Equipment Corp., (DEC), General Automation, Computer Automation, and similar minicomputer companies looked to protect their own minicomputer market base by making their own assembled microprocessing boards available to users. Most microsystem customers, however, are expected to look to the IC vendors for their microprocessor needs. Other users who have previously incorporated minicomputer and logic modules in their systems are continuing to turn to minicomputer companies like DEC and the others for their support requirements. Many classes of users are evaluating alternatives, waiting for the source that can deliver the faster part or system for the lowest price. Some are working with chip suppliers as a means of freeing themselves from dependence on minicomputers. There are big markets for both chips and boards. Many have elected to design their own processors from chips. They were not willing to pay a minicomputer manufacturer for software, design, and packaging. Most builders and users see the advent of the microprocessor chip as a "technology-inspired revolution in engineering" that will require design engineers to become familiar with firmware, microcoding, and microprogramming. There is obviously a technological revolution toward massive use of computers on a chip under way, but many devices have a bit of maturing to do. The semiconductor industry as a supplier of end-user products is rising fast along a short, steep learning curve.

Most user companies are primarily concerned with speed, reliability, cost, and second-sourcing of microprocessors. One company that manufactures traffic, process, and fluid control equipment is concerned about the question, When will price-performance settle down?

Another major end-product company is NCR, a good example of scores of others. A major micro market is the point of sale terminal at each checkout lane in supermarkets and department stores. These are linked to NCR in-store controllers. The Model 255 systems are now available with laser beam scanning. The first of these automatic scanning systems was installed in early 1974, and NCR had already installed thousands of the nonscanning 255 terminals. The main purpose of the microprocessor is to give the terminal stand-alone capability should the system's in-store controller experience downtime. The same type of microprocessor is used in the NCR bank tellers' terminals, which were recently unveiled. In this case, its function is to serve as the terminal control unit. NCR buys microprocessing chips and assembles its systems in-house.

Can practically anyone afford a computing system?

Indeed, practically anyone can afford a computing system. Business and professional applications of all types have largely contributed to the widespread use of computers. The technology is so common that minicomputer and microcomputer systems costing much less than traditional standard computers are available economically for all but the very smallest of private enterprises. Even the smallest operation or office will find computer assistance advantageous on a time-sharing basis . . . from service companies or at least by owning several "computer calculators." Functions where typically the greatest savings can be achieved are data storage, data collection, elimination of human error, reducing operating time, maximizing equipment utilization, reduction of labor content, and improving quality. It is now established that practically anyone can cost-justify a computer system, and a thousand software equipment suppliers can show them how. For example, microcomputer and minicomputer systems are now used prolifically in these applications:

Machine tool control

Shop management information systems

Typesetting

Industrial scales

Medical systems

Process controls

Point of sale systems

Power monitoring for electric utilities

Educational systems

Insurance proposal systems

Inventory management systems

Voice command systems

Radio and television scheduling systems

Multiple listing for real estate

Communications network systems

Automotive inspection

Taxi monitoring and dispatch

Material handling

Electronic test equipment

And thousands of others

In this era of micro/mini computers, it is a rare operation indeed that will not grow to the point of justifying a microcomputer—for a significant amount of its information-processing activities.

EDP systems will provide fast, reliable statistical and report data that can be digested while it is still current. They also are great educators and will eventually influence and permeate every segment of business and science. Monthly hardware system rentals typically average about .1 percent of sales, that is, sales multipled by .001. At first, many businessmen shied away from the supposed high cost of computers. Now they are analyzing how much they are currently overspending to support their office accounting functions without them. Most new users quickly realize the benefits of the efficiency and knowledge that would never have been attainable by using the old methods. In this world of increasing costs, as in wages and salaries and so on for people, facilities, and so forth, one of the few business costs that is going down is the cost of EDP hardware defined in terms of capability.

Impact of new technology on computer architecture, costs, and capabilities

The conventional concepts for the architecture and resource allocation in new computer systems are no longer based on the older conventional components and "standard" ratios between hardware and programming costs. Since the introduction to the third generation in 1967, new technology has again dropped the cost per hardware control function, this time by a factor of 100. A critical examination of the "sacred cows" of the mid-sixties unfolds some startling results. For example, it has become more efficient to abandon compiling (program translators) and to embed this and many other software functions in hardware (ROMs and RAMs) and to make systems multiple-redundant. Customers have voted with emphasis by buying not the fastest or "big-brand-make," but instead the most cost-effective machine available. Minicomputers and "standards" with micros embedded within them and the resultant great economy are not trends; they are the facts of life for most computer users today. Existing barriers between man and machine have been drastically reduced by directing the new flexibility in hardware and software toward meeting the user's requirements on his own terms without impairing system efficiency. MOS LSI microcomputer "smart" terminal designs have quickly won over.

CONCLUSION

Sociologists with human factors experience should join with engineers and management to make programming a more definite science rather than an individual art. Software systems of every type can be designed as ROMs and can be utilized with comfort and convenience to employees to complete, still very satisfactorily and efficiently, the clearly defined system requirements. Engineers, businessmen, and academics, in cooperation with scientists, should cooperate to develop better theories of programming based upon an understanding of new LSI-processor-ROM firmware "versatility options" in operations, such as data collection, handling, control and especially communications—all ideal for micropower.

Most sociologists agree that extensive automation of banks, supermarkets, hospitals, schools, offices, factories, and so on will dramatically alter the ways human beings will think, act and react, and adjust to the new forced life-styles. And there is little doubt also that computers are doing much more than modifying human behavior. Thousands of cases of innovative technology are leading inexorably to massive changes in the course of history and to much social and personal turmoil. History and technology are both irresistible and irreversible. And, in this decade at least, it is not immaterial whether we as individuals detest or cooperate with the omnipresence of the all-knowing computer memory and controls.

The technology moves relentlessly forward. We must first know what this technology is and what it does to exercise and control "machine intelligence." Only then can we judge its harmful or benevolent use. Only then perhaps can we learn how to protect ourselves from its current social misuse. Complaints and congratulations are equally irrelevant unless we can act intelligently and responsibly. Although the power, effects, and impact of computers are already manifold, the revolution they are causing has only just begun. Just where the computer is taking us is really beyond poetic insight, and anyone attempting to predict the long-range future of this technology will inevitably underestimate its psychological, social, and cultural impact, just as men did with all past major technological revolutions.

Wristwatch-sized calculators

Figure 4.5 shows a handy calculator with a 17-key unit. Its tiny keys and readout use a layer of conductive rubber. The trend toward microminiaturization in electronics has been pushed even further by the watch industry. Chomerics Inc., Hughes, and others responded by introducing a keyboards measuring only 3/4 × 1 inch with 17 keys of 5/32-inch centers.

FIGURE 4.5. Chomerics, Inc. manufactures tiny keyboards for calculator-watches. Several models are being marketed with significant success. *Courtesy: Chomerics, Inc.*

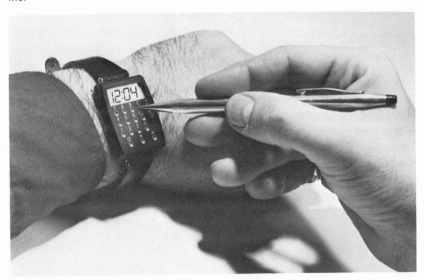

The key array includes a moving decimal point and constant, clear, multiply, divide, add-equal, and subtract-equal keys, which are as easy to read as a watch face. Some full calculator would probably have either a four-digit liquid-crystal display or a six-digit light-emitting-diode readout. Slightly larger readout areas could accommodate several "answer" lines, using an attached magnifier for improved clarity.

This pencil tip keyboard makes use of Chomerics' materials technology in conductive elastomers, paints, and inks, and its capability in full-size keyboards. The miniature keyboard uses the same materials as the large subassemblies, but they are put together differently. The keyboard consists of a tiny printed-circuit board, screened with a silver paint that provides a permanently conductive contact surface. Over this is laid a 0.005-inch-thick Mylar spacer with holes directly under the keys, a layer of conductive rubber, and a Mylar legend sheet that has the keys on it. When the Mylar is deflected, an electrical impulse that is set up in the conductive rubber travels through the holes in the Mylar spacer to the printed-circuit board. The keyboard was developed as a result of inquiries from watch companies, and samples were supplied to at least ten of them in mid-1974. In volume the manufacturer says the keyboards could sell for less than $2 each.

FURTHER DEFINING THE WORLD OF MICROCOMPUTERS

A/D analog-digital converter. Circuit used to convert information in analog form into digital form (or vice versa), for example, in a digital voltmeter and other devices.

Addressing capacity, microprocessor. Programming addressing range determines how large a program can be written without resorting to special external hardware and internal software techniques. A range that is too small means that extra hardware will be required to extend the addressing. Excessive capacity means that extraneous address bits will be carried in every instruction that refers to storage.

ALU (arithmetic-logic unit). The ALU is the heart of and one of the essential components of a microprocessor. It is the operative base between the registers and the control block. The ALU performs various forms of addition, subtraction, and the extension of these to multiplication, division, exponentiation, and so on. The logic mode relates to the operations of gating, masking, and other manipulations of the contents of registers.

Backplane, microcomputer. A typical bus-oriented backplane is used as the data highway between logic memory and process input/output modules. Some backplanes are configured so as to give each module plugged into it its own unique address.

Bipolar microprocessor slice, 4-bit. The 4-bit bipolar microprocessor slice is designed as a high-speed cascadable intended for use in CPUs, peripheral controllers, programmable microprocessors, and numerous other applications. The microinstruction flexibility will allow efficient emulation of almost any digital computing machine.

Boolean operator. An operator (gate) used in Boolean algebra as applied to logic units of computer architecture, that is, the result of any operation is restricted to one of two values, generally represented as 1 or 0.

Chip architecture. Functionally, the microprocessor chip includes the arithmetic logic unit (ALU), the general-purpose registers and the control-bus structure. The architecture is to some degree dependent on the partitioning of the processor between one or more chips, the number of pins each chip has, the chip size, the off-chip memory, and 1/0 bus structure. Speed or throughput is very dependent on architecture. Clock speed (or frequency) is not necessarily indicative of execution speed. Speed is a function of data and address patch widths, number of separate paths, and overlap in the fetch and execute cycles.

Clock. 1. The most basic source of synchronizing signals in most electronic equipment, especially computers. 2. That specific device or unit designed to time events. 3. A data communications clock controls the timing of bits sent in a data stream and controls the timing of the sampling of bits received in a data stream.

Command. 1. For microprocessors, an electronic pulse, signal, or set of signals to start, stop, or continue some operation. It is incorrect to use command as a synonym for instruction. 2. The portion of an instruction word that specifies the operation to be performed.

Control circuits. The digital computer circuits that carry out instructions in proper sequence. They also interpret instructions and apply the proper commands to the arithmetic element and other circuits in accordance with interpretation.

Control section. Refers to the primary sequence of instructions or data within a program that can be transferred from outside the program segment in which it is contained. The control section can be deleted or replaced with a control section from other program segments. Microprocessors are changing the structure and procedure of many such devices and systems.

CPU chip. A CPU chip may be visualized as one universal chip that performs the functions of numerous individual chips. The CPU chip requires two sets of input signals to generate one set of output signals. The input and output signals correspond to the chip inputs and outputs. The instruction signals tell the CPU chips which individual logic chip to emulate. In order for a CPU chip's versatility to be useful, it must emulate logic equivalents to more than one chip.

CPU chip circuit. Contained on some CPUs are an arithmetic logic unit (ALU), an accumulator, a scratch-pad memory, a status register, several bidirectional I/O ports, clock circuits to control all chips in the system, an interrupt control circuit, and a power-on detect circuit that disables the interrupt system and assures that processing starts from a unique address when power is first applied.

CROM instruction set. One specific chip has macroinstructions that comprise basic instruction sets that are implemented by one control read-only memory (CROM). Because these instructions are common to this series of microprocessors, these instructions may be used for program development for other series systems. The basic instruction set may be extended by the use of additional CROMs. (A socket is provided for a second CROM on the CPU card.)

Data bus components. A typical system data bus is composed of three signal buses. An example is a data bus that consists of 16 bidirectional data lines. The timing bus provides the basic system clocks as well as address and data strobes that indicate when data is valid on the bus. The control bus provides a priority system for bus access, signals to indicate whether the current transaction is a read or write from memory or a peripheral, an extended cycle signal, and a response line to indicate that a peripheral device has accepted an order sent over the system bus.

DIP (dual in-line package). 1. The most popular IC packaging in the mid-1970s in the plastic, dual in-line case, using plastic for economic reasons and the dual in-line package (DIP) configuration for manufacturing efficiency. 2. Chips are enclosed in dual in-line packages that take their names from the double, parallel rows of leads that connect them to the circuit board. DIPs are sometimes also called "bugs."

Gate. 1. A circuit having one output and several inputs, the output remaining unenergized until certain input conditions have been met. When used in conjunction with computers, a gate is also called an AND circuit. A gate can also be a signal to trigger the passage of other signals through a circuit. 2. An electrode in a field-effect transistor. 3. A device having one output channel and one or more input channels, such that the output channel state is completely determined by the input channel state except during switching transients. 4. A combinational logic element having at least one input channel.

General registers, microcomputer. A typical central processor module might contain eight 16-bit general purpose registers that can perform a variety of functions. These registers can serve as accumulators, index registers, autoincrement registers, autodecrement registers, or as stack pointers for temporary storage of data. Arithmetic operations can be from one general register to another, from one memory location or device register to another, or between memory locations or a device register and a general register.

Input-output channels, automatic. Automatic I/O channels transfer data between memory and external interfaces in blocks of any size without disturbing the processor's working registers. Word or byte count and current address for each channel can be held in memory; each transfer automatically updates them until the count is complete, in some systems. This use of memory for control registers lowers the cost of interfacing. Multiple channels can operate concurrently, with hardware priority control of each channel. Transfers can be full 16-bit words or 8-bit bytes in some systems, with automatic packing/unpacking.

Input/output port. A typical input/output port consists of an 8-bit latch with tri-state output buffers along with control and device selection logic. Also included is a service request flip-flop for the generation and control of interrupts to the microprocessor.

The device is multimode in nature. It can be used to implement latches, gated buffers, or multiplexers. Thus all of the principal peripheral and input/output functions of a microcomputer system can be implemented with this device. Some units require only .25 μA input current, permitting direct connection to MOS data and address lines of the CPUs.

Instruction path, microprocessor. The instruction path is a transfer bus for retrieving instructions from the program memory. Instruction word width is determined by the size of the instruction set that affects processing power.

Integrated circuits, basic processes. Basic integrated circuit processes include implementation of active devices (such as diodes and transistors) and passive components (integrated capacitors and resistors). The reading assignment focuses on considerations of importance in analog integrated circuits, where parameter tolerances and drift are of most importance (compared to digital integrated circuits). Various constraints are imposed on various electronic components (bipolar transistors, field-effect transistors, capacitors and resistors) by integrated circuit fabrication processes.

Interface, I/O. The type of interface and the I/O responsiveness of the microcomputer are factors in the organization of I/O activity. One method is to assign a specific class of interface to each processor. For example, one processor can do all decimal interface operations; another can handle high-speed I/O. In this way the designer can choose the most suitable. The second function, information concentration, improves efficiency—unlike the use of bytes or small records. Each data transfer requires less I/O software, and the data are easier to handle. Any form of concentration, however, implies the use of storage.

Interrupt priorities. Interrupt requests are frequently assigned priorities. Whenever two interrupts occur simultaneously, the one with the higher priority is considered first. Furthermore a higher-priority interrupt can interrupt the service routine of a lower-priority interrupt. Most microprocessors do not have built-in priorities, and these must be handled either with software or external hardware.

Interrupt types. Several types of microprocessors can accommodate single-line, multilevel, and vectored interrupts, and they save essential registers automatically. A complete saving must be programmed. In one single-line interrupt system, device-interrupt requests are ORed together to form one request line. The program identifies the device and resolves priority. A multilevel scheme employs several single-level sense lines to handle additional interrupts. For very fast response, the vectored interrupt directly branches to a memory location that corresponds to a specific interrupt.

I/O section, microprocessor. The I/O section consists of the necessary buffering and control interfaces for connecting the system to I/O devices such as teletypes, terminals, and other types of peripheral devices. The I/O area needs very careful consideration during the process of selecting a microprocessor system. I/O inherently creates a bottleneck in small systems for applications that require heavy I/O activity. The user must analyze his intended applications carefully to assure a satisfactory ratio between processing and I/O and to avoid having to build costly external I/O interfaces.

IPL (initial program loader). An initial program load or a program that reads the supervisor into main storage and then transfers control to the supervisor.

Loader, bootstrap (microprocessor). Enables users to enter data or a program into the RAMs from a teletypewriter, paper tape, or keyboard and execute the program from the RAMs. Often consists of a PROM that plugs into the phototyping board.

Loaders, microcomputer. A variety of loaders is available for entering programs produced by assemblers into read/write memory. The input media may be punched cards, paper tape, and so on. The format of the programs may be either absolute or relocatable modules for most systems. The following loaders are typically available: a firmware paper tape loader, which

166

in some systems can be activiated by LOAD PROG switch on the control panel and which loads an absolute program module via the paper tape reader; a card reader bootstrap, which loads an absolute hexadecimal card deck into memory; an absolute loader, which loads one or more absolute program modules via the card reader; and a relocatable linking loader, which loads one or more program modules via the card reader or paper tape, relocates them to any location in memory, and links them together via global symbols specified at assembly time.

Logic. As regards microprocessors, logic is a mathematical treatment of formal logic using a set of symbols to represent quantities and relationships that can be translated into switching circuits or gates. Such gates are logical functions such as, AND, OR, NOT, and hundreds of others. Each such gate is a switching circuit that has two states, open or closed. They make possible the application of binary numbers for solving problems. The basic logic functions electronically performed from gate circuits are the foundation of the often complex computing capability.

LSI technologies. The various LSI technologies are conceptually similar; most use the electrical properties of silicon dioxide and doped, crystalline silicon. Pure crystalline silicon has a valence of 4, and a regular, covalent lattice structure. Crystalline silicon can be turned into a conductor by adding a source of surplus electrons or by introducing electron deficiencies (holes) into the crystal lattice structure. Surplus electrons can be generated by "doping" the silicon with traces of a valence 5 impurity such as phosphorus.

Mail box. A "mail box" is often referred to as a set of locations in a common RAM storage area, an area reserved for data addressed to specific peripheral devices as well as other microprocessors in the immediate environment. Such an arrangement enables the coordinator CPU and the supplementary microprocessors to transfer data among themselves in an orderly fashion with minimal hardware.

Master control routine. Refers to various parts of programs consisting of a series of subroutines. It controls the linking of the other subroutines and may call the various segments of the program into memory as required. It is also used to describe a program that controls the operation of a hardware system.

Master scheduler. Refers to the control scheduler that permits the function of a control program that allows an operator to initiate special actions or to cause requested information to be delivered that can override the normal control functions of the system.

Master/slave configuration. A special system or compute configuration for business or scientific use (as production automation) in which one computer, usually of substantial size or capability, rules with complete control over all input/output and schedules and transmits tasks to slave computer. The latter computer often has a great capacity, and it performs the computations as directed and controlled by the master unit.

Memory board. A typical semiconductor memory board can be configured in 4K word increments up to 32K words. It provides addressing for up to 32K words, refresh and standby logic, the bus interface, and the first 4K words of memory. The system is driven by the microprocessor and contains up to 16K words per board.

Metal oxide semiconductor (MOS). 1. In MOS technology, amplification or switching is accomplished by applying a signal voltage to a gate electrode. The resulting electrostatic field creates a conduction channel between the two diffused regions in the silicon crystal structure, called the "source" and the "drain." 2. MOS is part of the acronym MOSFET, the FET meaning *field effect transistor.* Thus MOS/LSI are types of transistors for large-scale integrated (LSI) metal-oxide semiconductor components for computer memory units.

Microcomputer CPU. In general aspects, the CPU consists of the following: program counter (PC), instruction register (IR), instruction execution logic, a memory-address register (MAR), a general-purpose register (GPR) file, and an arithmetic and logic unit (ALU).

Microcomputer data base system. With the data-base management system, the user's computer and intelligent terminals can communicate with the disk file through high-level commands while the intelligent disk system carries out the detailed commands for indexing, searching, and deblocking operations required to access or store the needed data.

Microcomputer disk operating systems (DOS). A typical disk operating system is a complete batch-processing system optimized to reduce the time and cost of program development. It provides all of the file management and utility functions required for generating, debugging, storing, and modifying programs. Using DOS, programs can be developed either for stand-alone applications or for operation under real-time executives.

Microcomputer software. Microcomputers are the first level of programmable logic where available software is an important consideration. All microcomputers require an assembler. Owing to inherent efficiencies and available support features, most microcomputers are supported by cross assemblers on commercial time share systems enabling users to develop and debug microcomputer software on an easy to use high-level operating system. Some manufacturers package a microcomputer with power supplies, memory and I/O devices making it feasible to develop software on the microcomputer itself.

MOS (metal oxide semiconductor). 1. Refers to the layers of material and indirectly to a fundamental process for fabricating ICs. MOS circuits achieve high component densities. 2. The basic technology is a circuit structure called MOSFET, the FET representing field effect transistor or transfer. It concerns metal on or over silicon oxide or silicon. The metal electrode is the gate; the silicon oxide is the insulator, and the carrier-doped regions in the silicon substrate become the drain and source.

Nondestructive readout. 1. The copying of information from a computer storage device without altering the physical representation of the information in the device. 2. A particular storage area that cannot be erased and reused, for example, punched cards or perforated paper tape. 3. A reading process that does not destroy the data in the source.

Operating console, microcomputer. The operating console is generally mounted on the front of the processor enclosure and contains all controls and indicators necessary for the operation of the processor. The controls and indicators can include the following: run indicator, run switch, halt indicator, halt switch, reset switch, link indicator, interrupt on indicator, display switch, accumulator position, and so on.

Option boards. Option boards allow customers to implement miscellaneous basic system options: Typical options are a real-time clock, serial interfacing, and digital I/O. The real-time clock is often a crystal controlled interval timer, in which the intervals can be selected under program control.

Peripheral interface adapter (PIA) functions. Often three chip select lines are provided for selecting a particular PIA; two address inputs are used in conjunction with a control bit within the selected PIA for choosing specific registers in the PIA. The MPU can read from or write into the PIA's internal registers by addressing the PIA via the address bus and control bus.

PLA (programmed logic arrays). A PLA is an orderly arrangement of logical AND and logical OR functions. In application they behave very much like a glorified ROM, but PLA is devoted primarily with a combination logic device.

PMOS. P-channel MOS refers to the oldest type of MOS circuit where the electrical current is a flow of positive charges.

PROM programmer. A typical PROM programmer peripheral can program programmable read-only memories by plugging personality cards into the appropriate PROM programmer card socket. One PROM programmer includes provisions for two personality cards and corresponding zero-insertion force PROM programming sockets (one 16-pin and one 24-pin). When users plug the appropriate personality card into the PROM programmer mainframe, they can program and verify PROMs.

PROM programming. To store microprograms, the PROM has to be programmed, and machine language programming is the basic method of programming. The machine language user is expected to have a sound understanding of the microcomputer organization and the significance of the instruction set.

RAM (random access memory). Random access memory is random because it provides access to any storage location point in the memory immediately by means of vertical and horizontal coordinates. Information may be "written" in or "read" out in the same very fast procedure.

RAM capability. Semiconductor R/W (read-write) RAM memories are available with access times from 2NS to 3μsec and in sizes from 4 bits to 4096 bits per package. RAM R/W memories obviously play their most important role as the elements that provide the mechanism for software designers to program the logic of all programmable logic systems.

RAM card systems. RAM card systems are replacing core memory systems with less costly, higher density, faster solid-state systems built with 4096-bit RAMS. A typical card, for example, is a custom 16K × 18 system, complete with control logic, that is now used in a popular minicomputer as a replacement add-on for a more costly core memory with only half the storage density.

RAM operation. During a cycle, a logical "one" on a write/I-O line is interpreted by the RAM as a write enable command, and data on the bus will be written in to RAM. Generally, a RAM is a nondestructive readout device and, therefore, is always programmed to read; however, it must be instructed to "write."

Read-only memory (ROM) programs. Users have to be sure that their program is right before they enable it into a ROM. On most computers, once enabled, the program gives no flexibilities that are not an inherent outcome of the encoded instruction sequence. This can be inconvenient if users plan to load data from a peripheral device, process it in some ways, and then store it.

Registers, general purpose. Some microcontrollers provide 16 GPRs (general-purpose registers) and an ALU. If users assign one of the registers as the program counter, this still leaves 15 GPRs. Other circuits needed to complete the CPU are an instruction register, a memory-address register and instruction-execution control logic. To design the instruction-execution logic, users must define the instruction format and the execution sequence for each instruction. The instruction format determines how the instruction will be decoded.

ROM (read-only memory). A blank ROM can be considered to be a mosaic of undifferentiated cells. Many types of ROMs exist. A basic type of ROM is one programmed by a mask pattern as part of the final manufacturing stage. PROMs are "programmable" ROMs. ROMs are relatively permanent although they can be erased with the aid of an ultraviolet irradiation instrument. Others can be electrically erased and are called EPROMs.

ROM loader. A typical binary loader program is implemented in read-only memory. It eliminates the manual bootstrap loading procedure. Typically consists of a 3" × 2.5" printed circuit card that plugs into sockets located inside the processor enclosure and comes complete with documentation.

Semiconductor technologies. Various different semiconductor technologies are used for fabricating LSI arrays: bipolar, p-channel MOS and CMOS (complementary metal-oxide semiconductor). The bipolar and p-channel MOS techniques require load resistors through which the current passes when the transistor conducts. This wastes power and heats the chip, which limits the packing density by virtue of this "thermal barrier." The CMOS technique, however, uses both p- and n-type transistors in series. The signal that turns the n-transistor on, turns the p-transistor off— and vice versa. There is never a path to ground for the current except through an external load. This saving in operation power is particularly advantageous in battery operated devices.

Sensor-based computer. A type of computer designed and programmed to receive real-time data (analog or digital) from transducers, sensors, and other data sources that monitor a physical process. The computer may also generate signals to elements that control the process. For example, the computer might receive data from a gauge or flowmeter, compare the data with a predetermined standard, and then produce a signal that operates a relay, valve, or other control mechanism.

Service routine. Refers to a routine designed to assist in the actual operation of the computer and a broad class of routines that are standardized at a particular installation for the purpose of assisting in maintenance and operation of the computer as well as the preparation of programs as opposed to routines for the actual solution of production problems. This class includes monitoring or supervisory routines, assemblers, compilers, diagnostics for computer malfunctions, simulation of peripheral equipment, general diagnostics, and input data. The distinguishing quality of

171

service routines is that they are generally standardized so as to meet the servicing needs at a particular installation, independent of any specific production type routine requiring such services.

Shift. Displacement of an ordered set of computer characters one or more places to the left or right. If the characters are the digits of a numerical expression, a shift is equivalent to multiplying by a power of the base.

Silicon, processing. Basic techniques of forming a dielectric layer on a semiconductor surface sound complicated, but the simplicity of thermally oxidizing a silicone surface, the low diffusion coefficients of most dopants in the resulting silicon dioxide, and the ease of etching without attacking the silicon itself are key factors leading to development of the silicon planar process.

Slice architecture. In a "slice" architecture, a section of the register file and ALU in a computer is placed in one package. In some systems the registers are all four bits wide; others accommodate two bits. Each end of each register is accessible through the ALU at chip's edge; two or more of these "slices" can be cascaded together to form larger word sizes. Whether instruction lengths are identical to data word size or not depends upon how the control portion of the processor is organized. In some systems another chip in the set provides eight microprogrammed control sections.

Slices, bipolar. Bipolar/LSI microprocessor slices offer several advantages over standard MOS. The bipolar speeds of "bit slice" processors, or microcontrollers, assure a precise emulation of conventional systems, which employ standard-bipolar circuits. By using microprogramming techniques, designers can replace scores of SSI and MSI packages at reduced power. And in applications such as minicomputers, processor slices provide the hardware flexibility to reduce equipment size without changes in existing software.

Software, microcomputer (typical system). Standard software for many micros includes an assembler, loader, debugging utility, source edit utility, and diagnostic programs. The assembler translates symbolic assembly language programs into executable machine programs. The loader loads object tapes produced by the assembler or debugging utility. The debugging utility aids program check-out and features multiple breakpoints, instruction trace, and several other standard functions. The source edit utility is used to generate assembly language source tapes or modify existing source tapes. The diagnostics are used to verify processor operation. The cross assembler enables programs written for the micro to be assembled on IBM 360/370 and other series computers.

Time-shared computer utility. Generally refers to the special computational ability of time-shared computer systems. Programs as well as data may be made available to the user. The user also may have his or her own programs immediately available to the central processor or may have them on call at the computer utility, or he or she may load them by transmitting them to the computer prior to using them. Certain data and programs are shared by all users of the service; other data and programs because of proprietary nature, have restricted access. Computer utilities are generally accessed by means of data communication subsystems.

Transistor, MOSFET operation. The field effect transistor (FET), the metal oxide semiconductor (MOS), and the MOSFET operation have become very popular. Junction transistors are often called bipolar devices because two types of current carriers, the free electron and the positive hole, are involved in their operation. The MOSFET operates quite differently. The fabrication of the MOS device is based upon the planar technique. Because of its inherent construction features, the MOSFET can be fabricated in a smaller area than the bipolar transistor, allowing a higher element density and lower costs. The channels between source and drain can be used as a resistor whose value depends upon the gate potential and the transconductance of the structure. These resistors are smaller than bipolar resistors, allowing even greater density of elements.

Venn diagrams. Diagrams in which circles or ellipses are used to give a graphic representation of basic logic relations. Logic relations between classes, operations on classes, and the terms of the propositions are illustrated and defined by the inclusion, exclusion, or intersection of these figures. Shading indicates empty areas, crosses indicate areas that are not empty, and blank spaces indicate areas that may be either. Named for English logician John Venn, who devised them.

5

The Available
Microsystem
Products—
Systems
and
Criteria

THE MINICOMPUTER AND MICROCOMPUTER
INDUSTRY TODAY AND IN THE FUTURE

Minicomputer and microcomputer manufacturers are very aggressive, intensive, and inventive. The "technological imperative" is working most demonstrably in this area. The financial power of a score or more recent start-up microcomputer manufacturers is now extremely firm. Other strong leaders in the micro field are large, older instrument houses (Hewlett-Packard, Tektronix, and so on). This industry is strongly applications-oriented. The standard computer manufacturers were not for the last 20 years. The "big five" standard computer manufacturers—IBM, Univac, Honeywell, Burroughs, NCR (Xerox, GE, RCA, and others have now exited)—are beginning finally to receive heavy competition from these eager, now major, microcomputer and minicomputer manufacturers. But the toughest competition is coming from the makers of the components and "chips," such as Intel; Texas Instruments, Inc.; Motorola; Fairchild Industries; Rockwell International; National Semiconductor, Inc.; Signetics; Mostek; and so on. All are now fully in the computer business. With the recent announcement of $5, $10, and $30 micros (in job lot volumes), several companies are competing fiercely and are striving diligently with scores of new product introductions to capture big portions of the vast worldwide communications, point of sale, and machine tool automation markets. Also, new lower-cost, higher-reliability manufacturing processes such as silicon on sapphire, CMOS, I^2L, and so on, on chips and PC boards are being developed rapidly (See end-of-chapter definitions). The advantages of these new techniques are even higher speeds, greater reliability, and tighter compactness, as well as faster automated assembly. Although competition will increase among the micro manufacturing giants, many small size firms will join to innovate applications of these microminiaturized low-cost units further. Because they require very little power to operate and continue to use ROMs and RAMs to reduce complexity and costs of operating systems and applications programming, the ease of use, the mass availability of standard programs, and the relative simplicity of developing and "plugging" in new programs are so important to the micro revolution that a full chapter of this book is devoted specifically to microcomputer software.

The reducing cost of microcomputers

Reduced costs of microcomputers are based on (1) expanding varieties and increased unit demands of markets for the tiny, powerful, versatile solid-state devices; (2) new mass-production techniques for integrated circuits and silicon wafers containing them; (3) the realizable potential and consequent aggressiveness for further improvement of the systems; and (4) increasing sales. For example, experience has shown how the unit cost of an integrated circuit element has come down as production improvements have gone up. The ratio, according to a leading manufacturer, is about 10 to 1: "Every time we make 100 times as many units, the cost drops by a factor of 10." Integrated circuit memories, for example, in 1973 cost between 0.3 and 3 cents per bit; it is confidently expected that well before 1980 they may cost from 0.05 to 0.03 cents. Another trend that experience has signified relates to the complexity that can be almost routinely achieved in integrated circuits. For example, the number of elements that can be combined into a single device and the number of functions it can perform have practically doubled every year since the first such circuits were built a decade ago, and designers foresee no reason for this trend to stop.

Microcomputer applications: the field grows . . . and grows

The potential applications of microprocessors and microcomputers extend over the broadest spectrum of control and information products. Their largest quantity to date has been in electronic calculators—in extremely high volume quantities. This market segment has dictated much of the early architecture of many microcomputers. Terminals were the next major market area to utilize microcomputers. Low-cost data terminals now routinely use microprocessors for simple data-handling tasks. Remote terminals, by the addition of a microprocessor, become "intelligent" and perform many special capabilities, such as off-line editing, computing, and processing. Point of sale (POS) terminals add significantly to micro sales as they perform calculations and data storage and inventory control functions and control keyboard, tag reader, display, and printer peripherals, and so on, under microcomputer control.

Microprocessors are also very useful for tasks within and/or normally associated with large-scale systems. In addition to performing channel control and various switching and preprocessing communications functions, they relieve the large central processor of the overhead associated with scheduling, text editing, or file management. In a similar manner, microprocessors can be used for sequencing, control, formating, and error detection in tape or disk units. It is probable that more microprocessors will be buried in computer peripherals than will be used as computing devices. Other types of microprocessors, combined with low-cost memory and moderate performance peripherals like floppy disks, CRT displays, or medium-speed printers, can provide all the processing power needed for many applications. A large multi-user computer system may soon be needed only for accessing large, on-line data bases or for a few CPU-bound program tasks. Although the two final chapters are devoted to microcomputer applications, it will serve the reader well to note the ranges of applications listed as follows as he or she analyzes the control products defined in this chapter. In brief summary, microprocessors and microcomputers are now being applied to the following types of equipment, among many others.

1. Calculators, both programmable and fixed-function.
2. Small business/accounting computers.
3. Terminals, both keyboard and special-purpose.
4. Production and process control equipment and robots.
5. Measurement systems, from panel meters to full-scale monitoring and other instrumentation systems.
6. Automotive transportation and traffic control systems.
7. Medical equipment and hospital systems.
8. Education devices and terminals.
9. Communication.
10. Computer peripherals and system control devices.

In effect, microprocessors and microcomputers are substituting, enhancing, or replacing conventional minicomputers and controllers in many applications. This is especially true where minis or controllers are overpriced or overpowered. Speeds of minicomputers have increased over the years owing to changing technology rather than in response to an overall need. Very great cost reductions are being realized by producing massive micro power, thus forcing reexaminations of all types of computer price-performance trade-offs in the areas previously mentioned and new applications formerly not considered possible.

The milestones to microcomputer progress

To gain better perspective of the impact of the microcomputer on the total computer scene, one must carefully examine some specific milestones that have occurred in the immediate past. We have noted that large numbers of microcomputers are being sold and sales continue to accelerate significantly owing to sudden technological breakthroughs in computer logic and memory. Predictions of the numbers of products sold for the 1980 timeframe are occurring instead in the 1976–1978 period, especially as regards surprising new computer capabilities, nanosecond speeds, and reductions in sizes and costs of products. Totally unanticipated and very widespread are consumer applications of microsystems being successfully marketed currently, as noted more fully in Chapters 8 and 9. This is fully five, and perhaps ten, years before the original expectations. The surprising microcomputer developments have been considered by most experts to be "the leading edge of a new computer revolution," or "the pivotal point for tremendous advances" in the new, reinvigorated semiconductor industry. These advances spawned feedback and impact upheavals on practically every phase of computer memory, architecture, information systems, and device control. Many writers see the microprocessor as a phenomenal new invention with powers and capabilities that are well beyond current man's predictive attributes. Such bold capability claims and quite remarkable applications statements beg analysis.

Is it realistic to believe that we are at a major turning point of computer developments and applications? Two major conclusions can be discerned. First, micros have certainly provided a great many machine and information system control designers with effective new hardware and system capabilities that heretofore were too costly or complex to consider at all. The second blanket impact or conclusion is the clear fact that more actual working computers are being produced in one 18-month period than were sold in any previous decade. This totally unpredicted happenstance came about in stages. The impact of microcomputer proliferation and expanding microcomputer capability has been to capture and outperform many of the applications formerly restricted to the expensive and complex small, medium, and large computer systems. The microcomputer developed its own particular milestones, as noted further on.

A major event occurred in 1972, when the number of minicomputers in use in the United States exceeded the total of the classical or standard computers. It required only seven years for the minicomputers, introduced initially in 1965, to accomplish this. However, more significant was the introduction of the computer-on-a-chip in 1971. The micro was still at that point when it was considered as only a minor subsystem or a component in a growing number of devices—primarily in calculators, terminals, and communications devices. It required only three years, however, until 1974, for the total number of microcomputers produced to exceed the number of all mini, small, medium, and large-scale computers then in existence. Microcomputers are suddenly everywhere—embedded within thousands of devices, usable as control devices in supermarkets, automobiles, testing, and communication instruments and as stand-alone computers in their own right. As predicted 20 years earlier, computers have now very suddenly and dramatically impacted many segments of the consumer markets. Of major significance relative to the future, these events, in effect, point to the coming demise of the former very costly, large, or "maxicomputer" approaches to computer development, manufacturing, and marketing procedures and policies.

Along with the massive acceptance of the newest micro technologies have come drastic reductions in design and production cost, labor input, and time required to design and implement new computer systems. The new computer industry is characterized by the rapidly developed new designs, massive manufacturing quantities, very short lead-time to implementation, and quick prototype to marketable product successes. Equipment and new program designs have produced systems of easily controlled, new, and varied pragmatic applications. Where products and systems prior to 1972 might have required three to five years for development from concept to design to implementation, with microcomputers, such products and systems become "profitable" within a few months to a year. This is accomplished so often and by so many innovations that it has baffled the "traditionalists" and amazed even the "futurists."

As the first generation of microcomputers evolved, the champions of big systems and software complexity grudgingly agreed the micros were loaded with promise, but they maintained they were much too slow and almost totally lacked software support. However, these "progress doubts" were soon erased. The second generation of micros that appeared in surprising quantities in 1974 were ten times faster than the original micro powerhouses . . . with 2-microsecond instruction speeds for most and faster nanosecond speeds for others. Instead of their being handicapped by programming and software, the opposite occurred. A new prime consideration must be examined, which is the differential between the cost of executing an instruction and the cost of programming an instruction. Owing to the significant cost-effectiveness of microcomputer hardware, this gap has now grown to an enormous figure. This huge gap has led to the design of many new, more efficient software/hardware design combinations. In consequence, more and more hardware features have changed. Thousands of programs are now cast in hardware and are called "firmware" and are in the form of ROMs, RAMs, PROMs, CROMs, and so on. These very substantially reduce the cost and time constraints of program availability and new program development. The clear prognostication of the future is one of quite dramatic and unusual reductions in applications and control program costs. A proliferation of these thousands of "standard" and/or easily developed "pluggable" programs makes the "hardware" even more cost-effective and valuable. And it is already difficult to imagine how explosive the numbers and ranges of available software products might become. Already programmable calculator manufacturers, using many varieties of microprocessors very extensively, offer "software" such as cards, strips, cassettes, chips, ROMs, and boards at very low cost or "free" as sales enticers. Four major time-sharing computer service companies immediately collaborated with such major microcomputer manufacturers as Intel, Motorola, and others to offer microcomputer users simple programming techniques on their networks of hundreds of thousands of terminals in all major cities in the world.

We have already noted the sudden and dramatic reduction of hardware costs owing to the plunging costs of manufacturing microminiaturized logic and memory. Equally as significant was the use of microcircuits in peripheral equipment and communications terminals and devices. By the reduction of their size and complexity, costs also dropped quickly and competitively. While processors began selling in quantity for from $20 to $50, RAMs and ROMs were selling for from $8 to $15, also in large quantity lots.

"Smart" CRT terminals containing these components had costs that fell from original late 1960 prices of $3,000 to $5,000 for entry and editing types to from $700 to $2,000 in 1974. Similar reductions were realized in many sophisticated graphic and standard "intelligent" types. And because many types of software for standard systems still contained a great number of "human" costs, a strong trend was immediately begun to substitute much more of the highly reliable and less costly "firmware" to reduce these total system costs. Also RAMs, ROMs, PROMs, and other firmware or "wired software" are being used more and more in standard and minisystems. These are low-cost devices performing and replacing many of the high-cost, complex, less reliable items in (1) source data terminals; (2) data and file management systems; (3) operating systems and internal control functions; (4) applications software and programmable functions; and (5) error detection, correction, and miscellaneous functions.

The abrupt changes in software/firmware costs and availability

With the expanding use of more firmware and hardware and the additional advantage of the tiny size of the components, the new great power of miniaturized circuit boards represents odd-shaped but powerful and versatile computers. Many more achievements and innovations are now also possible in other system areas: (1) increased reliability and data entry availability is easily and quickly developed through the addition of more checking, measuring, and redundancy as through microprocessor fault-discovery and fault-tolerant features; (2) more dedicated systems are cost-effective with the practical elimination of much of the error-prone older user programs; (3) many systems can now cheaply and quickly be made into tutorial types making them much easier to use or to change, adapt, and expand; (4) owing to mass production and the ease of use of ROMs and RAMs, rapidly increased use of much more memory is certain because it is now also microminiaturized, cheap, and fast; and (5) primary shifting of current and future trends indicates extensive use of many microcomputers as minor subsystem components causing increased use of multiminis containing "stacked" micros with multiplied power, applications versatility, and system adaptability. All this seems to permit the very happy and safe economic dedication of large amounts of versatile logic and memory for the supply of "intelligence" to practically any imaginable operating, measuring, control, or information manipulation system.

Thus the "hard" software trends make it advisable and economical to put many complex subroutines and programs into hardware. The rapidly expanding programmable calculator markets clearly prove this. The unusual, very high popularity of these with consumers, engineers, and all types of professionals and general business has been most remarkable. The low cost, increased reliability, and easy integration have forced increased use of intelligent polysystems by small and medium-sized manufacturers and educational business, and government institutions. In net effect, microprocessors for $20 or $40 singly or as stacked into multiunits and grouped (at even lower prices per part) make most of the formerly automatic but "dumb" peripherals, automobiles, terminals, household appliances, and so on now able to become individually intelligent, that is, programmable. To those devices or components already made "smart" with processors, programmed ROMs, and so on, additional microprocessors provide parallel addition of even more computer power and versatility. And many of these electronic blessings as substitutes for other systems and energies are arriving just in time. The cost of paper and other communications media has been increasing exponentially while the costs of their new substituting devices of electronic storage and information dispersal are even more rapidly decreasing. A quick summary of some of these near miracles is presented later. A full discussion of microsystem applications (Chapters 8 and 9) is dedicated to the electronic developments in energy conservation and discovery. Dedicated, integrated, distributive information networks became cost-effective with the simultaneous use of microminiaturized electronics and satellite-provided, self-contained, and addressed packet-switching systems. Remote and interactive (real-time) teleprocessing hardware and software developments now also permit microprocessed on-line debugging, maintenance, and system alteration. The result is a totally unpredicated volume of terminals in use today and also in demand by the millions for the late 1970s.

It is a fact of life for all mini-based systems that the biggest system expense quickly became add-on memory. However, the microsystems' mass memory is less cost-dominating. The advantages of extremely tiny size and exceptionally low cost have also had beneficial effects on the need for a smaller number of memory modules. New micro memory architecture, very adequate ROM and RAM, increasing speed of access, and new very heavy but still low-cost memory densities are not all that difficult to organize with micros. Modular memory organization and new hierarchies of add-ons create significant microprocessor diversity in organization, structure, and distributed application utilization; thus many micros spread in more places require less costly memory than equivalent maxi systems. Microsystems, because of the speed and implementation from original design and quick progress from implementation to wide acceptance and simpler, cheaper, faster, easier-to-use software, allow bigger problems to be solved at much lower human and machine cost. These systems are also more reliable and transparent to the user. Thus much more sophistication and reliability are placed in the hardware instead of the expensive, complex software. Cost/performance effectiveness is fast and easily proved. This is contrasted with developments and trends of memory in standard systems, where advances were always very slow, usually requiring five to six years for changes in types and hierarchies. Price reductions or relief for designers from some of the constraints of large size, power, and refrigeration requirements and so on were rare. The "standard" manufacturers are now forced to copy from the micros and use ROMs, CCDs, bubbles, cassettes, and so on, all now rapidly being competitively developed and for very, very high production rates and low costs.

Managers and micro technology

Because microprocessor techniques of information control have become almost predominant in computers, terminals, communications, production, and almost all other automation techniques, most managers now require an understanding of semiconductors. Processing techniques force a willingness to experiment with new layouts and materials. The solid-state industry is already at sophisticated heights of 16-bit microprocessors, 32,728-bit and larger "chip" memories, 65,456-bit charge-coupled devices, and linear large-scale integration. Performance and bit densities promise to go right on climbing while prices fall.

MOS semiconductor technology has been developed into a formidable arsenal of fast, reliable, microminiaturized integrated circuit (IC) devices. These can be deployed to perform nearly any system function imaginable. LSI digital technology, using improved n-channel and complementary-MOS processing techniques on the one hand and revamped, high-density bipolar techniques on the other, are teaming with new linear-MOS capabilities to provide increasingly more powerful design options and to create unprecedented equipment performance. The five key items are as follows:

1. *LSI processors.* Basic 8-bit n-channel microprocessors offer the versatility of 70 to 90 instructions at 1- and 2-microsecond speeds. These bus-oriented CPU designs can be interfaced with matched input/output chips, such as modems and data-acquisition circuits, to provide a wide range of programmable computer-control applications. Latest to arrive were 16-bit microprocessors with improved n- and p-channel process on single low-cost chips that deliver economy and performance. Many are used in industrial applications as numerical controllers and data-acquisition systems and for monitoring car-engine and other parameters, and so on. Also TTL LSI processors have emerged in families of computer components to add automated performance to industrial and computer-system designs. Moreover, new bipolar techniques called integrated injection logic (I^2L) are developed for 8-bit and 16-bit single-chip bipolar processors that provide designers a strong alternative to today's n-channel and TTL devices. (See definition detail at the end of the chapter.)

2. *Bipolar LSI.* High-performance bipolar capability on large chips at reduced cost is everywhere. Many consider integrated injection logic to be an ideal technique in this respect. I^2L chips being readied at laboratories throughout the world may contain more than 3,000 gates operating at speed faster than 10 nanoseconds and generally dissipate only 1 nanowatt of power. And long-abandoned logic forms, such as resistor-transistor logic, have new life from such new LSI-processing techniques as implanted transistor elements and passive isolation.

3. *Linear devices.* I^2L structures have emerged in LSI linear devices, such as analog-to-digital-converter chips, digital tuners, and tone controls. Mixed processing techniques are now packaging single- and double-channel MOS structures on conventional bipolar chips to boost significantly the performance of operational amplifiers, digital-to-analog converters, comparators, and integrators.

4. *Standard logic.* LSI-circuit techniques are being applied to the fastest and most demanding jobs in mainframe controllers, megabit communications terminals, gigahertz counter circuits, and military and industrial computer equipment of all kinds. Schottky TTL and low-powered Schottky are now standard families. Complementary-MOS families, some built with space-saving, oxide-isolation processing techniques, can pack more functions onto small chips, and silicon-on-sapphire (SOS) substrates are boosting C-MOS speed into the TTL range.

5. *Memories.* Fast 1,024-bit to 32,728-bit dynamic n-channel random access memories are now into volume production, and static n-channel devices with high speed 300-nanosecond access times have become widely available. Bipolar RAMs moved in two directions: very fast 256-bit and 1,024-bit emitter-coupled logic devices with access times typi-

cally as low as 20 ns for the fastest cache and scratch pad applications and low-power versions of the 1,024-bit transistor-transistor-logic devices for heavy-duty mainframe subsystems. Complementary-MOS structures, in addition to their well-known logic capabilities, have united with silicon-on-sapphire substrates to create a new class of low-power, high-density memory devices for low-power industrial and aerospace systems; and charge-coupled memory devices that can replace moving disks and drums are competing successfully. The 32-kilobit and 64-kilobit CCD (charge-coupled devices) chips are revolutionary in themselves.

Microprocessors have been and are now making many mass-media headlines. No segment of semiconductor technology has moved faster in the last few years than semiconductor control devices and semiconductor memory types that now span whole new spectra of applications, from the microsecond and micropower requirements of today's terminals and portable memory equipment through 100- to 500-nanosecond mainframe and peripheral-controller applications all the way to the faster 20-nanosecond computer-buffer scratch pad communications switching functions.

Potentially the cheapest way of satisfying the needs of medium-speed mainframes and large peripheral controllers is to apply the capabilities of the 4,096-bit n-channel RAM, which offers four times as much memory on the same-size chip and operates at about the same speed as the 1,024-bit p-channel devices. RAMs built with C-MOS techniques are available in volume. Initially at the 256-bit level, they have now reached the 1,024- (and higher) bit level. Having low standby power dissipation, high noise immunity, and high power-supply tolerance, they are particularly useful in industrial and portable memory equipment. C-MOS RAMs are proliferating throughout the computer-memory hierarchy. The prospect of power-supply-tolerant, noise-immune, 1,024-bit and 4,096-bit static C-MOS-on-sapphire RAMs, operating off 5 volts at speeds below 100 ns is very real. Memory-component manufacturers are ready to use their established n-channel processes in combination with SOS substrates. These could be the next high-density memory technology—a massive 16-kilobit memory chip capable of 300-nanosecond access time.

There is now developing an increasingly powerful array of single-chip processors. They serve as the hearts of the new low-cost microcomputers, minicomputer controllers, and data-processing systems. The 12-bit and 16-bit n- and p-channel microprocessors offer minicomputer-processor capability on single, low-cost LSI chips. This is the technology needed for the complex real-time control jobs, such as automobile-engine monitoring, cockpit-panel control, high-speed chemical processors, and the like. The technology is moving to tighter n-channel designs, combined with such process innovations as using insulating substrates of sapphire and spinel to boost processing speed and lower-power consumption. Now, too, processor activities are the newly available bipolar LSI circuits that go to the heart of minicomputer-control applications. These LSI processor chips enable designers to emulate most of today's 16-bit minicomputers, as well as to build into their equipment sophisticated microprogrammable control capabilities. Typical cycle times of 70 ns and capacity of 120 and more instructions in a set make LSI bipolar-processor technology for the first time suitable for medium-scale computing applications, for both traditional minicomputer manufacturers and independent designers of control systems. These families have been greatly enlarged, both in types and performance. Standard TTL still dominates main-line logic applications—all the timing, processing, and controlling that make up the bulk of instrument and computer-mainframe and peripheral logic. Moderate prices for moderate speeds are generally the key. For LSI designs, new and revived bipolar circuits of integrated injection logic are making their impact. High-speed technology is still dominated by ECL (emitter-coupled logic) designs, though they are encountering some competition from Schottky TTLs. Finally, for the industrial environment, where noise immunity and protection from power-supply variations are the chief considerations, but high speed is rarely needed, C-MOS is still the best bet.

Of the many kinds of bipolar LSI available, the latest integrated injection logic caught the imagination of logic designers throughout the world with its high density and its high performance—nanosecond delays and microwatt power dissipation. I^2L circuits are appearing in a multitude of old and new applications: single-chip digital data processors, LSI logic arrays, watch chips, digital voltmeter circuits, high-frequency counters, digital tuners, read-only memories, shift registers, converters of all kinds, control logic for complex calculators, frequency dividers for electronic organs, and linear circuits for radio and television. Commercial production of 8- and 16-bit microprocessors and high-frequency watch circuits is plentiful.

At this early stage of microprocessor development, a wide variety of devices exist. These microprocessors may be classified as calculator chips, 8-bit processors, bit-slice devices, and emulators.

1. *Four-bit processors* are principally calculator chips and were the first microprocessors. They can serially process 4-bit words with binary coded decimal (BCD) arithmetic. Based on PMOS technology, they are generally pin-limited (16 pins) and relatively slow. However, they can be designed into microcomputers with instruction execution times in milliseconds. Examples of 4-bit microcomputers include Intel's Intellec 4 and Teledyne's TDY-52A.

2. *Eight-bit processors* capitalize on the current advanced technology. Intel and Rockwell began them with the PMOS 8008 and PPS-8. Newer 8-bit processor designs have switched to NMOS, bipolar, or CMOS

technologies. Instruction execution times are now comparable to those of minicomputers—less than $5\mu s$ per average instruction. Eight-bit byte handling applications are commonly found in communications systems. Compared to PMOS devices, NMOS chips offer improved speed and gate density. Furthermore, the number of pins per component has jumped from 18 or 24 to 40, which increases performance by transmitting address and data in parallel. New NMOS 8-bit processors include Intel's 8080 and Motorola's M6800. And an important competitor is RCA's Cosmac, which uses CMOS technology for low power dissipation and which will eventually be produced with silicon-on-sapphire substrates (SOS). Like Motorola's M6800 and unlike microprocessors from smaller suppliers, RCA's 8-bit processor has come with software and support hardware.

3. *Bit-slice processors* allow microcomputer organizations of variable word sizes, with processor units separated into 2-, 4-, or 8-bit slices on a single chip. These devices can be parallel to yield an 8-, 12-, 16-, 24- or 32-bit microcomputer when assembled with the other necessary "overhead" components of the system. Sixteen-bit microprocessors constructed from these components can be assembled into microcomputers that perform in the minicomputer class. Examples include National Semiconductor's IMP-16 and Teledyne's TDY-52B. Intel's 3000 series microprocessor chip set is a bipolar slice of two bits. National's 5750 is based on a PMOS 4-bit slice. Raytheon has a fast ECL (emitter-coupled logic) bipolar 4-bit slice—four of them and a CROM become the RP-16 microprocessor—which, like others with double precision, can operate in 32-bit configurations.

4. *Emulators* produce low-cost "versions" of the mini manufacturers' own products, but using microprocessors and "chips." General Automation, Computer Automation, DEC, and others are in this class of manufacturer of special microprocessor chips for emulation systems. Many micro manufacturers will undoubtedly copy several popular brands of minis. The bit-slice microprocessors can easily replace minis owing to greater production volumes and massive slashes in costs. CMOS units reduce power needs—and hundreds of thousands of micros will be sold to control and reduce energy uses.

See Appendix A for further discussion of competing microcomputer systems.

MODERN APPROACH TO CONTROL LOGIC

The development of microprocessors in the mid-1970s has spawned the use of microsystem technology in whole new ranges of design applications. The use of LSI technology to fabricate microprocessors has made low-cost programmable digital logic available for dedicated applications in data communications and control.

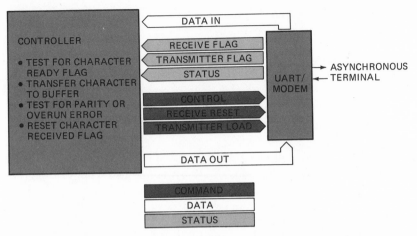

FIGURE 5.1. Data communications application. An asynchronous terminal data input and data output lines are connected to a universal asynchronous receiver transmitter (UART) circuit, which converts a serial bit stream to eight bits of parallel data and vice versa. The controller tests for a character received by testing the *receive flag*. An 8-bit character is transferred off the *data in* lines to a buffer memory area in the controller for further processing. Error conditions are tested to insure character integrity, and finally the *receive flag* is cleared, indicating to the UART/modem that the previous character has been transferred.

Classes of control applications

Device Control
    Computer Peripherals
    Machine tools
Data Control
    Switching
    Concentration
Process Control
    Discrete
    Continuous

Three of the many classes of control applications:

1. *Device Control.* A single machine tool or computer peripheral is sequenced through its different operations.
2. *Data Control.* Data from one or more sources must be moved to one or more destinations, or multiple low-speed data paths are concentrated into a higher-speed data path. Examples include multiple channel analog acquisition systems, data communication message switches, or data communication line controllers.

3. *Process Control.* Discrete inputs from measured process variables are used in a closed loop environment. Examples of assembly line control are automobile or appliance manufacture or continuous steel/aluminum smelting operations.

MICROPROCESSORS AND MICROCOMPUTERS: SPECIFIC PRODUCTS IN THE MARKETPLACE

In order to grasp and interpret the concepts of microprocessors and microcomputers more adequately, it is always advantageous to compare and contrast several of the products in being. This section follows this procedure. In early 1974, for example, Honeywell Information Systems had developed one called NUBLU, which is an acronym derived from *basic logic unit* (BLU). BLUs are being used in a number of different products, one being a banking teller terminal, BLU provides the terminal's built-in intelligence. Because BLU was designed to be application-flexible, some people called it an "information motor"; that is, just plug it in where information-processing power is required.

BLU flexibility comes from a read-only memory (ROM) containing a microprogram that defines the microprocessor instruction set and from a second ROM that contains an application program that uses the instruction set so defined. These ROMs are LSI chips and can be changed to alter a BLU microcomputer personality or intelligence. NUBLU is simply "new BLU," or new basic logic unit. It is an enhanced version of BLU and a test vehicle for experimenting with new LSI design techniques and technologies. BLU, the product version, served as Honeywell's base for improvement comparisons. The NUBLU chip's actual size is 3.4 millimeters on each side. That would be just slightly larger than twice the square area covered by the letter *M*. But many kinds of computer functions have been packed into that space, including a complete 8-bit arithmetic unit with a binary adder, carry-look-ahead logic, shift matrix, an accumulator, two special 8-bit registers, jump control logic, and lots of miscellaneous control.

A logical question would be, How many components would be required, using pre-LSI technology, to duplicate NUBLU's functions? The Honeywell answer: TTL (transistor-transistor logic) in small-scale integration form as it existed a few years ago would require 140 packages with some 2,000 external connections. The NUBLU chip has only 40 connections. With that much functionality packed into a 3.4 mm square, it would seem that microelectronic packing density is approaching that of nerve cells in the human brain. In two dimensions, their best localized storage density now is about one million bits per cm^2. That is about the same as nerve cell density in a thin slice of brain tissue. But designers have not done much with three-dimensional packing yet, and they lose much of the area density when they package and connect a chip to other electronic components. A packaged NUBLU chip, for example, is 50 mm × 12.5 mm.

It is interesting to note that one of the vacuum tube computers built in the early 1950s by ElectroData contained 1,500 tubes and used 15,000 watts of power. It executed about 50 different instructions, and it performed one addition in about 300 μs. How does NUBLU compare? This requires some explanation. So far we've only discussed the arithmetic unit in NUBLU. Other circuits are usually needed to form a complete microcomputer for application program and data storage, other registers, input/output circuitry, and control. Even a "one-chip" calculator has other chips in it for power, for generating timing signals, for driving its display panel, and so on. A microcomputer needs more components, mostly because more I/O and memory are involved. A "computer on a chip" exists only in a restricted sense. The whole NUBLU microcomputer, then, would be a relatively powerful machine compared to some commercially available microcomputer versions. With that qualification, a minimum useful configuration might consist of three circuitry boards: one for the CPU, one for program and data storage, and a third for circuits to interface with peripheral devices. The separated functions into these three boards are to allow a user to configure the amount of memory and I/O capability he wants in his system. The CPU board has some support circuits, the ALU (arithmetic-logic unit) chip and three other LSI chips. This computer can be compared to the ElectroData computer of the early 1950s as follows: if one considers one MOS transistor within an LSI chip to be equivalent to a vacuum tube, then just one NUBLU-ALU chip contains the same number of "tubes" as did the old ElectroData computers. The NUBLU instruction set, being defined by microcode, is not fixed to a specific number of instructions. The BLU chip applications, however, in 1973 used about 40 instructions. NUBLU add time was about 50 times faster than ElectroData's was. And only 10 W to 20 W as opposed to 15,000 W of power would be needed for the three-board configuration.

One must remember that the design approach must have a high level of interaction between people doing system design, logic design, circuit design, and chip layout. LSI allows an entire subsystem to be put on a chip; so the circuit and subsystem design trade-offs become intermeshed. Minimizing the number of transistors is not the game anymore. It is much more important to design logic that interconnects readily. Continuous interaction between the logician and the layout designer is a must. With MOS circuitry, a "breadboard" simulation may be useful to check the logic, but it cannot test electrical performance. That is where computers come in. A lot of logic and electrical simulation is done to prove a design before it is built. Computer programs help on chip layouts, too; the more layout done automatically, the fewer mistakes. Design automation programs are used to check manual layouts for dimensional mistakes.

Most designers believe LSI circuits will become the basic components of all computers in the future. This technology is moving the computer industry in many new directions. The level of integration on a single chip is continuing to get higher, and LSI, as defined today, will become the basic technology of future computers. LSI today is the cheapest way to implement large volume applications. How many new computers use discrete transistors for logic these days? Very few. In the future, most see microcomputer chips being used as standard components in various parts of electronic data-processing systems. Initially, these microcomputers will be invisible to the user except when used to create "intelligence" in terminals; that is, they will appear as one-for-one replacements for traditional hardwired logic subsystems such as I/O device control logic. The real impact will occur when the distributed intelligence potential of all these microcomputer subsystems can be harnessed. Perhaps more significant in the near future is that microcomputers are finding their way into a host of new applications that one does not usually associate with computers. This will introduce the concepts and feel of computers to a vast new group of people. This truly creates exciting new possibilities for many other industries as well.

AN ANALYSIS OF SOME MAJOR
BRANDS OF MICROCOMPUTERS

To understand the needs of microcomputer markets, we will briefly examine some of the products of the large semiconductor firms that have joined in fierce competition. Fairchild Camera and Instrument Corporation, one of the largest, has developed a family of microprogrammed MOS/LSI microprocessor blocks called the PPS 25 (Programmed Processor System). Equipment engineers have long recognized the desirability and flexibility of designing digital systems, using a microprogrammed processor as the heart of the design. Such systems are very practical in that they can be readily programmed around specific system requirements. The size and cost of minicomputers no longer limit their application to relatively large systems. With the availability of the PPS 25 and other similar units, extremely small microcomputer systems can be readily and economically designed. In fact, it was already possible for the equipment designer to develop small programmable digital processing systems for under $50, according to a Fairchild technical bulletin in 1974.

The PPS 25 microprocessor system was designed to fill the gap between intermediate to upper-end calculators and minicomputers. It substitutes a few MOS/LSI packages where normally several hundred TIL, MSI, or SSI packages (of larger, more expensive chips) would be required to implement the system function. The PPS 25 system has a versatile instruction set that permits the system to perform a wide variety of different functions. The

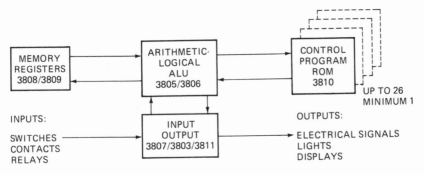

FIGURE 5.2. PPS 25 block diagram

general description: Fairchild's Programmed Processor System (PPS 25) is a microcomputer system that provides all the building blocks needed to construct a digital system that performs combinatorial and sequential logic and data storage. The heart of this bus-oriented system is comprised of two chips—the 3805 arithmetic unit and the 3806 function and timing unit. These two chips together perform all timing, control, and arithmetic functions. Auxiliary to these chips is the 3810 ROM, which stores microprograms and data look-up tables. The 3808 and 3809 shift register memory devices store data. Keyboards and control panels may be attached by using 3803 and 3807 input devices while data output to displays or other information-processing equipment is provided by the 3811 (see Figure 5.2).

The PPS 25, which is designed to be used as a digital arithmetic or control processor, may be used in several applications. These include business machines, desk top computers, cash registers and point of sale terminals, industrial positioning and sequencing controllers, elevator controllers, traffic light control systems, instrumentation controllers, electronic scales, hospital monitors, and medical analyzers.

Intel Corporation's popular model 8080

The original micros were based on many of the desirable architectural features copied from minis. But they were short on important characteristics of processing speed, multiple interfaces, and compatibility with other peripheral and memory devices. The second generation of microprocessors and microcomputers overcame these disadvantages and now match most minicomputers in all aspects. The Intel 8080, introduced in April of 1974, has a very fast typical execution time of 2 microseconds. It is a more powerful, versatile, single-chip, 40-pin TTL-compatible microcomputer that enjoys a speed improvement of ten to one over its immediate predecessor and is 100 times faster than the original device. The new micro also defeated the former interfacing problems and lack of multiple interrupts.

191

Even with these greater capabilities, the 8080 achieved lower costs because of newer production techniques, which placed the entire processor and all its complex functions as implemented in only about 5,000 transistors. It was initially priced at $360 in quantities up to 24, with significant discounts above that number, but the price dropped rapidly in 1975. It has 14 control lines, an eight-line bidirectional data bus, and a 16-line bus for addressing memory and for input-output selection. All systems controls are decoded on the CPU chip. Through its bus structures, the CPU directly accesses up to 64 kilobytes of memory. It can operate up to 256 input and 256 output channels (eight bits per channel) and handle up to eight interrupt levels. Although the 8080 can be used with standard logic and memory circuits, Intel also later introduced a family of memory and peripheral circuits designed specifically for the 8080. Thus it is an n-channel (NMOS) processor unit available with a set of software development packages. Source programs for the 8080 can be written in either Intel's programming language for microcomputers or PL/M, its new macroassembler language.

PL/M was also available initially on the terminals of several time-sharing networks: United Computing Systems, General Electric (more than 100 computers interconnected in 400 cities worldwide), and Tymshare, as well as from Intel on magnetic tape. The unit can process data in a decimal mode almost as fast as in binary mode; a number of CPUs would serve as peripheral controllers for an 8080 microcomputer system, with the CPUs sharing a common central memory. It has capability for double-precision arithmetic involving two 16-bit numbers. The software includes ROMs, RAMs, PROMs, communications interfaces, and so on in the form of assemblers, editors, simulators, and so forth, all available by remote terminal. A simple schematic of its components and operations is shown in Figure 5.3.

The new n-channel MOS devices outdid the first generation of p-channel microprocessors [1] in speed and instruction power. Needing fewer memory and peripheral support chips, they also economize on space and assembly costs, as both Intel's 8080 and Motorola's competitive chip set, the M6800, prove. N-channel silicon-gate technology also brought enlarged capacity and greater versatility because this technology can pack many more memory and logic structures onto one CPU chip. It also operates at high speed from 5-V (TTL) power supplies, and the new n-channel memories are also directly compatible. Practically all the other competing companies also were bringing out n-channel devices—economic feasibility with

---

[1] If the higher mobility of electrons versus holes were the only difference between the n-channel and p-channel technologies, only 2.4:1 improvement in speed could have been expected. But n-channel's power threshold allows use of a 5-volt supply for internal logic, with a 4:1 improvement in speed-power product. Also the higher substrate concentration of the n-channel starting material, combined with the lower supply voltage, allows channels to be shorter than with p-channel technology, so that input capacitance is lower and size is smaller.

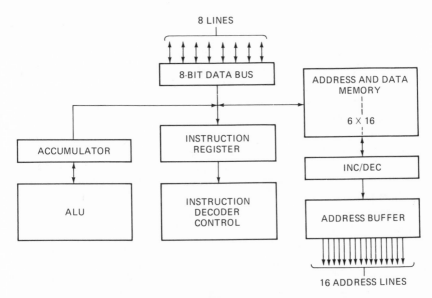

FIGURE 5.3. One of the first n-channel MOS microprocessors, Intel's lead microcomputer in 1974, set the pace for increased speed and improved instructions
Courtesy: Intel Corporation

small chips and conventional packaging. The interfacing requirements were
simplified because n-channel technology allows a big reduction of the
power dissipation of individual output buffer circuits, so that the 8080 Intel
unit could be packaged in a 40-pin package to include 30 buffers as against
the 12 on its predecessor. With 30 new instructions added to the original 48
of its predecessor, the 8080 had a speed improvement of 10:1 and 20:1 with
much smaller or dedicated storage requirements. In the unit, memories are
combined into a single internal 16-bit-wide memory with paired 8-bit register organization. The 8080's accumulator and its associated circuitry have
been moved into the arithmetic logic unit (ALU) section to speed up the
operation of the processor (data transfers between memory and ALU on the
internal data bus are, therefore, not required for arithmetic and logic operations). The 8080 memory is double-ended—information can be transferred
from the internal bus eight bits at a time, and 16-bit transfers can take place
from the address register. And the addition of decimal correction to the
ALU section enables binary and BCD arithmetic to be performed at about
equal speeds. The addition of many new, easy-to-use control and status signals simplifies interfacing, allows direct memory access, and helps in program debugging.

Instructions in the 8080 use one, two, or three bytes of storage. Each
instruction requires from one to five machine (or memory) cycles for fetch-

ing and execution. Machine cycles are called M_1, M_2, . . . M_5. Each machine cycle requires from three to five states—T_1, T_2, . . . T_5—for its completion. Each state has the duration of one clock period (0.5 microsecond). There are three other states (WAIT, HOLD, and HALT), which last from one to an indefinite number of clock periods each. At the maximum clock frequency of 2 megahertz, this means that assembly-language instructions can be executed in 3 to 9 microseconds. The 8080 will be used in new systems that were not feasible before because the first-generation microcomputers were not powerful enough.

The implications of all these microprocessor activities are tremendous for the computer industry. Many observers feel that the MOS microprocessor families now just emerging will have a bigger impact on the entire electronics industry than any other development in its history. Other LSI structures in 1974 brought out single-chip microcomputers combining the CPU, I/O, and memory in one LSI device—and these compete with the same sort of exciting new developments surrounding bipolar LSI processor work. This is now a priority in many semiconductor laboratories. The older very basic bipolar technology has also progressed to the point where full instruction microcomputer capability on a few LSI chips, but at even faster speed, is possible.

In brief, the great promise that programmable LSI circuits had just a few years ago for all types of control applications has indeed been fulfilled with the second generation systems now selling heavily around the world. The microprocessors are completely self-contained and have high power and versatility and are very easy to use—in thousands of cost-effective applications. They are designed to work nicely with a minimum number of memory and peripheral support chips, and all of these are supplied in coordinated families to permit utilization and operations off the same voltage and power-supply conditions as the CPU chip. The typical set contains the CPU chip, a RAM for fast scratch pad logic control, a ROM for storing the system's program parameters, and a set of input-output chips. The I/O chips enable the CPU to control a large variety of industrial, processing, and communications equipment—in management information systems, automated data capture, process and manufacturing control systems, peripheral and terminal hardware, testing, and measuring the parameter control systems of all types—from microcomputers in automobiles to control systems for traffic monitoring and interactive supervision and practically anything else that random-logic computers can be used to optimize. In all of the second generation systems, system designs and board layouts are neatly simplified. The complex interconnections required for large numbers of conventional ICs are replaced by highly reliable, low-cost ROMs. The only interconnect wiring on the printed-circuit cards runs between the various address and data buses and the I/O devices. The cost savings are not limited to direct circuit components costs; they also relate to other extensive sys-

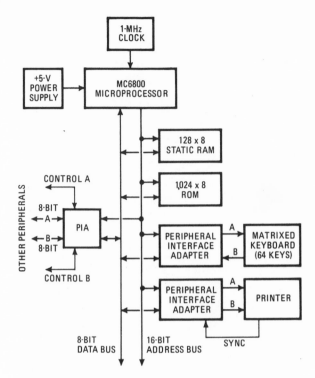

FIGURE 5.4. N-channel MOS technology yields new genera-
tion of microprocessors. *Reprinted with permission from*
Electronics, *April 18, 1974, copyright McGraw-Hill Book*
Co., all rights reserved.

tem hardware costs. Connectors can be decreased in number, cabling is
simplified, and the card cage is reduced in size, and so on. Associated indirect costs also have been considerably decreased because assembly takes
less time, documentation is simpler, and maintenance is very much easier
and less costly.

Further interpretation of the popular Intel 8080 microproces-
sor/microcomputer system is developed with the two diagrams shown in
Figure 5.5: (a) the basic, straightforward functional organization, and (b) the
state diagram showing the progress steps for the completion of an execution.

Motorola's n-channel 8-bit M6800

The Motorola n-channel 8-bit M6800 was announced about the same
time as the Intel 8080 microprocessor and competes with it in price and capability. These second generation n-channel units expanded system bene-

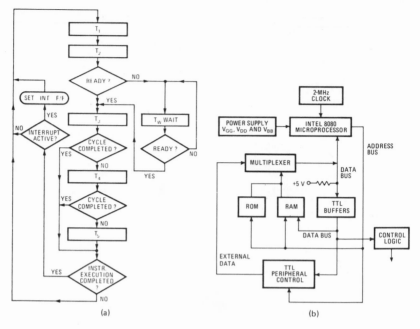

(a)   (b)

FIGURE 5.5. The Intel 8080 n-channel microprocessor. *Reprinted with permission from* Electronics, *April 18, 1974, copyright McGraw-Hill Book Co., all rights reserved.*

fits substantially over the first generation p-channel units. They offered more than 70 instructions versus the 40 previously available and required as few as four packages to build a complete 8-bit microcomputer. The M6800 further reduced its need to only one +5-volt power supply instead of Intel's three.

Besides other advantages such as speed and so on, board space, fewer packages, and lower components costs were the prime advantages, and total system capacity was increased. Besides cost savings in hardware, and so on, system engineers can also build proposed design changes very quickly. In most cases, hardware logic need not be simulated, optimized, or breadboarded.[2] The logic design portion of the cycle simply becomes the manipulation of functional building blocks; that is, the control sequence

[2] A breadboard is a gate-to-gate implementation of the CPU, employing basic gates and flip-flops, usually on 10 by 10-inch boards containing, for example, 400 to 500 packages. An engineering model is a functional implementation of the design and makes extensive use of logic packages and programmable ROMs to reduce package count. Microprocessors replace much of this by using single, as Intel and others, 40-pin packages containing a CPU chip—substituting for many formerly complex computer functions.

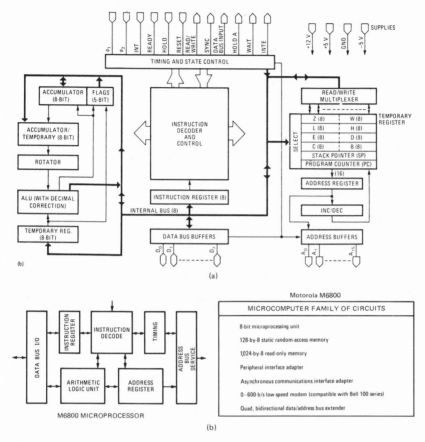

FIGURE 5.6. Functional organization comparisons: the Intel 8080 and Motorola M6800. *Reprinted with permission from* Electronics, *April 18, 1974, copyright Mc-Graw-Hill Book Co., all rights reserved.*

takes the form of writing a software program into an external ROM. Breadboarding consists of interconnecting a few LSI packages. This is also the case for modifying control programs, thus avoiding designing and laying out fresh logic. By simulating, most of the design can be verified even before it is committed to hardware, cutting design time by an estimated 90 percent. Typical instruction time for the M6800 is under 5 microseconds, and there is direct memory access on the chip. Up to 64 bytes of memory can be addressed in any combination of RAM, ROM, or peripheral registers. The adapter can interface with Teletype, displays, cassettes, test equipment, and so on, and even large computers for time-shared expansion of computer capability or modems for communications.

197

Texas Instrument's low-end microchip offerings

Texas Instruments approached the microprocessor chip market with a bipolar family of high-performance parts in early 1974. The Dallas-based company entered the lower end of the performance scale with p-channel metal-oxide semiconductors. The initial vehicle in 1975, the TMS 1000 microprocessor, is a derivative of TI's earlier work on calculator chips. Besides an arithmetic-logic unit and input/output circuitry, the device includes a 256-bit random access memory for data storage and an 8,192-bit read-only memory for program storage. This is an exceptional amount of capability in a chip measuring only 200 mils square. Moreover, although the TMS 1000 is roughly comparable to the Intel 4004 in terms of instruction set and execution times, the on-chip memories with which the device is furnished may well undercut Intel system costs. Price of the TMS 1000 will start at $20 and range down to $10 for 10,000-piece quantities, according to TI. Already in volume production, the microprocessor had as its first customer TI's own Calculator Products division, where it has been used in the recently announced SR-16 slide rule.

As with its calculator chips, TI's MOS microprocessor is mask-programmable during the final gate-mask step. The ROM and output logic array an each chip can thus be tailored to meet the user's applications. Applications, as defined by TI, cover a broad range of possibilities, including appliance controls, point of sale terminals, flow meters, automotive control instruments, consume arcade games, intelligent instruments, telephone dialers and controllers for serial or parallel printers. A credit card verifier could be implemented with the TMS 1000, along with a TMS 6011 universal asynchronous receiver/transmitter to convert the parallel data to serial for transmission over phone lines and eight transistor-transistor logic packages, including latches and digit drivers. The logic accepts 4-bit parallel input, and there are 64 4-bit locations in the RAM to store working data. The chip's 8-kilobit ROM will accept up to 1,024 8-bit instructions, and TI provides a set of 43 instructions that include conditional branching capabilities that give it a single level of subroutine nesting. Instruction execution time is 12 microseconds; adding two 8-digit numbers takes 1.2 milliseconds.[3]

INTEL BIPOLAR FAMILY

The Intel Corp. family of bipolar microprocessors represents "an order of magnitude" improvement above their 8080 family. The two units, the 3001 micro control unit (MCU) and the 3002 central processor element (CPE), are the major components of the bit/slice microprogrammed computer.

[3] From *Electronics*, copyright McGraw-Hill Book Co., all rights reserved.

The 3001 and 3002 are Schottky bipolar LSI elements that the firm expects will become standard components in high-performance systems. Typical cycle time is 125 nsec/microcycle. In terms of raw compute power, this is about 15 times faster than Intel's 8080. The minimum slice is two bits wide, and slices can be stacked in parallel for as many as are required or up to 2^n bits wide. The CPE contains 128 microinstructions. The microcode enables the system to perform an operation, test the result, and branch on that result in one microcycle.

The chips and the cards

In a very heavy promotion in 1974, National Semiconductor Corp. of Santa Clara, California, advertised microprocessors for do-it-yourselfers, and they were on distributors' shelves in quantity then. They offered chips that contained P-MOS/LSI circuits that could be slapped together like building blocks to yield computer systems ranging from simple 4-bit processors for control functions to a powerful 32-bit system that handled complex calculations. The building blocks are the register and arithmetic logic unit (RALU) and control and read-only memory (CROM). Together they contained all "the gates and flip-flops needed to wire together to build [the user's] own processor."

The "thing" that does the work is named the RALU. It is a 4-bit slice of the register and arithmetic portion of a general-purpose microcomputer. In one 24-pin package using standard +5V and −12V supplies were crammed all of the following: seven general-purpose registers, a status flag register, an arithmetic logic unit, an I/O multiplexer, and a 16-word LIFO stack that improves speed and performance while conserving main memory. The RALU number is IMP-OOH/520D. The "thing" that tells the other things what work to do was labeled a CROM. CROMs are souped-up ROMs that translate binary instructions into operational commands. A single instruction to the CROM triggers a series of commands to the RALUs. CROMs are currently available in three varieties: a standard-instruction 16-bit CROM, IMP-16A/521D, with 43 instructions; an extended-instruction 16-bit CROM, IMP-16A/522D, which speeds up processing with 17 additional powerful instructions, including divide, multiply, and double precision add/subtract and so on.

For people who want to save time, National also offers its "ready-mades." These are complete, fully debugged 8- and 16-bit microprocessors on 8½ by 11-inch PC cards ready for application programs. Their big micro, the IMP-16C, is a 16-bit microprocessor built around four RALUs and one or two CROMs. The one-CROM version has a standard-instruction-set CROM and an empty socket for another (IMP-16C/200). "Add the extended instruction-set CROM, and you've got the IMP-16C/300." The IMP-16L/300 card is similar to the 16C/300, but optimized for high performance applications with a direct memory access bus controller and multi-level interrupts.

National's little one was the IMP-8C, an 8-bit microprocessor—a flexible, low-cost, self-contained processor and controller containing two RALUs, an IMP-8A/520 CROM, and provisions for the addition of a second CROM to expand the instruction set. It includes eight addressable control flags—control jump multiplexer provides 16 programmable branch conditions—plus an 8-bit buffered data-out bus; memory addresses 16 bits wide to provide a memory address range of 65,536 bytes; on-card memory expandable to 2,304 bytes, consisting of read/write memory and up to 2,048 bytes of read-only memory (ROM/PROM).

Single-chip 16-bit microprocessors

A 16-bit data length for microprocessors facilitates interfacing with 16-bit minicomputers. This increases efficiency of hardware and software. When the device is on a single chip, it adds advantages of lower cost with higher reliability and system density. A single-chip 16-bit microprocessor is National Semiconductor Corp.'s PACE. It is a system for processing and control elements. It processes either 8-bit or 16-bit data and handles tasks that require 16-bit instructions and addresses. It is built with p-channel MOS silicon-gate technology. PACE is a general-purpose microprocessor that integrates, on a single chip, the control logic, a stack, four accumulators, and interrupt-control circuitry. The instruction set consists of 45 types

FIGURE 5.7. ECL slice. *Reprinted with permission from* Electronics, *April 18, 1974, copyright McGraw-Hill Book Co., all rights reserved.*

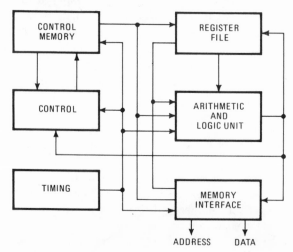

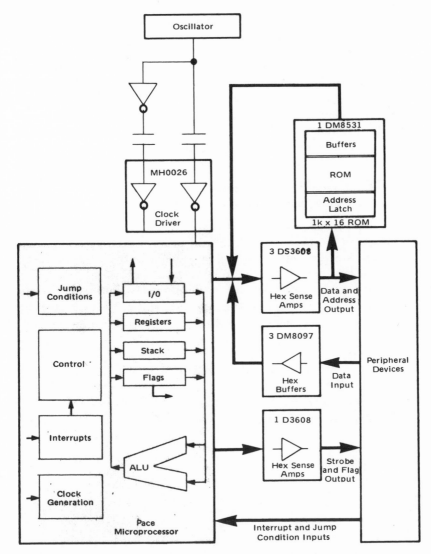

FIGURE 5.8. PACE microcomputer. *Reprinted with permission from* Electronics,
April 18, 1974, copyright McGraw-Hill Book Co., all rights reserved.

with 337 individual instructions. National offers an extensive array of software and hardware products to support systems designed with PACE. Software support includes assemblers, loaders, a debug program, an editor, diagnostic, and software for programming programmable read-only memories.

A prototyping system also aids in development and debugging of both software and hardware. Built in an instrument-sized case, the system has a front control panel that allows the engineer to examine or alter the contents of any register, the stack, or memory location. The prototyper, which provides single-instruction execution and bootstrap loading, also interfaces to a card reader, line printer, or tape reader for high-speed input and output. PACE was originally marketed as a single component in a 40-pin package that sold for about $140 each in quantities of 100 and was also available on a printed-circuit card of 4.5 by 4.5 inches, along with enough other components to form a complete data-processing controller.

Single chip programmable processor
uses N-channel Si-gate technology

An 8-bit parallel processor fabricated on a single chip, the programmable integrated processor (PIP), developed by Signetics Corp., Sunnyvale, California, is a complete, general-purpose computer. N-channel silicon gate technology is used to achieve density and performance. Customer shipments began in 1974. Support logic and memory required to implement a given function have been minimized. Hardware is common to many applications, with specialization residing in software, and interfacing problems are eased.

A PIP chip is made up of three basic elements, as shown on the block diagram in Figure 5.9. The address logic section handles all instruction, branch, and operand addresses. It includes a return address stack that allows nesting of subroutines up to eight levels deep. The register and ALU sections contain four general-purpose registers. Each is eight bits long and

FIGURE 5.9. Simplified block diagram of a programmable integrated processor (PIP) chip, showing the three basic sections and I/O paths *Reprinted with permission from* Electronics, *April 18, 1974, copyright McGraw-Hill Book Co., all rights reserved.*

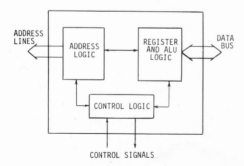

may be used for indexing and as sources and destinations for arithmetic operations. The ALU is an 8-bit parallel unit that executes all arithmetic, Boolean, compare, and rotate operations. The control section manages the operation of all external control lines, decodes all instructions, and coordinates the activities of all other internal circuitry. Memory, I/O, and interrupt operations are handled directly by the control lines using request/acknowledge format. Forty interface pins include three for power, seven for input, seven for output, 15 for the address lines, and eight for the data bus. Seven input lines include clock, reset, pause, sense, and interrupt signals; seven outputs are used to specify the nature of the functions being performed by the processor, in order to discriminate between memory, interrupt, and I/O operations.

Data bus signals form an 8-bit bidirectional data path into and out of the processor. Memory operations use the data bus to transfer data to or from the memory. I/O operations use the same bus to transfer both control and data information. Address signals form a 15-bit path out of the processor. For memory operations, the address lines allow direct addressing of up to 32 kilobytes of memory. For I/O operations, the low-order eight bits of the address lines are used for device addressing. All addresses remain valid for the duration of an operation so that no external address register is normally required.

Because memory costs will often dominate small processor system costs, the PIP chip instruction set is designed to minimize the instruction memory space required to implement a given function. Good coding efficiency also improves performance by decreasing the number of instructions to be executed. The most complex direct instructions are executed in less than 10 μs. More than 64 PIP instructions, divided into nine groups, are of variable length and may be one, two, or three bytes long. Several addressing modes are used to define the operand addresses for the instructions. Register, immediate, relative, absolute, indirect, and indexed modes provide both flexibility and efficiency in implementation of programs. Branch addresses are formed using a relative or absolute mode and may be direct or indirect.

Fabri-Tek Inc. had been a manufacturer of computer memories for many years. It suddenly entered the microprocessor competition and is an example of how a great many other memory, component, peripheral companies have jumped in because entry is easy and not costly. Fabri-Tek's microprocessor, the MP-12, performs like a minicomputer. The MP-12 helps users get application systems up and running fast and easy. As is true of other microprocessors, its performance in data acquisition, automated assembly, point of sale, and other dedicated digital control applications is quite universal. It is shipped completely operational. The MP-12 is self-contained with all the digital electronics needed, built in along with 4K of core memory, an operating console, power fail-auto restart, and more. Everything comes in a compact 2.0″ × 9.5″ × 15.0″ package. The user also gets the software needed to develop and check out application programs. MP-12 supplied programs are completely documented and include assembler, debug, loaders, 360/370 cross assembler, source edit utility, processor diagnostic, and utility subroutines. Instruction set is PDP-8 compatible. (The Digital Equipment Corp.'s PDP-8 is the largest selling mini in the field—up to 50,000 have been sold.) The MP-12 comes with all the timing and control necessary to interface with almost any peripheral. And it has enough power to drive up to 64 peripherals—printers, teletypes, CRTs, card equipment, and on- and off-line storage devices. It is a most useful component for hundreds of systems, games, and so on.

Digital equipment corporation's microprocessors spur competition of other mini manufacturers

Digital Equipment Corp. entered the microcomputer market to protect a place in a market segment that was not being covered by its minicomputer products. Its big-block print, double-page newspaper ads read: "Introducing Digital's New PDP-8/A Computer on a Board—only $572" (100 quantity price).

The chips were designed for the 8-bit MPS (microprocessor series) and 12-bit medium-scale integration with its PDP-8 equivalent PDP-8/A minis. They initially came from microcomputer chip leader Intel Corp. But that changed when DEC realized large sales volumes from the products. The MPS consists of five modules; an 8-bit CPU capable of addressing up to 16K of memory; a semiconductor read/write memory module expandable from 1K to 4K 8-bit words; a programmable ROM, expandable from 256 to 4K words; an external event detection module to monitor low voltage or to implement priority interrupt schemes; and a monitor control panel serving as a diagnostic check-out and program entry device. A 1K RAM and CPU sold in 1975 for $445 in 1,000 unit quantities, or $745 each. The PDP-8/A was highly competitive. For $150 in additional price (unit quantity), users got 12-bit addressing for up to 32K of 1.5 usec memory. The units were also fully compatible with all of the PDP-8's software and peripheral products, a fact that will count heavily with OEMs.

The Micro-one by Microdata Corporation, Irvine, California, is a high-speed microprogrammed microprocessor designed to sell for less than $1,000 in small quantities. It is well suited for dedicated volume applications and can be microprogrammed to emulate other general or special-purpose computers. It is a microprocessor version of the Microdata 800/1600 series computer. With 1,024 words of ROM and 1,024 bytes of MOS memory, it occupies one 8½″ x 11″ board. The small size is achieved by utilizing ROMs for the control logic of the CPU. Features and operating characteristics of the Micro-one include bipolar circuitry; CPU and common ROM on one board, memory addressing to 65K bytes; compatible with MOS or core memory modules; 1.2 microsecond full cycle memory; and an 8-bit arithmetic/logic unit. Additional features of the new unit include 15 general-purpose file registers; 220 nanosecond microcommand execution time; 15 basic microcommands; real-time clock, power fail/auto restart firmware; and an operating temperature range of 0°C to 50°C. The Micro-one is designed for use in applications ranging from phototypesetting and process control to file management and intelligent terminals.

Foreign micros

An interesting advertisement in *Electronics* magazine (December 1974) [4] ran as follows:

> We've developed a microcomputer that's ahead of its time. The MYCRO-1 is a truly complete computer on a single printed circuit board. Simply connect a teletype or display and a power supply and the computer is ready to work.
>
> Need more memory? Add on a 4K byte RAM or erasable PROM modules, any mix up to 64K. On the connectors, the MYCRO-1 has a 16-bit address bus, an 8-bit bidirectional data bus and all the necessary signals for memory read/write, input/output control, eight interrupt control lines and DMA control. All TTL-compatible and buffered for output drive and low input load.
>
> Power supply and cabinet? If you don't plug it into your own system we can also supply a small complete box. If you're interested in new developments in microcomputers, we think you'll be interested in the MYCRO-1 and associated modules. For further information write to Data Industri Pilestredet 75 C, P.O. Box 7175H, Oslo 3, Norway. Our microcomputers are available from stock at prices you'll like.

German microcomputer has four chips and needs no external circuits

West Germany's Olympia Werke AC in Wilhelmshaven has a new concept that treats the microcomputer as a special function and partitions it into four large-scale integrated circuit chips. Unlike most of today's microcomputers, these LSI chips operate only with each other. The chips are self-contained and do not require additional standard memory and I/O interface circuits for implementing most microcomputer applications. The first units of what Olympia calls its CP-3-F chip set are sold as a desk-top computer with printer—basically a calculator with memory. (Olympia is a $270 million subsidiary of AEG-Telefunken, the German electronics giant. A Telefunken spokesman asserted that some 25 European equipment makers are interested in the chips for their own products.)

[4] The ad was placed by Data Industri, a member of Norway's largest electronics group, Elektro Union.

Significantly, all circuits are interchangeable even though dfferent MOS technologies are being used to implement the designs. The 4-chip system consists of an 8-bit parallel CPU containing a 48-byte RAM and 8-bit I/O channel, a microprogrammable read-only memory, a data RAM, and a combination microprogrammable ROM and data RAM chip. These chips have been designed so that a functional system can be built without the use of external logic or control registers. The minimum configuration consists of the 8-bit CPU chip with a 48-instruction set having a minimum cycle time of 5 microseconds plus the microprogrammable ROM chip. These two chips contain all the logic, binary, and decimal operations, as well as other processing functions necessary for simple controller systems. The set of 48 instructions is sufficient to handle instructions for most controllers and many processors—for example, logic, binary and decimal operations, shifting, constant multiplications, and subprograms. The microprocessor set can be used for even more complex systems, for it is possible to expand the memory capacity to 16,000 8-bit words without additional I/O circuits. Along with the system, Olympia will supply a FORTRAN cross assembler, a simulation program, and necessary test equipment. All circuits are supplied in a 40-pin dual in-line package and operate from −5-volt and −17-volt power supplies.

NEC introduced microprocessors in 1973 and 1974

In 1974, Nippon Electric Co. (NEC) introduced an 8-bit microprocessor to compete against Intel's Model 8080. The Model μ PD 753 D, an n-channel silicon-gate device, is NEC's second microprocessor. The firm introduced a 4-bit device in 1973. The 8-bit microprocessor consists of a one-chip CPU capable of 8-bit parallel processing, an 8K ROM, and an 8-bit latch driver for input-output devices. The software for the Intel 8080 can be used in the NEC CPU without modification. Sales began in October 1974, with list prices set at $216.67 for the CPU, $10 for the 404D Ram, $23.33 for the 412D RAM, $48.33 for the 465D ROM, and $8 for the 754D latch driver in quantities of 100 to 249 pieces. The software is priced between $833 and $1,166. Mask charge is $1,000. NEC hoped to sell about 5,000 kits per month during 1975 and about 20,000 kits per month in 1976. Although there were no plans in 1974 to sell the microprocessor in the United States, an NEC executive said he may consider exporting individual components without software.

Japanese micros

Toshiba and Nippon Electric are leading the way among Japanese manufacturers in the development of microprocessors. In 1974, Toshiba claimed sales of about 200 kits a month of its 12-bit microprocessor at an average price of $600. By the middle of 1975 it expected volume to expand and average price per kit to halve. Toshiba figures that Intel Corp. is the leading U.S. competitor in Japan, initially selling about 1,000 units a month. But by fall 1975, Toshiba had a line of n-channel microprocessors both faster and smaller than the current Intel devices. NEC also expected much from microprocessors. The company had a 4-bit unit that it used inside chip bonders built for its own assembly plants. And it had an 8-bit unit that is software-compatible with Intel's 8080, though pinout is completely different. NEC developed a 16-bit microprocessor, which was due to arrive on the market in 1976. Hitachi had a microprocessor CPU, and Mitsubishi introduced an 8-bit device similar to the 8080.[5]

STACKED MICROPROCESSORS: A BETTER WAY TO GO?

Exciting, low-cost, and extremely fast throughput advantages have led to coordinated groups of microcomputers that already outperform many of today's standard computers. The difference between a multiprocessing system of, say, 16 microcomputers and 16 standard computers working independently is that the multimicroprocessors share memory; that is, some of the primary memory can be addressed by two or more machines. A more common technique in today's standard computing world is multiprogramming. Multiprogramming means that more than one program can reside in main memory at a time and the central processor can switch among them. This means that the CPU does not have to remain idle while waiting for a job's input/output to be completed. Whenever a job must wait for an I/O operation (it sometimes takes a long time to read some data from a file into main memory), the operating system looks over the set of other jobs in main memory and chooses one whose I/O operation has been completed. If there is more than one CPU, many problems are solved and the user has— multiprocessing. If a job starts running on one processor and is stopped while waiting for I/O, it may be restarted later on another processor. Generally, multiprocessing systems come in two types: master/slave or symmetrical. In a master/slave system, one processor (not necessarily similar to the others) controls the rest. From the user's point of view, the maxicomputer, the Control Data Corp.'s (CDC) 6600 is an example of such a machine.

With LSI, speed limits are imposed only by the speed of light. Electric current moves only one foot per nanosecond.

In England, several of the units have been combined to share the work load. In addition to the truly modular systems in which processing capability is added in units rather than by system replacement, the use of multiple processors of the same design has added greatly to system reliability. Low-

5 *Electronics*, November 28, 1974.

cost processors easily operate in tandem and choose jobs in priorities. Several "spares" are added, and, in the event of one unit's failure, to ensure system integrity, the next "spare" takes over. This is not the case for many large computers that use multiprocessor designs. Several units in the micro systems are always identical. They might as well be built of many of the same units because they are so cheap. Systems may use one microprocessor for a storage manager; another, for communications; and still others, for compilation, execution, and job scheduling. They provide performance equivalent to current million-dollar systems for only a few thousand dollars. Although the speed of individual microprocessors may be limited, several units now easily run out of phase with each other to provide smooth, fast, and powerful processing. Races between memory speeds and processor speeds are forcing new architectures to evolve utilization of the latest technological states of the art, as they have in the past.

Economies of scale have been obliterated. Function alone no longer defines the types of computers that are purchased. Ranges of systems from pocket-calculator types through centralized giants do share technology but not design. Micros have new functions, new power, new component speeds, and great new system capabilities. Wide ranges of user firms have been seeking new ways to use new microcomputers—to control very fast processes like graphic displays, plotters, radar, and so on.

Advantages of stacked microprocessor systems

Most considerations for the use of "stacked micros" are much the same as for multiminicomputers with the exception of three characteristics: shared memory, low cost, and microprogramming capability. Many microcomputers have limited execution rates; that is, the system throughput is limited by the processor rather than memory. This means that several micros can share the same memory without seriously degrading individual execution rates. Their low cost (compared to costs of memory and peripheral devices) allows the use of many microprocessors in one system. This more than offsets the lower throughput of a single processor and reduces the importance of utilizing each processor to maximum capability. Microprogramming further allows the use of special instructions that aid in satisfying control requirements. The advantages of implementing systems with many micros solve several system control problems and offer approaches to solving many others. Many of these advantages may be realized with multiprocessor systems. In general, it may be said that

1. Throughput often increases almost directly with the number of processors although system cost increases by only a small amount.
2. Shared system resources offer an economic advantage by eliminating devices that would need to be duplicated in separate stand-alone systems.

3. Shared resources provide direct access to data that might otherwise require transmission from one system to another.
4. With many processors, the cost of a standby is small.
5. A spare processor that can be switched into the system to replace a failed processor may be provided.
6. Functionally equivalent processors are treated as unassigned system resources to be allocated as required to process incoming tasks (symmetrical multiprocessors can be used in general-purpose environments where processing requirements are constantly changing).
7. Any currently idle processor may be used for the next task to be executed, eliminating the need to wait for the availability of a dedicated processor specialized to that task.
8. Failure of an individual processor causes only slight degradation in system capabilities rather than complete failure of an assigned system function (symmetrical systems require that every processor have full capabilities).
9. Systems are able to assign any task to any processor and set up interprocessor communication when required without the complications of software of single large systems processors.
10. Individual processors can have fixed specialized processing functions; that is, the asymmetric class is typically used in dedicated applications where type, frequency of occurrence, and relative importance of tasks are known in advance; processors may be specialized to carry out one particular type of task. For example, one processor may perform all I/O operations; another may provide floating point arithmetic capability; a third may provide file maintenance; and so on.
11. Specialization may occur via the software programs executed, as well as the microprogram (which implements the processor's instruction set) and hardware architectural features (for example, number of registers, interrupt capabilities, and stack processing).
12. Each specialized processor is kept busy a sufficient amount of time to justify its cost. When low-cost microprocessors are used, utilization does not have to be exceedingly high to justify addition of a new processor.
13. Simplication of programming is developed because each task can be treated as an independent module, with no provisions required for execution of other tasks by a given microprocessor.
14. Switching matrices can connect any processor to any memory (or peripheral) in the system. This allows many processors to utilize simultaneously many different memory modules, reducing memory reference interference between processors.
15. All processors, memories, and peripheral devices can be multiplexed over one data bus (or a limited number). This is a very low-cost approach, and cost increases negligibly with the number of processors.

The infrequent memory reference characteristics of stacked micros makes this organization attractive.

16. The asymmetric processor with multiplexed bus appears to offer the best cost advantage for stacked micro implementations and is of simpler organization than the others.

THE IDEAL MICROCOMPUTER

An ideal microcomputer should be built from a wide range of interchangeable and compatible components that can be custom fit to the user's application without any problems. The technology to build this ideal micro is here. Vendors have too long taken the tack of developing minicomputers within the emerging technology, and it is time to design microcomputers that fit the users' needs more precisely. The basic machine concepts such as registers, instruction sets, and basic I/O formats should be removed from the direct user interface.

Users today do not want to spend more money debugging an application than they would if they could buy a more user-compatible unit that can be built with today's technology.

Many of the "bells and whistles" may just not be necessary because people predicate a whole structure on the past without knowledge of what the future technology will be. We are producing improvements faster than this technology can be put to effective use.

Up to this point, the main thrust in minicomputer design has been to use the emerging technology to build a smaller, more compact copy of some of the original computers at a lower price. Minis are slowly taking on all the attributes of larger machines—more data types, larger memories, more peripherals, multiprogramming—as long as they do not violate some basic cost constraints. The drop in mini prices over the last seven years has been at 37 percent compounded a year, but new and different micros are now here!

There has been a persistent ongoing controversy to define the difference between a minicomputer and a microcomputer. Many micros, for example, are dedicated systems without complicated operating systems, without complicated general-purpose I/O, but with the capability to have instructions and data in independent storage units for data security. Micros have been proved the "most economical for data processing." But probably of greatest importance, the micros of the future should be modularized so that applications could be run on a number of systems. For example, big files can be broken into segments, each to be handled by a small system. Micro hardware is not as much a problem as software, systems design, and the handling of data. Two main things users want to see in hardware are throwaway modules and fault identification procedures, so that anyone can

TABLE 5.1. A convenient purchase criteria check-off list.

Documentation and application notes

Software commitment
Complete microcomputer cards or systems
Pricing and second source

Hardware

Reputation and availability
Power supply requirements
Clock and cycle time
Semiconductor technology
Interfacing requirements
Packaging

Microprocessor architecture

Word length
Addressing capability
Registers, ALU, stack instruction set,
addressing modes and I/O

Microprocessor system

Bus control capability
Direct memory access
Interrupts
Compatible functions
   Memory
   Buffers
   Clock generators
   Input/Output
   Communications interface

Microprocessor software

Stand-alone assembler, editor, debug monitor
Cross assembler for batch and time sharing
Software documentation
Simulator
Higher-level language

fix a micro. Micro equipment is priced low enough so that there is no need to "twiddle" with attempts to save memory.

Ideal micros for the college and business environments should utilize a variety of I/O devices to construct architecturally any type of machine a user could desire. Standard basic micro machines should be similar in some respects to an automobile in which a variety of components built by various manufacturers can be connected to the device. The CPU is the heart of all computers; I/O is the soul of computers; and the computer's reason for being is to be useful to the outside world. Software written for one vendor's mini or micro should be usable on other machines. To do this, emulation through microprogramming is highly desirable as the solution to program compatibility.

The executive command, which enables the programmer to call for the execution of a particular instruction, is vital to all machines. Another area that could use improvement is memory—it must have the capability to be very big if and when it is needed and to be addressable without wasting extra address bits. When a micro goes down, it must also be able to come up quickly. There should be something in the micro so that a malfunction can be exactly diagnosed, and the micro should be designed so that the problem can easily be repaired.

The Unibuslike structures seem to work pretty well in the ability to interface with a number of I/O devices; that is, the common bus tends to be a problem for the machine during high-speed I/O operations. Other micros have architecture whereby each memory module has a direct access channel into it. Communications capability is becoming more and more important. Micros now have improvements in the ability to interface with other computers and network environments. A code conversion box that automatically converts to ASCII when needed—possibly even in the control memory—is also helpful.

MICROPROCESSOR SUMMARY: SOME ABCs FOR USER SELECTION

The importance of individual microprocessor characteristics depends heavily on the application. A checklist of key features should be considered before making a selection. All microprocessors use large-scale integrated circuit technology. Silicon-gate, p-channel MOS initially was the most commonly used process. But manufacturers now routinely employ n-channel MOS, silicon-on-sapphire MOS, and bipolar processes for increased speed. And they use complementary MOS for lowered power dissipation.

1. *Programmability* is a flexible feature not usually found in random-logic designs. It can be obtained on one of two levels. A very detailed level of control is provided at the microinstruction level. These microinstructions may be used to obtain a macro, or machine-language, instruction set, which is then used to write control programs for the microprocessor. New machine-language instructions may be defined by coding new microroutines. In this way, an instruction set can be tailored to an application.

2. *Control programs* can also be written in microcode. This provides increased execution speed and more detailed control at the expense of more difficult programming. Microprocessors that are not micropro-

grammable contain fixed, general-purpose instruction sets, which are not often adequate for most applications.

3. *Word length* should be the first feature to consider. The determining requirements are computational accuracy, character length, and width of parallel digital inputs or outputs. Microprocessors are structured for fixed word lengths or for modular expansion by a parallel combination of building block chips. In the latter category, some suppliers have 4-bit "slices" of a CPU, or central processing unit. In some microprocessors the word lengths for addresses exceed those for instructions. A large address word eliminates the need to manipulate smaller—4- and 8-bit—data registers to obtain 12- to 16-bit addresses. In general, longer word lengths for either addresses or instructions provide higher system throughput and more powerful memory addressing, whereas shorter word lengths require somewhat less hardware and smaller memories.

4. *Architectural features* include general-purpose registers, stacks, interrupts, interface structure, and choice of memories. General-purpose registers are used for addressing, indexing, and status and as multiple accumulators. They simplify programming and conserve main memory by eliminating memory buffering of data. Multiple accumulators are especially important for ROM programs that have no writable memory. Stacks can be used for nesting subroutines and interrupts and for temporary storage of data when programs reside in ROMs. Stacks consist of read/write (RAM) memory locations maintained by software—called pointer stacks—or by registers built into the processor chip—called hardware stacks. The pointer stack generally offers size restricted only by the external RAM, but it must be maintained by software. The hardware is faster, but its size is limited. An additional advantage of the hardware stack is that RAM is not required.

5. *Interrupt capability* for applications where asynchronous or unpredictable events occur (a variable interrupt capability) is valuable. Throughput increases are important, because the processor can perform useful work concurrent with I/O (input/output) operations. The major characteristics of this capability include interrupt latency (time to recognize the interrupt and branch to the service routine), response (time to identify the interrupted device and begin execution of the device service code), and software overhead (to get to the service routine and return to the main program).

6. *Memory choice.* The choice of memories is important because the memory section often represents a major portion of hardware cost. Read/write memories are commonly used for variable data storage and for program storage during software development. Field-programmable ROMs have become quite popular for program storage in small and intermediate-volume systems and for high-volume prototype systems.

MOS PROMs may be erased by ultraviolet light and then reprogrammed. For ease of design, memory modular blocks should be used; the memory-address bus width determines the upper limit of expansion (maximum number of addressable locations). Available microprocessor cards include ROM, PROM, and RAM memories and eliminate the need to design or specify a memory system for limited storage requirements.

7. *Interfaces.* The interface structure should be easy to use for simple, low-cost applications (parallel or serial). Separate buses for data, addresses, memory, and peripheral input and output are most appropriate in this case. Although the type of control depends on the processor, higher throughput results from the use of a direct-memory-access (DMA) bus. In this arrangement, a peripheral device communicates directly with memory without disturbing the CPU. Interfacing is more complex because request and acknowledge signals must be exchanged between the device and an autonomous bus controller. When a single bus is used, data and addresses must be time-multiplexed, and latches must be provided to hold the address stable while memory or a peripheral are accessed.

8. *Operating measured speed.* Cycle time, minimum instruction time, time to add two numbers, and interrupt response time are often named to measure speed. But these numbers do not measure the power of the instruction set. Benchmark programs for a specific task should be coded, and the execution times should be compared to determine which microprocessor meets the speed requirements. The degree of programming flexibility can be determined from an examination of the instruction set. Multiple addressing modes conserve main memory, simplify programming, and increase speed through single-word memory-reference instructions. For programs stored in ROM or PROM, indexing or pointer addressing are the only means to access data tables in program loops. Other useful capabilities include bit and byte manipulation, multiply and divide, double-precision arithmetic, normalize, and I/O control instructions.

9. *Microprogramming.* Custom instructions through microprogramming can upgrade performance by optimizing the microprocessor architecture. In some cases, other processors, including minicomputers, may be emulated with the microprogram control technique, thereby enabling software built for a larger machine to run on a microprogrammed microprocessor.

10. *Prototyping procedures.* Prototyping systems are essential to develop and debug hardware, firmware, and software for the end product. The ingredients of such prototyping systems include expanded memory capability, a teletypewriter or card-reader interface, power supply, chassis, control panel, and support software (assemblers, compilers, loaders,

and debug and edit packages). A PROM programmer provides very fast turnaround time when control programs are modified. With a processor card, users get an assembled and tested microprocessor system, complete with memory. Cards are often more economical than chips for low-volume applications. They may be used for development of early production models for high-volume applications before they are replaced by an in-house design.

11. *Microprocessor support.* Support should be provided by the manufacturer to simplify the application of the processor and the development and prototyping of the end product. This category includes documented manuals, application literature, area field specialists, prototyping systems, and so on.

Applications, characteristics, and word lengths

Generally, various standard word length processors fit specific applications. A list of eight examples for each of three types is developed below.

Four-bit machines with arithmetic or simple control functions:

1. Display controls for calculators.
2. Electronic cash registers.
3. Business and accounting systems.
4. Credit card verification.
5. Intelligent instruments.
6. Appliances.
7. Game machines.
8. Intelligent terminals and instruments.

Eight-bit machines with controllers:

1. Data concentrators or front-ends (communication preprocessor).
2. On-board computers (automobile).
3. Process, numeric, and machine control.
4. Text-editing typewriters.
5. Traffic control.
6. Education—computer science courses.
7. Computer design projects.
8. Medical electronics.

Sixteen-bit or general-purpose machines:

1. Measurement systems.
2. Data acquisition systems.
3. Process monitoring and alarm systems.
4. Supervisory controls—gas, power, water distribution.
5. Navigational systems.

6. Automatic test systems.
7. Word-processing systems.
8. Peripheral control.

FURTHER DEFINING THE WORLD OF MICROCOMPUTERS

ACIA (asynchronous communications interface adapter). An asynchronous communications interface adapter provides the data formating and control to interface serial asynchronous data communications information to bus organized systems. The bus interface of some systems includes select, enable, read/write, interrupt, and bus interface logic to allow data transfer over an 8-bit bidirectional data bus.

Arithmetic registers, microprocessors. Arithmetic (or ALU) registers are those on which arithmetic and logic functions can be performed; the register can be a source or destination of operands for the operation. Registers that can supply but not receive operands for the ALU are not considered arithmetic registers by many evaluators.

Assembler advantages. A useful characteristic of an assembler is evaluation of expressions at assembly time, which permits the programmer to specify certain parameters algebraically instead of numerically or symbolically. Then when a program is assembled, the assembler evaluates the algebraic expressions and inserts the correct values in the machine-language program. The process requires the variables to be specified ahead of time, but it permits the programmer to alter these variables by changing their specification only once, rather than every time they are used in the program. It is a great time-saver and bug-killer. Although these characteristics are not uncommon in advanced assembly languages, high-level languages that can handle them are quite rare.

Bipolar microcontroller. Desirable features of both stored program controllers and high performance microprocessors are included in a bipolar programmable microcontroller designed for use in high-speed instruments, control, and data-processing/collection systems. One single-board unit offers a powerful and efficient instruction set, flexible and performance-oriented I/O structure, and versatile machine architecture.

Bus driver. Generally refers to a specially designed integrated circuit that is added to the data bus system to facilitate proper drive to the CPU when several memories are tied to the data bus line. Such circuits are required because of capacitive loading that slows down the data rate and prevents proper time sequencing of microprocessor operation.

Bus priority structure. Because many buses are used by processors and I/O devices, there is a priority structure to determine which device gets control of the bus. Often every device on the bus that is capable of becoming bus master is assigned a priority according to its position along the bus. When two devices that are capable of becoming a bus master request use of the bus simultaneously, the device with the higher priority position will receive control.

Chips, I/O. To complete his microcomputer product line, each manufacturer tries to offer a complete set of I/O interface chips. I/O chips are implemented in MOS or bipolar technologies depending on the requirements. Those designed to fit a particular device to a microprocessor save the designer-programmer time in development and reduce the overall number of chips in the microcomputer. The next step was to make these interface chips parameter selectable so that several models of one kind of peripheral could be handled by one chip.

Clock rate. 1. Refers to the rate at which a word or parts of characters of a word (bits) are transferred from one internal computer element to another. 2. The time rate at which pulses are emitted from the clock. The clock rate at which logical or arithmetic gating is performed with a synchronous computer.

CMOS applications. Because CMOS offers low power and low voltage operation, it has opened new markets for ICs in battery-operated systems such as watches and portable equipment. Operation over wide supply and temperature ranges with good noise margin make it a natural for automotive electronics and machine or process control.

CPE (central processing element). Refers to elements that contain all the circuits representing a 2-bit-wide or 4- or 8-bit-wide slice through a small computer's central processor. To build a processor of word width N, all that is necessary is to connect an array of N/2 CPEs together.

Data paths and I/O capability. Some systems provide an extremely fast elementary input/output capability. The data paths and control functions are often simple elements that are sequenced from the control memory with flexible disciplines. The fact that the control memory is very fast means that microprograms (firmware) in the control memory can implement facilities with a high degree of versatility in timing, data paths, and I/O capabilities such as priority interrupts, fully buffered data channels, macroprogrammable transfers, and special purpose communication multiplexer channels. This basic I/O element is always the I/O bus and varies for cell systems.

Diskette operating systems. Diskette operating systems substantially reduce the time required to assemble, edit, and execute programs. On many systems a diskette operating system is available to speed the microcompute development cycle. One diskette operating system includes an intelligent disk controller, a diskette drive, and a powerful software system called IDOS.

Dynamic MOS circuits. Dynamic circuits use the absence or presence of charge on a capacitor to store information, typically with three or four transistors per cell. Fewer transistors give higher packing density and lower cost. Because the capacitor that stores the charge has a leakage current, the stored information degrades slowly and, therefore, must be refreshed (normally by simply addressing the memory periodically so that every address is covered eventually).

ECL microprocessor. A typical ECL microprocessor set contains five chips: a 4-bit slice, a control register function, a timing function, a slice memory interface, and a slice look-ahead. The various chips can be used as building blocks to construct a microprocessor with capabilities larger than four bits.

FPLA vs PROM. The structure and use of field programmable logic arrays can be understood if one compares them more to memory than to logic. An FPLA is basically a PROM with one very important difference—its versatility makes it a great deal more useful.

Instruction register, current. The control section register that contains the instruction currently being executed after it is brought to the control section from memory.

Integrated injection logic (I^2L). I^2L is characterized by some observers as the bipolar LSI of the future. Its primary advantages are increased density, good speed-power product, versatility, and low cost. The technology is capable of squeezing 1,000 to 3,000 gates, or more than 10,000 bits of memory, on a single chip. It has speed-power product as low as 1 picojoule, compared to 100 pj with TTL logic. It can handle digital and analog functions on a single chip and is made with a five-mask process without the need for current-source and load resistors.

Interrupt capabilities. Many applications require asynchronous or unpredictable events control and an interrupt capability. Throughput increases, because the processor can perform useful work concurrent with I/O (input/output) operations. The major characteristics of this capability include interrupt latency (time to recognize the interrupt and branch to the service routine), response (time to identify the interrupted device and begin execution of the device service code), and software overhead (to get to the service routine and return to the main program). Single line, multilevel and vectored interrupts offer various speed-hardware trade-offs. Cascaded interrupt capability (interrupting an interrupt) is essential if slow and fast devices are to be mixed in a system. Interrupt enable flags are used to mask or unmask individual levels.

Interrupt vectoring. Handling interrupts in some systems is a problem of software polling. A polling sequence usually has a corresponding program. Such a polling approach is usually the lowest cost alternative for identifying interrupts, but may in some instances be too slow. For many applications, hardware may be added to the system to achieve priority encoding of the various interrupt requests. The encoded value of the interrupt request can then be used as a system address to transfer control to the appropriate response routine. This is referred to as "interrupt vectoring."

I^{2}L. A new kind of bipolar LSI integrated injection logic, I^{2}L chips may contain as many as 3,000 gates operating at less than 10-nanosecond speeds, dissipating just 1 nanowatt of power per gate. These are appearing in electronic wristwatches and as single chip controllers for industrial, automobiles, and computer systems. Some scientists feel that I^{2}L because of its tremendous speed-power ratios (100 times smaller than other bipolar logic) will have as much influence on the way logic is built as TTL had in the 1960s.

I^{2}L microprocessor. One of the first LSI digital circuits built with nonisolated I^{2}L logic is a microprocessor chip slice designed SBP 0400, which stands for "semiconductor bipolar processor," 400 series. It is a 40-pin, 4-bit microprogrammable binary processor element containing more than 1,450 gates—one of the most complex standard product bipolar logic chips built.

Mask. 1. Usually a device made of a thin sheet of metal that contains an open pattern used to shield selected portions of a base during a deposition process. 2. A machine word that specifies which parts of another machine word are to be operated on.

Masking. A technique for sensing specific binary conditions and ignoring others. Typically accomplished by placing zeros in bit positions of no interest, and ones in bit positions to be sensed.

Microcomputer control panel functions. A programmer's control panel is supplied with most systems to provide access to the CPU registers and memory. It generally includes an array of data switches, data and address indicators, and function switches. Using the programmer's panel, the operator may address, load, and examine memory and CPU registers and control the operation of the microcomputer.

Microcomputer development peripherals. Latest microcomputer development systems combine both hardware and software design tools. They constitute complete microcomputers with the capability to interface with a host of peripherals that speed development. Newer prototype "boxes" can interface with disk-operating systems and high-speed readers and printers. They have extended debug capabilities, being able to check internal μP registers and memory locations and exercise a system one or several steps at a time. And they now allow in-circuit emulation, permitting the very early isolation of trouble spots in an end product.

Microcomputer development system advantages. A microcomputer development system provides cost savings, efficiencies, and speed in product development and system test. An OEM product designer can use a single self-contained system that supports him throughout the entire development cycle, from the initial concept of a microcomputer-based product through its final production and field test. Using the system over the entire design cycle saves considerable time and expense in program development, hardware prototyping, in-circuit hardware and software debugging, production testing and actual in-use field testing of the product.

Microcomputer prototyping system. Prototyping tools are developed for the microprocessor user to devise hardware and software systems around their microprocessors. They include a chassis, programmer's control panel, power supplies, and generally one or more 8K-byte RAMs (random access memory), in addition to the microprocessor cards themselves. With a Teletype, the system provides all equipment and software necessary for the immediate evaluation and use of microprocessor cards and LSI devices. The prototype system is especially useful for the development of application software and equipment interfaces.

NMOS development. The silicon-gate n-channel MOS process, introduced in memory chips in 1973, has about a dozen laws of physics favoring it over PMOS. It makes components smaller, faster, cooler, and more amenable to working with standard power supply voltages.

Nonvolatile PROM. The PROM is a member of the standard ROM family of memories. Once it is programmed, its memory is nonvolatile, which means that if power is removed from and then reapplied to the PROM, the stored information remains intact. By contrast, a RAM (random access memory) has a volatile memory; if power is interrupted, when it is again applied, whatever information was stored in the memory will be erased.

Pushdown list. A list of items in which the last item entered becomes the first item of the list and the relative position of each of the other items is pushed back one.

RALU (register, arithmetic, and logic unit). The RALU differs from the discrete ALU package in that it contains a number of special registers as well as the arithmetic and logic units.

Read-only memory programmer. A microprocessor ROM programmer is a versatile option for microprocessor series (MPS) users, providing a capability for writing programs into chips used on a programmable read-only memory (PROM) module. Operating as an on-line peripheral device to a microcomputer system, the unit can be a fully self-contained subsystem that will load and verify user-generated MPS routines in individual PROM chips. Source data for loading PROMs is binary code, previously generated by an assembler or the debugging programs. The code can be in the form of paper tapes or a previously programmed PROM.

Register complement, microprocessor. The number of registers in the microprocessor is considered by many to be the most important feature of its architecture. Registers in a computer have varied and different uses. The ways that they may be used are embodied in the instruction set. The most important resource to many programmers that allocate in software is the set of CPU registers. The more registers there are, the less likelihood there is of main storage references.

ROM emulator. In a typical evaluation system, all pertinent signal, control, address, data, and I/O lines connect to each board. Either a customer-furnished ROM emulator or a PROM evaluation module can be used for microprogram development. If a ROM emulator is used, then the address and data bus go to the bus and to the TTL interface module for converting the MOS dynamic signals to TTL static signals.

ROM simulator. A ROM simulator is a general-purpose instrument that is used to replace ROMs or PROMs in a system during program debug. Because it offers real time in-circuit simulation, it can be used in the engineering prototype, preproduction version, or production model to find and correct program errors or add new features. The ROM simulator provides the software documentation required during debug, and often a user configured assembler makes program development a relatively simple task.

Schottky bipolar LSI microcomputer set. A typical set includes microprogram control units, central processing elements, and bipolar PROMs (256 × 4). Various updating programs ensure that kit owners are kept abreast of bipolar microcomputer set developments. This service includes priority mailings of additional design aids—application notes, specification sheets, user manuals—and often free samples of new members. Such free samples that are often sent to development kit owners are

Look-ahead carry generators.
Multi-Mode latch buffers.
Interrupt control units.
Inverting bidirectional bus drivers (some companies).

Transistor logic circuit families. A variety of logic circuit families have appeared on the market, each with its special features, advantages, and limitations. They are variously labeled as RTL (resistor-transistor logic), ECL (emitter-coupled logic), DCTL (direct coupled transistor logic), DTL (diode transistor logic), TTL (transistor-transistor logic) and variations of these. From the logic designer's viewpoint, a logic system can be designed using functional "black boxes," each with well-defined input and output characteristics.

Vector, interface. In some systems, the interface vector is the input/output path between the microcontrolled system and the user equipment. Each bit in the interface provides a program-addressable, buffered, bidirectional path. Both the microcontroller and the user have simultaneous access to each bit for read or write operations. Bits are grouped into 8-bit interface vector bytes to simplify user control of the interface and access by the program.

6

Microcomputer Kits, Development, and Testing Systems

PART I: THE KIT "CRAZE"—
WHAT DOES IT PORTEND?

One of the most unusual and perhaps important characteristics of the microcomputer revolution is the striking differences between the users of micros and the users of its predecessors, the standard and minicomputers. First, there will be millions more of them, and they will be able to use micros with much less knowledge of the workings of the hardware and the systems software. Hundreds of thousands of microcomputer kits have been sold to hobbyists, laboratories, high schools, and toy and appliance makers, for example. Secondly, the very low cost of micros will permit their use for special purposes, thus eliminating the cost of difficult programming support for the great majority of them. The millions of users, in most cases, will either develop their products with the most rudimentary programming or they will purchase "ready-made" or dedicated programs, which are pluggable, insertable, or read in from low-cost tape cassettes. The concept of "firmware" or hard-wired "software" will dominate in the instruction of amateurs as to how to use microcomputers.

Most kit developers and users are amateurs or at least novices concerning computers and even electronics. For this reason, we will begin this chapter with a review of the basic concepts of microcomputer operations and capabilities. As with all computers and regardless of the technology designed to manufacture chip microcomputers, the devices fundamentally operate by receiving information, processing it by manipulation and interpretation, and sending it on to other input-output devices in the form of

223

data to be stored or instructions to be executed. Thus one can quickly conceptualize microprocessors as the central processing units (CPUs) that receive sequential or parallel binary coded information and store it in addressable memory locations, usually in ROMs (read-only memories) and/or RAMs (random access memories) included in the same chip set or circuit board. The sequential information entering the microprocessor initially or later is the program, and there are thousands of standard programs and hundreds of thousands of specialized programs.

Because the CPU is required to keep track of the program and where (locations and addresses) data are stored in RAM or ROM, it needs its own memories or depositories, called registers. One CPU depository—an instruction register—stores instructions to be executed, thus keeping the CPU informed of what it is doing at any particular instant. A second basic CPU memory performs the functions of a program counter register, storing and then divulging the address of the next instruction to be read from ROM. A third basic CPU memory or register, called the accumulator, provides a place to carry out the operation called for by the instruction. If the CPU (microprocessor) generates information that must be stored for a longer length of time, it sends the data out over a bus to a RAM or other type of read/write memory.

The microprocessor control unit (CU)

As the instruction register receives an order (command, fetch, and so on) from the program stored in ROM, a CU (control unit) in the microprocessor system decodes (deciphers) that instruction. An ALU (arithmetic logic unit), also part of the microprocessor, executes the decoded information, and the bus operation begins. Binary coded signals move to and from and within the CPU, along a path known as a *bus.* The bus connects or permits the communications commanded by linking memory with the accumulator, program counter, and instruction registers through the control units. Thus the CU essentially makes the microprocessor system operate by directing traffic in the various registers. Basically, the CU executes an instruction by performing the following system operations:

1. It interrogates the program counter, which contains the memory address of the next instruction, using binary code, and, in effect, asks where it should go.
2. It decodes those binary numbers that specify the addresses in memory.
3. It contacts the specified address, using the bus system. The instruction stored at that address location is fetched and placed into the instruction registers.
4. It then signals the program counter to indicate the memory address of the next program instruction.

5. It then asks the information (instruction) register for the next instruction, decodes it, and sends out the instruction for execution.

The essential elements of a microcomputer kit

Generally, the kit contains LSI chips with MOS or other type logic to be mounted on one or several printed or plain circuit boards. Besides the performance of data control, data storage, program storage, and program control, the CPU performs input-output buffering (temporary storage and device speed matching and so on) and the previously mentioned data busing. The microcomputer is usually mounted on a chassis (metal box) or rack, which furnishes space for the power supply and the terminations and other necessary hardware to insert the parts (data control bus modules) according to correct spacing. The chassis also provides for I/O ports, control panel, peripherals, or the connections to them.

Kit buyers have many purchasing criteria to evaluate as new technologies are introduced with increasingly important advantages in speed, smaller size, lower power requirements, and so on. Generally, the substrate of the chips is silicon, and the basic device types are bipolar and MOS. The bipolar structures include EPI collector, triple diffusion, and isoplanar; and the circuit forms are TTL, ECL, Schottky TTL, I^2L (ion injection logic), and so on. The MOS structures include MOSFET and CCD, with circuit forms of PMOS, NMOS, and CMOS. (See definitions at the end of the chapter). The comparisons go something like this: Schottky bipolar and CMOS are faster, but NMOS and I^2L have greater density and lower power requirements. Schottky bipolar and PMOS are more tested and older types, and PMOS and NMOS are less complex. CMOS is quite expensive whereas Schottky bipolar, though fast, is relatively larger. And the judgment evaluations go on.

I/O channels, interfaces and memory—the extra costs

The basic functional components are control, memory, and I/O channels—the CPU receives the interrupts and is the control; the memory contains the addresses and data that are communicated through the paths (buses) and I/O channels. The channels interface with the buses and are external to the computer for input and output of data. The interfaces control, interrupt, sense, and alert the lines external to the computer. This provides the logic to control the information flow to and from control and to and from memory; some micros contain a special device, a direct memory access (DMA). DMA substitutes for the control unit and contains the logic to determine the address at which information is to be accessed as required. Computer words with fixed numbers of bits per word are arranged sequentially in memory. As noted, control fetches instructions from memory and decodes, times, and counts the next instructions. Control also handles adder and logic operations related to interrupts, condition flagging, and other data manipulation through register and bus transfers, as well as with clocking and start-up (and reset).

I/O channels and multiplexing

Many firms now offer flexible interface chips to work with all processors and peripherals. Some standard peripherals for microcomputers are keyboards, tape readers, teletypewriters, LED (light-emitting diode) displays, disk memories, CRT displays, communications modems, and so on. The basic functions of I/O channels are to assemble and format data, reconcile timing requirements, develop appropriate interrupt and status signals for the CPU and DMA, devise control signals, perform "handshaking" functions with the peripherals, and drive external lines. Flip-flops are clocked and are set and operated to hold data through the latching process. Thus data is sampled at the input, and the "clocking" is determined by the control signals from the CPU. Latching is mandatory on some buses because buses also carry nondata information on different clock phases.

Buffers (tri-state gates) are connected to flip-flop outputs. When disabled, they are effectively open circuits. These gates allow several signals to output to a single data bus without interfering; thus they are "multiplexed." Microcomputer attachments are controlled and line driven by interrupts and status words available to be read by the microprocessor. Typical 4-, 8-, 12-, and 16-bit words are often "paged," that is, divided into blocks of memory of 256, or 2^8, words. Addressing is then required only within the enabled page. The enable of a page is accomplished by control signals or a "page counter" register. Some systems then operate 8-bit pointer counters in the CPU with external 8-bit page counters and operate with last-in/first-out (LIFO) (16 8-bit) stacks with multiplexers and page counters, 8- or 16-bit address buses. Others operate with first-in/first-out (FIFO) stacks.

The timing is the orderly sequencing of computer logic events and is usually associated with the CPU control of a free-running oscillator (clock), which furnishes time reference signals. The basic features are the clock period, which is the time between pulses from the clock, and the next phase, which provides a different timing rhythm because the clock may put out more than one logic line of timing pulses (each line of pulses is a phase of the clock). Thus a richer set of time references allows the microprocessor more complex timing schemes. The instruction cycle, as noted, is the time required to fetch a simple instruction from memory and execute it— although many instructions in reality take several cycles for the simpler microprocessors. Some instruction cycle times require up to eight clock periods, for example. Some systems permit or implement instruction decode by basic hardware, others have special hardware called programmed logic arrays (PLAs), and still others have control ROMs or CROMs.

A PLA has many input lines and large numbers of AND gates and OR gates for output lines. In many microcomputers the CROM is on the microprocessor chip and contains the microprograms that give the sequence of actions necessary to execute single instructions. The better microprocessors use PLAs and CROMs for control, thus precluding the redesign of the CPU chip when more complex logic functions are required or varied. A microprocessor handles subroutine and interrupts considerably differently from standard or minicomputers through the specialized use of RAM. For example, on some systems the main program issues a call for a subroutine or interrupt handling routine, and with a RAM, the call instruction simply records the return address into a return address instruction in the subroutine. With ROM, the return address must be saved by the microprocessor, and a program counter stack is almost universally used. An interrupt or subroutine call causes the stack to be pushed down, the next instruction address of the present program ends up in the "first return" or return 1 position, and the first instruction address of the subroutine is placed in the program counter (PC). After the subroutine is completed, the stack is "popped," and the next instruction in the calling program is addressed by the PC. Different models have specific capability design registers. One type of register gives one subroutine level on the chip; another, the address of the lower-level stack, which is in the RAM, and so on.

ALU, accumulator registers, general-purpose registers

Generally, accumulator registers provide the source and destination for data to and from memory, as noted. Also the accumulator typically provides the location for one of the operands in two-operand arithmetic and logic operations. The arithmetic-logic unit (ALU), as the name implies, performs addition, subtraction, complementation, shifting, AND/OR/exclusive OR, and so on, plus BCD addition. In many systems, the ALU sets 1-bit registers according to the result of operations, such as overflow, carry, zero, and so on, to be used for logic branching flags and for bit manipulations. The general-purpose registers, located on the micro chip, are designed to be used together with the accumulators for fast-data manipulation. These can be accessed with a larger instruction set and with greater speed than main memory.

The tie-in of interrupts and priorities remains as a fundamental microprocessor control operation. Interrupts are the signals to the computer that demand special attention and are designed primarily with peripheral equipment to inform the CPU via I/O ports when specific data are arriving or when they have been received. The microprocessor reaction to various interrupts generally results in the interrupt signal's entering control; and, when the instruction cycle is completed, the PC stack is pushed, and the program flow branches to an interrupt handling subroutine, and the interrupt is disabled until the subroutine is completed. Further interrupts are locked out, and all register saving must be done by the interrupt subroutine. There are generally many levels of priority interrupts, three at the barest minimum. After completing a cycle, the machine starts executing at the determined interrupt level, locking others out; and control is returned to the CPU.

Static memory interface chips ("ROM family") generally have internal and external interrupts that can be forwarded to the microprocessor. Internal interrupts on some systems are activated from a software activated clock to permit software controlled timing. ROMs can be chained with control lines to allow priority determinations. Interrupts can also themselves be interrupted with higher priority interrupts. A register on some systems is associated with each interrupt, containing the address of the subroutine used to service that interrupt—a feature called vectored interrupt.

Microprogramming as an aid to the kit user

Microprogramming, where each machine instruction initiates a sequence of more elementary instructions (microinstructions), is an approach that permits replacing of fixed, conventional CPU control logic with a control memory. Addresses in control memory represent unique states in conventional control logic, and each memory output represents control lines from conventional logic. Stored in this memory are basic microinstructions, including the fundamental control, testing, branching, and moving operations. For an LSI machine to perform higher-level operations with ease, microinstruction sequences corresponding to common higher-level functions are stored in a separate read-only memory (ROM) to be accessed, decoded, and executed on command. These high-level sequences are called macroinstructions, the medium in which system programmers usually code. Macroinstructions in a microcomputer correspond to the basic instructions of a minicomputer.

Microprogramming permits a systems designer to adapt standard hardware to specific applications. And this is one of the most useful characteristics of microcomputers. The designer can construct macroinstructions that are best suited for the particular functions to be performed and incorporate them into the microprocessor as "firmware." We have noted that the instruction set of practically any existing minicomputer can be completely or partially emulated to minimize software development. Alternatively, a machine can be built to perform functions peculiar to an application such as an automated bank terminal, word processing (WP), or data acquisition. The capability to adapt a standard set of hardware modules to a variety of problems is a distinct cost advantage. High-volume, low-cost chip production adds more computing efficiency to the tailored instruction sets.

Microcomputer kit users find that the CPU or control unit, when totally microprogrammed owing to its user programmability, allows the general-purpose microcomputer to be tailored to custom, that is, specific requirements without necessitating special hardware design—and this is the key to economy in time and funds. Also many computer suppliers offer such standard and inexpensive options capabilities as extended-arithmetic and floating-point instructions, among the most basic, and special disk, diskette, and other operating systems and compilers as well.

Microcomputer kit selection criteria

Users quickly discover that they cannot get all of the advantages out of their systems with only the few processor and control chips. Generally, unless the whole family of chips is used, they cannot develop all the versatility hoped for—or the superior performance that the various systems are capable of providing. If, for example, the design of a specific system does not use the parallel and serial integrated circuits for interfacing, users lose the programmable interface feature that makes many systems so easy to interconnect with outside devices such as terminals, printers, disks, and so on. Some ROMs of the "family," for example, provide automatic loading and operating systems compatible with other systems using standard, widely sold evaluation sets. As owners of some of the major microsystems, kit buyers automatically become eligible for membership in user's groups providing access to large libraries of programs that will run on their modular systems. Editor and assembler programs are available directly from kit developers as well. Users who know they will be expanding their systems should check the amount of memory that can be added and at what cost. How many additional interfaces can be added, if any, is also an important consideration. How much of the desired system can be run off of the power supply provided with the kit is an important question. Can the system desired be expanded in the standard cabinet? Can a respectable number of I/O boards be plugged in? Memory expansion will be essential if the user intends to use a resident assembler or higher-level languages such as APL or BASIC. Assembler programs alone typically require a minimum of 4,096 words of memory and higher-level languages require even more. Users should be able to enter data by Teletype, CRT terminal, and so on. Very few system developers would seriously consider a major computer application by attempting to enter data from a switch and status light console. These may be educational, but they are not really practical. Calculator keypads and digital readouts are not too much better. There is really no substitute for a full alphanumeric keyboard and terminal system display for serious work.

There follows a chart of system components that potential microcomputer users develop as a checklist. Besides this, the new user should examine input lines and determine if the signal present can be readily communicated. Compare a number in RAM to a known threshold. If available, the A/D converter should be tested with a comparison of input to a particu-

FIGURE 6.1. A DEC kit interfacing package is plugged into the Unibus ® of Digital Equipment Corporation's PDP-11/10 mini-computer. The kit features a prewired backplane and accommodates from six to 18 standard interfacing logic modules and is one of a series being offered as part of the company's Scientific 11 marketing plan, which enables users to develop their own low-cost, expandable systems from new and standard PDP-11 hardware, peripherals, and software. *Courtesy: Digital Equipment Corporation*

FIGURE 6.2. Two complete prototyping and programming systems for Intel micro-computers, MCS-4 and MCS-8. Each includes prototype card at front and PROM programming card at rear, both plugged into control chassis for program assembly, simulation, PROM programming, prototype operation, and debugging. *Courtesy: Intel Corporation*

lar level; temperatures should be compared to a maximum level. Input data should be read and confirmed; controllers can be checked by reading dials or sets of buttons to determine if final values are reached. Overhead, timing, and multifetch instruction cycles can be checked by using basic tasks. The software should include programming manual; applications manual; systems reference and data sheet manual; evaluation module brochures; evaluation module users guide; linear interface manual; support software brochures; pocket programming cards; compiler offerings; and the available assemblers, editors, and interpreters.

As regards kit size, many users do not want to have most of their rack filled up with the CPU, power supply, I/O system, and little else, especially if they can find a kit to do the same job in just a few inches of rack space. Different systems require different amounts of main memory, and again users do not want to be paying for capability they do not really need. A dedicated system, for example, may require only up to 32K words of main memory. Another information management system application may require 128K words of main memory. Users might then consider at the outset that they want a system capable of being expanded as additional needs arise without the necessity of trade-offs of physical memory space for I/O controller space. Microcomputers should also be able to match closely to

FIGURE 6.3. Intel in-10 semiconductor memory system stores 4K 18-bit words per card. Chassis holds eight cards plus power supply to form 32K × 18 system with 450 ns cycle time. *Courtesy: Intel Corporation*

the number of peripherals required by the particular application. If the user needs four, he should not be required to pay for twelve I/O slots.

Criteria for microprocessor evaluation

Physical characteristics
    Technology
    Word length
    Package size—number of chips
    Voltages required
    Physical specifications

Control section
    Number of registers
    Size and type of registers
    Control and sense bits

Instructions
    Number and type
    Length
    Decoding method
    Speed of execution (min, max)
Addressing
    Modes
    Capacity
    Special features (for example stacks, and so on)
Control lines
Subroutine capability

Input/Output
    Number, size of I/O paths (buses)
    Device specification
    Drive capability, levels
    Interrupt system
        Number of lines
        Priority selection
        Handling methods
        Return technique
    Other signaling lines

Other system elements
    ROMs
    RAMs
    PROMs
    Clock chips
    Interface chips
    Special-purpose chips

    Additional circuit requirements
    Latches
    Buffers
    Drivers
    Reset circuitry
    Interface
    Multiplexers

Software support
    Assemblers
    Simulators
    Time sharing
    Other support
        Higher-order languages
        Debugging aids

Hardware support
   Development systems
   ROM simulators
   Other support
Costs and availability
   Processor
   System elements
   Other requirements
   Software development
   Hardware development

Typical kit components

A typical kit contains a family of devices designed to operate from a single +5V supply with a single bus architecture that encourages ease of system expansion. They are word-oriented families of RAMs and ROMs specifically designed for general applications that offer compatible memory interface devices and programmable logic peripherals for I/O task management. They should be true sets of building blocks designed for optimum parts count regardless of system application. Peripheral interface adapters (PIAs) prove very helpful for many systems and simplify I/O interface. The systems should have programmable logic communications interface adapters and modems and have instruction sets designed for efficient execution of both control and communications data. Users should be able to start with a clean, clear configuration and then add their own expertise and experience to create unique and personalized microcomputers designed for particular as well as general applications. Even nonprogrammers should be able to use the various kits and their versatile power.

Besides providing erasable ROMs and programs that can be entered, modified, examined, and executed under control from switches or typed commands, some suppliers offer cassettes filled with other useful information and/or programs to help debug and demonstrate microcomputer kits. Users' manuals explain everything the new customer needs to know and provide hints on how to expand systems for specific needs. Often wall-chart schematics are provided for easy reference to components and operations. Other suppliers offer expander boards that come with space for more edge connector sockets to allow for the addition of more cards. Some kits often contain double-sided circuit boards with edge connectors to allow all cards on the bus to be extended out of the card rack and for easy maintenance. Electronic distributors offer kits containing all popular microprocessors, peripheral support circuitry, and memory. Microcomputer interfacing kits permit customer interfacing of user peripherals, production control units, and laboratory instruments, for example. Such kits feature prewired backplane units that accommodate typically from six to 18 logic modules. The user selects the necessary modules and wires the proper mating connector to a standard 40-conductor cable. Kits for user assembled power supplies are also available.

The kit operations diagram in Figure 6.4 represents a package of components, software, and design documentation for building a full capability microcomputer based on Motorola's MC6800 single-chip microprocessor.

FIGURE 6.4. A typical kit—the Motorola 6800 microcomputer

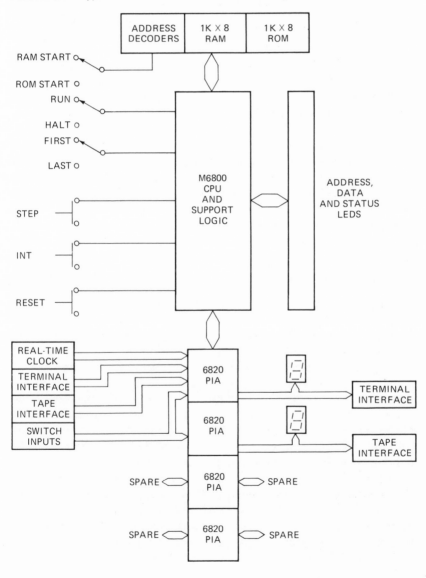

Custom software development and testing on the kit are supported by an array of CPU controls and displays, a variety of peripheral interfaces, special debugging circuits, and a system monitor that handles software-development peripherals. With the optional PROM programmer kit, the monitor will transfer programs directly into erasable PROMs. The kit design includes a master clock that is crystal controlled and uses a clock driver. Peripheral interface adapters (PIAs) are used for all I/O. All CPU buses are buffered, and ample address decoding is provided so that extra RAM, ROM, and I/O can be added.

Field alterable ROMs work with many popular micros. Packaged on a single PC board, some 256-by-1 bit field-alterable ROMs (PROMs, EAROMs, and so on) can be reprogrammed at the single-bit level. With this capacitive type unit, the alteration is almost as simple as a pencil erasure. Any discrete bit in storage can be reprogrammed repeatedly, even while the system is operating. Larger capacity systems to 16K bits can be accommodated on the same PC board. Models are available for most popular systems. Cost of the 16K memory is less than two-tenths cent per bit.

Among the many companies also announcing kits was RCA with its CMOS microprocessor family including its 8-bit processor. The Microkit hardware, manuals, and software development packages include the CPU, 1024 words of RAM, 512 words of ROM, space for additional memory and user-designed interface cards, input/output decoders, an I/O interface for teletypewriter or other terminal, and power supply.

Microcomputer user seminars and educational institutes

Most major manufacturers and distributors of microcomputers offer special training courses by correspondence, by traveling seminars, or by localized "institutes" that provide intensive hands-on training for standard fees. The courses last for from one to three days—others continue for a week or more. Key topics are logic design, microcomputer applications, specific system analysis, storage alternatives, interfacing, LSI technologies, and so on. Also many microcomputer implementation companies—those that build systems from chips supplied to them in large quantities—offer kits, peripherals, and special educational opportunities, again in local areas, with distributor or company-provided staffs. Many of the efforts designed to bring in more customers by updating them to the latest systems and developments have proved very successful—and hundreds of thousands of new computer users are becoming total enthusiasts, including a substantial number of high school students. Many microcomputer clubs have sprung up throughout the United States and Europe. Rapid development of very simple BASIC compilers, many new programs, and new computer-controlled toys and appliances have followed in this wake and new onrush of persistent curiosity.

"Stacks" of high-capability computers

Stacked micros or multiple minis are often called load sharing, minimultiprocessing, networking, hierarchical computing, and so on. The concept is distributed computing. Using multiple small computers to solve a complex computing problem quickly gained acceptance. It is a serious competitor for the traditional large-scale central computer. The battle is more than economic and technical. It is a gigantic run for vast unplanned markets. The advent of the minicomputer brought a valid alternative to the centralized-computer concept of the fifties. And the micro is doing battle with the minis of the late sixties and early seventies. Basic differences exist today. Decisions must be made as to whether to use a number of micros or minis or single central computers. But the sinking prices and growing capabilities of small and tiny computers make more compelling cases of distributed computing than ever before. Software and experience are catching hardware development. And all are out for expanded markets. All are trying to close new gaps. The system designers are investigating the potentials of distributed computer systems and are embarking on many new projects.

MITS—Leader in hobbyist equipment

Considerable credit should be given to the strong leadership in kits and hobby computers developed by the makers of the Altair models. For several years this firm almost single-handedly carried the concept and offered the products (as low as $400 for complete kits) that enticed thousands of beginners into a growing home computer revolution. With deep confidence in its products, prices, and the public's curiosity and desire to "do it yourself," the brave gamblers from New Mexico began to nationally advertise their wares and surprisingly accept and handle thousands of mail orders within the first year of their "personal computing" drive. The company was assisted by a cover picture on the magazine, *Popular Electronics* and a send off story of their products and company efforts. The company expanded rapidly, holding their prices low and keeping their advertising strong, until they achieved a commanding lead in the field that was maintained throughout 1976 and shows no sign of letting up. Their lead models in 1976 were the Altair 8800b, using the popular 8080A Intel chip family, and the 680b, using the Motorola 6800 chip family. These two leading microcomputers, now being used extensively in schools, colleges, small business, laboratories, and professional offices around the world are described briefly below along with the expanding line of peripheral equipment now available. The firm sponsored the first national users convention in Albuquerque and markets its products aggressively at all shows, conferences, and by large ads in practically all computer and electronics periodicals. It sells most of its equipment by direct mail but also makes its products available through a score or more "computer stores" and other distributors. Tens of thousands of home computer users have "grown up" on their Altairs.

In early 1976 strong positive customer feedback and alert managers of MITS brought out one of the first home systems using the biggest seller CPU chip system, the 8080A, while others continued with the initial 8080 chip set. Equally important were the many system improvements made over the first Altairs and the compatibility maintained for all the early purchasers. MITS also offers one of the most extensive lines of peripheral and support equipment, and although it was practically snowed under with orders during its first years, in late 1976 it was catching up—and introducing many new capabilities in a rapidly expanding line.

Other hobby computer makers

The biggest competition and one of the strong leaders is the IMSAI 8080 computer system from IMS Associates, Inc. of San Leandro, CA. The rugged, reliable, industrial type IMSAI 8080 is optionally expandable to a substantial system with 22 slots in a single printed circuit board, up to 64K of memory, plus a floppy disk controller, with its own on-board 8080, and a Disk Operating System. Other items as described below include audio tape cassette input devices, printers, video terminals, teleprinters, and so on. These peripherals function with an 8-level priority interrupt system, and IMSAI BASIC software is available in 4K PROM. A 4K RAM board with software memory protect is available for less than $140, and the system can be designed for low-cost multiprocessor shared memory capability. As many as six processors can share a common memory. The firm offers a variety of I/O interfaces plus 256 I/O ports. The variety of I/O interface boards includes serial I/O for synchronous and asynchronous RS232 or current loop operation. Or users can choose a versatile multifunction board with both serial and parallel ports, plus a tape cassette recorder interface.

Southwest Technical has listed questions and answers that are helpful to potential customers.

QUESTION: The 6800 system doesn't have any console switches on the front panel to enter data. How do I use it?

ANSWER: The 6800 system loads the initial data needed at "start up" automatically from an internal ROM. Instead of spending several minutes entering a "loader" program each time you use the machine, this is done for you automatically when power is turned on. System control is turned over to the control interface at this point and you are ready to enter information, or work with the machine from any 20 mA. Teletype, or video terminal.

QUESTION: What type terminal do I use?

ANSWER: Any terminal that outputs ASCII coded data may be used. The ASR-33 series Teletypes, or any video terminal using a serial interface will in general work with the 6800. Our CT-1024 terminal system is a good low cost terminal. You cannot use terminals having the old five level Baudot code, or terminals having the "IBM Corp." EBCDIC code.

QUESTION: Why is this method of data entry used on the 6800 system?

ANSWER: Because the 6800 system was designed to be convenient and easy to use. Entering programs in binary form with console switches may be educational, but it is certainly not convenient. With the 6800 system addresses are entered in "Hexidecimal" form, which is far simpler and less confusing. The data is also on the screen where it may be inspected and changed if desired. You don't have to write down each line of data from a row of lamps, or LED readouts to keep track of things.

QUESTION: What will I need besides an input/output (10) device to use the 6800 computer system?

ANSWER: Nothing—you will not be in for any nasty little surprises. The 6800 kit is complete with 2,048 words (BYTES) of memory a serial interface and diagnostic program information to help you test the completed computer. You will not find that you must purchase additional memory or other plug-in units to make the system useful and practical to use.

QUESTION: What about software and permanent storage.

ANSWER: In addition to our test programs, a resident editor and assembler is available for the 6800 system. The editor and assembler requires 8K of memory and is available to anyone purchasing the memory necessary to use the program. Cassette tape, or paper tape inputs are usable with this system.

QUESTION: What if I want additional memory, or more interfaces? The basic kit price is reasonable, but will I pay an arm and a leg for additional equipment?

ANSWER: Additional memory is $125.00 for the 4K kit. Additional interfaces are $35.00 per interface kit—serial, or parallel. Users can economically obtain a BASIC program for use on your SwTPC 6800 and other computers. An extensively tested "Tiny BASIC" interpreter is available from Itty Bitty Computers, Box 23189, San Jose, CA. 95153. This program has twelve commands and will run in 4.096 words of memory. A twenty-four page manual describing the program with sample programs written in "Tiny BASIC" and the punched paper tape to be used in loading the program into the machine is available for only $5.00.

A complete JOLT microcomputer in a single CPU kit includes:

An MOS Technology MCS 6502 NMOS microprocessor

512 bytes of program RAM, and 64 bytes of interrupt vector RAM

1K bytes of mask programmed ROM containing DEMON, a powerful debug monitor

26 programmable I/O lines

Internal RC clock, or crystal controlled clock with user supplied crystal

Serial I/O ports for use with a teleprinter current loop drive/receiver, or an EIA standard driver/receiver

Expandable address and data buses

Hardware interrupt

Control panel interface lines available on card connector

Complete assembly manuals and sample programs

JOLT accessory kits are:

JOLT RAM Card—Fully static 4,096 bytes of RAM with 1 microsecond access time and on-board decoding.   **$199.95**

JOLT I/O Card (Peripheral Interface Adapter)—2 PIA LSI chips, 32 I/O lines, four interrupt lines, on-board decoding and standard TTL drive. Fully programmable.   **$95.50**

JOLT Power Supply—Operates at +5, +12 and −10 voltages. Supports JOLT CPU, 4K bytes of RAM and JOLT I/O card—or, CPU and 8 1/O card.   **$99.95**

JOLT +5V Booster Option—Fits onto JOLT Power Supply card. Supports CPU, 8K bytes RAM and 8 I/O CPU and cards.   **$24.95**

JOLT Universal Card—Same size (4¼″ × 7″). Same form factor as other JOLT cards. Completely blank, drilled to accept 14, 16, 24 or 40 pin sockets.   **$24.95**

JOLT Accessory Bag—Contains enough hardware to connect one JOLT card to another, flat cable, connectors, card spaces, hardware, etc.   **$49.95**

JOLT Resident Assembler—Fully symbolic, single pass resident assembler, all mnemonics compatible with timesharing assemblers. Delivered on seven 1702A PROMs, ready for plugging into JOLT PROM card.   **$395.00**

JOLT 1702A PROM Card—Sockets for 2,048 bytes of PROM memory. Place anywhere in memory with jumper selectable addresses.
        $149.95 Assembled Only

Video Terminal—ASCII keyboard to video monitor or home T.V. Many other features.
        $450.00 Assembled

KIM series

The KIM-1 is a complete 8-bit microcomputer on a single printed circuit card, completely assembled and tested with a ninety day warranty. It contains an MCS 6502 microprocessor, 1K bytes of static RAM, 2K bytes of ROM containing a system executive program, a 20ma serial terminal interface, a 23-key control and data entry keypad, a six digit 7-segment LED display, and 15 bidirectional I/O lines. A programmable interval timer and an audio cassette interface are also included. The KIM-1 can be used as a stand-alone microcomputer or form the heart of a complete system when used with the KIM-4 motherboard and other expansion modules. It is 10.75" × 7.85" single PC board. Terminals are provided for mounting an additional keypad remotely. Functions are:

0–9,	A–F:	hexidecimal data entry
	AD:	enter address mode
	DA:	enter data mode
	+:	increment address
	PC:	restore program counter
	ST:	(STOP) generate interrupt
	GO:	begin program at current PC
	RS:	reset to monitor control

The KIM-1 characteristics are:

LED Display:

Six seven-segment displays, 0.6" character height. When used by the monitor, the leftmost four hexidecimal digits display the current memory address, the rightmost two digits display the contents of that address.

Subroutines are provided in ROM for user-control of the display and keypad.

Retail store competition

Before the total of hobbyist computer stores reached 300 in early 1977, Intel Corp. and several other major semiconductor manufacturers that were leading in microcomputer chip production began to see the size of the "personal computing" market grow to significant proportions. Intel began advertising directly to hobbyists and major distributors began to supplement this action with promotions of their own. A great many small businessmen began to frequent the retail computer stores—and they began buying units and systems for office and home use. Soon observers of a very big competitive battle saw National Semiconductor take an early lead with the claim of selling 8000 SC/MPs in a period of four months in 1976. Fairchild's competitive F-8 system, with equal power, also started to move in large volume—and the two companies started a price-performance war. Digital's

FIGURE 6.5. Digital Equipment Corporation LSI-11, PDP-11/03 and PDP-11V03 microcomputer configurations

LSI-11 available to hobbyists made a big splash—particularly because of the huge pools and availability of business, educational, and scientific software throughout the world—requiring only minor adaptations for wide "personal" and small operator use.

Multiprocessing advantages

Multiple microcomputers and minicomputers are bargains for many reasons: (1) they cost far less to purchase, (2) they are easy to program and install, (3) they are much less difficult to use, (4) single large computers are linked to various operating departments via cables or communications links and remote time-sharing terminals, and (5) they also are often considerably more convenient and economical than time-sharing bureaus with their tie-ups and high overhead.

Small computers are distributed to different departments of a company and individually work on order entry, inventory control, sales analysis, accounts payable and receivable, employees payroll, and other statistics and reports. In such configurations, each micro or mini is responsible for processing the data for its own department, then sending summaries or results to a supervisory computer whenever required. But overall hard results can be summarized:

1. *Start-up simplicity and system flexibility.* Multiple computer systems are usually installed in segments according to corporate, not system, priorities. Each computer can be installed, programmed, and started up before going to the next. Segmented system installation fits with budgets also. These new computers are less costly and are added as more money becomes available. Often programming or interfacing problems can be handled by company people.
2. *Processing economy.* Small computers can be designed to develop, analyze, and format their own local data, cutting costs of the central computer. This saves processing time for more important uses; and, if data are being transmitted through rented telephone lines, it can cut carrier line usage, or new company-owned microwave or laser systems can be used.
3. *Quick and easy system expansion.* When new hardware must be added to a multiple computer system, ongoing operation does not have to be halted. New software can be developed and tested off-line and can be transferred to those computers on which they will run.
4. *Fast response.* A small computer dedicated to local data processing can react much faster than a large computer that must handle many different applications. In a retail selling environment, this could mean inventory reports instantaneously vs.—with a batch-processing system— waiting until the next day for a reply. Similarly, errors that otherwise would turn up in the overnight batch process routine of the central computer are discovered at once.
5. *Reliability.* There are several ways to distribute the risk of downtime by interconnecting small computers to achieve redundancy without having to buy more computers.
6. *Systems can be built in segments.* Small computers can be purchased singly and first installed in the least complex or most critical areas of work. Installation and programming experience gained by setting up these machines can be applied to other parts of the system as more com-

puters are added. Once the small computers are performing their local-ized jobs, they are connected to the supervisory computer to complete the system.

7. *Uninterrupted operation.* Small computers (and the supervisory compu-ter) can be interconnected to provide backup should any computer fail.

8. *Using different types of processing simultaneously.* Dual medium-scale processors supervising a number of distributed satellites in microcom-puters or minicomputers may be an economical alternative to single large systems. The satellites could do all local processing, sending only final statistics to one supervisor, perhaps running in real-time, that could send back inventory reports and accounting or price changes as they are called for by the satellite. A second supervisory computer could be batch-processing companywide data and turning out manage-ment information reports while acting as "hot standby" for the primary processor in case of failure.

9. *Winning the battle of very high incoming data rates.* Busy-hour peak data loads can slow down computer response times. A multiple com-puter system can be configured so that the primary data-handling pro-cessor can keep response time fast. Then, when the data load returns to normal, the secondary machine can return to its own processing tasks.

10. *Multiple interconnections can vary in many ways.* The data-handling potential of multiple computers is helpful for the different ways they can be interconnected, as well as for the hardware options that facilitate specific types of connections. Many installations can effectively use a dual-processor, shared disk configuration, and so on.

The I/O bus switch is a hardware ingredient that is used for complete redundancy among interconnected computers. For high-speed multicom-puter applications, where any computer in the network must be able to communicate with any other computer, a multiprocessor communications unit permits large volumes of data to be transferred directly between mem-ories. They are used in front-end message switching systems to intercon-nect data concentrators for performing control functions.

Schottky bipolar LSI microcomputer set: an example of "bit slice" architecture[1]

The Intel® bipolar microcomputer set is a family of Schottky bipolar LSI circuits, which simplify the construction of microprogrammed central pro-cessors and device controllers. These processors and controllers are micro-programmed in the sense that their control logic is organized around a sep-arate read-only memory called the microprogram memory. Control signals for the various processing elements are generated by the microinstructions

---

[1] © Intel Corporation, from sales literature.

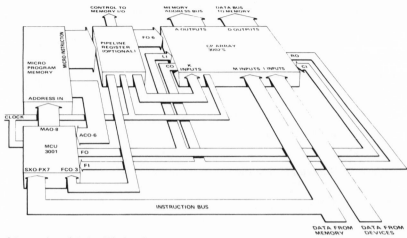

Other members of the Intel bipolar microcomputer set:

Microprogram Control Unit	Priority Interrupt Control Unit	Schottky Bipolar ROM (512 × 8)
Look-Ahead Carry Generator	Inverting Bidirectional Bus Driver	Schottky Bipolar PROM (256 × 4)
Multimode Latch Buffer	Schottky Bipolar ROM (256 × 4)	Schottky Bipolar PROM (512 × 8)

FIGURE 6.6. Block diagram of a typical system. *Courtesy: Intel Corporation*

contained in the microprogram memory. In the implementation of a typical central processor, as shown in Figure 6.6, the microprogram interprets a higher level of instructions called macroinstructions, similar to those found in a small computer. For device controllers, the microprograms directly implement the required control functions.

The Intel®3002 central processing element contains all of the circuits that represent a 2-bit-wide slice through the data-processing section of a digital computer. To construct a complete central processor for a given word width N, it is necessary to connect an array of $N/2$ CPEs together. When wired together in such an array, a set of CPEs provide the following capabilities:

2's complement arithmetic.

Logical AND, OR, NOT, and exclusive-OR.

Incrementing and decrementing.

Shifting left or right.

Bit testing and zero detection.

Carry look-ahead generation.

Multiple data and address buses.

High performance—100 ns cycle time.

TTL and DTL compatible.

N-Bit word expandable multibus organization.
3 input data buses.
2 three-state fully buffered output.
Data buses.
11 general-purpose registers.

Full function accumulator.

Independent memory address register.

Cascade outputs for full carry

look-ahead.

Versatile functional capability.
8 function groups.
Over 40 useful functions.
Zero detect and bit test.

Single clock.

28-pin DIP.

Time-sharing microcomputers; microsystem monitors and keyboard pads

One of the first to announce microcomputer time-sharing systems, Digital Equipment Corp., the largest supplier of minicomputers, startled many computer traditionalists. The time-sharing microcomputer systems will broaden significantly the opportunity for computer usage among both new and experienced users. The system, the MU/11V03, is an easily transportable, fully programmable system that serves up to four users simultaneously. The economy of time-sharing systems provides a practical and useful experience for great numbers of people, schools, labs, and so on with limited means and little experience, extending computer access to practically all ages and levels of society.

The system is disk-based, housed in a compact, roll-about cabinet 25 inches high, 19 inches wide and 25 inches deep. It weighs approximately 200 pounds. Any combination of up to four video display or hard copy terminals can simply be plugged into the system, which operates on standard 115–120 or 230-volt alternating current. Users can write and execute programs in BASIC, FORTRAN IV, or MACRO assembly language, which run the RT-11 real-time operating system. One FORTRAN IV or MACRO program may be executed simultaneously with up to three BASIC programs. It contains 28K words (56K bytes) of main memory, with dual flexible disks adding more than one-half million bytes of mass storage. Users can choose among several terminal models. Addition of a graphic display terminal provides interactive graphics capability. Terminals can be situated up to 25 feet from the system without additional hardware or in any remote location with appropriate interfaces.

FIGURE 6.7. Martin Research's Mike 3. *Courtesy: Martin Research*

Martin Research Inc. offers its Mike 3 system based on the Intel 8080 microprocessor chip. It has a calculator-type keyboard; instructions are entered in octal form and are displayed automatically on the six bright digits. The user can rapidly address any location in memory and display the contents at that address. The unit has a short stack option and a monitor and will accept seven PROMs; and, with a Teletype interface board, users can type in programs symbolically and receive symbolic or numeric program listings and many other functions. The monitor is in a PROM that plugs into a socket and allows the user to program the microcomputer with the system's 20-pad keyboard, addressing memory at any location, writing into RAM, and stepping through memory one location at a time.

**PART II: MICROCOMPUTER DEVELOPMENT
AND TESTING SYSTEMS**

Microcomputer development systems MDS combine both hardware and software design tools. Most designers must spend considerable effort getting both hardware and software to function properly, but then they often find that they do not work together properly in the final product. Development systems constitute complete microcomputers with capability to interface with a host of peripherals that speed development. Very welcome prototype "boxes" can interface with disk-operated systems and high-speed readers and printers. These systems have greatly extended debug capabilities and are able to assist in checking internal microprocessor registers and memory locations—and to do this in a system one or several steps at a time. Also they allow in-circuit emulation, permitting the early isolation of trouble spots in an end product or specific application. Development systems are now available for practically all major microprocessor chips, and the manufacturers strongly state that these development systems will not become obsolete, but that many of them will form the nucleus of "universal" design and debug centers.

Basically, the design aids are quite alike—one microprocessor residing in the prototype box generates the code and performs the fundamental software-development chores, such as editing and assembly. An additional processor, part of an add-on unit, tailors the box to a specific microprocessor and replaces the system processor. It thus monitors and controls the system, tracking down errors and simplifying diagnostic tests. Many other efforts are coming to fruition on the software front, some coming close to erasing the need for users to have a working knowledge of different assembly languages to use the different micros. Intel Corp. has pioneered the PL/M language, as previously discussed. Other software designs are types of cross compilers. Some of these can accept a popular assembly language for one processor and output code for another microprocessor; others translate assembly language and also handle higher-level languages. Such in-circuit emulators as Intel's ICE and many other microcomputer development systems are being copied most successfully by both large and small microcomputer companies. Thus resources can be applied to an end product at an early design stage, that is, as soon as the bus structure is defined. The development module can be plugged into an actual system prototype in place of the microprocessor. Thus various trouble spots may be checked out by a "transparent" mapping from the prototype to the MDS. Malfunctioning memory module or software problems or errors can be located quickly. The MDS solution disconnects the module and replaces it with an internal memory; the system does not know the difference. The program is then executed. If the system works, the hardware is at fault; if not, software must be the culprit, in most cases. Other debug tools are also included in various development systems as well as special "breakpoints" that suspend the execution of the processor and permit examination of bus activity during the previous many machine cycles. Also the breakpoints can and often are set "symbolically" rather than at specific locations. These development systems accommodate competitive products. Motorola's Exorciser prototyping system already does so. LSI testers plug into development systems and perform incoming inspection on all microcomputer ICs, including memory. National Semiconductor's prototype box, the IMP-16P, is a disk-operating system and can be used to design systems involving the company's 16-bit multichip MOS processor as well as its single-chip PACE microprocessor. Pretested, preprogrammed memories in many kits provide fixed-instruction sets that eliminate the need for a great deal of microprogramming for new users and inexperienced amateurs.

A flowchart for a popular software development system is shown in Figure 6.8.

A large and rapidly growing new subindustry has quickly grown because of the boom in microcomputers. The microcomputer systems development industry is no longer a fledgling, owing to the wide popularity of the "in-circuit emulator" concept and the pioneering by the major manufacturers. Special microcomputer shops and "stores" are springing up in practically every state in the land—and a considerable number of microcomputer program development courses are in vogue for many calculator users who have graduated to microcomputer systems.

See Appendix B for Additional Analysis of Design and Testing Tools: Software Support Systems

FIGURE 6.8. Software development through a process developed by Millennium Information Systems does not entail the printing of the entire program listing to determine assembly errors. Instead, only statements containing assembly errors are printed. *Reprinted with permission from* Electronics, *April 18, 1974, copyright McGraw-Hill Book Co., all rights reserved.*

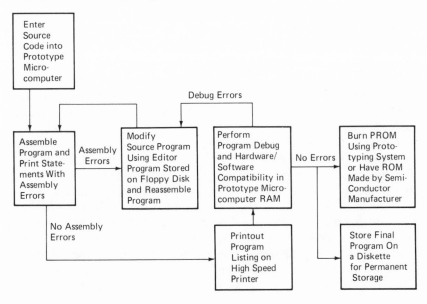

Testing programs by simulator

Some users elect to test programs on the many available simulators on the market. Often this does not yield a thorough test because simulators are limited in their ability to represent accurately peripheral devices and the hardware that the microcomputer is intended to control. Also simulation of program execution involves many operations and may develop lengthy reports on what happened during the simulation.

A great many programs have been tested to virtual completion on microcomputer development systems, and debugging programs are used during this stage while the program being tested is kept in RAM. The various debugging programs allow the user to modify and examine the contents of memory locations and set up data and register conditions for the program being tested. The most often used peripheral device is the Teletype (usually, the old ASR-33) because it includes a keyboard, printer, tape reader, and tape punch.

It is beyond the province of this book to analyze all the hundreds of testing routines that are required for all components of microcomputers, from integrated circuits through ROMs and PROMS. However, the reader may be interested in the total cycle and the intricacies of the problems concerned with the quest for quality and reliability of microsystems. A block diagram of the stages and processes is reproduced in Figure 6.9. A further breakout of the testing procedures of a microcontroller is shown to demonstrate the use of tape cassettes in the various procedures, in this case the automatic PC board tester. (See Fig. 6.10)

Simplified tester system

Most kit users, and smaller system developers, to conserve funds, might turn to low-cost module testing procedures. Such system testing procedures can be arranged properly to test each module of standard microcomputer systems. If there is a malfunction in one of the modules being tested, lights on the system console will indicate this by not turning on and off in a defined unique sequence. As an example, one basic tester consists of a tested CPU, RAM and PROM modules, power supply, and regulator module; other modules and programs can be added for testing other modules. For example, a D.C. output module is needed to test a D.C. input module. To operate the module, first the tester must be equipped with the necessary modules and programs. The PROM in the tester is programmed with the necessary test programs, and these programs can be executed by selecting the test number of the module on the thumbwheel switches. If the module under test is defective, then the lights on the console will so indicate by turning on and off in accordance with the test program outputs. The CPU of a good microcomputer system has a powerful and versatile in-

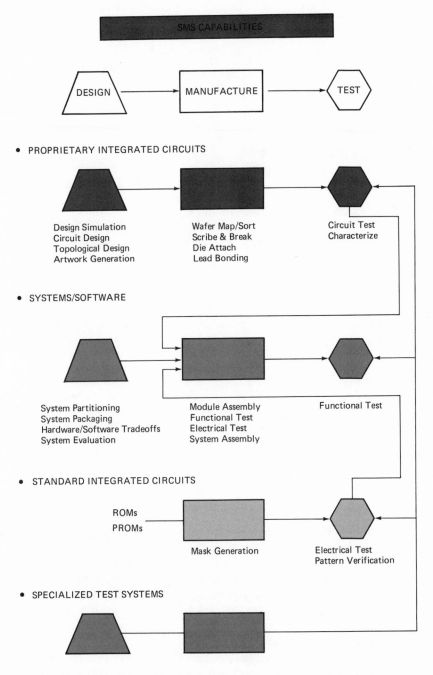

SMS CAPABILITIES

DESIGN ⟶ MANUFACTURE ⟶ TEST

• PROPRIETARY INTEGRATED CIRCUITS

Design Simulation	Wafer Map/Sort	Circuit Test
Circuit Design	Scribe & Break	Characterize
Topological Design	Die Attach	
Artwork Generation	Lead Bonding	

• SYSTEMS/SOFTWARE

System Partitioning	Module Assembly	Functional Test
System Packaging	Functional Test	
Hardware/Software Tradeoffs	Electrical Test	
System Evaluation	System Assembly	

• STANDARD INTEGRATED CIRCUITS

ROMs
PROMs

| Mask Generation | Electrical Test |
| | Pattern Verification |

• SPECIALIZED TEST SYSTEMS

FIGURE 6.9.

251

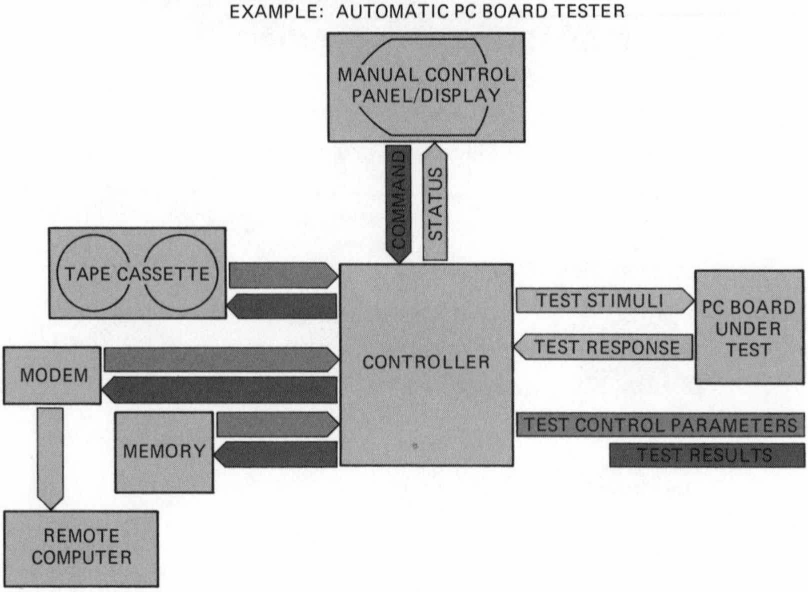

EXAMPLE: AUTOMATIC PC BOARD TESTER

FIGURE 6.10. Automatic PC Board Tester. Minicomputers have traditionally been used for this kind of application, which is an overkill and expensive solution to the problem. It has elements of data communications, device control, and process control. The PC board under test is connected to A/D and D/A convertors where test stimuli are applied and test responses monitored by the controllers. The testing sequence is specified by formated data contained on a tape cassette. These data are transferred to an external memory before the testing begins. The controller reads and interprets test sequence data from the memory and implements appropriate test to the PC cards. Alternatively, the test sequences may be supplied by a remote computer connected via a modem or through a manual test panel and display.

struction set that allows the system to perform a wide variety of arithmetic, control, and decision functions. The PROM, with microprogram, allows users the power of designing custom computers with standard components.

An interesting case of a specific individual's attempt to master the development of his first microcomputer is offered on a following page. Because it represents so many "at first" frustrations of users, it is reproduced here. It also says much about how development systems and testing devices often spring from the most common users or from serendipity.

The reader is advised to read carefully the definitions on the following few pages and to consult product manuals, applications notes, and microcomputer dictionaries to understand better the progress of microcomputer development systems.

HOW I GOT FAKED OUT BY THE MICROPROCESSOR MAKERS.

(Or, they didn't tell me I had to be a programmer.)

I was a hardware-oriented engineer who had spent years doing analog circuit, hard-wired semiconductor, and relay logic designs. I had an elementary knowledge of computers and no knowledge of programming, but I thought I was ready for microprocessors.

Last February I attended a seminar on microprocessors. Very interesting, but I didn't know enough to ask a question. (Don't think my classmates did either.)

When I got back to the lab, the boss let me order a kit. I got chips, a connection diagram, and a lot of confusion. How do I connect the chips to demonstrate microprocessor operation? (The system interconnect schematic presupposed the knowledge of how to write a program in the 256-word PROM.) How do I program the PROM? How do I write an intelligent program about a device I know next to nothing about?

Finally, I got my hands on a user's manual. It suggested several systems configurations. It became apparent that program memory could not be contained in ROM. I needed to alter program memory during the learning process.

I told my boss about the problem; he suggested one of those "microprocessor test" units he'd seen advertised. "Too costly—$3 to $4K. Too advanced—had to be a programmer. Too specialized—good for only one processor." That's what I told him. My boss wasn't too happy. I guess he would have been lots less happy if I'd spent $4K for a program verifier I couldn't use.

At this point I drew a block diagram, then listed the characteristics of a system that would let me write and check a program: (1) Program memory address and data should be easily entered in machine language (ones and zeroes). (2) Program memory address and data should be displayed by panel indicators. (3) Program memory address should be capable of being incremented, decremented, and force loaded. (The contents of the memory program can thus be altered or examined in sequential steps for easy program verification or forced to a high order address location without going through the lower order addresses.) (4) At least one output port should have front panel indicators. The contents of the port could be readily examined to display the results of a CPU operation. (5) Single step operation must be provided for program debugging. (6) The machine must be capable of executing all instructions in the CPU manufacturer's set.

Then, I set out to build my own trainer. Configured eight chips into a 256 × 8 memory array. Two 4-bit binary counters for address. Chips and switches and lights and everything else I needed was scrounged—and voilà!—in two weeks— a minimicrocomputer.

They laughed when I sat down to play my microprocessor trainer. But, in short order I was off and running—programs, that is. Arithmetic and logic manipulation came to life. Instruction set meant something. Hardware and software came together. Programs were written with mnemonics. I could write short subroutines in high order program memory locations and jump them with conditional or unconditional jump instructions. I could write finite and infinite program loops. I understood on-board index registers, the push-down stack, the data RAM scratch pad memory, the function of the accumulator. In short, I understood how a microprocessor operates, what its limitations are, how to program it, and how it might be used.

Pretty soon, the rest of the gang found out about my machine—and I had them waiting in line to unravel the mysteries of the microprocessor.

Now, look what my boss has done to my baby. Named it μPrimer 4/8. Had it gussied up and designed to train engineers on 4- or 8-bit microprocessors. Come up with modules for the most popular 4- and 8-bit microprocessors on the market—so it's really versatile. (Can be used for simple prototyping, too.) Each card can carry chips from a set.

Courtesy of: Technitrol, Inc., 1952 E. Allegheny Avenue, Philadelphia, Pa. 19134

FURTHER DEFINING THE WORLD OF MICROCOMPUTERS

Assembler development systems. Various assemblers run software development systems. Some of the many approaches to system development permit the use of full macro capabilities, which means that a programmer can define special pseudoinstructions in the main program during the assembly process. Macros are line subroutines, except that the main program executes them as it comes to them, instead of branching out of the main stream and then returning, as it does with subroutines.

Battery pack. Battery packs generally provide backup power to support components as RAM and so on. Time of support is dependent upon the amount of RAM, for example, to be kept under power; 4K bytes can be supported for eight hours. 20K bytes can be supported for one hour in some systems.

Benchmark. In relation to microprocessors, the benchmark is a test point measuring the performance characteristics of products offered. A benchmark program is a routine or program selected to define or compare different brands of microprocessors. A flowchart in assembly language is often written out for each microprocessor, and the execution of the benchmark time, accuracy, and so on is evaluated.

Breadboard. Usually refers to an experimental or rough construction model of a process, device, or construction.

Breadboard, I/O interface. A typical board is designed for data transfers to and from the data line under program control with or without interrupt. Generally, the area included on the board for custom interface can use 14, 16, 24, 36, and 40-pin IC packs as well as discrete components. Vcc and ground are available on the breadboard area. Usually, two 44-pin edge connectors on the top of the board are available for either I/O cables or card interconnect jumper boards.

Breadboard kit. Breadboard kits usually come with an assortment of sockets for custom circuitry. A number of circuit kits are available that allow the user to add special functions to the modular microcomputer system. Designed for insertion into a breadboard, in general each includes a collection of parts and sockets and full instructions. Such kits are available for interfacing to ASCII keyboards, to 8-bit parallel TTL input/output sources, to the ASR33, and to other makes of printers.

Card cage. Many suppliers offer a variable connector card cage with a basic microprocessor. It is often prewired to hold the CPU, memory cards, a front panel interface, and a card reader controller. Additional card cages may be installed for expansion. Generally, if still more expansion is required, the power supplies may be removed and remotely installed, thus providing space for additional card cages in some systems.

Chassis assembly. The optional chassis assembly in many systems mounts in a standard 19-inch rack and provides convenient mounting locations for the processor, power supply, and often up to 15 (or more) peripheral interface cards. The chassis assembly is often designed using a printed circuit backplane for all interconnecting wiring.

Chip testing. The design engineer not only designs the chip, but determines diagnostic programs associated with the chip instruction set in a number of steps. First, he places the diagnostic programs into a computer that has implemented the chip logic and checked it out with a simulation program. The computer compares the chip output with the input to the chip from the simulation program. In the next step, the designer sets the computer to exercise the chip with the diagnostic programs he has prepared.

CMOS logic. CMOS appears to be an answer to power supply costs and noise immunity. When operated with a 10 V supply, it has a worst-case noise immunity of 3 V. Even when operated at 5 V, A.C. and D.C. noise immunities are superior to those of other logic. The power dissipation is essentially zero at D.C., climbing to that of lower power TTL at a few MHz. The low-power and regulation requirements allow power supply costs to be cut significantly.

Cross assembler. 1. Refers to a program run on one computer for the purpose of translating instructions for a different computer. 2. Programs are usually assembled by the same assembler or assembly program contained within or used by the processor on which they will be run. Many microprocessor programs, however, are assembled by other computer processors whether they be standard, time-shared, mini, or other microcomputers.

This process is referred to as cross assembly, and the programs are not designed for specific microprocessors but are to be used on other computers. They are known as cross assemblers.

Debugging, microprogammed system. The designer of a microprogrammed system during the debugging phase must have at his disposal (1) a way of setting and locking the ROM address register of his microprogrammed device, (2) a way of monitoring the contents of the address register, and (3) a ROM simulator. The ability to set, lock, and monitor the ROM address register provides a convenient means for identifying the location of errors and documenting individual program changes. The simulator enables the user to insert the hundreds of little changes he or she will make during the debugging of the program. Some of these changes will be made to correct actual errors in the microcode. However, the majority will be inserted in an effort to locate and diagnose mistakes.

Debug, microinstructions. Most microinstructions operate on data stored in the system, or they test system conditions and respond to these. For example, if a set of microinstructions controls an arithmetic element, then in order to determine if the add, subtract, AND, OR, and so on instructions are working, data must be present in certain registers so that results can be generated and checked. Many microinstructions test the condition of arithmetic unit and determine if a carry, overflow, or other indicators are present. Before these microinstructions can be tested, it must be possible to set up the conditions that will be checked.

Debug program. A debug program provides the programmer with an on-line conversational utility for use in a program debugging operation and offers a wide variety of inspection and control. The commands include memory search/inspect/modify and memory print, memory and/or register initialization, memory-to-memory copy of specific regions, a set of selectable relocation registers to provide listing/memory address compatibility, the ability to execute selected program segments using up to two breakpoints, and an automatic escape return to debug from a runaway program.

Debug program, assembly. If a program is written in assembly language, there is a close parallel between the source and object program instructions. While users are making corrections, they will execute the object code under a debug program, which allows them to control execution via commands entered at the teletype. Debug programs permit users to execute programs one instruction or a few instructions at a time and to display the contents of selected memory words at the Teletype or other output device.

Diagnostic test. The running of a machine program or routine for the purpose of discovering a failure or a potential failure of a machine element and to determine its location or its potential location.

Diagnostic trace routine. A particular type of diagnostic program designed to perform checks on other programs or to demonstrate such operations. The output of a trace program may include instructions of the program that is being checked and intermediate results of those instructions arranged in the order in which the instructions are executed.

EAROM (electrically alterable ROM). Electrically alterable read-only memories are commercially available as MNOS EAROMs. These nonvolatile memory devices, with operating power down to $3\mu2$/bit, are programmed much like ordinary RAMs. They have no fusible links and do not require UV irradiation.

ECL (emitter-coupled logic) advantages. Some designers predict computer logic will eventually be designed completely around ECL (emitter-coupled logic). The ECL approach often is preferred because the devices are inherently very uniform and very stable and are excellent for driving lines. ECL is very fast; so users must design with the higher speed in mind and follow certain layout rules. The approach also can necessitate use of multilayer printed circuit boards. That is advantageous in terms of packaging density. ECL is also advantageous because it requires only a 1-volt swing in 3 to 4 nanoseconds, whereas a typical Schottky T^2L requires a 5-volt swing in the same time frame. ECL also inherently generates less noise, which is a benefit.

EEROM programmer. A device that provides a means of programming a single EEROM or an EEROM module from paper tape or from an integral hex keyboard and display. EEROMs are electrically erasable and, therefore, need not be removed from the module or socket to be erased and reprogrammed. Included is a RAM buffer, which permits editing of any EEROM. The equipment may also be used as a ROM emulator.

EPROM erasure. Electrically programmable read-only memory (EPROM) is ideally suited for uses where fast turnaround and pattern experimentation are important. Some types are packaged in a 24-pin dual in-line (DIP) package with a transparent lid. The transparent quartz lid allows the user to expose the chip to ultraviolet light to erase the bit pattern. Therefore, unlike a metal mask read-only memory, where a pattern cannot be changed, a new pattern can be written in to the EPROM devices.

Error detecting code. 1. Refers to a system of coding characters in a computer such that any single error produces a forbidden or impossible code combination. 2. A code in which each expression conforms to specific rules of construction, so that if certain errors occur in an expression, the resulting expression will not conform to the rules of construction, and thus the presence of the errors is detected. Synonymous with self-checking code.

Evaluation module. An evaluation module, incorporating a specific micro-computer family of parts on a printed circuit board, permits users to evaluate these parts in a typical configuration. They may run simple programs on the module and interface the module with a peripheral device and become familiar with the microcomputer family or parts and operating characteristics.

I²L advantages. I²L circuit techniques offer capabilities that make next generation high-performance, low-cost systems possible. Because it is manufactured with today's TTL bipolar technology, it does not require major new technology research; the process is in production now. Because I²L is made from a standard bipolar process, I²L circuit designs can be made to interface with many other circuits.

These characteristics make I²L a universal logic form for medium performance, minimum cost applications. Internal logic can be totally separated from the interface, resulting in optimum density, correct logic interface; thus ease of use for the system logic designs.

ICE. ICE is an in-circuit emulator, which is plugged directly into the user's system in a real-time environment. ICE is used to control, interrogate, revise, and completely debug a user's system in its own environment. For Intel Corp. 8080-based products, ICE-80 is provided, and ICE-30 is used to develop products with the bipolar microcomputer set.

Input-output module exorciser. The input/output module provides the Motorola Exorciser with a flexible means of interfacing with the user's defined process or peripheral device. The module provides the user the option of interfacing directly with the module's two peripheral interface adapters (PIA) or of constructing customized interface circuits. The PIA input/output lines are TTL voltage compatible. Space for 12 wire-wrap pockets on the module permits the user to construct interface circuitry to meet his specific interfacing needs between the PIA and his peripheral device. The microprocessor addresses each PIA as if it were memory. Switches on the input/output module enable the user to select the base memory address for each PIA.

Interface debugging. Some microprogrammed interfaces can be checked out in part by writing short programs to see if portions of the interface work. Suppose one wished to check out the interface to a paper tape reader. A short loop can be written that advances the tape and checks for data. This loop can be executed in a single step mode. The final routine for driving the tape reader will be considerably more complex than this one because it will have to time out the interval between characters and so on. The short routine determines that the circuits were working. In this way, the problem of determining whether the bugs are in the microcode or in the circuits is coped with easily.

Interrupts, external. External interrupts originate with device controllers or interrupt modules on an I/O bus. An interrupt module provides control of many external interrupt signals. Device controllers may generate interrupts to signify individual data transfers, end of operation, or error conditions.

Isoplanar oxide-isolation. A novel variation applicable to all bipolar processes is oxide isolation. This technique primarily results in higher packing densities and slightly higher speeds and is accomplished by using silicon oxide to isolate the various components. A common form of oxide isolation is called isoplanar. The other bipolar processes achieve electrical isolation of the circuit elements with reversed biased P-N junctions, but these junctions occupy more space and have higher capacitance than applied to the complex. N-channel MOS is almost as fast as oxide isolation circuits, yet is considerably less expensive. Oxide isolation will not be an important memory technology. The technique will probably be applied to the complex bipolar products to achieve cost reduction. Because this memory market is not particularly cost-sensitive in the near term, oxide isolation will be adopted slowly.

Kit assemblers. A typical kit assembler reads a source program from an external device and converts it into binary form in the MPS memory. Input can be read from any device, including the Teletype keyboard. A second pass of the source can be made to generate an assembly listing. The assembler itself occupies approximately 3K of memory in some systems.

Kit processor cards. With a processor card, kit boxes include an assembled and tested microprocessor system, complete with memory. Cards are often more economical than chips for low-volume applications. They may be used for development of early production models for high-volume applications before they are replaced by an in-house design. Chips represent the ultimate in low cost and small size, but the designer or user must interface them with additional components and perform the necessary tests. The components selected must meet exact speed, power, and functional specifications.

Kit reliability. Reliability is of importance to any microcomputer user. It is especially important in such areas as telephone switching or measurement/control applications where minimum downtime is essential. In all other areas, however, it is certainly desirable to have a reliable microcomputer. And in the event that a component does fail, it should be easy to replace the failed sybsystem and get the system back on the air as soon as possible. For many applications, reliable operation even under abnormal power-line conditions is also important. The system should be able to operate normally if the power-line voltage dips as much as 25 percent indefinitely and be able to withstand complete loss of line power for short periods of time. Some applications also require power-fail-auto-restart capability; an example is a system monitoring data in an unattended location. In addition to these considerations, the computer should be able to run normally over a wide range of temperature, humidity, and vibration conditions.

Logic analyzers. Logic analyzers generally fall into three categories: state analyzers, timing analyzers, and trigger generators. State analyzers display digital data, in the form of 1s and 0s on a cathode-ray tube or via light-emitting diodes, in a word-versus-event format. This concentration on word sequences makes state analyzers useful in examining the functional behavior of binary systems. They are especially useful in the design of microprocessor-controlled digital products for examining the flow of command and data words on multiline buses.

Logic card. Refers to a group of electrical components and wiring circuitry mounted on a board that allows easy withdrawal and replacement from a pocket in the equipment. Each such card is related to a basic machine function, and on discovery of a bug in that function the card can be replaced.

Logic tester, field. Once a product leaves the factory, a new set of testing ground rules comes into effect. In the field, size, weight, and operating speed become the chief concerns. The kind of equipment required for field service varies with the firm's approach to such service. The kind of instrumentation needed to troubleshoot, test, and repair on-site differs considerably from the kind needed in field offices where instruments might be returned for service.

Logic tester, production. Digital test equipment for the production line should be relatively simple to use, with little or no need for an operator to interpret the output data. Where production volumes are relatively small, the simplest go/no-go indication of basic board parameters—checks of power supply continuity and freedom from shorts, for example—may suffice, and engineering can be given the responsibility for troubleshooting more subtle faults at a higher assembly level.

LSI board tester. New automated testers have been designed for low-volume production and troubleshooting and repair stations. A typical system(s) processor provides stored program capability that permits the testing of boards, devices, and the entire module with the exact patterns and timing necessary to do a function test. With the new stored program capability, testing of LSI boards and devices, as well as very complex sequential logic boards, is more easily possible.

LSI board tester components. One model tester consists of a memory board, personality board, and processor; permits stored program testing of the device-under-test. Buffers permit isolation or level translation to accommodate most logic types and protect the test system. Alternatively, fixed code generators may be connected to the device-under-test, and in either mode a transition counter and display may be used as part of the test process.

Macro cross assembler. A typical cross assembler runs as a conversational program on a time-sharing system; batch versions are also available. One system is a functional equivalent to the software provided by the manufacturer; however, various enhancements have been added.

Macro facility. A macro facility is often a deluxe feature in assemblers. It is very useful when similar sections of an assembler itself are written in FORTRAN. With minor modifications, the program can be run on any computer that compiles FORTRAN programs. Thus the designer prepares source programs, assembling them on some other computer, to obtain the object tape for the microcomputer. The FORTRAN-written assemblers are often made available to users through various national time-sharing, computer-service companies.

Microcomputer box. A typical system is provided with a full function, front panel power supply, Teletype and tape I/O connectors, a 12-slot card file, and an I/O buffer for driving external card cages. The specific CPU memory and controller configuration are at the user's option. Many printed circuit boards are 6.6 inches by 9.6 inches.

MOS microcomputer development systems. As a vehicle for integrating hardware, developing software, and debugging them both, many firms have offered microcomputer development systems to satisfy the combined needs of engineer and programmer. These systems can compose programs; emulate the product's central processor, memory, and I/O subsystems; and automate hardware/software debugging operations. The programmer need not use a separate software environment, such as simulation with a time-shared computer; and the engineer need not use a laboratory model equipped with homemade diagnostic aids. Equally important, the designers can debug with prototypes that operate in the same environment as the production model. The system can, in effect, reverse the traditional product-development flow, which has usually forced hardware-software integration to be postponed until late in the cycle. Many basic systems can be adapted to work with a variety of microprocessors, whether MOS or bipolar.

MOSFET (metal oxide semiconductor field effect transistor). When a voltage (negative with respect to the substrate) is applied to the gate, then the MOSFET is a conductor; and, if a potential difference is applied between source and drain, there will be current flow.

NMOS technology applications. NMOS semiconductor technology has made inroads into high density/high performance circuit design. The one-chip microprocessor, random access memories, and read-only memories are changing system implementation from random logic designs to software and firmware programmable microcomputing systems. Such systems frequently require relatively large amounts of memory.

One-step operation. Refers to a method of operating a computer manually, in which a single instruction or part of an instruction is performed in response to a single operation of a manual control. This method is generally used for detecting mistakes and other debugging procedures.

Operator interrupt. In some systems the operator interrupt trap is armed, and fixed interrupt location is patched each time the monitor receives control. When an operator interrupt occurs, control is given to a routine in the monitor. This routine signifies to the operator that the type-in is desired by ringing the bell, returning the carriage, and typing.

Package, ceramic. Refers to an industry standard high-performance, high reliability package, made of three layers of $A1_2O_3$ ceramic and nickel-plated refactory metal. In some types the cavity is sealed with a glazed ceramic lid, using a controlled devitrified low temperature glass sealant. Package leads are of Kovar, nickel-plated and solder-dipped, for socket insertion or soldering.

Package, plastic. A typical plastic dual-in-line package (DIP) is the equivalent of the widely accepted industry standard, refined by manufacturers for MOS/LSI applications. Many packages consist of a silicon body, transfer-molded directly onto the assembled lead frame and die.

Panel, removable. Some systems are designed with a removable front panel. Removing the front panel exposes the LSI modules and cables. This enables replacement or installation of a module from the front. The power supply is often located on the right-hand side when viewed from the front.

PC board diagnostic test systems. The primary purpose of testing printed-circuit boards is to identify the assembly and component faults that could cause the boards to fail later at systems test. Various test systems isolate and diagnose such faults and provide direction for their repair. Suppliers back up the systems with techniques and procedures that help.

PC testing, personality board. Output registers on personality boards permit generation or serial and/or parallel test patterns of various lengths; and, with appropriate test program control, they also generate pseudorandom codes and other types of shift register codes. The transition counting techniques can be used whether the device under test is exercised by the fixed program or the stored program. The stored programs also allow for a limited number of signal lines to be verified with data in the internal register.

Peripheral interface adapter (PIA), configuration. The peripheral interface adapter generally provides the universal means of interfacing peripheral equipment to the microprocessing unit (MPU). This device is often capable of interfacing the MPU to peripherals through two 8-bit bidirectional peripheral data buses and four control lines. No external logic is required for interfacing to most peripheral devices.

Personality cards. Inside some PROM programmers, a microcomputer tailors the program to the PROM the development team has decided to use. A programmer often directs the data to be stored through "personality" cards that provide the appropriate timing patterns, voltage levels, and other requirements. The programmer is partitioned so that new personality cards can be inserted as new PROMs are developed.

Plugboard. In a computer, a removable board having many electric terminals into which connecting cords may be plugged in patterns varying for different programs. To change the program, one wired plugboard is replaced by another.

PMOS. P-channel MOS refers to the oldest type of MOS circuit where the electrical current is a flow of positive charges.

Power supply kit. A typical power supply provides two +18, a +16, and a −16 volts. These voltages are unregulated until they reach the individual boards (CPU, front panel, memory, I/O, and so on). Each board has all the necessary regulation for its own operation. In some kits power supply allows users to expand their computers by adding up to 16 boards inside the main case. Provisions for the addition of a cooling fan are part of the design.

Prototype printed circuit board kit. A typical kit PC board is double-sided, plated through for designing custom interfaces to the MPS. It usually includes a 5-volt regulator and associated filters.

Rack. Refers generally to the metal or other type of frame or chassis on which panels of electrical, electronic, or other equipment may be mounted, such as power supply units, amplifiers, and so on.

RAM testing (IC). The advent of large-scale integrated circuits intensified the need for multichannel signal sources to permit functional tests. The need for electric parametric tests also remains. The effects on circuit performance of bias voltages, pulse amplitudes, signal delays, and so on must be evaluated to be certain that a device meets its specifications. For example, testing a semiconductor random access memory (RAM) requires that address, data, memory-enable, and write-enable signals all be applied with appropriate delays. A typical RAM is guaranteed to operate properly as long as the set-up and hold times are no less than the minimum values specified by the manufacturer.

ROM testing. Circuits that use ROMs to replace hard-wired logic tend to have many feedback loops. In many cases, technicians troubleshoot the ROMs along with the rest of the circuit—a practice that can lead to confusion. Therefore, it is best to install sockets for the ROMs so that the memories can be checked prior to installation on the board. This not only simplifies the test, but also provides a breakpoint in the loops. The sockets can also be used to connect to the test equipment during check-out. Thus the test system can be directed to generate ROM patterns while the system monitors the results coming back as inputs to the ROM. (Inputs to the ROM for address lines are usually a function of the previous ROM address pattern.) Circuits with ROMs also tend to have many jumps and subroutines so that it is often difficult to verify whether the instruction sequence follows the right course. Single-step capability is easy to implement at points where an external break is advisable.

Schematic diagram, electrical. Refers to specific representation in graphics of an electrical circuit in which symbols are used for each circuit element, that is, resistors, capacitors, inductors, transistors, diodes, transformers, switches, and so on; and wires are represented by lines. The schematic permits tracing of current paths for power and signals. Such diagrams most often are furnished by manufacturers of equipment for assistance in repairs or diagnosis.

Schottky bipolar multimodel latch buffer. A typical buffer is a versatile 8-bit latch with three-state output buffers and built-in device select logic. It also contains an independent service request flip-flop for the generation of central processor interrupts. Because of its multimode capabilities, one or more of them can be used to implement many types of interface and support systems for bipolar computing elements, including:

Simple data latches.
Gated data buffers.
Multiplexers.
Bidirectional bus drivers.
Interrupting input/output ports.

Simulation. 1. A type of problem in which a physical model and the conditions to which the model may be subjected are all represented by mathematical formulas. 2. The representation of physical systems and phenomena by computers, models, or other equipment, for example, an imitative type of data processing in which an automatic computer is used as a model of some entity, that is, a chemical process. Information enters the computer to represent the factors entering the real process; the computer produces information that represents the results of the process and the process itself.

Three-D process. The triple-diffusion process consists of three sequences of entirely nonepitaxial impurity depositions and profile distributions. The major advantage of the technique: the pnp transistor and its npn complement can be merged into the same region, whereas resistors terminate directly on the collector of the assembly, which is a simple extension of the collector region. This feature of coalesced complementary structures having common potential in a circuit not only results in extreme compactness; it reduces the intraconnection complexity.

Thumbwheel switches. Thumbwheel switches are often found on consoles of small systems and are internally connected to the input/output module. Each thumbwheel switch is in BCD code. In some systems four lines per switch are used to decode the 0 to 9 digits. The input-output module works as an interface between the switches and the CPU module. From a specific mounting rack position extra modules can be added, depending upon the test modules desired.

Transistor power supplies. Power supplies are changing rapidly and radically in design. Many power supplies now quite frequently use semiconductors in a switching rather than a linear mode. Such supplies operate at a much higher efficiency than linear supplies and exhibit great size and weight reductions. Though until recently only aerospace power supplies contained high frequency switching regulators, the availability of high-speed transistors has now made such supplies feasible in commercial applications as well.

Wire wrap. Wire wrap was developed in the 1950s by Bell Labs as an alternative to soldering. Wire-wrapping consists basically of winding a number of turns of wire around a metal post with at least two sharp edges. In practice, the metal post has evolved into a standard 0.025-inch square pin. With the correct wire and tension during wrapping, a clean metal-to-metal contact results.

Wire-wrap advantages. Wire-wrapping offers the advantage of ease of design, freedom of layout, easy maintainability and parts replacement, ease of design change, good performance, and good density. But unless users can justify wire-wrapped interconnection for applications on the basis of economics, there is no point in using it.

Wire-wrap tool. A wrapping tool is a pencil-sized shaft with two holes in the end. The larger hole fits over the wrap post; the smaller hole fits over the wire. Wire sizes are 26, 28, and 30 gauge. The tool can be turned by hand, or there are a variety of power drives available. For production work, electric and pneumatic tool drivers are common. In prototype work, battery-powered drivers avoid the inconvenience of a trailing cord.

Worst-case design. The worst-case design approach is an extremely conservative one in which the circuit is designed to function normally even though all component values have simultaneously assumed the worst possible condition that can be caused by initial tolerance, aging, and a temperature range of 0°C to 100°C. Worst-case techniques are also applied to obtain conservative denoting of transient and speed specifications.

7

Microcomputer Software: Why the New Systems Are Easier to Use— ROMs and RAMs

The "user revolt" brought not only smaller, cheaper, and simpler microcomputers and scores of types of new programmable calculators with power and versatility equal to many computers, but it also brought a hoped for beginning of an end to many terrible software bottlenecks in standard systems. The price of hardware for the older complicated systems fell fast because of new microsystem competition from many sectors. In early 1974, for example, computer leasing companies were reporting that the equivalent computer power that rented for $10,000 per month in 1969 was renting for $5,000 per month, and this per-computation-cost downward spiral was expected to continue and accelerate each year in the foreseeable future. The result of quite drastic cost reductions was the sudden opening of large new markets.

Potential users who had previously thoughtfully considered computers for their operations, but declined to order because of cost, were now again very active. And the totally new customer base appeared unlimited. Manufacturers were offering new systems that were much pleasanter for users to operate and control, and they were able to prove with more "dollars and cents" reasons the advantages for purchase or lease. Many customers were still cautious, however, because they seemed to know that "it will be possible to do next year's processing at even less than this year's costs." But most customers could not wait any longer because competitors were reducing their costs and product prices rapidly. Without automation of various types, inflationary labor, overhead, and material costs were cutting deeply into operating profits at an accelerating rate. New users, therefore, quite eagerly, but still carefully, analyzed computer systems to determine, for sure, that the old operating headaches and software bottlenecks were gone—or going.

Data indicate and many potential users are aware that 70 percent of the development and operations costs of new applications areas are still tied to people—salaries, office space, fringe benefits, turnover, new positions, and so on. Hardware costs are obviously dropping, but are as many people still needed? An analysis indicated that in older "standard" systems, 80 percent to 90 percent of the people costs relate to operations, maintenance, and programming. The largest markets of new user revenue for small system manufacturers will come from present nonusers, especially those representing medium and smaller unsophisticated enterprises. And the "forward march" of computer salesmen is moving in the direction of capturing these customers. Their first objections—people and software costs of computer systems—are being attacked to remove these sales obstacles.

Problem-oriented languages for customer use had to be made simpler. Very basically, the computer operates internally and finally on its own "machine language." This is the language in which each single microprogram statement is represented by a single microinstruction to a computer. To make programming much more efficient, a single program statement, or macroinstruction, is routinely used to cause one statement to result in many instructions to the computer. These are the statements of high-level languages, such as FORTRAN, COBOL, BASIC, and so on. Our discussion in this chapter concerns programming and the use of languages in microcomputers. A rerun of some software concepts is developed first. This is followed by an analysis of programming in ROM and RAM. But how rapid is this progress?

Microcomputer software as offered came on fast by following the calculator leads. Programs are in great abundance and variety for the huge calculator market. The software developed for the first microcomputers did not remain primitive for long either. Microcomputer assemblers and special sets of FORTRAN programs that enable users to develop and run code (in simulation) on time-sharing or batch systems are available around the world. The history and progress of the latest microcomputer software developments are very remarkable and unusual. Many microcomputers are specifically designed or made "smart" for applications of great importance, such as intelligent communications or preprocessing terminals, point of sale terminals, factory automation devices, calculators, and so on. The addition of processors to computer terminals enables local error checking, data formating, and immediate editing and also considerable other processing to take place before the central computer receives the input. One of the first "intelligent" terminals came from Datapoint Corp., as previously noted. It resulted in reducing the entire processor to a single circuit and changed the "form" of a minicomputer to the appearance of a visual display unit. The reliability, utility, and compactness proved to be equal to Datapoint's standards, and the firm became a leader and power in the market very rapidly.

MICROCOMPUTER HIGHER-LEVEL LANGUAGES PROGRESS RAPIDLY WITH ROM/RAM CAPACITY ADVANCES

In addition to remote and easy-to-use language assemblers, micros have higher-level languages available that enable programs to be written more rapidly and by persons with lower levels of programming skills. They also have disk, "chip," or mag tape operating systems and easy interfaces for many other peripheral devices. Most of this development happened in three years, 1972–1975. The area of progress since then remains rapid and is increasing. Competing designs from more and more suppliers serve expanding application ranges. The kind of microcomputer that a new application requires depends upon the kind of work the product must perform. There are sometimes limitations on the amount of hard-wired logic circuitry that can be mass-produced in a unit at a low price, but microcomputers are very versatile and can satisfy the needs of many varieties of users. Software or firmware for micros can tailor general-purpose instruction sets to practically any problem, and the number of instructions required remains at relatively low cost. Microinstruction sets may now grow very large with stacked micros to be used when needed.

Many types, sizes, and speeds of solid-state memories in various components technologies are now available. Memories for developing new processors are also being rapidly reduced in size and cost to satisfy many needs that are well established, such as those of terminal makers. Additionally, they provide some operating system instructions and interfacing advantages that make their products superior in several markets, such as process control, education, and data communications. The necessities of new control products and differences in automation product concepts are evident in the demands by many different firms in businesses, professions, and so on. Microcomputer software development is being pushed ahead rapidly by semiconductor manufacturers and other firms with the capability of making the micro kits and full system units. Engineers and product planners "all over the field" are not waiting to gauge the market impact of the first microcomputers. They have received great encouragement and large budgets. Most of the projects from various competitors are far more ambitious than the initial microcomputer projects. They have much more management and user support, and many proved markets exist to make them profitable. In addition, the high technology fabrication equipment used in making microcomputers is not generally committed to or shared by other products, and it continues to be reduced in cost, even as efficiency increases.

269

The very strong competition dictates that all or most manufacturing firms make extensive efforts in software, or they will lose out. They are producing assemblers, loaders, other utility programs, and elementary operating systems and plan many applications programs. Some chip manufacturers are going into the end-user world with their own calculators, point of sale terminals, and so on, using processors and attractive and utilitarian architectural designs. New memory technologies are optimizing microcodes on current terminals and other products. Parallel developments of machines using different generations of circuits enable many firms to bring application- or user-oriented gear to market, independent of the production risks formerly associated with original microcomputer developments while "hoping" markets might develop.

But without plentiful, simplified, and low-cost software, these efforts would be seriously inhibited. ROMs, RAMs, PROMs, strips, cards, cassettes, and whatever media of firmware the public wants are happening.

IMPROVED RELIABILITY AND SECURITY USING
MICROPROCESSORS AND FIRMWARE

The extremely low cost of logic, hard-wired memory, and multimicroprocessors has made security and reliability cheap and simple instead of complex and expensive. The micros make it easy to use extensively many new error-checking, error-correcting, and economical redundancy routines, such as the use of many duplicate systems either as spares or as positive and simultaneous checks on the correctness of programs and systems. The merging of computers and communications has proved the adequacy and effectiveness of these procedures in telephone and satellite systems in thousands of applications. Direct digital systems (DDS) as contrasted with voice communication (analog) systems have "uncomplicated" many of the expensive and complex multiplexing, converting, and "front-end" handling of communications.

But equally as important has been the use of multimicros in developing protective security and reliability through multiprogramming and multiprocessing. The interleaved execution of two or more programs, now becoming standard on most small and minicomputers, works very well with multi- or stacked-micros. The former procedures needed for multiprogramming were often awkward and required large, sophisticated, error-prone operating systems. The performance overhead was excessive and far too complex for managers to control or understand. As a result of the making of thorough analyses of operating systems for controlling multiprogramming and multiprocessing operations and the incorporation of these features in ROMs and RAMs of microprocessors, these formerly complex operations become automatic and standard. Because the ROMs and RAMs are microprogrammed (that is, each low-level instruction required is coded to accomplish each small internal processing step), they are easier to change and design and their programs are much faster to execute.

The microprogrammed ROMs and RAMs in the microcomputer systems provide the real efficiency for the very powerful multimicro systems. Thus correcting, protecting, and monitoring systems for increased security can be accomplished with little extra cost and difficulty as contrasted with conventional systems. Integrity, validation, and security procedures can be incorporated in even the very low-cost systems—mitigating much of the public bitterness that too many errors, too few corrections, and too much delay have already caused.

THE BASIC DESIGN PROCEDURE BLOCK

Because of the availability of tested and proved CPU chips from scores of component manufacturers, practically any applications engineer's imagination is the only limitation to the devices, systems, and processes that he or she can control with a microprocessor/microcomputer system. The entry into the computer industry has suddenly become very easy and wide open. The "better mousetrap" syndrome is now intriguing and tempting whole new generations of inventors, innovators, and system designers. And this is all to the good—of major industrialized countries and of "third world" countries as well. (See Figure 7.1.)

MOS/LSI microcomputer coding and programming procedures

The primary task for engineers and other users who incorporate MOS/LSI microprocessors into their designs is the conversion of system algorithms into the instructions that can be loaded directly into the system's memory. Micro manufacturers are making every attempt to assist these users with this coding by providing improved tools and techniques to simplify the designer's tasks. These tools include assemblers, editors, loaders, compilers, and other special microprogramming capabilities. The software phase generally calls for performance of the following major tasks: system definition; equating definition to programs; program design; charting of functional flow and detailed flow; instruction writing (coding); debugging; editing; and final program layout, or ROM stacking.

Although program design for micros is generally more detailed than that for conventional computers, it is also easier. ROMs are generally used to store the entire program. System definition involves the major tasks to be performed by the microprocessor, which is the central control device for

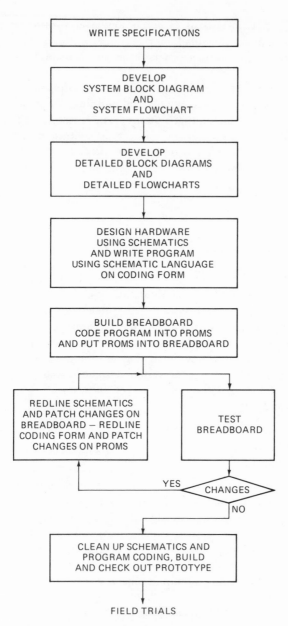

FIGURE 7.1. Design procedure with microprocessors
Courtesy: Pro-Log Corporation

the system. Data formats need to be designed to judge functions against time constraints. It is on these formats that the basic program structure can be designed. Each input channel to the microprocessor represents a major program, assuming the use of more than one input device. Also the executive program or ROM should be designed or written to control the overall operation of the system. Various routines—based on the different functions or command codes supplied—can further subdivide the main program. The 8-bit bus is general, and the program can be most efficient if it operates with a maximum of eight bits per message, eliminating the need for multiple-word processing for data control. The program design is the single most important part of the software assembler development because it bridges the gap between hardware and software. It is firmware when it is put into ROMs. The program design then should define every step of the system operation from the point of view of the microprocessor. It definitely establishes the necessary "handshaking" between the peripherals and the microprocessor and between the peripherals and the external circuitry.

Some of the specifics that the program design should include are system timing, code structures between the system and circuitry and to and from the microprocessor, sources of microprocessor data during all phases of its operation, method of executives and other program controls, and method of program interface and interaction. Most of this is based on memory structure and operation as designed into the functional flow chart, that is, the sequential analysis of the detail to allow for smooth program writing or coding. Other detail charts are derived from the functional flowcharts. They establish the command codes and the manner in which each command code works within the system. The detail charts tell step-by-step every operation that must be performed; and, therefore, for the instruction writing or coding, the programmers need only know how to program the microprocessor. Most engineers trained in assembly language for any computer can generally fulfill this requirement.

Program debugging is a more difficult task, but it can be simplified with good software aids. Most computer manufacturers supply quite complete software packages with their computers. Other software aids include all of the items on the list above. FORTRAN assemblers, simulation programs, and program editors set the proper sequences within a program and combine the various programs into one suitable for firmware. They add the proper address locations to the subroutines that have been developed.

The assembly language, the most common for microcomputer programming, has these features: symbolic operation codes; labels that refer to memory locations—instruction or data—and symbolic names for operands, such as registers, condition flip-flops, and test conditions of conditional instructions.[1] Assemblers are programs that must be run on some computers.

[1] See explanation of symbolic coding on pp. 278–79.

273

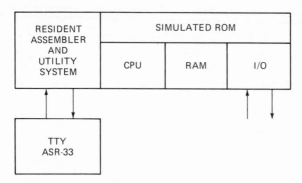

FIGURE 7.2.

For example, one assembler program from Intel can be loaded into several PROM or ROM chips and executed by a microcomputer of the type for which it is assembling. These are called "hardware assemblers" because they run on the hardware itself. (See Figure 7.2.) A more common situation is one in which the assembler itself is written in FORTRAN. With minor modifications, the program can be run on any computer that compiles FORTRAN programs. Thus the designer prepares source programs, assembling them on some other computer, to obtain the object tape for the microcomputer. The FORTRAN-written assemblers are often made available to users through the time-sharing companies in all major cities as indicated earlier. The ability of assemblers to detect and point to a variety of errors in source statements is one of their most valuable features. These errors are generally syntactic—they deal with misuse of the actual language. Assemblers normally cannot catch logic errors in the program, errors of intent, or other subtle problems. A statement that contains an error is printed in the list file with a code letter—a flag—beside it. Or the entire error message may be printed. Some common errors that can be detected include duplicate address labels, undefined labels, and unrecognized instruction mnemonics (owing perhaps to the misspelling of an operation code).

Editors are interactive systems that allow designers to prepare a program or text or to make changes with simple commands. Time-sharing services, which provide remote access to microcomputer assemblers, have such editor systems. Hence designers can prepare assembly-language programs and correct them. They can add documentation and store, combine, and retrieve programs. And they can output programs onto paper tape and printers with relative ease. Once a program has been written, assembler-flagged errors corrected, and a binary object tape or file created, the program must be loaded into memory of the microcomputer system.

Assembled programs can be loaded into mask or field-programmable

ROMs. They can also be loaded into RAMs, in which case a small bootstrap loader is required. The latter may be a minimal program loaded into several ROMs or PROMs. This bootstrap program has just enough capability to read an object tape of a compute loader program, which is placed on a tape of a complete loader program-reader under microprocessor control. More often the bootstrap loader contains the entire loader program, and all RAM space is available to load the application program. Application programs can be conveniently tested in RAM before they are committed to ROMs or PROMs. However, if they are to be used in RAMs in the final system, a start-up or restart procedure is needed. The procedure permits bootstrapping of the microcomputer into operation. A permanent loader is required in ROM.

The most elementary binary loader simply reads successive words on the object tape and writes them into successive locations of RAM memory. The loader generally starts at a fixed origin. A relocating loader is more complex and uses a special object tape and the desired origin data to adjust the program addresses automatically and load the resulting binary instructions. With a basic binary loader, the same flexibility can be achieved by reassembly of the original source tape or file, but with a change of the origin, using a suitable *origin* pseudo-operation. Another feature of the more advanced loader is linking capability. Here program segments or routines with undefined labels or names can be loaded. The loader supplies missing cross-references between the separate routines. Again this feature can be achieved by reassembly of the entire collection of programs.

Compilers are programs that accept as input data another program, written in a so-called source language. The compiler then outputs another program, written in what is called the target language. The latter can be either the assembly language or a machine language. The source language is usually a high-level language, in which instructions or commands are much more powerful than those of the target language. Examples of source languages are FORTRAN, COBOL, APL, ALGOL, BASIC, PL/1, PL/M, and so on. PL/M is a compiler from Intel that has a subset of IBM's PL/1 instructions as its source language. The subset language statements are converted by the compiler into a sequence of assembly-language instructions. Some microcomputers can be tailored to design requirements where the designer can choose, within limits, the basic machine-language instruction set of another computer if he or she writes the microprogram. This flexibility simplifies use of microcomputers as emulators of other computers. The instruction set of the other computer is microprogrammed into the microcomputer control ROM. Execution of a program instruction corresponds to selection of the equivalent microroutine. Microprogramming can also be used for critical, short routines in applications where speed is of the essence. The routines can be executed faster when written in the basic control language of the microcomputer. A single machine-language instruction triggers the routine. The microprogram instructions are more elemental than the usual machine-language instructions. Each instruction controls limited, simple operations in a microcomputer. A sequence of instructions is required for most machine-language instructions. Hence many instructions are required for an entire computational routine.

When the overall programs take final form, they can be tested within the system. If ROMs are to store instructions, an erasable field-programmable type can be used initially. Erasable PROMs permit full program test and correction prior to the use of top-mask memories. Erasable PROMs are also a more economical alternative when there are too few systems to warrant the high cost of top-mask development. In the final program layout, the total program can be reedited and stacked into one large program for final ROM commitment. ROMs are available with up to 16 Kbits on a single chip. Programs placed on large ROMs can result in significantly reduced size; for example, two 16-Kbit ROMs can replace 16 2K-bit PROMs. In addition to the hardware reduction, there is an appreciable saving in power. And expected shortly are larger capacity ROM and RAM ICs that require even less power per bit.

After selecting the microcomputer for various jobs, users integrate it into their products or systems. A series of *assemulators* with assembler-simulators offer a complete stand-alone microcomputer development capability. Applied Computing Technology, Inc., of Irvine, California, can build *assemulator* development systems for the Rockwell International and Intel series of 4-bit and 8-bit microcomputers. The *assemulator* features real-time microcomputer simulation, including ROM simulation up to full-system capacity. A resident assembler transcribes machine language directly into the ROM simulator memory from mnemonic instructions inputting via the Teletype. A resident utility system allows quick display and change of simulated ROM and RAM. Input-output channels within the *assemulator* provide for interface with external electronics. Integral programmers allow direct memory transfer to programmable read-only memories.

Programs in machine language are awkward and tedious for the great majority of users. They prefer to express problems and programs in "Englishlike" languages, high-level languages, or the even simpler "inquiry languages" discussed on pages 279–81. A good definition of a high-level language follows: a set of characters and the rules for combining them that (1) require no knowledge of machine code by the user, (2) are significantly independent of any specific computer, (3) cause the computer to execute many (machine-coded) instructions from single Englishlike statements, and (4) offer notation that is fairly natural to the problem and is not embedded in higher mathematics or stringent formats. Although most of these languages can be learned in a month or so, they are not understandable to most of the pool of noncomputer or nonprogramming-prone people. Besides the "inquiry languages" noted further on, many manufacturer-developed "entry" languages are now available, including job-control languages; string languages; data management languages; file management and editing languages; special information-retrieval, question-answering, management-information systems; and other simpler-to-use types. These are helpful and assist in gaining many new customers. But most of these are still not either sufficiently easy or efficient.

As we will note in the later chapters, programmable calculators are much further ahead in developing very easy software for noncomputer-educated people. Their strips, cards, stripes, and so on are quite quick and simple. However, the growing thousands of major computer system users and specialist newcomers need more. Faster development must be and fortunately is being done. People in various professions, for example, are using more specialized languages that relate very distinctly to the functions they perform daily. Some of these specific cases are as follows. Civil engineers have at least four languages oriented to their own daily needs: COGO, for coordinate geometry; STRESS, for *structural engineering system solver*; and ICEs and STRUDL. Movie and line-drawing creators have five special languages. Computer-aided instruction (CAI) coursewriters have at least eight special languages. Production automation and machine control people have at least six, including the popular automatically programmed tool (APT I, III, AdAPT, and so on). There are ten simulation languages, five linear programming languages, three social science languages, even seven equipment check-out languages, and so on. But the amateur and novice "general" users need even more help.

Some of that extra help is already here, and more is just a year or so away. Generally, these are modular languages or language assistance techniques. They fall into three primary categories: (1) generalized application packages, (2) firmware or direct execution high-level and problem-oriented languages, and (3) automatic programming and goal-directed techniques.

The best general applications packages are designed to eliminate programmers by providing computer users with an "automatic" capability of handling many special options. These packages are regularly sold, rented, and swapped and concern the often used cost applications, such as, payroll, inventory control, data base inquiry, and so on. They are ready-to-go packages designed so that the user merely specifies which options or special requirement he or she needs and what particular values (data) must be used. Examples of successes of these techniques are the IBM Small Scale System/3 "applications customizer" and the Burroughs' software specifically designed for their B1700, B700, and L small computer series. NCR also has very simple procedures for creating programs, often with minor assistance given users by salesmen.

Practically every company thought they needed their own unique payroll program, inventory program, purchasing program, accounts receivable and payables program, and so on. For years programmers have been working on these projects for each individual company, ostensibly because each company wants secrecy. Accountants, owners, or managers had their own special requirements, different from all others; and most often they believed no two programs, systems, or operations were exactly alike. They were too sure that other programs would not work for them if they were sold or designed for some other specific computer or for some other particular business, and so on.

In the earlier days it was often painfully found that one company's program would probably be worthless for another company. And so, needless "reinventing of the wheel" efforts continued and often still do, with more wasted time and money. In the great majority of cases, however, there are now a great many "generalized applications programs" that can be used by thousands of businesses with only slight modification. Many have mutually exclusive options, but also have the same basic control provisions that permit tremendous diversity and versatility within a given application, company, or group of "unique" users. Each user chooses his options, decides on his values, inserts his parameters (numbers, ranges, and so on), and either makes simple adjustments to his operations or to the "generalized" program; and they work very well indeed. Computer software companies, service companies, and/or consulting companies are profiting nicely with these programs, which often require no "user" employed programmers to originate, adjust, or be on hand for their operation.

SYMBOLIC CODING

It is obvious that machine-language coding and binary are tedious and burdensome for human operators. Keeping track of where everything is stored and developing unique addresses for each data word in absolute or machine language are cumbersome indeed. The location identifiers and operation codes are difficult to remember and reconstruct.

To overcome this difficulty, computer manufacturers almost without exception provide symbolic code substitutes. These symbolic combinations are, in effect, mnemonics. These are memory helpers because they suggest the nature of the operation. For example, MPY is a symbolic operation code for *multiply* instead of a numeric code or a string of digits. Each symbolic code is usually distinct and unique for each model and brand of machine. Symbolic addresses are provided for identifying memory locations used in storing instructions. Programmers themselves invent symbolic addresses for these combinations, which are subject to specific restrictions by the manufacturer to avoid duplication and internal coding problems. Therefore, symbolic tags identify memory locations, but a tag is required only if such instructions are to be referenced or used again in the program. Certainly, each absolute storage location must be assigned for each instruction, but the symbolic tag is not necessary at all times because instructions are assumed to be stored sequentially.

As previously mentioned, computers operate only with binary numbers. Therefore, the mnemonics codes and symbolic addresses mentioned earlier must be translated into these absolute binary codes and addresses before the computer will operate on them. This translation is completed by sets of computer programs called an "assembly system." Assembly routines are designed to read symbolic instructions from cards or tapes and so on and to translate the operation codes to binary or machine operation codes. The routine also assigns memory locations for the symbolic tags. The ultimate result is a translation of symbolic or mnemonic codes to machine or binary language programs that the computer can use directly.

The advantages of symbolic codes are that they are easy-to-remember abbreviations and tags; are easier for changing, checking, and reassembling; are easier for diagnosing or detecting errors. It must be remembered that the assembly system does not reduce the amount of coding because the translation is still on a one-for-one instruction basis, but, because many programs have some segments in common that are also used repeatedly, many programmers write short program segments for insertion for these repetitive actions instead of rewriting specific readings, error checking, or scaling values. These program segments are added to the symbolic system for convenience. When these type program segments are inserted in the asssembly system, they are referred to as macroinstructions. The word simply means that one symbolic instruction (segment) results in many computer instructions. Such macroinstructions relieve the programmer from rewriting standard routines and repetitious operations. Macros are most commonly used for input/output program operations.

The reader will probably make the next step in his or her thinking, which suggests that large groups of program segments or macroinstructions can be combined into a complete language. This is true, and such coding languages have been developed and have become machine independent. In other words, macroinstructions graduated into "automatic coding systems." These are often referred to as pseudocodes, and large groups of these have been built into higher-order languages. These languages can be procedure-oriented or problem-oriented rather than machine-oriented. Each of them, however, as with assembly languages, must be translated into binary before the machine can run.

LANGUAGES AND TERMINAL TECHNIQUES OF MINIS AND MICROS

The languages and terminal techniques of *minis and micros* have the big advantage of not requiring executive typing skills. Examples follow:

Englishlike languages. Englishlike languages provide the managerial interface between the executive and the system. These languages, such as QUEST, allow the manager to ask questions without the need for analysts and programmers, who cause delay and distortion. This access aid is loaded with imperative commands. For instance, QUEST uses basic verbs such as *retrieve, update, sort,* and *enter.* In that sense, it is an imperative style language. But through the use of conjunctions such as *and, or,* and *if,* phrases are also actually constructed, making it more like an Englishlike language.

Tabular languages. It is suggested that many of the expected managerial questions can be preformated and displayed on the CRT. The manager merely chooses the question he or she wants answered by indicating his or her choice through the use of a light pen or even by touching with the fingers or tapping typewriter keys, and the machine is programmed to respond with the correct answer.

Handshaking. Handshaking is analogous to programmed instruction procedures. The computer "leads" the executive through a course of inquiry, and the terminal demonstrates its abilities and advantages. Gradually, it takes the executive from the "show-and-tell" stage to the point where the executive realizes what kind of information is available from the computer and what he or she must do to get at it.

Dictionaries. Dictionaries refer to the computer's ability to store and output information concerning data base names and addresses. For instance, descriptive data field titles are usually precoded on the basis of length, and, therefore, "customer credit rating" becomes *CCR* or worse *XXABO.* The dictionary allows the executive to learn the computer's "language" for retrieving information. It is not a dictionary in the sense of a book, but rather in the sense of indexed information capable of being projected to a CRT.

Personal data structures. A specific case might be the situation when one manager calls and thinks of CCR from the previous use as an abbreviation for customer credit rating. Another might call it "buyer rating" and make his notes accordingly. The personal data structure allows each manager to use the terms he or she is most familiar with when manipulating the data, according to his or her own "code" book, which is input as a program—his or her own—to the computer.

Situation center. Situation centers, veritable "control centers," can be much like a "war room." At such a location, the top executives all get together to "rap" and play "what if" games with the computer concerning various decisions that have to be made. Each executive has a CRT, and often there are large screens to display whatever information is developed on the walls for "conferencing" with the computers. Management information systems, called MIS, will facilitate more and more centralized decision making.

Moreover, access to "information utilities" provides small and medium-sized firms with the ability to compete with larger firms without the disadvantage of lacking the information resources of these large competitors; that is, competitive information parity is now possible owing to low information costs.

THE ADVANTAGES OF LOW-COST MEMORY
AND HIGH-LEVEL LANGUAGES

With lower memory costs, a significant change has occurred that concerns the cost and use of programmers. Cost of program development specifically concerns the ease or difficulty with which new personnel can enter the work flow by "getting on" the computers. Either machine (low-level) or problem-oriented (high-level, as FORTRAN, BASIC, and so on) languages can be used and have advantages and trade-offs that should be carefully weighed. But because computer memory costs have dropped in recent years, the scales have increasingly tipped toward high-level languages as the faster, more effective, and—in many cases—less costly medium of communication both for and between managers and staff using small, mini, and micro computer systems.

Traditional arguments on behalf of low-level programming have centered on the fact that assembly and machine languages use main memory space far more efficiently than high-level languages. High-level languages use extra memory to store the additional instructions for translating conversational English into assembly language. For the same reason, low-level languages usually are capable of faster program execution because there are fewer instructions to execute. To the small computer owner, though, programming in a low-level language has always posed certain problems. For one, a programmer must be hired and given a thorough briefing on what the system is expected to do before attempting to write the programs. This can be costly because assembly and machine-language programmers command high pay for their skills—they typically earn 25 percent to 50 percent more than high-level language programmers. In addition, the low-level programmers must carefully document every detail of the program so that a successor will be able to understand what has been done. This sounds reasonable in theory, but, in reality, it rarely is done.

Low-level programming can be costly in other ways. A low-level programmer in a computer room probably knows little about the business procedures to be done on the computer. He or she must receive direction from accountants and managers who know little about computers, let alone low-level languages. This can result in various series of programs that are far less efficient than they should be. Also, if the programmer leaves the firm for another job, chances are the computer will have to be furloughed until a new low-level programmer can be hired, briefed, and turned loose on the previous programmer's existing notes and documentation. If these are incomplete, whole new programs may have to be written.

The arguments for using memory efficiently were strong ones until 1973–1974, when several computer and components companies underscored the trend in lower-cost memories by developing the low-cost 4K ROMs and single 16,384-word (16K) memory boards for their line of minicomputers and microcomputers. Words for minis (and several micros) are generally 16-bit word lengths. Until 1973, the maximum core memory contained on one printed circuit (PC) board was 8,192 words; 32K of memory required four boards; and the more PC boards used, the higher the purchase price. The new, 16K-word memory meant bigger, cheaper memories for original equipment manufactures (OEMs). Users could switch to high-level languages being offered by mini makers without the cost penalty in using additional memory. For example, a user writing in machine language for Data General's then current Nova 1220 model with 16,384 words of memory had to pay $10,000 for the hardware. But a newer Nova 2, complete with twice the memory, cost him only $10,150 total, and he got enough memory to switch over to a high-level language like FORTRAN, which is much easier to use; that is, twice the computer for the same expenditure. Thus it became easier to buy a bigger memory. This made the small minicomputer feasible and available to scores of small businesses that previously could not have afforded to buy a computer and pay for low-level programming. (Other competing systems were even less costly.)

This "price elastic" market meant many new small business firms or persons who had watched the small computer or minicomputer move within budgetary range could call it a dream-come-true. To the small business firm or person, a good part of their desires was the sophisticated array of high-level languages—and their inherent advantages over low-level programming. These are available with minicomputers—and now also with the significantly lower-cost microcomputer. Some of the advantages of easier-to-use, high-level languages are as follows:

1. *Ease of operation*. High-level languages are easy to learn because of their Englishlike statement format and their conversational nature. Because it takes a relatively short training time to become proficient in, say, FORTRAN or APL—and especially BASIC—a high-level programmed system will typically be put into operation far sooner than a comparable assembly language system.
2. *Reduced programming time*. As a rule of thumb, one high-level statement does the work of ten assembly-language statements. Yet it takes the same amount of time to write a statement in FORTRAN as it does in assembly language; so the programming time saving is clear.
3. *Reduced documentation costs*. High-level programs are far easier to document because of their compactness and because they can be documented by merely writing in comments next to the statements on a printout. This kind of documentation results in highly visible, easy-to-

understand program logic and encourages a "teamwork" approach to program writing—and long-term software compatibility—among the management staffs.

4. *Program language commonality.* Assembly language statements vary from computer to computer, but a high-level language can provide a common data base for use with a number of different computers. This can be a blessing in a business environment, where data can be transported for processing to the data-processing center, or in a division that wants to add a more powerful computer. In the same vein, system hardware changes, such as adding disk memory or input/output (I/O) terminals, are easily supported by high-level languages. They would necessitate time-consuming software changes if the system were programmed in a low-level language.

5. *Elimination of the specialist.* Programming in a high-level language ends the need for a highly trained computer specialist, one who cannot be expected to stay with the system during its life-span. This brings the system's operation closer to the people who understand the business work and whose first loyalty is to the firm, not the computer. With assembly language, the reverse is often true; so programs sometimes end up altering the components priorities to fit the computer's convenience. It generally takes only a minimum of training to get a staff member ready to program in a high-level language—most technicians have been exposed to FORTRAN in college. FORTRAN is now also being taught in high schools.

6. FORTRAN compilers do the work. FORTRAN is probably the most widely used compiler-type language, except the business-oriented COBOL. A programmer working in FORTRAN or other high-level languages develops the program by describing the data that will come into the computer and what the computer will do with them. The FORTRAN compiler then sets aside the necessary memory space for the program; lists the name, location, and characteristic of each type of data; translates the procedures that will act on the data; and determines what computer instructions are required to carry out the job. It further generates the instructions, puts them into memory, and lists the data addresses for the finished program.

7. *On-line interpreters.* An interpreter, as in the BASIC language, interprets and executes the statements individually. This is useful for programming in a conversational language on-line, while the computer is running the program, because it allows the programmer to make immediate alterations to the program. Also helpful to on-line programmers is the interpreter's ability to note any programming errors as they occur, so that they can be corrected immediately. From the user's point of view, the chief distinctions between compiler and interpreter languages are execution speed and capacity for user interaction. Because

BASIC interprets Englishlike instructions on a statement-by-statement basis, it is slower but more accessible to the user than FORTRAN, which compiles whole programs at once.

8. *Real-time processing.* This concerns controlling an operation by reacting to an external stimulus fast enough to have an effect on the incoming information. A version of FORTRAN is generally used because BASIC cannot respond quickly enough to control any but the slowest experiments. Real-time versions of BASIC have recently been developed, but their slow execution speed initially remained a distinctly limiting factor.

9. *Running the operating system.* A vital part of any computer system and the relevant elements in any discussion of high-level programming concern the operating system software that coordinates programming and hardware activities throughout the system. The operating system (or executive) is chiefly responsible for facilitating data transfer between the computer and its peripherals, scheduling I/O services in the most efficient manner, scheduling tasks for multitasking program execution, and organizing data files. The level of sophistication of the operating system depends on the complexity of hardware and software, ranging from the simplest stand-alone operating system to the comprehensive real-time disk operating systems. A small computer's operating system usually supports all the languages, low- and high-level, offered by its manufacturer. Often the builder of a specialized turnkey system will rewrite the computer vendor's operating system to the turnkey system's more narrow specifications to get better performance out of less memory storage space (smaller operating systems reside in main memory; larger ones can reside on disk or a combination of core and disk).

10. *Program consistency.* Ideally, all operating systems offered by a computer vendor should support all that vendor's computer models. This way, a user could run FORTRAN programs and BASIC programs, add disk memory and other peripherals, expand to multiple computers, transfer programs developed on large systems for execution on smaller systems (under compatible operating systems), and purchase new computer models as they are developed—all without having to rewrite drastically operating systems or existing programs. Until the day when computer programming is standardized throughout the industry—the computer manufacturers' intense competitiveness seems to guarantee this might be a long way off—the decision to program in high- or low-level languages poses a basic question that can set off a never-ending array of competing answers. The ultimate answers will have to be determined by comparing all company offerings against one another and evaluating them in the context of specific user abilities and processing requirements. The first step, however, is more easily dealt with by understanding what high-level programming can mean to specific applications and by keeping abreast of the continuing stream of high-level lan-

guage development and refinements coming from today's computer industry.

MANY USERS ARE EXCITED ABOUT APL

Some users claim APL could change the programming habits of the entire computing community because the language is proving just as useful for business applications as for scientific work. All the indications are that APL is something different from current user languages. It may be that it is, in fact, a quiet harbinger of a real revolution. The signs are there. It could be as important as FORTRAN was in 1956.

APL is a new kind of interactive computer language—powerful, easy-to-use, versatile—and strongly used for time-sharing applications. With APL, users talk to the computer in terms of the functions they want it to perform, not in the artificial definition and procedures of languages like FORTRAN and COBOL. If users want to add up a row of figures (or a column or both), they just strike two keys to "program" the operation. The same applies to complex mathematical functions like, say, transposing or multiplying matrices. To illustrate APL's power: IBM's ECAP (electronic circuit analysis program) is 7,000 FORTRAN statements long and required eight man-years to write and document. The equivalent APL program on some systems was written by a novice programmer in less than six weeks of part-time effort. It has less than 700 APL statements.

With APL, users can write and debug special purpose programs in a few hours—sometimes even in minutes. The program the user wants may already exist in various public libraries, which the user can use without charge. Programs can be written in a "conversational" mode to guide users through every step of the way, so that it is virtually impossible to make a procedural mistake. APL users can command computers from typewriter terminals, which serve as ordinary typewriters when they are not talking to the computer. They are often 50 percent faster than teletypewriters. Reports can have nearly twice as many columns as TTY reports. APL can be used for on-line systems, such as order processing and inventory control; the management of large data bases, such as personnel files; statistical computations; scientific analyses; engineering problem solving; and so on. Several companies offer a commercial time-sharing service using APL nationwide. APL programmers help users get started and/or will do contract APL programming at reasonable costs.

THE USER INTERFACE WITH MICROPROCESSORS

As previously noted, the major microcomputers can be programmed, using various programs supplied to time-sharing networks. The user's specific program is entered, simulated on a cross assembler resident in the GE computer system, bringing forth a debugged, edited, ready-to-use program. Most microprocessor manufacturers now supply the software required to program their devices in a form usable with readily available computer systems. The software programs for the Motorola MC 6800, for example, are also available on the GE net. Working with the GE stored editing programs, the designers enter specific program instructions and parameters; and, after obvious errors and/or violations are discovered and indicated, corrections are made. The designer then can make use of the large GE host computer for other tests, adjustments, or extensions. If he or she chooses then to simulate and if his or her program works, he or she can go directly to the hardware state. The designer can go through the simulator loop to pinpoint problem areas or try new techniques until he or she is satisfied that he or she has what is wanted. Motorola has an exorciser to assist further with the debugging stage. A panel switch enables the flexible RAM to look like the appropriate ROM.

If the program does not run, the Exorciser can save the designer from six to 12 man-months by providing him or her with a method of communicating with the microcomputer. With this and other programming systems that are cheaper to use than former trial-and-error "human" methods, users can create many new economies and end many frustrations. Designers also quickly realize that systems based on microprocessors are cheaper to manufacture, require shorter design cycles, and are certainly easier to modify, upgrade, and adjust to customization desires. Various functions of the system can be changed by simply adjusting the master control program. For market testing, systems can be adapted in the customer's own environment; and, for the first time, a manufacturer has the capability to make his product "smarter" and add features at any instant simply by expanding—again the master control program. Whole ranges of products become potentially available by simply adding more LSI modules with their associated features. System flexibility generally depends on the various types of memory, and they are inexpensive and easy to develop. For example, read-write buffer memories could be used in conjunction with a cassette or a floppy disk for very low-cost systems requiring moderate speed. Faster systems, for modem interfaces, might require ROMs, dynamic RAMs with battery backup. And, in this instance, the very widely available 4,096 RAMs appear to offer a most acceptable speed/cost trade-off.

SOFTWARE USERS GROUPS

Most manufacturers of computers, including minis and micros, "swap" software programs. For example, users of Wang equipment have a forum where they can exchange ideas and get helpful hints. The Wang user group, known as the Society of Wang Applications and Programs, or "SWAP," is based on a sharing or swapping of software. The main purpose of SWAP is to make available a large, powerful, extensive, and useful multidisciplined Wang program library by user-to-user swapping. SWAP also provides direct user feedback to Wang Laboratories concerning both equipment and programs. Membership in the user group is open to any owner or user of Wang equipment for a small fee. The members are entitled to vote on all SWAP policies and on the election of officers. Several special interest subgroups (SIS) have been formed to promote common interests by all user groups. These include SISs in accounting, agriculture, automobile sales, income tax, electrical engineering, and medicine and real estate, among others. Communication among members is maintained through official newsletters and annual symposiums of the 50 or so user groups expanding nicely yearly. The largest groups are IBM's SHARE and DECUS (Digital Equipment Company Users' Society).

THE NEW COMPUTER WORLD OF
ROMs AND RAMs—AND PROMs.

Although some ROMs are erasable, "patchable," and otherwise alterable, generally they contain fixed control programs. They are relatively cheap, almost totally trouble or "bug" free, and highly reliable. They do not wear out, are very tiny and "pluggable" and thus solve many problems and create great convenience for computer users. In massive quantities, as for a manufacturer's production run or a large order of standardized point of sale terminals or an individual model "fixed-design" calculator, they can cost as little as $8 to $12. We are more concerned at this point with the customized ROMs, that is, those designed to fit specific users' desires, and with the wide variety of customer "programmable" ROMs, or PROMs.

Custom design of ROMs does not cost nearly as much as previously. Most companies can deliver them at very low, highly competitive prices. Scores of component companies received considerable experience with customer desires and tailored production very rapidly in 1976 and 1977. Supplying ROMs has now become very big business, as we shall note. Designing a ROM does not take as many months as previously. Even as recently as early 1973, it normally required up to a year from start to full production of customized ROMs. Now it is much faster—a week, perhaps; some companies can produce them in 24 to 48 hours. By early 1974 many companies were developing ROMs in monthly volumes in excess of one million devices, and these rates were climbing steadily.

Customized ROMs allow users to choose their own specific design to fit their applications exactly—whether it is a calculator of standard or exotic capability, a dishwasher or some other household appliance, a digital watch or

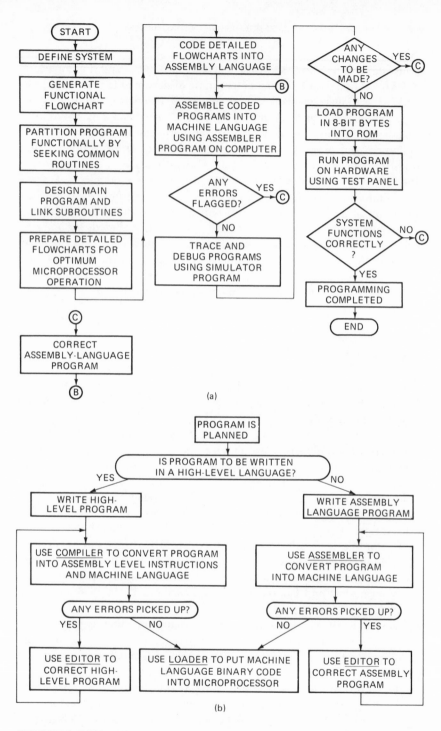

FIGURE 7.3. ROM software design procedures and coding of programs using compilers, editors, and loaders *Courtesy:* Electronic Design, *April 12, 1974*

clock, or whatever, that needs a control device. When users are looking for proprietary control circuits that will give them a jump on their competitors, the easiest, cheapest, fastest way to go, for many, is the route of customized ROMS. Four to six weeks from design delivery to receipt of even the most complicated ROM—for even several types of microprocessors—is now common in the trade. And thus software has ceased to be a problem for most mini, micro, or programmable calculator users.

Programmable ROMs or PROMs are available or completed as custom products by suppliers, service organizations, distributors, software houses, or users themselves. Service organizations can accept almost any format of the program, that is, on format paper, with only zeros entered for each address location. The program sheets are read optically, and the program is printed out for verification, or punched paper tape can be used in an 8-bit code, each tape line corresponding to an address location, codes listed sequentially, 000 through 255. For maximum flexibility and security, designers should complete the programming. Aids are available that allow both initial program writing into the PROM and copying from a completed PROM to a new one.

Several companies have offered PROM programmers that automatically blank check, program, and verify field programmable ROMs. They adapt to all PROM configurations by changing personality modules that are available for most PROMs now on the market, both bipolar and MOS. The operator inserts a preprogrammed PROM in a master socket, then loads a blank PROM in a program socket. The instrument can be cycled through blank check, program, verification, and so on, to assure that the pattern is correct and that the next blank is inserted. Go-no-go indicators show PROM status. Manual cycling is also possible. All procedures are initiated by individual lighted pushbuttons, and cycle light indicators display status at all times. PROMs and ROMs are so fast that they can emulate all operations of a computer, including I/O operations. PROMs and ROMs also allow older computers to use existing programs at greater speed and less expense. Also with inexpensive ROM options, designers and users can add hardware floating-point capabilities to minis and micros, or intelligence to controllers, data communications, and so on.

The flow chart in Figure 7.4 and the supply capabilities shown in Figure 7.5 demonstrate the relative ease with which programs and applications and control software can be developed. These systems relate to the MC 6800 Motorola unit, but the same or similar facilities are available for the Intel units and those of other manufacturers—from remote time-shared terminals of first three, and now many, computer service companies around the world. In addition to the capabilities described on other pages, "exorcisers," hardware, and programs are provided by most manufacturers to verify breadboard operations. The designer chooses the cards required (see Figure 7.5) to breadboard his or her system, plugs them into the machine,

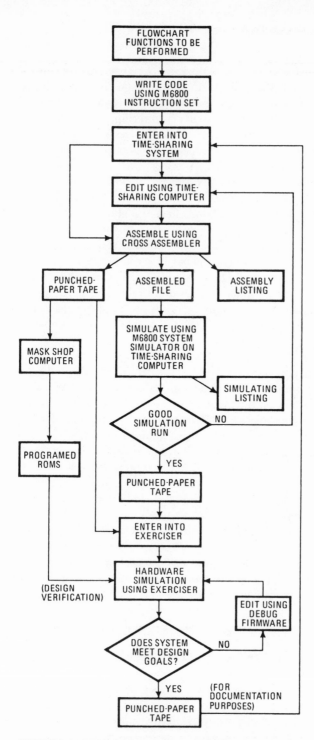

FIGURE 7.4. Working up the software. This design
sequence, which is organized for ease of use with the GE
time-sharing network, allows the designer to enter his specific program, which is then simulated on a cross assembler resident in the GE computer. *Courtesy:* Electronic
Design, *April 12, 1974*

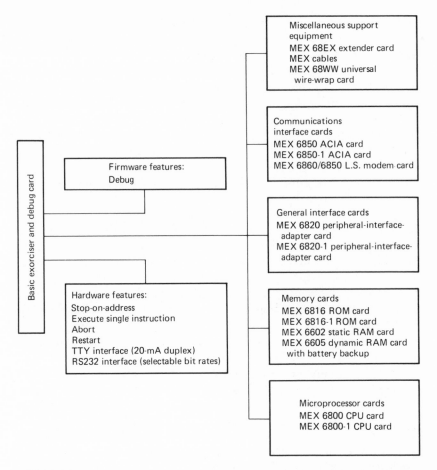

FIGURE 7.5.

cables the I/O cards to his or her various peripherals, and reads his or her program in through the TTY (or equivalent) network that interfaces to the debugging card. His or her program is contained in the read/write memory until debugged.

In debugging, a panel enables his or her flexible RAM to look like the appropriate ROM—if the program will not run, the "exorciser" will help modify it.

Programming PROMs

Field-programmable read-only memory (PROM) was brought out to the market in April of 1970. It has become widely acceptable and used in production designs. A score or more manufacturers have entered the field with proprietary and second-source PROMs. The original product was a 512-bit device. Now, users can find capacities from 256 to 2,048 bits. PROMs with 4,096-bit capacities began to appear in 1974 and are now available from many manufacturers. Several different techniques are used to make the bit changes involved in programming. One original technique, which is still used, is the bipolar "fusible-link" method wherein Nichrome (NiCr) fuses are "blown" by the introduction of programming pulses. These pulses range from 11 V to 25 V, 150 mA to 250 mA, and last from 10 to 800 msec, depending on the specific PROM being programmed.

Another technique is the "avalanche-induced migration" transformation of a transistor function into a resistor of fixed value. A third method is "stored-charge MOS," developed by Intel, wherein a permanent electric charge is stored within a cell. The charge can be erased, but only through exposure to ultraviolet or X-ray radiation. Because of the different techniques for retrieving stored data, some PROMs contain all logic-level *zeros* (that is, output low) in the unprogrammed state, whereas others contain all logic-level *ones* (output high). Many users program ROMs themselves. There are a number of steps involved in programming a PROM. Costly errors can occur at each step. Some typical errors to be avoided are (1) truth-table errors, (2) errors in translation, and (3) operator errors.

Any manufacturer's PROM—using currently available technologies—can be programmed automatically with several programmers when modified by appropriate "personality cards" and optional equipment. Most units have been equipped with a paper-tape option. These can be purchased with the capabilities for working with virtually any type of PROM and have options for accepting input from not only keyboard-punched paper tapes, but also mark-sense cards or preprogrammed ROMs. Price of the units with punched-tape options are below $2,000. Additional PC "personality cards" for adapting the programmer for use with different makes and organizations of PROMs are available for about $250 per card. Memory manufacturers will do the programming if the quantity of parts is large enough—well over 1,000 pieces, as a rule.

Another alternative is to have the programming done by a distributor who sells PROMs. Most distributors who sell memories are now set up to do programming. Many distributors charge for programming, but some offer the service free with orders above a certain size. Users can expect to pay about a $25 setup charge with each variation of their truth table. After the setup charge, additional units may range from $5 to nothing for programming, depending on the complexity of the PROM and the policy of the distributor. All will charge the setup fee if users send them their program in truth-table form, but many will reduce or eliminate the charge if users can send them the program already prepared on punched paper tape or mark-sense cards. Responsibility for correctness of tapes, of course, rests with the customer.

In general, this is what users can expect the distributor to do with each PROM he programs:

1. He will verify that the PROM is a new (unprogrammed) unit in good condition for programming.
2. He will program it with the information users supply him. Faulty units and errors, either human or equipment, are his responsibility. Users pay only for reliable, properly programmed PROMs delivered.
3. During the programming, he verifies each bit as it is done to ensure that the digit is fully and properly programmed.
4. He verifies the total program for correctness.
5. He marks, packages, and delivers the completed PROMs.
6. Performance of a leakage test on every programmed PROM.
7. Performance of an exclusive interrogation of each programmed link to ensure that it is completely programmed. If the bit being programmed is not completely altered, the equipment will automatically repulse the bit as many times as necessary until programming is completed.
8. Ability to offer this service completely free to all PROM customers, regardless of quantity ordered. Because the system will program any PROM made, some firms can also offer programming at a reasonable cost to people who have bought competitive PROMs.

Taking the programming operation out of the users' own plants does not necessarily mean they have to accept extended delivery schedules. With the systematized, automated approach used in the system described, it is possible to provide same-day turnaround on almost any PROM order received. It is not unusual to deliver parts to a customer's plant within six hours from the time the order was received.

SOME DISTRIBUTORS' SYSTEMS ACCEPT ALL INPUTS

A totally automated approach to programming has been developed by many electronic distributors. One system accepts input program information from all possible sources. For example, the customer may send in a truth table or supply punched tape through the mail, by TWX, or by computer time-share compatible terminal. In addition, simple mark-sense cards are supplied on which the customer can mark his or her program with a soft pencil. From the card, the program is then introduced into the system by means of an automatic card reader (also part of the system). Often another ROM is used (either of the masked variety or a previously programmed PROM). This can be plugged directly into the system to supply the programming information.

After the programming data are introduced into the system and translated into electrical form, they are fed into a large buffer memory (RAM),

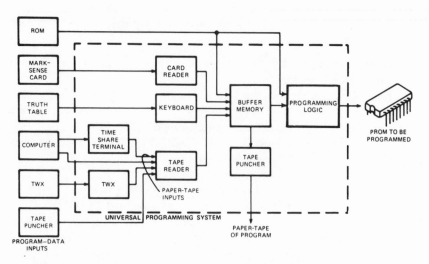

FIGURE 7.6. Data from a number of sources are fed into a large buffer memory for storage. If a paper-tape input is not used, the system produces one for an accurate record of the program. PROMs are programmed with data stored either in the buffer memory or a master ROM.

which stores the information for further use by the remainder of the system (Figure 7.6). If the program has not come in the form of a punched tape, the buffer (after automatically verifying the completeness and correctness of the program) feeds the program through a tape puncher to produce an accurate record of the program. The data are then sent to the programming logic as many times as necessary to prepare the required number of PROMs.

FIRMWARE AND DIRECT EXECUTION HIGH-LEVEL PROBLEM-ORIENTED ROMs FOR CALCULATORS

Strongly led by the calculator manufacturers, massive libraries of programs developed on cards, blocks, strips, boards, or several other "pluggable" media are available for sale, rent, swap, or "as adjustable" on tape cassettes. They are "standards" as wired, fixed, or preprogrammed. Hundreds of them for all types, varieties, and ranges of professions, special interests, processes, academic areas, and so on are becoming available rapidly and continuously. They are called "firmware" because they are software made "firm" by being electronically fixed or burned into ROM chips. But even they can be adjusted, expanded, and corrected because they can be transferred to RAMs, then adjusted and reburned into ROMs; or input to tape cassettes and adjusted, and so on. And many ROMs are erasable, field-programmable, and so on.

The calculator manufacturers offer "user definable function"—blocks, cards, strips, and so on "for any discipline." Users can literally design the functions used most and need only the touch of a single key for execution of the entire procedure, routine, or program. To continue the message from one leading calculator manufacturer, "With the user definable function block, you can customize individual keys for the operations uniquely important to you. For example, the electrical engineer will probably want voltage, impedance, capacitance, and true RMS functions; the physicist, his mass, velocity, and acceleration functions; the chemical engineer, his fluid flow and heat transfer functions. With one definable block, you can specify five, 15, or 25 keys depending upon whether the remaining banks are being occupied by other ROMs."

The trade and traffic will soon generate a very large new industry with noncomputer-oriented customers. There will be hundreds of thousands of users inventing, buying, selling, and swapping programs like phonograph records or books. Public libraries will have them available in wide variety. And the user revolt has gained considerably—again at the expense of the programmer—but for the very measurable savings of masses of computer and programmable calculator users. Certainly, the millions of students, managers, engineers, and so on, who have learned to program in FOR-TRAN, COBOL, BASIC, and any of the 200 other languages, can, if they choose, "cash in" on their abilities by developing marketable programs on ROMs, RAMs, cards, and cassettes; or they can carry pocketfuls of strips, boards, and so on to program instantly their computers or calculators for the "problem of the moment."

FURTHER DEFINING THE WORLD OF MICROCOMPUTERS

Addressing modes, microprocessor. Common addressing modes include direct, immediate, and indirect. In the immediate mode, the instruction includes data, whereas in the indirect mode, an address preloaded into a register increases the address bits in an instruction. Variations and extensions of these modes are also used; so a basic instruction can be manipulated several times and ways.

Address path, microprocessor. The address path is the selection path for memory and I/O data. For data processing, memory and I/O often use separate addressing or selection schemes. This suits the need for maximum memory and extensive peripherals. For logic processors, a combined addressing path for memory and I/O is the most efficient. Interconnection is simplified, and the package pin limitation is not overextended.

Assembler error messages. The ability of assemblers to detect and point to a variety of errors in source statements is a valuable feature on many systems. These errors are often syntactic—they deal with misuse of the actual language. Assemblers normally cannot catch logic errors in the program, errors of intent, or other subtle problems. A statement that contains an error is often printed in the list file with a code letter—a flag—beside it. Or the entire error message may be printed.

Some common errors that can be detected include duplicate address labels, undefined labels and unrecognized instruction mnemonics (due perhaps to the misspelling of an operation code). Other detectable errors include undefined operand field names, wrong number of operands, and an invalid number in the number system chosen. In addition, an assembler could be made to detect the error of an address referred to the same ROM page, as in a short JUMP when a long JUMP is required. Not all errors of syntax are flagged in current microprocessor assemblers. For example, when the labeled address for a JUMP or CALL instruction is not the start of an executable instruction, the error is not generally detected.

Assembler, hardware. A hardware assembler is a program that translates a symbolic assembly language into bit patterns suitable for a microcomputer control storage programming. It operates on the microcomputer system with an ASR-33 Teletype by plugging various PROMs into the board. The assembler accepts input source text from the Teletype keyboard or paper-tape reader on each of the required passes. A name table and source listing are created on the first pass. On the second pass, the source text is reread, and a programming paper tape and associated listing are generated. The programming tape is suitable for programming of PROMs using the dedicated programmer system. The same tape may be used for programming other metal mask ROMs.

Assembly testing. Refers to the testing of a group of functionally related programs to determine whether or not the group operates according to specifications. The programs may be related in that they have access to common data, occupy high-speed storage simultaneously, operate under common program control, or perform an integrated task.

Bucket. Refers to a slang expression used to indicate some portion of storage specifically reserved for accumulating data, or totals; for example, "Throw it in bucket 1." is a possible expression. Commonly used in initial planning.

Check problem. 1. A test problem that can indicate an error in programming or operation of a computer. When it is solved incorrectly, an error in programming or operation is indicated. 2. A problem chosen to determine whether the computer or a program is operating correctly.

Check register. A feature in some computers that temporarily stores information for comparison with a second transfer of the same information to verify that the transferred information agrees precisely.

Common programs. Programs or routines that usually have common and multiple applications for many systems; that is, report generators, sort routines, and conversion programs that can be used for several routines in language common to many computers.

Crippled leapfrog test. Refers to a standardized variation of the leapfrog test, so that it repeats the tests, and it does this quickly from a single set of storage locations rather than a changing set of storage locations.

Editor, microcomputer. Editors permit designers to prepare the original assembly-language programs and to change or correct them with simple commands. They can add documentation and store, combine, and retrieve programs. They can also readily output programs onto paper tape as well as printers.

Fetch phase, microprogram. Some microprograms provide a "fetch" phase to form an address, to access the machine instruction from the system memory (external to the CPU), and store it in the CPU instruction register. Also the microprogram has an "interpret" or "execute" phase to carry out the operations specified by the instruction. Microprogramming techniques can be extended to other programmable storage means besides conventional memories and to systems that include a number of programmable control sections operating in parallel or in a hierarchy.

Indirect address, microprocessor. Indirect addresses allow a named location to contain, instead of data, the address of data. Thus the instruction refers to a word or words that, in turn, refer to the datum. This is particularly important in generalized software. In some systems one of the bits of the address that has been fetched indirectly may further specify indirection.

Inserted subroutine. 1. A separately coded sequence of instructions that is inserted in another instruction sequence directly in low order of the line. 2. A directly inserted subroutine to the main line program specifically where it is required. 3. A subroutine that must be relocated and inserted into the main routine at each place it is used.

Instruction control unit. Many systems operations are controlled by the instruction control unit (ICU), which contains a read-only memory, in which the microinstructions are stored, and address control logic to allow microprogram branching.

Instruction cycles. The number of cycles that a computer requires to execute a program reflects the time and effort that the computer designer puts into designing his CPU. Simple machines may require four, five, or more cycles to execute an instruction, whereas a better designed machine can execute the same instruction in one or two cycles.

Instruction groups, microprocessor. Most CPUs have many instructions that are extremely useful and extend their ranges of applicability. The instruction groups are as follows:

> Data register and memory transfers.
> Conditional or unconditional branches and
> subroutine calls.
> I/O operations.
> Direct load/store accumulator.
> Save, restore data registers, accumulator and
> flags.
> Double length operation in data registers
> include: increment/decrement/addition,
>> direct load/store (H and L).
>> load immediate.
>> index register modification.
> Indirect jump.
> Stack pointer modification.
> Logical operations.
> Binary arithmetic.
> Decimal arithmetic.
> Set and reset interrupt enable flip-flop.
> Increment/decrement memory or data registers.

Instruction, microprocessor. A typical instruction can be from one to three bytes long, depending on the addressing mode used with the instruction. The first byte always contains the operation code, which designates the kind of operation the MPU will perform. In single byte instructions no memory address is required, because the operation is performed on one of the internal MPU registers. In multiple byte instructions the second and third bytes can be the operand or a memory address for the operand.

Instruction modification. Refers to an alteration in the operation code portion of an instruction or command such that if the routine containing the instruction or command is repeated, the computer will perform a different operation.

Instruction sets, microprocessor. From a programmer's point of view, microprocessor instructions break down conveniently into the following:

> Data movement.
> Data manipulation.

Decision and control.

Input/output.

Data can be moved about between a variety of internal sources and destinations. The most complex locations are those in memory—usually a RAM or RAM bank—because a variety of addressing modes can be used to specify location. The effective address of a memory location to be read or written can be given immediately by bits in the instruction being executed. In current microprocessors the immediate data may be 4, 8, 12 or even 16 bits long. Immediate data may be interpreted as a location (or displacement) in a previously selected page (or location) or memory.

Instructions, microprogrammable. Generally, all instructions that do not reference main memory (do not contain a memory address) can be microprogrammed, allowing the programmer to specify several shift, skip, or input/output transfer commands to be performed within one instruction.

Instructions, variable-length. A feature that increases memory efficiency by using only the amount necessary for the application and increases speed because the machine interprets only the fields relevant to the application. Halfword (2 bytes), two-halfword (4 bytes), or three-halfword (6 bytes) instructions are used.

Instruction words, location. Computers manipulate memory data according to a list of instruction words stored in the same memory. The program counter (PC) defines the location of the next instruction to be executed. The instruction register (IR) holds the instruction word for the current instruction being executed.

Interleaving. 1. In a computer, to insert segments of one program into another program so that the two programs can be executed essentially simultaneously. 2. A process of splitting the memory into two sections with two paths to the central processor to speed processing. Main memory access takes longer than logic or arithmetic operations, but a second word can be read during the half-cycle when the previously read word is being written back into the memory.

Interpreter operation. An executive routine that, as the computation progresses, translates a stored program expressed in some machinelike pseudocode into machine code and performs the indicated operations, by means of subroutines, as they are translated.

Interpreters. There are occasions when neither assembly language nor a compiler language is adequate. It will take too long to write and debug short programs whenever users want to run another trial-and-error calculation. An interpretive language fills this need. An interpreter is a program that operates directly on a source program in memory. The interpreter translates the instructions of the source program one by one and executes them immediately.

Interpret program. 1. A computer program that translates and executes each source language statement before translating and executing the next one. 2. A device that prints on a punched card the data already punched in the card. 3. To translate nonmachine language into machine language. 4. To decode.

I/O interface software. I/O interface software development involves specific memory, and additional hardware. A Teletype-based program assembler and PROM-programming system—put together with programs and modules from the vendor—help to simplify program development. Some systems read paper tape containing assembly-language programs and translates them into machine-language programs, also on paper tape. The latter tape can be reread to program the control PROMs.

I/O memory addresses. It is almost always possible to use memory addresses for I/O devices. I/O ports are considered as if they were RAM locations; an input is performed by reading memory and an output by writing into it. Though a program may look somewhat more obscure (I/O operations become more difficult to spot if the program is not documented), operations performed on input data can be those associated with RAM data. For example, add, compare, and test bits. This technique also allows for a number of I/O devices, limited only by the size of the memory that can be addressed by the microprocessor.

Link (L). In some systems, the link is a 1-bit flip-flop that serves as a high-order extension of the accumulator (AC). It is used as a carry flip-flop for 2's complement arithmetic. A carry out of the ALU complements the link. Link can be cleared, set, complemented, and tested under program control and rotated as part of the AC.

Linking loader. The bootstrap loader can be used to load a linking loader into main memory. The linking loader is a relocatable loader—it completes memory address calculations that were partially processed by the relocatable assembler, allowing users to load and execute a program anywhere in memory.

Literal. 1. A symbol that names itself and that is not the name of something else. 2. A symbol or quantity in a source program that is itself data rather than a reference to data.

Look ahead. Basically look ahead is a feature of the CPU that permits the machine to mask an interrupt request until the following instruction has been completed. It is also a feature of adder circuits and ALUs that permits these devices to "look ahead" to anticipate that all carries generated are available for addition.

LSI board testing. LSI boards and devices have complicated testing because often the programmer is unaware of the logic activity within the device. In fact, often this information is proprietary and not available. Only by function testing can these boards and devices be tested. This input pattern requirement, although difficult or impossible with fixed programs, is very simple using the stored program feature. Common bus logic is another area peculiar and difficult to test. Each board that connects to the common bus has its own address and must be addressed properly before testing can commence. Again, this is a difficult task with a fixed program tester but very simple using the stored program feature.

Macroassembler. A macroassembler simplifies coding when similar sections of code are used repeatedly, but variations preclude the use of conventional subroutine techniques. With a macroassembler, a single instruction yields the necessary expansion without undue complexity.

Macroassembler, resident. The resident macroassembler enables users to translate assembly language programs efficiently into the appropriate machine language instructions. The full macro capability eliminates the need to rewrite similar sections of code repeatedly and simplifies user's program documentation. And the conditional assembly feature of the macroassembler permits users to include or delete optional code segments that may vary from system to system.

Macro coding. Refers to procedures for providing segments of coding, which are used frequently throughout a program and can be defined at the beginning and used and referenced by a mnemonic code with parameters. This increases coding efficiency and readability of the program.

Macroinstruction design. Many efficient designs result from considering three steps together to ensure that the macroinstruction set formats are compatible with the microcomputer family members and that operation-code formats result in the simplest microprogram flow. The macroinstruction set may be register or stack-oriented and may be original or a copy of another machine. In general, lower cost and higher performance will result when an original macroinstruction set is developed to use the microcomputer family features most effectively.

Map. 1. Refers to activities to transform information from one form to another. 2. A listing provided by a compiler to enable a programmer to relate his or her data names to the memory addresses within the program.

Microcoding. Alterable machine structure is often called firmware. The trend toward standardization of LSI products on just memory and processor is being accompanied by a trend toward microcoding, especially for the sake of simplicity and flexible uniformity. Lower cost and ease of debugging processor hardware are the driving forces that favor microcoding.

Microprogramming techniques. There are very few techniques that have been widely publicized for writing efficient microprograms or developing efficient microcode. A few of the more frequently used techniques discussed often that are finding application in microprogramming are (1) indexing, (2) subroutines, and (3) paramaterization. Many arithmetic operations are made up of a sequence of repetitive operations. For example, a multiply is made up of a sequence of adds and shifts. This sequence will be executed over and over again until the operation is completed. Index registers have been used in computers to count the number of times one goes through a sequence of instructions. The same technique is applicable to microprogramming.

Microprogram principles. The basic principle is to segment the microprogrammed control into two parts—one for operating the gates that control the data paths and the other for selecting the next step in the control sequence. All microprogrammed devices are organized in a similar fashion. The essence of designing a good microprogrammed system is the selection of the proper strategies for data paths and logic function control as well as the implementation of the control sequence section.

Monitor, operating system. Generally, most monitors exercise primary control of the routines that compose the operating system. It is the operating system that turns the computer into a flexible tool, allowing the user to achieve maximum use of the hardware's advanced design features.

Nesting. 1. Concerns subroutines that are generally enclosed within each other. Those in the inner ring are not necessarily part of the outer ring or loop. Nesting is an important programming technique. 2. The inclusion of a routine or block of data within a computer inside a larger routine or block of data.

Nesting loop. Refers to nesting loops that usually contain a loop of instructions, which then also contain inner loops, nesting subroutines, outer loops, and rules and procedures relating to in and out procedures for each type.

Operating system. 1. A basic group of programs with operation under control of a data-processing monitor program. 2. An integrated collection of service routines for supervising the sequencing and processing of programs by a computer. Operating systems may perform debugging, input-output, machine accounting, compilation, and storage assignment tasks.

Overlay. A popular technique for bringing routines into high-speed memory from some other form of storage during processing, so that several routines will occupy the same storage locations at different times. It is used when the total memory requirements for instructions exceed the available high-speed memory.

Overlay tree. Refers to a specific graphic representation showing the relationships of segments of an overlay program and how the segments are arranged to use the same main storage area at different times.

Page addressing. Refers to a specific procedure of memory addressing utilized with some specific computers. The addressing capability is limited to less than the total memory capability available. But, using page addressing, memory is divided into segments (pages), each of which can be addressed by the available addressing capability.

PLA instruction fetch. During an instruction fetch, the instruction to be executed is loaded into the instruction register. The PLA is used for correct sequencing of the CPU for the appropriate instruction. Once an instruction is executed, the major state generator scans the various request lines through an internal priority network. The state of the priority network decides whether the machine is going to fetch the next instruction in sequence or service one of the request lines.

PLA vs ROM. The availability of low-cost ROMs has led to new concepts of digital systems design, specifically the "regular" design approach (or microprogramming) rather than the use of so-called "random" logic. The PLA offers an alternative to the ROM in many cases and allows regular design concepts to be used in situations wherein ROMs are impractical. The PLA concept is used in combinational and sequential digital systems in contrast to ROM usage.

PL/M compiler language. PL/M is a high-level language concept developed by Intel Corp. to meet the special needs of microcomputer systems programming. Programmers can utilize a high-level language to program microcomputers efficiently. PL/M is an assembly language replacement that can fully command the 8080 CPU and future processors to produce efficient run-time object code.

PL/M Plus. National Semiconductor has developed PL/M Plus, an extended version of PL/M, to simplify programming of its microprocessors. The compatible version can compile programs on micros, eliminating the need to use large systems for compilations.

Pointer. 1. A word giving the address of another main memory storage location. 2. Pointers automatically step through memory locations. Automatically stepping forward through consecutive locations is known as autoincrement addressing; automatically stepping backward is known as autodecrement addressing. These modes are particularly useful for processing tabular or array data.

Polling. Refers to an important multiprocessing method used to identify the source of interrupt requests. When several interrupts occur simultaneously, the control program makes the decision as to the one that will be serviced first.

Polling list. Concerns a specified list containing control information and names of entries in the terminal table. The order in which the names are specified determines the order in which the terminals are polled.

Pseudocode. 1. Refers to an instruction that is not meant to be followed directly by a computer. Instead, it initiates the linking of a subroutine into the main program. 2. Refers to various codes that express programs in source language, that is, by referring to storage locations and machine operations by symbolic names and addresses that are independent of their hardware-determined names and addresses.

Pushdown nesting. As data are transferred into storage, each word, in turn, enters the top register and is then "pushed down" the column from register to register to make room for the subsequent words as they are assigned. When a word is transferred out of the storage, again only from the top register, other data in the storage move back up the column from register to register to fill the space left empty. This is accomplished either through programs or the equipment itself.

Pushdown stack (p-stack). A register developed to receive information from the program counter and store address locations of the instructions that have been pushed down during an interrupt. This stack can be used for subroutining. Its size determines the level of subroutine nesting in a 16-word register. When instructions are returned, they are popped back on a last-in-first-out (LIFO) basis.

Queue, automatic. Concerned with a specific series of interconnected registers that are designed to implement either a LIFO (last-in-first-out) queue or a FIFO (first-in-first-out) queue without program manipulation. For a FIFO queue, new entries to the queue are placed in the last position and automatically jump forward to the last unoccupied position while removal of the front entry results in all entries automatically moving forward one position. Also called pushdown storage and pushup storage.

Quoted string. Refers to assembler programming, a character string enclosed by apostrophes that is used in a macroinstruction operand to represent a value that can include blanks. The enclosed apostrophes are part of the value represented. Contrast with character expression.

Reenterable. Refers to a special attribute of a program that describes a routine that can be shared by several tasks concurrently ("reusable reentrant") or that can "call" itself or a program that calls it. Special provisions are required: (1) to externalize all intermediate variables used (the "prototype control section" of the calling program) and (2) to avoid destruction of the return address by circular calling sequences.

Register, memory-address (MAR). A special location in memory is selected for data storage or retrieval and is determined by the MAR. This register can directly address all words of the standard main memory or in any preselected field of extended main memory.

Report generator. 1. A special computer routine designed to prepare an object routine that, when later run on the computer, produces the desired report. 2. A problem-oriented language capable of automatically generating the machine instructions required to transform an input file into a desired report.

Report program generator. Refers to a type of processing program that can be used to generate object programs that produce reports from existing sets of data. Abbreviated RPG.

Semantic error. 1. An error that results in ambiguous or erroneous meaning of a computer program. Most programs have to be debugged to eliminate these errors before use. 2. Refers to errors in meaning or intent of the programmer and are definitely his or her responsibility. Consequently, he or she is provided with an extensive set of debugging aids for manipulating and referencing a program when in search of errors in the logic and analysis.

Shift instructions. Numerous variations of the shift instruction are implemented on different computers; typically, you can shift right, or you can shift left. A right shift is more useful, because it is equivalent to dividing by two, whereas the left shift is equivalent to multiplying by two and can be reproduced by adding the contents of a register to itself. A shift may be continuous through a status bit or branched, or it may bypass the status bit. The shift may also be arithmetic and propagate the high order bit (sign bit) to the right.

Simulator, cross. Cross simulators are also used on larger host computers to simulate actions of the microcomputer programmatically. The primary problem, however, is that extensive program testing and simulation of real-time external events, such as signals input from a device controller, are tedious and expensive. Thus cross simulators are principally used to step-through subroutines and program modules independently of the electronic environment. A simulator is extremely useful, however, when exact execution time must be determined for time-critical program segments.

Software cross assembler. Cross assemblers translate a symbolic representation of the instructions and data into a form that can be loaded and executed by microcomputer. A cross assembler is defined as an assembler executing on a machine other than the one used, which generates code for the desired unit. Initial development time can be significantly reduced by taking advantage of a large-scale computer's processing, editing, and high-speed peripheral capability. Programs are written in the assembly language, using mnemonic symbols both for instruction and for special assembler operation. Symbolic addresses can be used in the source program; however, the assembled program will use absolute address. Most assemblers, designed to operate interactively from a terminal, are written in standard FORTRAN IV and can be modified to run on most large-scale machines.

Software development system, in-circuit emulator. An in-circuit emulator for various microprocessors replaces the specific microprocessor in the user's system and allows the designer to examine, alter, and control the microprocessor system. It is a real microprocessor and requires no special design considerations. Many of these units weigh about 16 pounds in basic configurations. They provide easy portability for use at the bench or in the field. When a major software effort is required, the base unit can be expanded with a variety of hardware and software options to give the user a full-scale software development system. Hardware designers can start using the emulators as soon as their breadboard has working clocks. A typical unit will read and write memory and perform input and output without the need for a program executing in the user's memory or even without user's memory working.

Software stack. Some microprocessor units use software stacks—an area in read-write memory set aside under program control. An on-chip hardware stack provides increased performance. For hardware stacks to be generally useful, there should also be on-chip indicators for stack full and stack empty, which increases chip area. However, the on-chip hardware required for a software stack consists primarily of a stack-pointer register and appropriate increment/decrement control. An indication of overflow and underflow is not so critical as for an on-chip hardware stack, for the software stack can be easily expanded in system memory.

Translators. Translators, a generic term for assemblers and compilers (also interpreters that have not been used much with microcomputers) are programs that allow the programmer to express his program in a language closer to his or her native language for later translation to a language acceptable by a machine or subsequent leader. Sometimes translators only translate from a higher language (closer to English, for example) to a lower language like assembly language (closer to machine language). Translator tools are designed with features to enhance program expression, to provide programmer services, and to remove as much clerical burden as possible.

Virtual machine techniques. There is an increasing use of virtual memory and virtual-machine techniques. Memory systems, already up to ½-million bytes, can go to 250 million words in a virtual memory, and it also has the advantage of simplified software and increased reliability. A virtual machine implies virtual memory and more. It maps memory plus instructions. So when a user executes, say, an I/O instruction, the machine traps and implements it directly.

Virtual memory, user-coded. Virtual memory can be provided by a user-determined form of code segmentation. This approach permits a program to be larger than the main memory and avoids the thrashing between disk and memory that often results when segmentation is totally machine determined. Some systems automatically eliminate swap out of segments that are in frequent use. A hardware-implemented variable stack design can sharply reduce the amount of memory required to execute programs.

8
Microcomputer Applications: Distributed Intelligence in Business, Banks, and Factories

FOUR MAJOR MICROPROCESSOR APPLICATIONS AREAS: POS, EFTS, CAM, AND WP [1]

The microsystems revolution that is bringing the power of electronics to retail stores gained added impetus during 1975 and flowered into full bloom in 1976. The surge had been made possible by the development of powerful new computerized point of sale terminals, freestanding electronic cash registers (some of which are minicomputers or microcomputers in their own right), and automatic scanning equipment for capturing merchandise and customer information. The ability of these advanced new systems to provide up-to-the-minute sales information, faster customer service, and improved inventory management has created a market that may well exceed $2 billion in the United States alone over the next several years. In 1974, NCR alone had orders for over 75,000 computerized point of sale terminals and freestanding electronic cash registers of various types, having a total sales value of more than $250 million.

Department stores, discount stores, and other general merchandise retailers have spearheaded the electronic revolution. Riding the crest in this wave of systems change are such giants of general merchandising as Montgomery Ward & Company and J. C. Penney Company. Ward's in 1974 was embarked on a three-year $60-million program to install 16,000 NCR 280 terminals, together with scores of NCR store computers and associated equipment. Penney's planned to install up to 17,000 NCR 280 ter-

---

[1] POS stands for *point of sale systems;* EFTS for *electronic funds transfer systems;* CAM, for *computer-aided manufacturing;* and WP, for *word processing.*

minals (plus 10,000 others); 10,000 OCR (optical character recognition) scanning units, which automatically read merchandise price tags and credit cards; and 300 NCR computers. Many different options are offered the user of this equipment. These include stand-alone terminals for stores planning to computerize their operations at a later date, terminals that collect data on tape cassettes or computer-compatible magnetic tape, and fully computerized on-line systems. Free-standing, fully electronic cash registers were developed for smaller department stores, apparel shops, and other retail stores as early as 1973.

Book stores, clothing chains, shoe stores, record stores, men's wear shops, and catalog showrooms are among other segments of the retailing industry currently installing check-out computer terminals or electronic cash registers. Even transactions at post office windows will eventually be handled by microprocessor-controlled point of sale equipment. The U.S. Postal Service has launched a pilot program using NCR terminals to test their potential for speeding up the nation's largest point of sale business. As in retailing, other new types of electronic payment systems point to major changes in the way financial institutions will conduct their businesses in future years.

There has been a growing interest in electronic funds transfer systems (EFTS). These are systems for transferring funds from one account to another with electronic equipment rather than with paper media such as checks. Larger commercial banks and thrift institutions were experimenting in 1971–1974 with EFTS for two basic reasons. At that time 123 billion checks circulated through the U.S. banking system annually, and this was expected to exceed 40 billion by 1980. These checks pass through many hands, and processing costs are high. One of the promises of EFTS is a substantial reduction in this nonproductive paperwork, which, according to one recent study, costs the economy about $10 billion annually. Equally important is the potential that EFTS systems offer in terms of improved financial services, with advantages for consumers as well as financial institutions. The evolution of EFTS will be closely linked with system changes now occurring in retail stores. This is because electronic point of sale equipment makes feasible the transfer of funds from a shopper's bank account to the store's account at the time of transaction. Although the concept of "less-paper" EFTS is relatively simple, its actual implementation will be highly complex. For example, broad-scale EFTS developments will require changes in the current regulatory aspects of banking and the establishment of systems that are mutually beneficial to financial institutions, retail stores, and their consumer customers.

Computer power now reaches from accounting and management all the way to the plant floor. Computer-aided manufacturing (CAM) goes beyond the computerization of functions such as capturing, updating, and disseminating inventory and production information. With CAM, computers are used in the "make," "move," and "test" operations. Computers are becoming parts of every production process. CAM includes (1) support for the equipment, process, and employees that constitute the production function in manufacturing facility and (2) indirect technical efforts of manufacturing and quality engineering functions that specify and maintain capital equipment and also the related procedures that thereby seek to achieve management as well as process and quality control.

One of the most widely talked about computer terms is *word processing*. It is defined as a term for automated production of the written (or printed) word. The concept has as its core any of several alternative technologies permitting automatic typing, text editing, and a whole series of other information-handling procedures. The movement toward word processing began to assume ground swell proportions in 1973, and it raced ahead in 1974 and 1975. Various estimates place the number of word-processing units then currently in daily use as high as 100,000, with a tripling of this number by 1976. The forecast is an eightfold growth rate during the remainder of the decade. Users of word processing report cost savings of a magnitude at least equal to 25 percent to 50 percent of the salaries of the typists who would otherwise be manually producing the documents now generated automatically by microprocessor-controlled word-processing equipment. But reduced salary costs may be only a fringe benefit. The primary advantages appear to be the reduced amount of executive time required to produce a document and the minimization of errors and the ease of error correction. All this and more is further facilitated by new speeds of turnaround time for practically every type of document in the business and professional environments.

Word-processing operations technology is actively extending the scope of word-processing hardware from tape controlled "power typewriters" to more complex systems that employ microcomputer control, disk storage, and multiple input/output stations. Instead of word-processing machines, therefore, like the IBM STS/MTS equipment, which offers one typewriter with magnetic storage and limited editing and justifying capability, today's word-processing systems offer considerably more versatility, operating ease, and very rapid throughput. This is accomplished by organizing low-cost processor-controlled tape and disk storage systems. They accommodate hundreds of stored and indexed "standard" paragraphs, many different form letters, and other reusable documents and so on. These can be assembled simultaneously on an array of input/output stations. The equipment can also compose research reports, legal documents, proposals, and other lengthy material; hold it on disk for final editing (via CRT terminal, for example); and then use a computer-output printer for high-speed document preparation. In this kind of application, uppercase and lowercase printout is invariably mandatory for producing multipage comprehensive reports. The consensus at a recent American Management conference was reported in press releases and by several writers to be as follows: The private "typing" secretary will all but disappear. She will have become as much of an anachronism as the village blacksmith—an unneeded craftsman in an age of automation. The letters and services she crafted for her boss will be accomplished in more specialized, productive ways.

Although there are already hundreds of distinct areas of microprocessor applications—and the previous chapter briefly indicated many of them—this chapter relates to and explains four primary "sectors" of changes. Retailing, banking, manufacturing, and office automation are very basic sections of our total economic system. Drastic changes in operating procedures in any one of them would be of major significance. Revolutionary changes in all of them simultaneously—owing to the simplicity, speed, low cost, and versatility of microprocessors—are fundamental to our total life-style.

THE DISPERSED BUSINESS DATA-PROCESSING MARKET

To understand the dispersed business data-processing market, one must briefly review the basic structure of the overall data-processing market, drawing a distinction between two basic types of applications—scientific and business—and between two methods of data processing—centralized and dispersed.

Scientific data processing.[2] Scientific data processing includes applications such as solving complicated mathematical problems for engineers, physicists, or chemists and process control, that is, use of a computer to monitor and control such things as chemical processes or machine tools. These applications generally involve complex calculations and short time periods. There may be varying amounts of data entry, but data output volumes generally are small compared to those of business data processing; for instance, the output required for a very complicated computation may be a single numeric answer. Scientific data-processing applications usually have relatively low data-storage requirements.

Business Data Processing. Business data processing includes the majority of data-processing applications such as accounts payable, payroll, inventory control, billing, material control, production record keeping, and management reporting systems. These applications generally require considerable amounts of data entry; they usually do not involve such complex computations as do scientific applications; large data output volumes almost always exist (for instance, the output from one payroll processing may consist of thousands of checks plus related documents); and data-storage requirements in business data-processing applications are almost always

---

[2] The distinctions have now blurred considerably; many business planning problems relating to management science are very complex. Industrial control, in many cases, has become "simplified" and not really "scientific."

substantial. Because of the differences between scientific and business data processing, the two applications are best served by different types of computer systems, and different companies have tended to be dominant in the respective markets. For example, IBM, which clearly dominates the centralized business data-processing market, has not been successful in establishing a similar degree of dominance over the centralized scientific data-processing market.

Centralized Data Processing. Centralized data processing is the performing of all data entry and computing in centralized facilities using powerful and expensive large mainframe computers. Detailed data are transported to a centralized computer room, and summarized data are returned to dispersed locations. More than 80 percent of the large mainframe computers installed today are used in business applications rather than in scientific applications, and virtually all these business computers are in centralized facilities. Because of the high cost of large mainframe computer systems, centralization has been the only means by which most such installations could be justified.

Dispersed Data Processing. Although centralization provided cost justification for large mainframe computers, it created many problems for users, including long turnaround time for feedback reports, an increasing rate of human-induced errors owing to centralization of data entry, and increasing difficulties in hiring and retaining competent data entry and operations personnel at centralized locations. These problems, as well as significant advances in solid-state electronic component and data communications technologies, are creating new and expanding opportunities for manufacturers of data-processing equipment designed and priced for use at dispersed locations. Such systems permit the people who originate, work with, and best understand the data to capture and process business data at dispersed locations on a cost-effective basis. It is here that the detailed data for entry are understood and feedback reports are needed. Successful penetration of this market requires addressing all three of the functions that constitute dispersed data processing—data entry, computing, and data communications—at dispersed locations. Many companies currently are successful with products for source data entry or remote batch data entry, which encompass only two of these functions—data entry and data communications. These companies should achieve long-term success; the dispersed data-processing market is large enough for a great number of companies with varying approaches to be successful.

Market evolution

Before computers came into widespread use, almost all business data processing was done on unit-record (punched card) equipment that was slow and had limited processing capabilities, but was low enough in cost for data processing at conveniently dispersed locations. The advent of large mainframe computers led to centralization of this function; and, as computers became larger and larger, the trend toward centralization accelerated. With centralization came the emergence of a handful of large companies that today dominate the market for data-processing equipment. These companies have concentrated on developing large systems for centralized applications. As mentioned earlier, IBM dominates centralized business data processing, but other industry giants have established strong positions in selling to certain industry segments of this market and in centralized scientific data processing.

By the mid-sixties, problems emerged concerning centralization of both business and scientific data processing. They became the rule rather than the exception. Economies of scale inherent in large computer systems began to be offset by many specific problems, including the rising cost of data entry, excessive human-induced errors, unnecessary delays, unacceptable turnaround times, and inadequate flexibility imposed by overall system complexity. The problem of service deterioration caused by centralization to the user of the system output was attacked initially by the time-sharing concept, first with teletypewriters and then with cathode-ray tube/keyboard terminals.

Although time sharing allows a number of dispersed users to share a large centralized computer, it was initially applied almost exclusively in scientific applications where input/output traffic tends to be low and in remote inquiry/response applications like airline reservation systems where the data communication cost is acceptably low. Other new products, such as key-to-tape and shared processor key-to-disk systems, which were developed to mitigate the problems that had evolved under centralization, were and are not generally communications-oriented and deal primarily with data entry. They have generally been used as direct keypunch replacements in centralized data-processing facilities.

The breakthrough: dispersed scientific data processing

A radical departure from centralized data processing occurred in the late sixties when advanced semiconductor technology was used to develop the minicomputer. This made computerized process control viable; it allowed individuals or small groups of engineers to have their own computer and brought scientific data processing back full circle to the dispersed locations where it began. Then came the microcomputer. The resulting microcomputer and minicomputer markets, which primarily dealt originally with dedicated industrial process control and other dispersed scientific data-processing applications, experienced explosive growth. The small company that initially pioneered in this market, Digital Equipment Corp., currently has sales of about $400 million per year and has become the "little giant" in dispersed scientific data processing. It now has a market position that has withstood subsequent competition from other small companies as well as from the largest manufacturers of data-processing systems. They have also joined in the microcomputer business. Thus both microcomputers and minicomputers have now been used to a great extent in business data processing because peripheral equipment and software needed for these applications have quickly become generally and economically available.

Dispersed Business Data Processing

Advances in semiconductor technology, particularly in silicon on sapphire (SOS) and metal-oxide silicon (MOS) devices, and advances in data communications technology, have created the opportunity for the same thing to be done for business data processing that the microcomputers and minicomputers did for scientific data processing. The relative magnitude of this opportunity can probably be expressed by the fact that minis now outnumber all standard systems and micros far exceed the numbers of all computers, including minis. The centralized business data-processing market is about ten times the size of the centralized scientific data-processing market; as the dispersed business processing market matures, it is likely to grow significantly larger unless the dispersed scientific market might include the education and medical markets. Because it has only recently become practical, the new dispersed business data processing does indeed represent a revolution rather than an evolution. Technology is simply permitting an economical return to past practices of performing at remote or dispersed locations the data processing that should logically be done there. Centralization of the total data-processing function has resulted in an information flow that is the inverse of most good management structures—detailed information is concentrated at the top and only summary data are available at other locations.

Dispersed business data processing enables a return to the concept of making detailed data available to the operating people who understand and need it while supplying summarized data to the central locations at which senior executive management and staff are normally located. However, it also permits personnel at the central location to have ready access to detailed data and allows personnel at dispersed locations to use the powerful centralized mainframe computers when such needs arise. Because of the relative newness of dispersed business data processing as a practical reality, direct statistics on market size and growth are not available.

Microcomputers within terminals offer flexible, total-systems approach to the dispersed business data-processing market by developing systems that perform the three necessary functions of data entry, computing, and data communications. Initially, companies competing in this market generally had products that could address only one or two of these functions. As a result, microcomputers have the potential to provide better solution to a customer's dispersed data-processing problems, particularly if the customer recognizes the need for flexibility and the ability to increase system capability at very low cost. Microcomputer companies are following product strategies that are based on five primary elements: evolutionary product development using the most advanced technologies available, major commitments to software, maximum utilization of each hardware component, upward system compatibility, and system flexibility. Microprocessors designed within minisystems change a minicomputer into a mainframe computer in miniature—a general-purpose, communications-oriented data-processing system that performs the three basic functions of dispersed business data processing at a price that justifies its use in remote locations. These systems are designed for use in ordinary offices, plants, or warehouse environments rather than in a special computer room and for use as part of the normal work routine by people without extensive specialized training.

The support software available for many microsystems is becoming as broad in scope as that provided with many large mainframe computers. The importance of these commitments to software cannot be overemphasized. Good software is essential for effective use of the system by production and clerical or other office personnel in dispersed locations. The comprehensiveness of software substantially increases the value of the system to users because it gives them the ability both to write applications programs for a wide variety of jobs and to make frequent changes in applications by simply inserting another program; thus it also increases the user's reliance on software for continuity of his or her operations.

Supermarket and department store microcomputer sales multiply fast

More than 30 manufacturers are vying for the multibillion-dollar computer business bonanza for check-out counter and point-of-transaction equipment terminals around the world. Electronic cash terminals and electronic games and scales were the first computer systems to invade America's and the world's supermarkets. This rich territory opened up properly only in 1973, when the supermarket industry agreed on a universal standard product code (UPC) (see further on) for identifying all products and their manufacturers on machine-readable tags. The 10-digit optical bar symbol quickly appeared on 5,000 to 10,000 items on the supermarket shelves by late 1974. Electronic scales are also programmed to weigh different types of meat, produce, and so on and direct a printer to produce coded tags and an alphanumeric label—the first for the scanner, the second for the buyer.

Competition was intense for clear-cut leadership. The equipment centered on five types of equipment: minicomputer-controlled store systems,

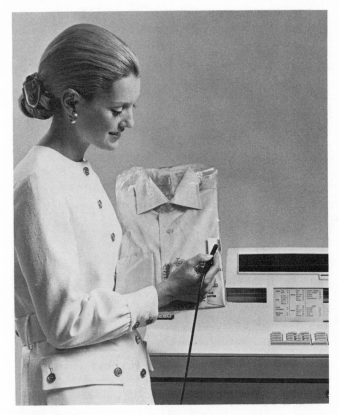

FIGURE 8.1. NCR 280 retail terminal with wand reader. *Courtesy: NCR Corporation*

stand-alone electronic cash registers with key entry, fixed-head slot scanning with either X scanners or raster scanners, hand-held scanners, and store-level UPC symbol-printing equipment. The scanners are generally sold as part of a register-and-checkstand package, which may include a place for an electronic scale tied directly to the register.

Conversion from electromechanical to electronic check-out was enthusiastically supported by industry's powerful Supermarket Institute. Early trials showed improvements in customer throughput and employee productivity. Users were initially cautious, but the costs savings were most attractive. A very high percentage of most stores' total inventories were coded because the high cost of the ultimate system had to be justified.

The reaction of shoppers to the product code and the high-speed checkstands was difficult to anticipate. Individual price tags disappeared from the items on the shelves, which was bothersome. Once a complete store system was up and running, the items had code labels only. Prices were

FIGURE 8.2. Groceries are passed over the scanner and into shopping bags in one quick motion at this supermarket. By the time the computer-controlled terminal totals the food bill, items have been bagged and are ready for carry-out. *Courtesy: NCR Corporation*

maintained in the store-level computer and looked up when the item was scanned at the checkstand and the transaction recorded. Consequently, once the customer had taken an item from the shelf, he or she did not know its price until he or she saw the itemized receipt at check-out time; and that created two tasks for the supermarket. First, shelf prices had to be prepared and mounted more carefully than in the past. Secondly, consumers had to be informed via promotion programs.[3]

There are scores of areas where the electronic checkstand activities benefit. The top two are increased productivity and accuracy, but the others offer direct cost decreases. These benefits promised from the universal product code are now part of the standard pitch of the hardware manufacturers.

Product or system companies have emphasized scanners. Sweda International, Bunker Ramo, NCR, National Semiconductor, MSI Data Corp.,

[3] Some stores added an extra "pricer" checkstand that customers could use to determine their total bill before going to the check-out clerk.

Singer, and Data Terminal Systems are some entries. IBM and Sperry Univac had previously demonstrated UPC-scanning systems as early as 1973. Many companies have developed laser scanners that are supplied to practically all of the companies making front-end systems. ✳

A number of the stand-alone registers can be upgraded to laser scanners, thus making it possible for a supermarket to enter sales data by register keyboard until enough goods on the shelf carry the UPC tags. Most stores estimate a 2.2-year payback on the investment, with the number of customers checked out per hour jumping from 16 to 19. Scanning systems have yielded a 45 percent improvement throughput. The savings were real enough to stop the buying of electromechanical registers very abruptly.

Executives of many supermarket firms have learned that they have a requirement for much more than replacement of the cash registers to increase productivity and reduce store operating costs. They need full systems that can link headquarters locations with branch stores with full data communications.

✳ The scanning units automatically identify the symbol-marked items that are pulled across them, and the checker can use a fast two-handed motion, simultaneously bagging items. As the scanner identifies each item, the terminal automatically retrieves the item's name and price. The terminal also (1) displays a description of the item and its price; (2) performs all the calculations for tax and change; (3) prints a customer receipt containing descriptions and prices of all items, totals, and a promotional statement that can be customized for each store; and then checkers can enter items that are not symbol-marked either by keying the item number or letter (and the system supplies the price) or by keying in the price of the item directly. And, most significantly, at the end of the day, or at most any other convenient time, summarized data can be transmitted to division or corporate headquarters for processing of scores of management reporting and analysis routines. ✳

Examples of ten very direct advantages are

✳ 1. *Misring control.* Computer terminals are very accurate check-out systems. They will accurately calculate the correct individual unit price for multiple-priced items and for mix-and-match items. The correct tax will also be calculated automatically. Human errors will be virtually eliminated for items that are symbol-marked, and customers themselves might operate self-check-out systems with alarm-ringing pilferage controls at exit doors (if items do not have a check-out magnetic spot on them).

2. *Merchandising.* Data provided by these systems can help manage new merchandising plans. Point of sale capture of item movement data, for example, can assist in advertising and promotion analysis; new item tracking; better vendor analysis, particularly for items that are direct

319

delivered; price management; demographic merchandising; extended departmental control; and immediate implementation of price changes.

3. *Price marking and re-marking.* With the universal product code and supermarket systems, prices and price changes go into the computer once, but not onto every item. This can save a considerable amount of time because the volume of price marking will be greatly reduced. And item price re-marking? For items that are product-coded, it is eliminated. When users change a price, all they change are shelf labels.

4. *Labor scheduling.* The supermarket systems provide the operating data needed for improved scheduling of store employees: dollar sales in 15-minute time period, customer counts, transaction data, and other store labor activity. This can improve the results of existing labor scheduling programs by providing more accurate and complete data as an automatic by-product of the check-out function. It is also an excellent tool for setting up advanced computer-based labor-scheduling programs. Either way, it can result in more effective use of personnel and substantial cost reductions.

5. *Store ordering.* Store ordering can be done automatically. Users can program their computers to determine when it is time to reorder. Supermarket systems keep track of item movement and transfer summarized data to the reordering program to order new merchandise automatically. This can mean significant savings plus greater control and accuracy and central control, relieving store managers of this chore.

6. *Store inventory management.* The typical supermarket stocks up to 10,000 items, and that number is growing. With the automated systems, management can know exactly what is moving—a clearer, faster, and more accurate picture than warehouse shipments give. The automatic reordering capability made possible by point of sale data capture can also help to lower backroom inventory and provide better control over pilferage and shelf allocation. And this can result in increased profits.

7. *Warehousing and transportation.* Systems programs can be written to assist with work load delivery balancing because the system provides the data needed to calculate an item's recent movement against the probability of its becoming out of stock before an order is delivered.

8. *Register balancing.* Supermarket systems help in register reconciliation, calculate the correct ending tender position, and transmit daily reports to the central office, including counts of cash, checks, store coupons, and vendor coupons. This can mean additional savings plus more timely and accurate central accounting of store funds.

9. *Check-out electronic scales.* Attaching scales to the system gives checkers fast, accurate prices on produce. The scale can increase the pricing accuracy of variable-weight items—and increase profits on these items.

10. *Time saving.* Because the supermarket systems can do so much of the pricing, repricing, and ordering work, they save on management time. Because the terminal and scanner are so simple to use, they can reduce checker training time.

Microprocessors in point of sale terminals

A mathematics, engineering, or programming student of the late 1960s, if asked to design, program, and implement a point of sale system with a terminal containing its own computer would certainly have immediately and indignantly thrown up his hands in despair. And these same individuals will today be almost totally amazed at the relative simplicity of the system block diagram in Figure 8.3, and they certainly will never believe its low cost unless they have been ardently following the progress of microprocessors.

The new n-channel micros address themselves to many parts of systems, as we are discovering. Families of circuits are designed to minimize components and program assembly costs while increasing capability and capacity as well as speed. The typical small terminal for a generalized point of sale system is shown in Figure 8.3. All CPUs require several peripheral interfaces; minicomputers are very cost-effective by providing simplified input-output and memory interfaces, compatible with data-bus arrangements and specific addressing schemes. Micros like the one in Figure 8.3 are word-oriented, and a great many similar types are appearing to com-

FIGURE 8.3. With microprocessor design techniques, systems such as this point of sale installation are capable of being implemented with only five or six circuit blocks, which are designed to work directly with the basic CPU family. *Reprinted with permission from* Electronics, *April 18, 1974, copyright McGraw-Hill Book Co., all rights reserved.*

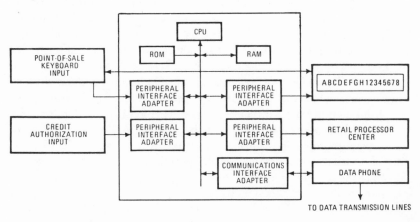

pete with the Motorola model M6800 depicted. These systems can maintain 1-MHz levels of operation even when they are expanded to ten or more modules that include memories, I/O devices, additional CPUs, and so on, on the principal data bus—with no external interface packages, using bus extenders. At slower speeds 30 or more modules can be handled. Micros in terminals of hundreds of types provide the "variable intelligence".

POS revolution at all cash points coming?

Emphasis should not be placed upon the changing technology of front-end POS operations. This is only the beginning of a transformation that is about to occur in management of supermarket operations. This change stems from the introduction of minicomputer and microcomputer capabilities at each store location. Supermarket executives see immediate future developments as follows:

1. Cashless transactions as promoted by the large banking institutions of the nation. The EFTS concept (electronic funds transfer systems), systems in which a customer presents a card at the register in a retail outlet that the retailer uses to ascertain the customer's balance in his or her checking account, is in live experimental stages. Accounts are debited and the credit transferred to the retailer's account within the bank in one instantaneous transaction. Automatic check-outs, computerized front-ends, and so on are causing management to accelerate the rate of introduction of such plans. For retailers this development poses some complex problems because in any area there will be a number of banks offering this. But will retailers decide to have POS systems tied into a number of banking outlets or opt for only a few?

2. Microprocessor control applications will include monitoring temperature changes in frozen food cases, minimization of energy usage, and monitoring other aspects of store operations. Robot-controlled and programmed in-store computer maintenance activities also open new sales.

3. New distribution methods by the jewel companies in Chicago (The Grand Bazaar) suggest the possibility of receiving at store level, direct from the manufacturer, pallet loads of merchandise without shipping cartons in which the individual packages are unitized by an overwrap of shrink film covering the entire pallet. This form of distribution could substantially reduce handling costs because there is no longer the need to price products individually when they arrive at store levels.

4. Sales management data will finally permit management to know how much Kodak film, lipstick, vitamin pills, and similar expensive, small, and pocketable items are on hand or lost through pilferage. This knowledge will lead to a rearrangement of store layouts and changes.

5. Communication systems between headquarters and stores will get out of rudimentary form, and the information collected about sales will develop automatic reordering systems to replenish store stocks.

The magnitude of the changes in this industry is already apparent. Computer capability has created new levels of efficiency in the POS revolution. A huge point of sale market already exists with several thousand systems installed in department stores and supermarkets in late 1974. Also an ultimate replacement market of over 3 million cash registers, and a realistic replacement market of over 1.5 million by 1980, make the point of sales (POS) market obviously a huge one. The companies now producing the new integrated POS systems total at least a dozen, led by the two major suppliers in the cash register market, NCR (80 percent) and Sweda (15 percent). Others are Singer, Bunker, Ramo, TRW, National Semiconductor, AMF, Motorola, MSI, General Instrument, and several computer makes, IBM, Univac, Data General, and Digital Computer Controls.

The federal reserve and ABA urge banks to adopt EFTS—fast

"Banks must stop merely talking about the Electronic Funds Transfer System (EFTS) and do something if they expect to stay ahead of thrift institutions which already have made significant inroads in automation techniques," according to the president of the American Bankers Association (ABA). (The Federal Reserve governors are also pushing EFTS.) The ABA president cited as evidence the successful instant payments transfer experiment being tried in Nebraska by the First Federal Savings and Loan Association of Lincoln and the Hinky-Dinky supermarket chain that is tapping "a new source of deposits—deposits that might have gone to local banks." Bankers must look around and "see what we must do to protect and increase our share of the market by laying the groundwork for EFTS."

Because granting all financial institutions direct access on equal terms to automated clearinghouses (ACH) would be the first step toward granting all financial institutions the power to offer checking accounts and because thrifts have given no indication of any willingness to relinquish any of their special privileges in the areas of deposit interest rates and reserves, "banks must oppose thrift institution efforts to win direct equal access to clearinghouses," the ABA president concluded. The automated tellers and currency dispensers shown in Figures 8.4 and 8.5 suggest that the savings and loan associations, savings banks, and other thrift institutions are well ahead of regular banks in using "striped" identification and "money cards." And legislation is in process, and some savings banks are already providing "automated" *interest-bearing* checking accounts on trial bases.

Many bankers now speak openly of the cashless, checkless society.

FIGURE 8.4. With the NCR 279 universal financial terminal, a teller can process account inquiries, checking transactions, savings transactions, loan payments, and utility bills without leaving the window. *Courtesy: NCR Corporation*

They also recognize that some form of cash and paper transfers will always be with us. However, some now use the more modest phase "the less check society." But all are convinced that they are crossing the threshold of one of the most exciting and far-ranging revolutions in the industry's history. The transfer of financial information will soon very certainly be accomplished very largely by electronic means. In Canada the revolution is already far ahead of the United States. The federal government's computer/communications task force estimated that banks are spending $75 million a year on their computer operations—that they employ about 1,000 systems analysts and another 5,000 supporting staff. They aim to have 70 percent of all branches tied in to an on-line system by 1977. "Banknet," a communications system developed by eight Trans Canada Telephone System companies, is expected to start operating in 1976. The system, which complements the Trans Canada Dataroute satellite system for computer data transmission, will permit instant transactions at any branch in the country as well as instant interbank transactions.

Besides the drive by the thrift institutions to initiate interest-bearing checking accounts (calculated instantly by computers), the vast credit union industry seeks even more "banking authority." The credit unions have outgrown nickel and dime operations. A curious phenomenon on the financial scene today is that the fastest-growing institute is not in banking, savings and loan associations, or similar houses; it is the credit union. Those "little co-ops" have had a meteoric growth rate of roughly 20 percent annually over the past decade. With mushrooming membership and swelling assets, they want to expand to include services to members that the big banks provide now almost exclusively. Many CUs want to pay higher dividends on members' shares (savings); make larger loans for longer periods at low interest; offer checking accounts (a real thorn of contention to bankers); have trust fund administration; group life, auto, and health insurance; tax-sheltered annuities; and participation in mutual funds. They also want to merge their resources into a central bank, at both state and national levels—and automated "instant" and remote transaction capabilities will certainly facilitate their drives.

New automated bank teller systems were specifically designed to simplify customer operations and increase public use of 24-hour unattended

FIGURE 8.5. The NCR 770 self-service banking terminal is activated by an embossed plastic card with magnetic-stripe encoding. *Courtesy: NCR Corporation*

teller equipment. The new systems have several operationally oriented features, including character displays that lead the customers through each step of a transaction. The displays work hand-in-hand with illuminated function keys.

When the system calls for specific customer action on the graphic display, the appropriate function and alphanumeric keys light up. As a customer waits for the transaction to be processed, the display allows the institution to show advertising/sales promotion messages on financial services not currently being used by that particular customer. A single drawer is provided for dispensing cash, receiving deposits, distributing checks or money orders, receipts, and so on, instead of multiple slots—again making it easier for the customer. The systems can handle up to 20 or more transactions with a single card insertion. This shortens the transaction times for individuals desiring more than one transaction and simplifies usage. The systems dispense bills in variable denominations with no prepackaging required, eliminating what traditionally has been a high operational cost. The secure cash cartridges can each hold up to 2,000 bills of any several denomination. There are also drive-up models and models that will offer the capability to open new accounts and make applications for credit cards and other services in a remote environment. The systems are also compatible with all financial industry magnetic stripe plastic card standards. One company had captured approximately 20 percent of the on-line teller terminal systems market in thrift institutions—savings and loans and mutual savings banks—in 1974 with over 1,000 terminals installed.

When the systems ask customers to select the type of transaction via the graphic display, the only function keys illuminated are those directly related to services available to that customer, such as *credit card, Christmas Club,* and *savings account.* This individual customer data is derived from the service restrictions magnetically encoded on the plastic card or from the central computer. Other messages on the display range from "Do you desire more time on this transaction?" to error notices that inform the customer of the problem and the appropriate action to take. This is opposed to simply timing out and starting the entire transaction over again.[4]

Perhaps the Bank of America is trying to tell all of its competitors something. A May 1974 announcement was:

> *Bank of America Plans to Build a $100 Million Computer Center.* Construction began in early 1975 on the facility, which will serve as a data bank for 500 of the bank's branches in northern California. B of A officials said that the complex would be the world's sixth-largest office building and would cover a full block on San Francisco's Market Street. About 8,000 persons will be employed at the new facility.

[4] Financial Data Sciences Inc. See *Communication News,* June 1974, p. 22.

REMOTE COMPUTING: MICROPROCESSORS AND NETWORKS

Predictions from most of the top professional research firms began in 1971 to predict that data communications markets would grow in revenue produced, customers served, and services offered "ten times" during the current decade. These predictions concerned equipment such as communications terminals, modems, multiplexers, processors, and so on, and they also related to satellite and "packet" switching (small user) capabilities. Huge numbers relating this progress read like some of the European and Latin American country national budgets—American Satellite Business to reach near $2 billion; data communications *services* to grow from $600 million in 1972 to $3 billion in ten years; data base services alone to reach $1.1 billion in 1978 and $1.7 billion before 1983; point of sale devices to grow from near zero in 1972 to the gigantic figure of $10 billion by 1983 (to $3 billion in Europe).[5] And the numbers like these go on and on. Some experts further predict that the computer industry and communications industry will, in effect, merge into one superindustry or that computers will become only a "subsystem" of massive communications "wheels of distributed intelligence" around the globe.

To consumers and small businessmen, the most visual applications will be from the time-sharing companies and information utilities. These entrepreneurs feel they are about to hit a gold mine of new business and opportunities. The huge multinational computer service networks, although initially competing among business, industrial, and specialized professional customers (banks, hospitals, colleges, and so on), are now strongly focused also to provide useful and convenient facilities directly to the small enterprise end-user. Customers are individual accountants, doctors, lawyers, engineers, factories, and people who are not program-oriented, computer-experienced, or even management types. Formerly, nontypical, but now big, applications areas are small libraries, TV and movie studios, museums, churches, and so on. And the now rapid progress of value added networks (VANs) has reached also into the vast personalized terminals in homes and into new neighborhood computer utility centers.

Microprocessors for communications

In several sections of this text, considerable emphasis is placed on the almost central part microprocessors are playing in a very sudden and massive communications revolution. Most of these sections relate to many specific applications as well as to hundreds of devices that contain the micros for control, sensing, measuring, directing, and so on. In this section we will

[5] Frost and Sullivan Inc., New York, N.Y.

very briefly analyze the micro itself in its specific design for access to any communications modem. Although few packages are required, the flexibility, versatility, and, above all, programmability of the micro is of great significance to the total communications industry and to the computer industry as well. The micro substitutes for a great deal of very expensive, complex, and difficult-to-design and manufacture hard-wired devices. The diagram in Figure 8.6 illustrates a typical communications system with an asynchronous communication interface adapter performing the basic serializing-deserializing function required for modem interfacing with CPUs. And, it also provides additional logic capability, such as start, stop, parity, compensation, and so on, as being used for line driver/receivers. Costs are reduced by two-thirds, and 116 former TTL and modem packages are reduced to only seven, but with format versatility.

Data communications, which now also include voice communications and new "packet" systems, as noted—each message unit contains its own address and can be routed, using the most economical or specific priority path—have made giant strides with satellites, microwaves, and soon lasers to reduce costs well below the conventional ranges. In most cases, these reductions have been more than 50 percent and even up to 90 percent, as in the case of the Canadian Anik satellite system. Two-way visual communications experiments and developments in the United States, England, and France have proved economically feasible, and significant progress continues. The use of microprocessors to substitute for formerly very complex and expensive switching, converting, multiplexing, and otherwise controlling, when combined with the new low-cost media used, has also had important impact on the costs and efficiency of time-shared computing both within various enterprises and on worldwide networks. Microprocessors have also provided the very vital cost-effectiveness for the many remote data banks now being established on a "crash" basis.

Time sharing is the simultaneous access to, and shared use, of single computers by many remote users and is a major factor in centralizing many processing systems and efficiently decentralizing others to reduce operating complexities and expenses. Primarily, various enterprises, educational institutions, and professional entities can "farm out" many capabilities they need or desire instead of purchasing or leasing the equipment and software necessary to complete exceptional, overload, or specialized computing functions. Powerful, heavily competing computer service networks act as software distribution sales, lease, and trade facilities. They also permit microcomputer people to program ROMs, RAMs, and so on remotely. For many companies and institutions they provide all the communications facilities needed by tying in branch offices, customers, suppliers, and into their own computers. Moreover, for the occasional computer user, they provide the facilities of large, very sophisticated computers at very low user costs, allowing the user his or her choice of languages, terminals, data bank facili-

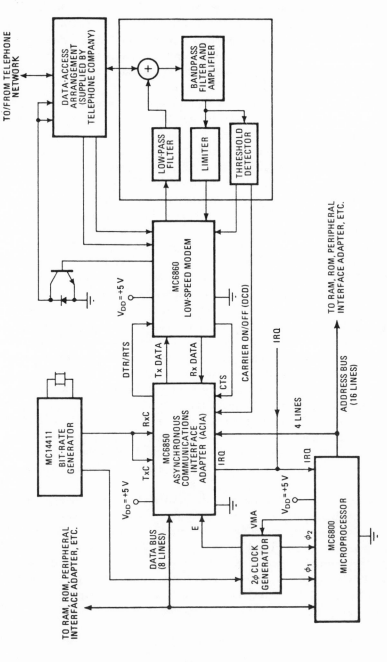

FIGURE 8.6. *Communicating.* A boon for communications systems, this microprocessor setup can be implemented using standard communication interface adapters (CIAs). These adapters' function is to give the CPU system access to any standard modem. *Reprinted with permission from* Electronics, *April 18, 1974, copyright McGraw-Hill Book Co., all rights reserved.*

ties, error-proof software, and so on. Also, giant "information utilities" service any individual doctor, scientist, hobbyist, businessman, and so on as these become accustomed to computer utilization and capabilities. Typical applications areas include on-line research in advertising, engineering, science, and so on and complete computer operations of facilities (your own company's) management (FM).

The hurdles of microprocessor communications have been cleared recently. Successful microprocessors have ROMs, RAMs, input/output ports, and the right interface plus effective hardware. As with any computing/communicating system, the peripheral devices for use with microcomputers must meet system requirements. They require an interface to the microprocessor. The right choice ensures that the advantage of minimal hardware—gained by the use of microprocessors—will not be lost because of an overdesign of the interface. The largest single cost of almost any computer system is still software. With low-cost microprocessors, the ratio of software-to-hardware costs can easily exceed that of conventional computers. Hence there is need for an efficient procedure to develop low-cost software. Emulation (discussed previously and further on) is one answer.

Microprocessors can operate with data links that are either direct or telecommunication types. Either type permits data to be transmitted serially or in parallel on a bus. Telecommunication links are not like direct links. They require modulator-demodulators, or modems, to interface the system to the links.[6] Basically, modems supply the carrier frequency and decode transmitted information. Modem designs can be simplified by the use of universal asynchronous receivers and transmitters, or UARTs. These are now available using MOS. For serial transmission, baud rates can range from D.C. up to 40 kHz. Baud rates [7] on the input channels also affect both the design of the interface and the handling of channels. A telecommunication channel can operate with baud rates up to 2,400 without conditioned telephone lines. But higher rates of 4,800 and 9,600 baud need conditioned lines.

A single microprocessor can handle several channels, each operating at a different baud rate. For example, systems can be built with telecommunication channels operating at 300 and 600 baud rates and with data links handling 10,000 baud. And the microprocessor provides simultaneous, asynchronous control. Keyboard inputs, both numeric and alphanumeric types, can also be used with microprocessors. Standard codes, such as ASCII, EBDIC and BAUDOT, as well as special codes may be employed, depending on system requirements.

[6] Unless the service is DDS (direct digital service) or all digital, which has just recently been introduced in some areas.

[7] A baud is a unit of signaling speed equal to the number of code elements per second. For practical purposes it is used interchangeably with "bits per second"; that is, a baud is equal to one signal element per second.

When the microprocessor is interfaced with a keyboard, the code can be written in the instruction format. For example, all 48 instructions of an 8-bit parallel microprocessor can be derived from a single keyboard. Microprocessors permit direct operation from teletypewriters. The prime consideration is one of level shifting to obtain teletypewriter-compatible input. The program of the microprocessor must be written to accept teletypewriter codes. Generally, any input device that can interface with a minicomputer can also interface with a microprocessor. The possible inputs include light pens—if a CRT is used—optical readers, sensors, and card readers. In addition, storage inputs, such as tape or disk, can be readily handled.

In the design of the interface, format compatibility is important. This includes both word length and field arrangement. The word length affects the amount of hardware required at the interface. A fixed word length can be standardized for a number of I/O devices. It is much easier to implement and control than a variable word length, which differs for each device. Channel priorities depend on the data and traffic rates. Many channels have varying levels of importance to the system. Some channels may have to be processed faster or more often than others. This would call for higher data rates.

Where many inputs and outputs are serviced, varying data rates are obviously preferable to a processor overload. However, this approach reduces the data that can enter the system at any one time, as well as the time for processing of the data. For example, an 8-bit serial data word with a start bit, a stop bit, and a parity bit—a total of 11 bits—operating at a 300-baud rate, requires 36.6 ms to transmit one word. A channel with the same data at 600 baud requires only 18.3 ms. Hence twice as many data can be transmitted in the same time frame in the second case. However, both conditions require a long time between words for processing. A channel with considerable traffic often requires more frequent processing than a low-volume data channel. The more frequent processing implies less backup of data at the output and less storage at the input prior to processing.[8]

Production and process control using microcomputers

Alert manufacturers were already spreading the word in 1973. Microcomputers are going to turn the industrial-equipment marketplace into shambles. The old technology is gone forever. Product planners at semiconductor houses are developing microprocessor-chip sets for the manufacturers of process-control instrumentation in crash programs. Early predictions are borne out by clear-cut developments in the industrial marketplace. Prospects for even further dramatic improvements are so

[8] *Electronic Design*, September 27, 1973, pp. 76–78.

bright that custom piece-parts manufacturing under varying microcomputer-programmable process control will also be commonplace, fast, and cheap. Model or design changes or slight alterations of sizes, shapes, and colors are all easy, very precise, and low in cost with microprocessor-controlled machinery. Microprocessors are the "brains" of many types of new industrial equipment—factory automation systems, machine-tool control, data-acquisition systems, monitors for processing food products, electronic tests, control of conveyor lines, machine control, robot manipulations in warehouses, data sensing, and component-insertion or environmental monitoring, phototypesetting, and so on.

Microprocessor-based systems are very flexible. They adapt manufacturing systems to changing demands and upgrade machines as production requires. All chips containing new instructions need only be inserted when designs are changed, equipment is added, or the system itself is modified. Changes and modifications were formerly very difficult, expensive, and time-consuming when conventional hard-wired circuitry needed to be replaced. Decreases in manufacturing costs result when a relatively few microprocessor chips replace expensive older computer control. Not only are fewer components required, but the microprocessors obviate the necessity to buy new equipment in most cases. They are installed within manufacturing or processing units or attached to them.

A sudden surprise is that the microprocessor is making it possible for manufacturers of process-control equipment and systems literally to go into computer manufacturing. Sharp designers and programmers point out that microprocessors seriously influence the make-or-buy decision. Many companies can buy micro chips, fashion them on boards, and are suddenly in the computer-manufacturing business without the expense of getting deeply involved in the technology. They make their own computers from "kits." Many systems-design firms offer expanding lines of microprocessor modules. Within a year or two, product designers who previously had not considered microprocessors in their systems will either be performing many very special applications or they are going to be very uncompetitive in hardware, productivity, and price. This is an explosive situation. Controllers that are cheap and reasonably powerful change things quickly. Most hard-wired electronic machines are out. All must consider microprocessors, or they may make big mistakes.

Some firms got a very early start. It has been reported, for example, that Comstar Corp., Minneapolis, first started using microprocessors in 1972 and in mid-1974 had more than 700 microcomputers installed. Applications included assembly-machine control, automatic weighing and batching systems, materials-handling systems, remote monitoring and control, data entry, and automobile-traffic control. Another example, this time in materials-handling, is Beatrice Foods' frozen-food warehouse in Chicago, which had Comstar install six microprocessor systems. Each controls 50 motors in a network of more than 300 conveyors that transport boxes from the freezer to trucks. On the way, they go through sorters, convergers, divergers, and conveyor-belt changes; but the controller keeps track of every box for its entire trip.

Major production automated equipment suppliers like Allen-Bradley Co., Bendix Corp., and Cincinnati Milacron Co. are heavily involved in microprocessors, and indeed there are very many smaller companies and even total newcomers to the "microprocessor control" field, with little or no obsolete product base and inventory to worry about, now jumping in. General Electric Co., the largest computer numerical control (CNC) supplier, in early 1974 announced that it had begun using microprocessors in its numerical controllers for various types of machines. Obviously, the biggest markets are the computer numerical control units aimed at applications that have been too expensive for N/C until now. Many new units operate point to point rather than on a continuous path and are aimed at simple positioning for such applications as insertion, wire wrapping, and machines for drilling. Low-cost controllers can position a tool to within .001 inch. Prices for such units are less than $4,000, including the controller. Many are built around the Intel 4-bit MCS-4 microprocessor set. The control and arithmetic units in the Intel 4004 chip allow the processor to acquire and manipulate control logic and data from the memory sections of the microcomputer and generate the outputs called for in the parts-making program. All active components in the control section are contained on a single plug-in printed-circuit board—a decided advantage for maintenance and troubleshooting. Moreover, because the control has fewer parts, supplier companies can deliver units in one month or even two weeks, as opposed to the three to six months it formerly required to put a hard-wired control together—and at about one-half the price or less.

Traffic controllers will use many microprocessors in networks to regulate streams of cars. And one firm predicts that intersection-control systems constitute the wave of the future for microprocessors. Controllers can be designed cheaply for each intersection's needs. In replacing the hard-wired controllers early in the game, the number of ICs (integrated circuits) had been reduced from between 500 and 600 to about 100. One company's controller used only 50 watts of input power, weighed only 41 pounds, and measured only 17 inches by 17 inches by 9 inches. The standard hard-wired models used about 200 watts, weighed about 80 pounds, and were twice as big. They are even smaller now. Many use the Intel 8008 microprocessor as a CPU. Comstar teamed with TRW Systems, Houston, on a single contract for 1,000 microcomputers for the city of Baltimore. This market is huge.

Microprocessors are naturals for providing information to improve the quality of the earth's environment. In many applications, microprocessors are being installed in remote data-gathering stations that are keeping tabs on such conditions as water and air quality, noise, and oil pollution at thousands of sites, preprocessing data and determining right at the remote site whether or not it falls within certain preset limits. There is consistent economy because data transmission is cut by sending back only important data. In addition to screening out unnecessary and redundant data, the microprocessor-based systems also run calibration and diagnostic tests of the remote instrumentation to determine whether or not it is functioning properly. This provides greater reliability than handling from a central site. The new systems also cost less. But even more important is the capability of programming the microprocessor to tailor the operation of each remote station to specific requirements. Changing the programmable read-only memory (ROM) in the field with a new program or using a read/write memory in the same basic physical hardware is cheap, simple, and fast.

Most types of data-acquisition systems are also feeling the effect of microprocessors. They expand the capabilities of systems for monitoring the operation of utilities. They partially process data and send necessary information to central computers. Many computers are designed in systems that monitor torque applied to fasteners on auto assembly lines. For example, micros also sharply expand the number of monitored points—as from 100 to 1,000, an order of magnitude increase over the capacity of many earlier hard-wired units. They also increase the kinds of parameters that can be monitored. New microprocessor-based monitors record D.C. voltages and currents, as well as thermocouple outputs, in such diverse areas as the textile, petrochemical, and pulp and paper industries. One company stated the microcomputer system handles as many as six different types of functional ranges at a time—double the capacity of older hard-wired systems. Moreover, it can send data out to many separate peripheral recording or transmission devices, such as magnetic-tape recorders or teletypewriters. In contrast, the older system handled only a single peripheral reporting device. This controller relies on an Intel 8008, with as many as three low-cost PROMs, four ROMs, and two RAMs in a simple bus-organized structure. The memories contain input instructions for handling data; for scaling; for reading out measurements directly in several scales; for activating limiting alarms; and, with use of scratch pad memory, for aiding in formating and reporting.

The microprocessor approach was quite a bit cheaper. With the microprocessor, changes are made by simply plugging in a new memory rather than substituting a costly hard-wired logic board. New microprocessors further expand the capability of these systems by offering new operations and calculations capabilities.

The reader will recall that a typical microprocessor-based system consists of a module containing all the processing and memory functions. Such early modules contained the Intel 8008 or the National Semiconductor Corp. IMP-16, for example. They, like others, offer large instruction capabilities plus the required programmable ROM, control ROM, and RAM, an input bus, and often printers and teletypewriter interfaces. The suppliers are able to add processing capabilities to their top-of-the-line products. And because they are cheap, they can be included in lower-end products as well. The results could not make management groups happier. Many engineers have built families of standard plus-in modules that they can just about pull off the shelf and apply to new products as they are needed, and most have decision-making capabilities. This could never have been accomplished at such low prices with the special-purpose minicomputers that many firms had been buying. The old mini was "markedly" more expensive and complex than even the full controllers and the modular families that even enable product designers to tailor the processing power to each application.

Other advantages are numerous. The new processors are far more compact and reliable, and their plug-in designs make it easy to troubleshoot and service in the field. Also customers seem to prefer the microprocessor design to hard-wired logic because it is easier to upgrade systems by adding features through a plug-in ROM. Microprocessors quickly began to have a tremendous impact on many industries that have repetitive processes to be controlled. In the future, their applications are limited only by the imagination of market managers and design engineers. Although cheap now, microprocessors will come down still further in price. Within a few years, an entire microcomputer with plenty of memory could cost less than $100. These prices suggest the devices will develop markets as large as those enjoyed by hand-held calculators—in the millions.

EXAMPLES OF MINI AND MICRO CONTROL APPLICATIONS

Industrial applications

Chemical:

Ammonia and Ethylene Processing. Identifies mechanical problems in large compressors used to manufacture ammonia, ethylene, and so on. Monitors bearing temperatures, operation of clearance pockets, compressor speed, power consumption, vibration, discharge temperatures, pressures, suction flow, and gas compositions.

Plastics. Acquires, processes, and provides stress analysis for a wide range of plastic materials. Calculates the product's strength, records and calculates material properties, and measures and computes elasticity and hardness.

Explosives. Provides data acquisition and analysis of explosive shock waves. Measures and calculates explosive force and duration.

Dyes. Monitors and controls the processing of dyes used in the textile industry. Provides accurate processing of color blending and matching to predetermined values.

Petroleum:

Gas Transmission and Distribution. Monitors and controls pressures and flows of gas transmission and distribution systems. Data are gathered, measured in the field, and transmitted to the system.

Manufacturing:

Production Machines. Controls and monitors automatic and manually operated production machines at a higher sustained efficiency rate. Monitors the actual piece-count production and machine status and signals out-of-limit conditions as they occur. Enables corrective action to be taken immediately.

Package Processing. Controls high-speed packaging equipment and prevents inaccurate operations and breakdowns. Controls the speed of the filling device, the amount of product in the package to be filled, and weighs each package accurately.

Shop Floor Data Control. Provides an economical data collection system for shop floor control validation of shipments, monitoring and testing goods, and the staging of goods for production monitoring; monitoring of plant facilities; monitoring of the attendance, productivity, and the efficiency of production personnel; and dispatching of jobs in a predetermined priority sequence.

Industrial Testing Systems. Monitors and controls complex testing sequences in an industrial testing system. Operations include product identification, selection of test sequence, calibration check of test equipment, automatic handling of units during testing, source collection and analysis of test data, accept/reject determination of testing units, and printout of test results.

Automotive:

Internal Combustion Engines. Acquires data recorded from sensors attached to the internal combustion engine. Measures water temperature, oil temperature, RPM speed, torque, oil pressure, exhaust temperature, manifold pressures, and timing.

Automotive Exhaust Emission. Identifies vehicle for record purposes. Analyzes samples of exhaust gas components during the test cycle. Computes the concentration and/or volume of each monitored gaseous constituent and compiles a test record.

Production Testing. Provides on-line analysis of automotive carburetors in a high-volume production assembly line. Significantly reduces the test time required while providing a greater yield of better quality carburetors.

Automotive Quality Control and Production. Testing systems and assembly line applications such as steady-state emission analysis, vehicle electrical check-out, carburetor testing, piston-to-engine-block size matching, engine performance testing, safety testing, fuel injection research, transmission testing, and production quality control data collection.

Electronics:

Peripheral Test. Computer interfacing and multi-unit control of input/output peripherals for large-scale computer installation. I/O units include a line printer, card reader, card punch, and magnetic tape.

Coil Winding Production. Control of automatic winding machines for the mass production of small coils for magnetic-latching reed switches. Winding patterns are stored in the computer's memory. All of the patterns can be run on up to 16 machines. Coils are wound on plastic inserts in a steel plate on an 8″ by 8″ matrix. Inserts extend from both plate surfaces and provide 64 winding cores on each side.

PC Board Production. Used for the automatic development, formating, and conversion of instruction programs for numerically controlled printed circuit board drilling machines. Complete patterns are stored in the computer memory to perform step-and-repeat operations accurately. Frequently repeated patterns for standard devices are entered into memory that will completely define all points in the pattern after only two points have been located by the operator.

Electronic Testing. Tests each of electric/electronic components in a high-volume production line. Executes tests at a predetermined maximum rate; variations in manual operator rates are eliminated.

Testing and Analysis of Circuits. Controls circuit testing and analysis systems. Coordinates the testing operations, specification, signals, and the test sequence of electronic speeds, including continuity, impedance, test stimuli, and measurement of the circuit output.

Aerospace:

Aircraft Wing Production. Controls and monitors riveting machines for manufacturing aircraft wings. Riveting patterns are stored in the computer's memory to perform step-and-repeat operations accurately and quickly.

Fatigue Testing. Acquires, processes, and analyzes fatigue stress data for a variety of metals as well as bonded joined materials. Prints out data for corrective action, thereby preventing potential accidents and malfunction due to fatigue stress.

Metals and Woodworking

Steelmaking. Controls and operates steel furnaces and produces the metal in exact accordance with present specifications. Calculates oxygen requirements, alloy additions, and power requirements.

Metal Analysis. Monitors and controls optical emission and X-ray spectrometers widely used in the metals industry for high-speed determination of the chemical composition of metal.

Tensile Testing. Provides quality control, production techniques evaluation, product classification, and customer certification. Calculates the product's strength and other characteristics, records and calculates vital material properties, measures and computes tensile strength.

Transfer Line. Monitors and controls transfer lines producing high production parts and consisting of many machining stations mechanically connected by work piece transfer mechanisms and closely interlocked with electric controls. Receives input from operator or sensors and then concurrently checks the operating conditions of line-mounted controls, takes protective action when required, prints out a report of the malfunction, and generates production reports.

Materials Handling:

Automated Warehousing. Provides optimum space utilization, significant manpower savings, and high turnaround for material requests in an automated "high cube" vertical storage warehouse. Keeps track of numerous units of merchandise and optimizes the movement of stacker cranes. Provides real-time inventory control and warehousing applications to be integrated into a plantwide information system.

Material Handling System. Controls complex material-handling systems including storage and retrieval equipment. Processes orders, prepares shipping documents and invoices, provides operator guidance, maintains accurate inventories, and provides direct control of transport facilities and stacker units.

Paper and Rubber:

Paper Mill Production. Regulates the average basic weight and moisture variables in each paper grade. Manipulates the steam flow valve, adjusts the stock valve to the regulated basis weight, and monitors and/or controls total flow and digital filtering of instruments signals.

Rubber. Controls in-process inventories and maximizes utilization of machine tools in the production of rubber products. Substantially reduces the time and personnel required to summarize and review the stripcharts of production activity and the manually produced shift-end reports.

Business and communications applications

Management

Financial and administrative. Financial reporting and analysis, accounting, payroll, and invoicing and billing.

Management planning and control. Capital investment analysis and resource allocation and mathematical model simulation.

Marketing operation. Sales forecasting, sales analysis and control, market research, and sales order processing.

Distribution operations. Warehouse operations, shipment order processing, traffic, and in-the-field inventory control.

Factory operations. Materials control, production scheduling, quality control, and in-plant inventory control.

Research, development and engineering. Product testing and product design and evaluation.

Continuous-process industrial product. Assembly operations, automatic processing or fabrication, testing, pollution control—reports and analyses.

Banking. Reads, analyzes, and tabulates check data for monetary transactions in real-time applications at branch offices. Central computer at the main bank processing center provides fast analyses and totals for management control.

Accounting. Acquires, processes, and prints out man-hours on-the-job for job/function/time evaluation.

Environmental control. Controls and monitors environmental conditions throughout a large office building. Evaluates and monitors temperature, humidity, pollen, airborne direct, and irritants and so on within the controlled environment.

Merchandise. Automates checkstand operations in large retail stores. Computes transactions for management accounting and inventory control.

Food. Computes transactions quickly and accurately in a fast-food service. Maintains "instant" inventory and management control throughout the food chain's operation.

Business communications

Synchronous data exchange. Remote minicomputers perform synchronous exchange of information on medium to high-speed data lines involving multiprocessor and multidevice complexes, process control of data gathering distribution task and provide the main or system computer with information and data for process and/or management decisions and commands.

Telemetry data acquisition. Monitors remotely the physical status of objects, animals, people, or the environment in space flights. Evaluates incoming data for relative importance and validity. Isolates useful data from "noise" and other spurious signals.

Broadcasting. Provides automatic timing-control of audio/visual processes for radio and television station-break advertising. Maintains time-of-day synchronization with the national networks.

Education. Provides audio/visual control of the instruction leader presentation and real-time data acquisition. Processes and tabulates student responses.

Television. Provides real-time data acquisition and processing of audience-viewer responses in audience participation shows. Tabulates and prints out responses for "instant" results while still on the air.

Printing presses. Monitors and controls the operation of large multicolor printing presses. Preset ink fountain and compensator positions are maintained during running, taking into consideration temperature, humidity, ink absorption, and so on.

Typesetting. Automates formats of typesetting in a high-volume newspaper operation.

Production. Minicomputers are part of custom and standard systems for such work as message switching, source data entry, order entry, data collection, cable TV control and monitor systems, and general telecommunications.

Petroleum/pipeline. The majority of these application areas concern proved approaches for controlling dedicated data acquisition devices for oil refineries; supervising reports for on-line engineering modifications; providing data flows for batch petrochemical cracking processes; supervising on-line, real-time control reporting of remote substation activities; developing hydraulic network analysis; and developing visual problem-solving solutions. Remote batch "intelligent" terminals provide decentralized control of remote substation and time sharing for on-line simulation; assist in providing flow distribution data analyses; and provide graphs, charts, and projections of current and future operations.

Display systems

External. Monitors and controls scoreboard displays located in sports stadiums, providing score information, animation displays, and audience messages. Stores repetitive messages and animation programs of all types.

Internal. Provides generation and control of architectural display, light, sound, and temperature effects of remote-site data from microphones and CCTV sets.

Automated processing quality control

Quality control systems have been developed for use in steam generating plant monitoring and control, wind tunnel data acquisition and control, environmental monitoring, heating and air conditioning monitoring and control, high-speed textile loom control, and chemical and physical analytical instrumentation monitoring and control.

Power and fuels

Substation monitoring and control. Monitors and controls high voltage and extra high voltage substations from centralized dispatching offices.

Plant power system. Assures proper distribution of available electricity, gas, or steam in utility systems. Monitors powerhouse facilities, schedules distribution of energy, and produces operating distribution logs.

COMPUTERS IN MACHINE TOOLS

Computer numerical control (CNC) provides an excellent example of the application of minicomputers into a manufacturing system at the point of control—the machine tool. This type of system, referred to as "soft-wired

340

control," has a distinct advantage over its hard-wired version because it permits lower costs and great flexibility to the machine tool builder as well as the user. With CNC, the users, such as foremen, section leaders, or workers, can now program the machine tools with less labor and at the same time introduce new efficiencies into their shop operation by using computing intelligence at the point of control. A microcomputer or mini-computer, employed in the electronics at the point of control, provides management with a link to metal cutting or other processes. It gives the manufacturer versatility and flexibility of features at a basic level. Benefits are reduction of off-line preparatory activities and increased machine "use time" through expanded troubleshooting capability. The more control features required, the easier it is to justify CNC. Moreover, the open-ended nature of computer NC allows system functions to be added modularly— even in the field—as machining requirements increase the need for more sophisticated control. Well-engineered CNC will also have the capability of fitting into a larger system of multimachine control directed by a large computer and, eventually, into an automatic factory plan.

Economic justification factors are reduced labor; fast amortization; tiny space requirements; easy, low-cost maintenance; great savings over wasteful, old, or other error-prone methods. Increased productivity and increased return on investment are assured. Taking these factors into consideration, users can quickly determine the economic impact, especially that the slashed net cash operating costs revenues permit a computer to then pay for itself in months, not years. Almost any cost comparison alone points to computerization. Better performance or how fast and how well the job is done are the other considerations.

WHAT MICROCOMPUTER AND MINI-COMPUTER PRODUCTION SYSTEMS DO

Computing systems easily and quickly solve many problems. Complex problems are increasing for business, manufacturing, professionals, government, and so on. Users recognize the problems, analyze them, and then set up requirements for a computing system to solve them. But many mini-computer and microcomputer suppliers eagerly offer the equipment, the people, and the expertise to show users how to implement the solutions. All computing systems also create some problems. Job skills change, reorganization may be necessary, or shifts in traditional departmental authority and responsibility may occur. Too many users try to plan their systems without considering what problems will be created. Both social and technical problems always arise owing to the particular way companies operate. Micro and mini systems for personnel organizational planning are important. Who in management will be in charge should be clearly displayed on a meaningful organization chart. Most firms have to train new operators. Others will train existing people. Many computer users look to the equipment company to assist or to provide all the training required. Space requirements will need to be figured well in advance of actual equipment installation. Easy access to the back of the equipment when installed in place allows for fast, uninterrupted maintenance if and when an emergency should arrive.

When one is planning a computer system, it is necessary to have a basic understanding of hardware capabilities. Several different hardware systems should be reviewed to acquire a general understanding of the cost versus capability gained by the various options available. For example, in the two megabyte range of disk storage, data stored on disk costs twice as much as the same data stored on magnetic tape because of the hardware cost. But the disk access time is ten times faster than on magnetic tape. A high-speed printer can cost two to three times the price of a low-speed printer. It is important to know what time constraints are present when selecting hardware. The ability to accommodate growth in volume and in new applications in the future is also a prerequisite in selecting hardware. For example, one manufacturer of electronic control systems was required to keep track of 10,000 printed circuit boards per month consisting of several hundred varieties. The boards were manufactured in-house and were assembled into finished control systems. In addition, this manufacturer also had to generate a list of "missing components" that were holding up production and had to keep management informed as to the status of production. The supervisor of testing realized that far-reaching benefits could be achieved by the use of a computer system, but the only way conclusive evidence could be provided was to put a system into use. The system consisted of a central processor unit and teletype and a CRT. I/O devices could display or input the same information: part number, shop order number, lot amount, amount received into the department, amount sent out of the department, and amount remaining in inventory. The CRT is a fast means of obtaining any of the processed data immediately, whereas the Teletype was used for a hard copy. As knowledge of the system grew, so did the use of the system by the other departments in the shop. Production and accounting control, for example, found the computer printouts from the test department useful in expediting printed circuit boards plus budgeting, accounting, automatic billing, purchasing, and so on.

Because of this increased interest and increased use of the computer system by other departments, the system was expanded into a full *shop management information system* over the next three years to include sixteen terminals throughout the plant providing such data as

Order status

Parts layup status

Receiving

Unit assembly and test

Printed circuit board assembly and test

Engineering revisions

Incoming inspection results

Quality control reliability figures

Maintenance

Scheduling.

Each of the sixteen terminal locations included either a teletype, line printer, or a CRT. Because much of the data was of a classified nature, such as pricing, a security system was also implemented to permit access of data on a "need to know" basis. The manufacturing manager's terminal is the only one permitted access to all data. The basic question, "Can I justify a computer system?" was quickly answered by this user through actual use of the system.

SOFTWARE SUPPORTS THE SYSTEMS

Software is generally the intelligence to operate the computer in the form of application programs and those specific programs that command and instruct full computer systems. It manages the computer's resources so that it can work efficiently. Systems that allow users to communicate with the computer, therefore, are of primary importance in planning. Some companies will provide a programmer so that they can create and maintain application software "in-house." Others decide to subcontract to a "software house" the job of creating programs. Still others decide to have their system manufacturer supply them with a "turnkey" operation or provide some parts of the software. A combination of the above mentioned approaches could be the cost-reasonable solution.

Operating system software is typically provided by the manufacturer. If users contract to have the application software prepared outside their organizations, it is extremely important to have, in writing, detail specifications that are understood and agreed to by the contract programmers and the company. These specifications should include a comprehensive testing procedure, perhaps even a parallel operation for a period of time, to ensure that the application programs perform as required. Plans for software maintenance are also necessary. Manufacturers should provide maintenance on the system software they provide. Software maintenance includes not only correcting a problem, but also changing and/or adding a function. Today in manufacturing and business there is a great tendency to put as much intelligence as possible in the hardware device. This approach requires special but low-cost microcomputer hardware design to connect computers to the other devices. When functional changes are needed, new low-cost design boards are plugged in, and the new design electronics are fast and cheap. A sound mini- or microcomputer system concept to remember is to have practical hardware-software trade-off. Users quickly implement in software that intelligence and those decision-making processes that are subject to the highest degree of change. And they implement in hardware that intelligence subject to the least degree of change. The soundest approach is to distribute the intelligence and decision-making process at the lowest level consistent with human control responsibilities, but eliminate as many human functions as possible in all processes and procedures because they are the cause of 95 percent of errors.

COMPUTERIZED CONTROL OF OPERATIONS AT SIX-STAND COLD-STRIP MILL

Automation of Europe's first six-stand cold-strip mill was accomplished with Siemens AC (Germany) controls. The plant, operated by Rasselstein AC in Adernach/Rhine, has a product spectrum from tinplate to car body sheets. Deviations in thickness of the strip entering the mill are reduced in the first two stands with the aid of automatic loops that control the active roll gap. These deviations are compensated also by controlling the strip velocity in accordance with the gauge/velocity relationship. Tensions between the individual stands and coilers are kept constant with the aid of high-precision tension control loops by means of hydraulic screwdown gear with secondary automatic control of the roll-separating force.

A Siemens process computer optimizes mill operation by providing the command variables in their optimum sequence for all the secondary conventional controls. To obtain optimum strip shape, the computer calculates the optimum pass schedule in each particular case from the entry dimensions, the desired final dimensions, and any additional technological conditions, such as electric load distribution and roll-separating forces at the last stands. Mill timing, all movements of the auxiliaries required for the automatic threading in and out of the strip to obtain an optimum coil sequence, is determined by sequence controls. A total of 200 working sequences is needed. Logs printed out by the process computer for each strip make many management controls possible. Sensor-responsive microprocessor-controlled measuring and responding instruments are required in systems such as these. An example follows:

Datalogging system handles 200 sensor outputs

The model 90GP34 Datalogger is a system used for measuring the output of sensors. It employs satellite stations, each capable of handling 200 sensor outputs. A typical 600-sensor system incorporates a central station and two satellites. The central station consists of a digital indicator to provide visual readout of data, a master scanner to sense each data point in sequence, a digital clock and scan interval timer to provide time of day and scan-cycle initiating outputs, six skip-scan modules to permit the selection of desired data points, and a data coupler to provide ASCII code output for connection to a teleprinter.

WORD PROCESSING: A KEY
MARKET FOR MICROPROCESSORS

Approaching word processing successfully consists of knowing the kind of work each company does, knowing who does the work, and then matching the machine to the work. Buyers must thoroughly understand their paperwork problems. Successful solutions for others might well work for them. Separating typing and administrative duties, however, is not enough. The study must go further and record times spent daily on each task. A more complete breakdown includes power typing, revision typing, switch-read typing, statistical typing, document assembly, and administrative duties. A WP system will work only if the firm knows beforehand about its machine needs. Dual tape and card systems can best handle a lot of editing and merging, and power typewriters are better for repetitive tasks.

For example, newly developed products provide increased operational simplicity to make users more productive. Correcting mechanisms on typewriters, improved magnetic card typewriters, and faster copies exemplify these developments. Investigations of the merits of computer-based systems will show that any firm using two or more stand-alone automatic typewriters will likely find shared systems less expensive, more productive, and versatile. Although they appear sophisticated, typists find them easy to learn and use.

Word processing is simple in concept—the use of computerized equipment and systems to facilitate the handling of words and text—but its great economies and efficiencies in practice are drastically shaking several whole industries. The office furniture, office forms and supplies, urban real estate, employment recruiting, and several industries—none of them small or unimportant—are all becoming quite alarmed. The replacement of people and all the "traditional" supplies, space, comforts, and so on, that they use by small "boxes" of microminiaturized electronics equipment really began in earnest in 1972 with an estimated $800 million "new" industry. The estimated growth rate places that industry at well over $2 billion by 1976 and reaching $8 billion by 1980. The primary purpose for the expenditure is to replace people and to decrease the time expended to complete the various editing cycles involved in creating an electronically "store and retrieve" document and in proofreading and transmitting the information recorded on such "documents." By the use of the computer to store words, sentences, paragraphs, formats, and so on, any of these can be called in split seconds. For example, the replacement of one word or phrase with another on a stored "to be reused" document is accomplished in one or two seconds. Automatic headings, footings, page numbering, page reference, paragraph and section numbering—automatic table-of-contents formation, hyphenation, and so on—are just a few of the capabilities of word-processing systems. The high speeds of low-cost printers work hundreds of times faster than the normal typewriter, and they do so while other materials are being entered, edited, retrieved, reformated, addended, and so on. The "orders" to the systems are received and forwarded from remote terminals as simple as the ten-key telephone and are processed by recorder-transcriber units with the completed documents transmitted by long distance facsimile (videofax) or by remote CRT (cathode-ray tube) terminal printouts or by making instant copies of documents appearing on its face—and there are no "waits" despite having the system accessed by scores or hundreds of users apparently simultaneously. (The magic of the microsecond operation speeds of micro and minicomputers!)

Many other nontext editing capabilities are being used in such systems. These include file structuring and analysis, budgets and information list analysis and manipulation, form letter generation, name and address list maintenance, label creation, automatic message forwarding, and so on. The costs and versatility of such systems are also remarkable. The micro- and minicomputers, teletypwriterlike printers, CRT display terminals, tape units are the main components and have all now become very low-cost. Highly competitive purchases are acquired with nominal lease cost arrangements. Such systems can (1) be quickly set up at the user's location; (2) can be the terminal's only system at homes, remote offices, and so on, with time-shared connections to the firm's major or primary computer center; or (3) a time-sharing system provided by an outside service company can be used without owning or leasing any equipment by simply paying the "time used" fees. All this makes it quite easy to agree with the very big numbers used in predictions of the huge equipment business that will be developed to replace office personnel, office space and fixtures, and many "normal" office supplies.

There are, of course, some few people involved in each word-processing operation. A few "automaton"-type low-skilled people, located for convenience of communication costs, are the unseen "parts of the machines" (as they describe themselves) who perform some key parts of the typing and editing process. One executive describes the environment as follows: ". . . peak efficiency is obtained 'in a fishbowl' environment, but away from the other fish—or you don't get your money's worth out of your equipment . . . and let's face it, word processing is a deadly routine." The word-processing typist does not know the users or dictators of documents; the people to whom the documents are addressed mean nothing to her; she has no idea whatever what effect, if any, the documents might have on the recipients; she has to contend with the literary quirks of individuals she will know only by their calling numbers. And because only human beings really ask about the "meaning" of what they do, perhaps these people—who usually can stand to work only on 4-hour shifts—do really become part of the machines. And because automatic equipment must be used efficiently—which means full-time, three-shift operations—the "human" aspects become overly stressful, and the "fifth" hour of a shift becomes inefficient. The jobs are dull, demanding, unrewarding, but there will be thousands of unemployed typists and secretaries eager to accept them to follow their deeply inbred "work ethic"—and, of course, to continue eating.

The reasons for using a computer word-processing system are fairly obvious. It reduces keyboarding and proofreading time in the preparation of large documents, facilitates revision and change, reduces typing inaccuracies, and can help level out the peaks and valleys in an unpredictable work load schedule. The advantages of a computer word-processing system are its fast processing speed, huge storage capacity, and high-speed output combined with the ability to process simultaneously work for users connected by a terminal typewriter located on different floors or even in different buildings or cities.

Today's automatic typing/editing devices can be grouped into five categories, each with distinct characteristics: (1) automatic repetitive typewriters, (2) stand-alone mechanical text-editing devices, (3) stand-alone display-editing devices, (4) shared logic text-editing systems, and (5) very rapidly rising time-shared text-editing services. In the last case, smaller offices use WP without purchasing or even leasing equipment. The WP service company (more than 50 of them even in early 1973) supplies this. It invites the customer to make its tape by phone, using its own data base of words, phrases, forms, and so on, and to expect its correspondence, reports, and so on to be mailed or even delivered the same day.

SUMMARY

In early 1974 the first single-chip, second generation (NMOS), high-performance microprocessors began to appear in commercial markets in large production quantities. This was the needed solid confirmation of acceptance by business, education, industry, and scientific users. These second generation microprocessors with matched or attached memory and customized logic circuits provided product designers with the full power of computer capability at unprecedented low cost. The implications of these

347

cheap "distributable intelligence" units were then only beginning to be understood. Some early applications examples of efficiency are as follows: (1) traffic light controllers were built with 12 microprocessor family packages instead of the former 200 electronic packages at more than four times the cost; (2) simple gas pump meters required only one microprocessor and nine subsidiary chips; (3) electronic scales required only eight relatively simple and low-cost chips, and (4) microprocessor control systems operated in several automobiles, monitoring dozens of parameters with component costs of less than $200. Performances of these and many other devices were never before possible at such practical costs.

Like the hundreds of calculator chips, these and a thousand other devices are no longer "dedicated" to single-purpose application. With microprocessors, they offer many more advantages, as we shall confirm. Especially noteworthy are the tininess and reliability of low-cost LSI circuitry and the welcomed ease of programmability and low power-supply and cooling requirements. The microprocessors replace standard computer hardwired logic and require fewer chips and connections; they simplify system reevaluation, redesign, and testing. Thus engineers are *not* locked into finished product design because of lengthy redesign time and heavy new costs. Reprogramming the micros is simple, cheap, fast, with totally new control capability—and this very drastically cuts the former quite high costs of assembly, inventory, and "mistakes." Is there any wonder engineers and product development people love them? Using software programs to affect the behavior and control factors is better than being forced to design and build hardware and logic interconnections of former fixed design for electronic system .

In computer-controlled production machines or measuring, testing, controlling devices, as noted earlier, simple new programs not only extend flexibility of these devices, but also strongly boost system performance. The new control is a typical software program consisting of a series of orders or commands to the processor stored in a companion read-only memory. Because these ROMs are very easy to program quickly and because programmable ROMs are very easy to reprogram, the micros' behavior can be most conveniently adapted to changed applications. New design can be used along with a different ROM program for each new application. And the microprocessors themselves require only from five to about 50 ICs, including clocks, control logic, memory, and peripheral buffering—with total costs, in quantity, at prices like $20 or $50. As we note in many parts of this text, they control point of sale systems, inventory-control systems, and so on in microcomputers, calculators, intelligent terminals, and so forth. We find them in navigational systems, electronic games, identification and credit card systems—there really is no defined domain for the microprocessor.

FURTHER DEFINING THE WORLD OF MICROCOMPUTERS

Alarm systems, microprocessor. CPUs scan input-output points at preselected intervals. When the A conversion is completed, data are read, processed, and checked against alarm limits. Critical deviations from normal operating conditions are detected and alarms are sent to the control/acknowledgment terminal. The CPU at the terminal formats and routes the alarm data to an operator's display panel. The operator on duty observes the detected alarm and takes the necessary steps to correct the problem.

Alarms corresponding to "crisis" situations can be detected directly by limit switches, circuit-continuity breaks, or by the manual depression of a button. Examples include floods, fire, burglary, or accidents. These conditions require immediate attention and would, therefore, be assigned as priority vector interrupts in the CPU monitor.

Industrial microcomputer. To install industrial microcomputer systems, users often require a full range of memories, interface modules, and peripheral equipment for the application. With this type of equipment, microcomputers can be used in the industrial computer control area, controlling test and assembly machines. They can be used in remote monitoring control for pollution monitoring, public utility control systems, and waste water and monitoring systems. Simple machine tool control systems are now using microprocessors and, as the microcomputer becomes more powerful, probably all machine tool control systems will be microcomputer based. Many industrial data entry systems are based on microcomputers that preprocess the data and forward them to a central computer for sophisticated management information systems.

Industrial microcomputer applications. Microcomputer systems can be used for intersection traffic control, local traffic congestion control, and traffic monitoring.

Modern material handling systems are using distributed microcomputers to control conveyors and packaging and palletizing equipment, as well as stacker cranes. Pallet-moving equipment such as robot cars is used to completely automate product movement in a modern warehouse. Thus the industrial microcomputers will be used for almost every control system where users need flexibility and future interconnect capability to large computer systems. In many cases, microcomputers now can even be cost-effective against standard relay systems.

Industrial microcomputer, peripherals. Peripheral equipment used with industrial microcomputer systems must be rugged, low in cost, and very simple so it can have long-life operation. The simplest types are push-button and L.E.D. indicators. The next level of complexity is keyboards and alphanumeric displays, usually gas plasma. At an additional level of complexity, users may obtain small alphanumeric printers and/or more sophisticated equipment such as floppy disk, magnetic tape cassette, or IBM compatible magnetic tape systems to store information for later data processing. In the next few years there will probably be a whole new array of low-cost peripheral equipment for industrial microcomputer systems because the processing section—CPU and memory—is becoming so cost-effective that the user is being forced to match the performance and cost of the electronics.

Microcomputer word processing. Microcomputer applications include an office equipment application, word processing, that is, controlling one or more typewriters that edit text stored on cassettes for floppy disks. Before the appearance of microcomputers, this application clearly required a minicomputer. To support a small system containing only a few typewriters, the minicomputer was relatively costly; the microcomputer helped bring the cost down to a reasonable level. Needless to say, this application also received a considerable boost from the development of the floppy disk as a relatively inexpensive text storage medium. Microcomputers are also appearing in small business-accounting and recordkeeping systems. A microcomputer can handle these functions in a relatively standardized format if the information traffic is not too heavy.

Microcontrolled modems. Modems can be interfaced using an assembly of characters from the bit stream. This is accomplished by the microcontroller without difficulty. The real key to truly economic solution of the control problem is to make the interfaces to all these devices simple registers. The control for these registers is then centralized in the microcontroller, which time-shares itself between many jobs. One reason for desiring a fast central control is so that it can be effectively time-shared between many registers. Many fairly simple slow jobs can be done by one central control device. This offers the designer a way of achieving a really economical solution to his or her control problem.

Microcontrolled terminals. Microcontrol is suited for use in remote batch terminals. In these applications, devices such as modems, card readers, and printers are frequently found. The control logic for each of these devices can be centralized, and one microcontroller can be shared between the various devices. For example, in the control of a printer, a set of output registers can be used with each bit controlling an individual print hammer. Input on the print wheel position can be fed into an input register and analyzed in the microcontroller, which can output appropriate bits to control print hammers. Similarly, a card reader can be interfaced by feeding data from the card into an output register. The code conversion from Hollerith to ASCII could be accomplished by analyzing input data using

JUMP INDEXED instructions. Control of the card reader can be handled by a register output.

Microcontroller. Another all-purpose word, microcontroller can mean a microprogrammed machine, a microprocessor, or a microcomputer used in a control operation—that is, to direct or make changes in a process or operation. But there is a narrower definition, more in keeping with the prefix, in which *microcontroller* refers to any device or instrument that controls a process with high resolution, usually over a narrow region.

Microcontroller applications. There are generally three classes of control applications: (1) *device control:* a single machine tool or computer peripheral is sequenced through its different operations; (2) *data control:* data from one or more sources must be moved to one or more destinations, or multiple low-speed data paths are concentrated into a higher-speed data path. Examples include multiple channel analog acquisition systems, data communication message switches, or data communication line controllers; (3) *process control:* discrete inputs from measured process variables are used in a closed loop environment. Examples of assembly line control are automobile or appliance manufacture or continuous steel/aluminum smelting operations.

Microcontroller control program. The first major step in the development of a microcontroller-based system is system design. Because the microcontroller is a complete control microcomputer system, users begin by considering the interface to the devices to be controlled. They characterize those device interfaces by the number of command, status, and data lines and then determine if any extra circuit components to the microcontroller are required. A major part of system design is to develop the control program. Because of the high performance available and the control architecture of the microcontroller, the amount of interface logic to devices is radically reduced—the control program replaces much of the hardware. Control program development begins by flowcharting the control tasks and their sequence and defining specific control functions and decision points in the sequence. The program is written in a compiler language to develop a symbolic representation of the control sequence. Once the program is written on paper in an easily understood symbology, the program is prepared for use in prototype development. The program is prepared by translating the symbology into binary patterns required for input to the microcontroller simulator by the use of the language compiler available on a nationwide time-sharing service. The program translation provides program documentation and a paper tape of the binary for direct input to the simulator.

Microcontroller design system. A microcontroller design system provides resources to aid in design implementation. Emphasis is placed on the designer's application knowledge rather than on his or her knowledge of component design. Software support is usually provided to facilitate programming and minimize errors during the design. In addition, resources are available to the designer to operate and diagnose a system in real-time at the hardware level.

RAM alarm functions and options. Diverse alarm functions are offered, by various systems, with everything from a simple alarm indication in red on the printout to a separate alarm relay on each channel and functions in between these possibilities. Alarms operate on a digital comparison basis. Digitized input data for a given channel are compared with digitized alarm set point values. Logic operates when limits are exceeded, placing that channel in alarm. A "print on alarm" feature adds to flexibility. The data system can be set to scan at its maximum rate over and over again without data output until a channel is detected in alarm. The microprocessor then prints out a complete data scan from memory, regardless of which channel is in alarm. A second mode is to set the system to scan (and print-on-alarm) all channels at the maximum rate and automatically print out all channels at a desired interval even if there is no alarm. An alarm condition triggers a priority printout immediately, giving the system an effective alarm scan at one rate, printout at another. In some systems, an alarm condition initiates a printout, with the alarm channels indicated in the record. The onboard printer prints the entire alarm line in red, inserting a period in front of the data to signal a low alarm or a colon in front of the data to signal a high alarm. The same data can be sent to any peripheral device with appropriate punctuation to indicate alarm data values. Each alarm scan initiates its own data printout independently; if an alarm is encountered in one scan and displayed on the printout, the next scan will not be printed unless an alarm condition is again encountered.

Servomechanism. 1. Closed-cycle system in which a small input power controls a much larger output power in a strictly proportionate manner; for example, movement of a gun turret may be accurately controlled by movement of a small knob or wheel. 2. Any closed-loop, feedback type of control system. A servomechanism consists of the following elements (which may be distinct or combined-function elements of hardware). 3. An input signal or command line, to indicate the desired state. 4. An output sensor, capable of monitoring the actual output state. 5. A comparator, which determines the deviation from the desired state, based on the above two signals. 6. An effector, which has the power to modify the output state or condition. It is not necessary for an explicit input signal to be provided, but an implicit signal must exist in those cases where an explicit signal is missing (for instance, as in the fixed-setting thermostats or automatic level-seeking devices). The important feature of a servomechanism is its four-part closed-loop organization as outlined previously. Its actual physical implementation or field of application is immaterial.

Servo valve control, hydraulic. A typical application of a hydraulic servo valve controlled machine using a microcomputer system is a multiaxis robot. The features necessary to control a robot are (1) *capacity:* The controller must control up to seven axes and execute up to ten selectable motion paths with up to 100 positional points per axis. Both external and record-play programming is required. Inputs, outputs, external computer control, and resistance welder control must be easily added. (2) *Programmability:* All functions must be programmed, that is, timing, acceleration, deceleration, velocity, and allowable error. External command must be able to control the unit on a supervisory level. Almost any feedback or external sensor must be able to be added and programmed. Programming by an external portable unit must be available as an option. (3) *Features:* Ambient conditions of 50° F to 120° and 1–95 percent noncondensing relative humidity must not affect operation. Inputs and outputs for 110 Vac must be isolated. Lights as an option can be used to monitor inputs and outputs for maintenance. A robot controller with this flexibility allows the robot to be applied in areas of low volume with rapidly changing applications.

Traffic control, microcomputer. A microcomputer at each intersection allows a large central master traffic control system to know the traffic flow at each intersection. The intersection microcomputer can implement light changes operating (1) on its own information, (2) in conjunction with a group of intersections, or (3) under central master control. This multimode control is now practical with microcomputers and has become low in cost.

Transducer devices. Refers to specific elements or devices that have the capability of receiving information in the form of one physical quantity and converting it to information in the form of the same or other physical quantities. This particularly relates to specific cases of devices such as primary elements, signal transducers, and various transmitters.

353

9

Microcomputer Applications Continued: Examples of the Wide Ranges of Microcomputer Utilization

The compatible 8-bit word lengths of most microprocessors simplify the interfaces for most applications and thereby reduce system costs. Additional chips complete the basic family—usually peripheral interface adapters (PIAs) and communications interface adapters (CIAs). They couple the microprocessor to its anticipated auxiliaries. Growing lists of these auxiliaries to microprocessors, microcomputers, controllers, programmable calculators, and so on and also the wide range of peripherals available attest to the versatility of the markets for these systems.

PIAs permit easy interface with teletypes; display terminals; cassettes and switching equipment; various keyboard, remote control panels; and with other standard computers, minicomputers, or microcomputers. These capabilities add time-shared expansion of "stacked" microcomputer power. The CIAs are the devices for coupling processors and modems for these necessary short- or long-distance communications with other computers. Microprocessor-controlled two-way TV systems provide great communications potential for new social gains, as well as new scientific and business opportunities. Because microcomputers are now available at tool prices, they have broadened the capability for electronics applications far beyond the experience and imagination of the electronics industry alone. The microcomputer explosion might well quite suddenly change the entire working world as more sophisticated electronic communications systems substitute for much journey-to-work transportation, extend their utility in resource discovery, and continue advances for "intelligent" robotic powers and, most notably, institute changes from the old "work for work's sake" Puritan ethic.

MICROPROCESSORS AS TOOLS
FOR EFFECTIVE MANAGEMENT

There is a continuous and increasing pressure on managers at all levels to achieve a higher degree of control over their resources. This specifically pertains to employees. The use of visual microcomputer control systems is taking on a new importance. Closer management control over people, machines, and facilities is needed to achieve the high degree of productivity required today in many fields of industry, business, and government. In recent years, there has been a rapidly increasing and very widespread use of visual control systems as management planning tools. Business has become deluged in paper work and far too many needless computer reports. It is difficult, indeed, to make decisions from piles of papers and masses of data. Perhaps it is the realization that, in order to control, one must have the total picture to make a sound management decision. This is creating a renewed emphasis on visual control systems.

Because of the reduced cost of terminals,[1] visual control systems are coming closer to meeting the management control needs of business today. A visual control system is a combination of entry hardware, a viewing surface to hold information in various forms, and reporting software. The means for the display of information are offered in different degrees of sophistication, capability, and cost. Most executives want the facts, stripped of excess words and details, in order to make prompt decisions. Training lower-level management people to make their own decisions is simpler when visual tools are used.

Management by exception is a successful technique that has become popularized in recent years. Management's chief concern is with the exceptions rather than every detail of everyone's responsibilities. A well-designed visual control system signals or transmits only those items that require urgent management attention and action. The manager using terminals can easily spot the few exceptions that require his or her attention; he or she reviews the system by checking related activities and makes his or her decision on the corrective action required. Good visual control systems provide "exception" reporting, for example, to specific customer orders being completed in a plant. The plant manager may only have to concern himself or herself with the ten or 20 orders that are behind schedule and

---

[1] The steep rise in computer terminals is borne out by the following report: Computer terminals in use by the end of 1977 will total 2.3 million, representing a compound growth rate of 31 percent during the five-year period 1972 through 1977, according to a report by Creative Strategies, Inc., Palo Alto, California. There were an estimated 586,000 computer terminals in use at the end of 1972. "If sold" revenues from installations by the end of 1977 are projected at $2.6 billion. Interactive terminals—the largest segment of the industry used for data base access, time sharing, and data entry—accounted for 475,000 of terminals installed at the end of 1972. An increase to more than 1.8 million units by 1977 is forecast.

signaled for his or her action. Problems can be avoided if signaled early enough so that corrective action can be taken before the crisis occurs. Budgets, accounting, supply items, and so on are handled similarly.

Management by objective (MBO) is one of the recent management techniques that sets short- and long-term objectives for each element of a business and then periodically checks actual performance against the programmed "computer alerts" of milestone progress toward established goals. This technique can be applied to projects, units, or departments using financial and other measurable units of performance. The high degree of performance of missile accuracy, submarine construction, and space programs were excellent examples of "management by objectives."

These computerized systems are now applied to business activities as well as defense. Such techniques as computerized as PERT (program evaluation review technique) and CPM (critical path method) have made vast improvements in many fields for managing complex operations. They can be used at all levels of business, applying the new methods of step-by-step objectives. Schedule setting and progress checking are a means of evaluation and control. The use of CRT multicolor charts to establish milestone performance targets or goals for each element of an operation are then visually recorded as progress against these established goals. Periodic visual computer-compared projections and progress reports show instantly deviations from the established goals and necessary corrective action to be made in order to avoid serious and costly errors or delays. The most complex job can be broken into individual elements, each of which can have milestones of progress and estimated completion dates established. Remedial steps can be taken to adjust for serious delays. Planning and control have become new elements of every form of project management and can pay rich rewards in reducing costly delays and in avoiding errors. In a more positive sense, computer-controlled project planning and control can also streamline operations to reduce costs.

Microprocessor firmware: a significant aid to users

Among the many computer headaches is this one: "You'll have to change your whole way of doing things just to accommodate those new computers you're considering." But microprocessors, minicomputers, and ROMs can instead change the whole way computers have of doing things to accommodate users better. Microprogrammable micros can be adapted to adjust to users' needs. Managers do not have to adjust to *them*. Micros combine the hardware and the software to provide "intelligence" built into firmware—and that firmware is structured to fit applications precisely and specific applications very particularly. They also offer built-in safeguards for open-ended software. They can make older pokey computer systems super-fast by preprocessing particular jobs. And they save time and a lot of money and increase productivity as well.

Simpler and better software makes life more comfortable for new customers. Minicomputer and microcomputer makers now work hard and spend more on software in their efforts to compete for systems builder customers. Most companies are tying applications software development to specially configured hardware packages. This allows their systems customers to be up and running very quickly with their purchased machines. Competition is no longer centered around cycle times and so on. Industry executives contend, at least privately, that one processor is just about as good as another. Competition is centered on the broad assortment of systems building tools they offer: more memory configurations, more interfaces, more peripherals, and more software systems and considerable offerings of applications software. The vendor most likely to sell hardware in today's market will have sophisticated software development aids to make the customer's applications job easier.

Applications and systems software is getting more and more important. Many firms' investment in software as a percentage of total development expenses has doubled over the past few years. The suppliers have also concentrated on operating systems and high-level languages for process control systems, general-purpose data communication, and data collection systems. They are trying to give their customers the best tools to get the job done quickly, at the lowest cost, and they want the customer to use the language most convenient for his or her application. Other firms are working on language processors that would allow virtually any customer to easily develop his or her own applications software, using the language of that customer's specific industry.

Many manufacturing firms will spend far more on software than on hardware development. The basic economics of the microcomputer business have changed. In the past, programmers were cheap, and memory was expensive. Now the opposite is true. Now software is labor-intensive; its cost can go up and up whereas the cost of hardware continues to come down. Although the cost of software support is rising, it is a service that people now can buy as firmware; so some of that expense is offset. Customers today are more interested in solutions than in buying hardware. They do not compare processor speeds, but want to run bench marks to check the operating system and total "system" reliability.

Computer systems' effectiveness relates to function and cost, and competition in the micro and mini business today is increasingly centered around function. A large majority of the features of a computer system are actually software features. In given markets, suppliers either have these products or they do not. The problem is to develop the software products that will sell hardware. Many new series of standard hardware packages can be used either for program development or as OEM building blocks. The trend toward packaged systems, typically take-it-or-leave-it affairs, priced lower than the sum of the separately priced components they contain, is now getting off the ground. Most competitors are not dismissing the strategy as merely a pricing gimmick. They admit price is a factor, but so are system cost savings.

Boxes are getting so cheap that most suppliers must make their money somewhere else. Increased emphasis on both software development and new secure and tested packaged systems is paramount. Users do not want to worry about fitting software components together, and each customer no longer wants something different. There are options within various packages.

Microcomputers have, to date, had their greatest "outside" impact on user applications and methods that include such fields as finance, health care, retailing, distribution, transportation, communications, and manufacturing. But in the science and technology of computer equipment, microprocessors have had tremendous effect on system architecture, with many significant innovations such as microprocessor control of fast auxiliary memory, mass storage, intelligent terminals, transaction processing, computer-communication interaction, distributed processing and networking, hardware/software trade-offs, structured programming, and program developments still being imagined. It is also expected that microcomputers will impact such areas as detection of computer crime (and its prevention), better computer security, preservation of personal privacy in data banks, new education innovations and standards, and electronic funds transfer, as well as two-way TV.

Microcomputers perform higher-level operations more easily with sequences of microinstructions corresponding to common higher-level functions. They are stored in a read-only memory to be called out, decoded, and executed on command. Such sequences, as previously noted, are called macroinstructions. In a microcomputer the macroinstructions correspond to the basic instructions of a typical minicomputer. Microprogramming provides microcomputers with this most useful characteristic: the easy capability of system designers to adapt standard hardware to specific applications. They quickly construct the macroinstructions best suited for the particular functions to be performed and actually "build" them into the microprocessor. Many already have emulated all or part of the instruction set of existing minicomputers to minimize software development. They have built machines to perform efficiently those functions that are associated with particular applications such as word processing, point of sale, data acquisition, and so on. The capability to adapt a standard set of hardware to a variety of problems, in very tiny, single, or "stacked micros," combines the low-cost advantages of high-volume chip production with the computing efficiency of tailor-made instruction sets. In general, microcomputers offer better price/performance of peripherals and lower power consumption, save space with their small physical size, and offer higher reliability. These advantages are further enhanced by the flexibility of microprogramming, which, for practically all applications, has very substantial value.

Microprocessor programming approaches are available that combine the macroinstruction set with microprogramming. Often a few specialized macroinstructions can add greatly to the speed of execution and efficiency of macromemory utilization. A good approach is to start with a macroinstruction set, eliminate some instructions, and add others to create a new and more appropriate instruction set. If the quantity of production will be high enough, a more cost-effective system can be developed, using a direct microprogrammed approach. All microprocessors can use numerous ROM chips for storage. If the designer can analyze the tasks to be performed and manage to define them in the allowable (but expandable) microinstruction space, substantial additional memory for macroinstructions will not be needed and the cost of the system can be reduced. The system will be smaller as well. If the microprocessor is being applied to a relatively simple, dedicated task, getting down to the microlevel will permit maximum efficiency and speed. In fact, often the required speed can be met only by a microprogrammed approach.

MICROPROGRAMMABLE SYSTEMS COMPUTERS: AN EXAMPLE

We have noted that microprogrammable systems for microcomputers and minicomputers offer new technological "firmware" advances and capabilities. Built into these systems are cards for extended arithmetic instructions, floating-point hardware, dual-channel direct memory access, power-fail interrupt, memory protect, and other basic features. Powerful instructions of many other types are implemented in high-speed read-only memory. Microprogrammability offers the capability of enhancing the microcomputer or the mini with microprograms in order to adapt the computer to user desires more specifically. Microprograms can be stored in hardware the same way that the manufacturer stores the basic instruction set. By using the microprogrammability, critical subroutines can be executed five to ten times faster than with conventional software. An example is the PROM writer (programmable read-only memory writer), which occupies one Hewlett-Packard 2100S I/O slot enabling users to load microprograms onto read-only memory chips permanently. Software is provided for checking microprograms prior to fusing them on chips and for verifying accuracy after the chips are loaded. The microprogramming provides other extensive advantages as follows:

1. *Speed.* Microprograms optimize the general functions of the 2100S to specific needs by using the same 196 nanosecond microprocessor that the 2100S basic instructions use.
2. *Memory savings.* Any routine coded in microinstructions occupies less memory space than the same routine would require in any other computer language.
3. *Power.* With six additional high-speed registers and the six-field instruction format, the programmer has expanded programming techniques at his or her disposal.
4. *Editing.* The microprogramming debug editors enable users to edit microprograms and then store the final version on permanent read-only memory chips.

An Eniac computer in your hand

A 600 to 1 difference in computer cost and 270,000 to 1 difference in size in 28 years! The new programmable calculators and new microcomputers have about the same power and capabilities of one of the first computers ever built, the *Eniac*. But what a difference in 28 years between cost and size. The Hewlett-Packard 65 and the PDP-8A cost about $795 and $895. This is a 600:1 difference from the $480,000 cost. The power requirements of the Eniac were 50,000 watts; the HP-65, 1/2 watt—PDP-8, a few—thus a 100,000:1 difference. The sizes—the Eniac $10' \times 100' \times 4'$, or 4,000 cu. ft., vs $3.2'' \times 1.4'' \times 5.8''$, or 26 cu. in., for the HP-65 and $15'' \times 9''$ for the PDP-8A—a difference of 270,000:1. What we have now is essentially an Eniac one can hold in one's hand! Twenty-eight years is not a long time, and the changes have been dramatic. What can we suppose will be developed in the next 28 years?

TYPICAL APPLICATIONS FOR MICROPROCESSORS AND MICROCOMPUTERS

A summary of typical applications for microprocessors and microcomputers follows:

1. Process control equipment for data gathering and reduction.
2. Medical equipment, from radiation measurement to lab analysis gear.
3. Intelligent traffic control for trains, autos, and assembly lines.
4. Measurement systems, from panel meters to process flow monitoring systems.
5. Automotive diagnosis and control systems of many types.
6. Education systems as CAI and library control.

7. Architectural controllers, for elevators, security systems, and environmental controls.
8. Calculators, all types—programmable and fixed functions.
9. Keyboard terminals for data entry to tapes and disks or for reservations and other uses.
10. Optical character recognition (OCR) devices.
11. Automatic time clocks and payroll systems.
12. Chemical and gas controllers, analyzers, and testers.
13. Manufacturing control systems.
14. Banking terminals, cash dispensers, and so on.
15. Point of sale terminals.
16. Multiprocessors for minicomputers.
17. Stand-alone desk-top computers.
18. Automatic typesetting control units.
19. Low-cost radio navigation equipment.
20. I/O channels for large computers.
21. Processing oscillographic data.
22. Special purpose terminals, such as badge or card plus tape readers and similar devices.
23. Terminal add-ons, which give intelligence to standard units, such as teletypewriters.
24. Small business computers of many types and varieties.
25. Intelligent terminals including display unit record and remote equipment.
26. Multiplexers, modems, and communications controllers.
27. Industrial appliance and utility output systems.
28. Multiprocessing engineering systems.

AN EXAMPLE: "DISTRIBUTED INTELLIGENCE" THROUGH INTERPRETERS

A new computer structured after a distributed-intelligence microcomputer concept was recently delivered by Burroughs for the Avionics Laboratory at Wright-Patterson Air Force Base, Dayton, Ohio. It is a new LSI computer called the Aerospace Multiprocessor. It has many of the architectural advantages developed by Burroughs engineers and others. "The system delivered to the Avionics Lab," says a staff engineer at Burroughs in Paoli, Pa., "is built on LSI chips. It is more sophisticated than the stark microcomputer that people are today putting on chips. And not only that. Since we're not so uptight about keeping them 100 percent utilized, our control software is greatly simplified. There are five interpreters in the Air Force computer system, with the logic partitioned to be compatible with a 1,000-gate-per-chip LSI device. Because LSI of that density was not initially available, the unit was built with 500-gate-per-chip devices. The function of the interpreters is to perform all the functions that any processing element in any type computer would have to process."

The interpreters are programmed with two levels of microprogramming. But the interpreter processors are all connected with multibus structures that permit many terminal connections through parallelism between all processors. All of the processors are allowed total access to the shared memory; so it is truly multiprocessing, not a multicomputer. As a result, the interpreter can perform a wide variety of decentralized as well as many central-processing functions. It can perform the function of an I/O control module and special functions like matrix arithmetic, communication control, and so on. The interpreter is versatile because of its structure and because all of the control is stored in microprogram memories rather than in wired memories.

MICROPROCESSORS HELP INTELLIGENT TERMINALS CHANGE BUSINESS ENVIRONMENT

Microprocessor-controlled "intelligent" terminals and their increased capabilities are in widespread use. They are an example of how hardware technology developments have changed the business environment. Many more changes are likely to occur as a result of new cost trade-offs and expanded capabilities. With recent advances in hardware and low-cost software availability for microprocessors, even very small businesses by the thousands can afford to use systems efficiently. Micros are also reducing peripherals and equipment necessary for rapid communications to costs well within their reach. There is no longer any functional reason for maintaining a data base in one central location, nor for centralizing the main computer. With increased availability of low-cost LSI circuitry, economics do *not* favor centralization of processing. There is already a consistent shift toward more processor functions being embedded within terminals and consequent localized control. The capability of new chip computers and calculators and their decreased costs have forced a reevaluation of the economy of scale, the old precept that the way to run an efficient operation was to keep the big CPU busy. In the next few years, the costs of intelligent terminals will drop rapidly and the demand for high performance processors will also decline. (Examples of microprocessor-controlled terminals are shown on the following pages.)

As new circuit economics and processing efficiencies are developed, the pressure switches to the peripheral makers to reduce their costs and prices. There will be much more localized processing at terminals, and finished data and reports will also be moved to the proper decentralized executives quickly. Computer-communications engineers now know how to design, maintain, and update distributed data bases and networks. Intelligent terminals are playing a major role in solving the expenses of the "people problems" by putting more programming into terminals. This allows access by less-trained, lower-salaried users. In addition, reliability of small systems is much greater now and at affordable costs. All users have now begun to think in terms of distributed processing, and this means a lot of rethinking for die-hard big computer user holdouts. One important implication of the use of intelligent terminals is the need for modular and "standardized" programs and more Englishlike inquiry languages, as previously discussed.

Micro chips aid design
changes in terminals

Many digital engineers are discovering the advantages of putting their logic in the form of software and using one of the new single-chip microprocessors as a major component in their designs. But few companies had initially taken this approach as far as Digi-log Systems Inc., of Horsham, Pa., a designer and builder of special-purpose and custom-designed computer terminals. Heretofore, the company had relied on hard-wired logic for a variety of terminal products. Included were two units displaying 16 lines of 40 and 80 characters, respectively, and each with a keyboard and an acoustic coupler for use with a telephone handset. There are also a terminal for use by travel agents that gives them direct access to an airline's computerized reservations system (still being tested by the airline); a CRT terminal with an attached tape-cassette drive, for use by insurance brokers; and a terminal for use in a chain of restaurants catering to motorists, enabling them to receive telephone messages while on the road by interrogating a central message center. But the necessity for a new design to build each individual product turned out to be too expensive when it came to a terminal earmarked for users of Western Union's Mailgram service—until Digi-log designed the terminal around Intel's 8008 microprocessor. Digi-log has now shipped several hundred units made in that configuration to Xonics Corp., the contractor building the terminals for Western Union. Digi-log has also used the same idea in designs for other customers.

Basically, its entire design approach has been reduced to a set of printed-circuit boards: three kinds of read-only memory; a read/write memory; synchronous and asynchronous input/output cards; a set of display drivers; a keyboard module that can generate any 8-bit code from any of 110 keys; and, last but not least, a processor board called Microterm, which uses either the 8008 or the faster version of it, the 8008-1. "We have no standard product," according to the director of product applications, "but we use the Microterm to emulate any other product we want to." He cited one Digi-log customer who uses a single terminal design for three different applications, each of which is programmed for the Microterm and its microprocessor.

Perhaps the most effective use of the Microterm is in a program-development center built by Digi-log for its own use. Here the Microterm runs in three modes: to load a new program into a read/write memory, to emulate the processor while debugging that program, and, finally, to transfer the program into a reprogrammable read-only memory (ReProm). For the last, it uses Intel 1702 memories, which can be erased under ultra-violet light. It can also copy the contents of a known ReProm into a new one, thus doubling as a low-volume production unit. For larger volumes, the box can also drive a paper-tape punch to generate the data for the program mask of an Intel 1302, the mask-programmed equivalent of the 1702 memory.

Multilingual terminals

Recently, a computer terminal was developed to read the numerical data first and then read the textual data from a data base. Because of this simplicity, it was a trivial matter to replace the textual information displayed in English with other languages. Both the original program and its new multilingual display characteristics were developed at IBM.

The program is designed to be language-independent. Using the program, one can solve a problem in one language and communicate the results in another, a boon to multinational companies and international trade. All of the languages initially substituted used the Roman alphabet: French, German, Italian, and Spanish. But because a vector display also can have a programmable character generator, it also is possible to write in other alphabets, notably Hebrew and Arabic. The Semitic alphabets differ because they read from right to left. To match this characteristic, data tables should be transposed, but this flexibility is not built into the program. Arabic also concatenates (links together) letters forming new symbols, but, for convenience, the concatenated form is not used. When Japanese is substituted, a hexidecimal coding is used because the Japanese alphabet contains about 47 characters.

Application ranges—how and where
micros are being used today

Some specific and very early cost-effective applications of microcomputers are briefly examined further on. The first group are Intel micros. The broad range and increasing versatility are indicative of many benefits to customers—if the savings outlined by the users are passed along in lowered prices.

1. A laboratory is using an Intel microcomputer in an instrument that measures the protein content of blood, printing a separate quantitative reading for each of several different proteins. The microcomputer translates the raw data from a sensing instrument into medically meaningful numbers. The people at the lab were quoted as saying that the microcomputer on one PC board replaced three PC boards plus a power supply, cutting the overall size of the electronics package in half. They estimated that using the microcomputer reduced the cost of the electronics about 30 percent.

2. A general-purpose data-processing machine for small businesses, built by Omni Electronics, uses an Intel microcomputer as the heart of the system. Suitably programmed, this machine tabulates accounts, types invoices, writes checks, and produces personalized form letters. Omni says they saved about $3,000 by using a microcomputer in place of a mini. Moreover, the micro enabled them to reduce the whole system to typewriter size. The microcomputer has more speed than they need and offers the extraordinary reliability they require in this application. The integrated CPU does all central processing, using Intel's electrically programmed PROMs for bootstrap programming and RAMs as the central memory, a memory that stores up to 16K 8-bit bytes. Peripheral memory is supplied by one of the eight Omni tape decks, which store 15,000,000 bits per cartridge.

3. Another Intel microcomputer does the "thinking" for an automatic bottle-loading machine. The system was built by Comstar Corporation of Edina, Minnesota, for Conveyor Specialties. It "tells" the machine how to load bottles of different sizes and when to perform each step in the loading process. The tiny computer in a $6'' \times 6'' \times 1\ 1/2''$ space replaces several racks of counters, timers, and relays that would otherwise have been required. According to Comstar, the computer's flexible programming is a major advantage. Programs on PROMs can be changed in half an hour. Comstar estimates that the microcomputer halved the cost of the control portion of this system and reduced the time required to build it by a factor of two or three. The company is now building other types of systems with microcomputers, including an automatic meat-weighing and packaging machine.

4. Action Communications Systems of Dallas used Intel microcomputers as front-end processors in a high-speed dial-up communications controller built for the Bekins Company. Action adapted microcomputers in order to save both development time and system cost. The Bekin system was fully developed and delivered only 90 days after Action decided to use microcomputers. And Action estimates they saved about $10,000 in overall cost. The Bekins controller, located in Glendale, California, is the heart of a nationwide multiterminal system that carries administrative messages, financial data, shipping notices, and customer

inquiries. A microcomputer on each of five lines puts messages in a binary synchronous format, checks for errors, and signals for retransmission when an error is detected. Action did the final programming with PROMs.

5. An Intel one-chip computer performs as a microprocessor in the character recognition system for an optical scanner. The builder said the one-chip computer does the work of about 100 discrete components and replaced an entire $9'' \times 10''$ PC board otherwise required. He also estimates that the microcomputer reduced the cost of the character recognition system by about 20 percent.

6. The microcomputer was selected on the basis of cost and performance, according to the manager of Terminal Equipment Development. He added that the equivalent computing functions cost at least three to four times as much and required three times as much board area and somewhat more design time. The on-line display terminals made by Sycor of Ann Arbor, Michigan, are flexible enough to stand alone or operate in clusters connected to the central processor via a remote control unit. Sycor engineers have equipped the series with ample ROM plus 6K bytes of user programmable memory. As a result, the programs can be tailored for applications-oriented field validation and error detection.

7. Datatype Corp. used standard logic cards to develop an optical page reader for automated typesetters, providing an outstanding price/performance ratio, but then switched to Intel's microcomputers. Datatype's marketing relations manager stated, "When our engineers switched to micros, they were able to pack more logic into a single PC card than in a dozen standard logic PC cards. The results were a 50 percent reduction in unit size which greatly improved portability, and enhanced controller reliability. The microcomputer added considerably to an already outstanding price/performance ratio of increased savings in time and labor for the graphics industry. Our customers concur that the microcomputer is easier to program and has reduced programming time by 60 percent to 75 percent. The microcomputer can also store string commands, which means one or two typewritten characters are sufficient to "call out" up to 256 code commands on a typesetter control tape. This makes it possible to set repetitive copy or make major format changes with one or two key strokes."

The Datatype system generates perforated tape for controlling automated typesetting machines. The system input utilized typed copy with Datatype-designed print elements that have bar codes beneath each character. These bar codes are read optically to produce virtually error-free perforated tape for automated typesetters. Because of its superior economy and low error rates, the Datatype system is widely used in data-processing communication and in printing and publishing industries.

8. The Porta-verter terminal design required software development and tests. Intel delivered ROM components in prototype quantities six weeks after specification and production quantities two weeks later. They worked as expected, predicted, and intended. As a result, the Porta-verter went into production within five months after switching to micros. The Porta-verter, made by Iomec of Santa Clara, Calif., is a source data collection terminal for accounting and point of sale applications. Using the Porta-verter keeps two running totals, checks for errors, and prints hard-copy and a cassette record for all computations. It can also batch transmit over voice-level lines and can operate for eight hours on batteries, still within the user requirements of low cost and portability.

9. Six months after the design of the Series 1230 Digital Gas Flow Computer with a calculator chip, Daniel engineers switched to microcomputer components. "Using Intel components, it now computes the gas flow equation in one second as compared with ten seconds required for the calculator chip," according to the manager of Daniel's Electronics Division. The unit also has much greater programming flexibility, resulting in extended user applications. After switching to the microcomputer, the engineers completed the new design in four months and eliminated a large number of components. The microcomputer chip made the system more portable and less expensive. The Digital Gas Flow Computer, made by Daniel Industries, Inc. of Houston, Texas, uses Intel's microcomputer components and the gas flow equation to compute volume flow for up to four meter tubes with an accuracy of 0.1 percent. Because of its high accuracy, the system is now used extensively for monitoring industrial gas flow processes.

Generally, MOS and LSI have reduced the size and complexity of microcomputers. And programmable controllers have become very sophisticated. There is now a big boom in small controls for industrial tools, similar to the one for the hand-held electronic minicalculators. Computerized numerical control (CNC) is expected to continue its lead over direct numerical control (DNC), or hard-wired systems. Software can now be reduced to a "chip"—and the computer-on-a-chip has arrived. Solid-state controls have extended from the lowest level of factory automation up the hierarchy through the higher ones. This trend came into vogue very quickly. The reasons are because solid-state controls allow machines to operate faster, more accurately, and more cheaply and to offer longer life.

Lines of "microperipherals" introduced rapidly

The microprocessor has rapidly come all the way to the business DP user with the announcement of a line of low-cost microperipherals for the computer-on-a-chip systems. The new microperipheral I/O devices are hardware- and software-compatible with the microprocessor systems available from most semiconductor firms, such as Intel and National Semiconductor, and soon the rest. They are adaptable to most. It was expected that initially the microprocessors operating in end-user environment would be limited to scientific applications and process control. But that changed fast. Industry experts point out that the minicomputer was initially utilized in scientific areas long before it became part of the business DP repertoire.

An example of microperipherals is a paper-tape reader that can interface to the Intel Intellec series of 4-bit and 8-bit microprocessor systems. The paper-tape reader costs well under $1,000 and interfaces directly with the I/O boards of the Intellec systems. It is being supplied by iCom, Inc., a firm formed to provide a full line of microperipherals. The systems initially were mainly restricted to use by OEM users, many of whom utilized them to develop experimental dedicated applications systems.

The iCom firm will provide specific interfacing and software for each type of peripheral system. Because Intel was the largest supplier, at least through 1975, the first microperipherals were compatible with the Intellec series. Initially, the microprocessors that originated from semiconductor suppliers, who are mainly chip vendors, offered little customer support. But that changed fast. Microsystems available from DP vendors usually include a level of hardware and software support in addition to compatible peripherals.

The iCom microperipherals include a line printer on tape. The iCom paper-tape reader operates at 80 char./sec, using a photoelectric reader. It was followed by a high-speed punch and shortly after that by the line printer. The first units included their own power supplies and interfaced with the ribbon cables on the Intellec I/O boards. Later, iCom developed a compatible floppy-disk operating system, and the available microperipherals were interfaced to other lines of microprocessor systems.

Although direct comparisons between the microprocessor systems and existing computers are difficult, many sources indicated that, with the microperipherals, the new systems have "slightly less performance than available minicomputers but with about a 50 percent savings." Among the most logical applications are multiprocessor systems, communications control, process control, and similar dedicated uses. The microprocessor systems may see the emergence of special system architects who will all perform this development work. It is expected that the more sophisticated users will be the first to utilize the microprocessor systems at their DP sites. Beyond that, microprocessor systems could come into widespread use the same way that minicomputers have evolved. The iCom firm has correctly identified a need; other firms quickly followed. The calculator peripheral cycle moved ahead first with many auxiliary devices—and the microcomputer users demanded many more.

Handwritten graphics and voice-transmitted terminal

Voice messages, schematics, or equations can be transmitted with equal facility between any two standard telephones equipped with a telecommunications device. Using microprocessors and called Telenote, the system enables users to write, draw, or talk over any telephone in a normal matter. Extremely useful for transmission of technical information, as anyone who has tried to describe a circuit in words alone will recognize. The 19-pound units are completely portable. The manufacturer suggests that, in many cases, an audiovisual teleconference can actually replace costly intercity travel. A second potentially valuable application is transmitting written authorizations between offices, divisions, or companies. In operation, the user simply calls the other party in the usual matter. Either party may then originate a graphic message by applying a send-pen to the writing surface of his or her unit. The set at the other end will automatically duplicate the message, diagram, or signature. (The manufacturer is Talos Systems, Inc., Scottsdale, Arizona.)

Microprocessors for automobiles

By 1978 automobiles will be testing on-board processing systems to handle such functions as electronic fuel control, ignition control with automatic spark advance, generator control, and cruise control and more items as noted further on. The auto industry will probably have a system in which all vehicle communications are handled via digital multiplexing. The same box for on-board processing systems could also be part of a closed-loop servo control for the throttle position, for the distribution of cylinder-to-cylinder fueling and ignition selection, for signal processing for the dashboard tachometer, for diagnostic functions, and for some emissions control—perhaps direct exhaust gas feedback. With digital multiplexing, vehicle wiring harnesses will be reduced to perhaps four wires: positive power (battery), data bus, control bus, and negative power (ground). The problem is not in the complex areas like LSI, as formerly believed, but in the sensing function and the development of actuate functions. The actuate functions are particularly difficult because the load used by the automobile manufacturers for electric window motors and for electric seat controls are subject to large transients in current and voltage. Electronics will dramatically improve safety, emissions, and economy; and, in the long run, electronics will decrease the cost of cars.[2]

[2] Edward N. Cole, president and chief operating officer of General Motors Corporation, delivered a major address in June 1973 at the National Computer Conference and Exposition in New York. He stated: "Computers and their applications are becoming increasingly intertwined in virtually every area of automotive research and development, manufacture and

Automobile minicomputers and microcomputers

The potential applications for microprocessors in automobiles can be divided into many categories as listed further on. With the existing emissions-related regulations and possible future fuel economy legislation, a logical first application for an on-board computer is the engine control function. The monitoring/diagnosis and functions that are directly related are as follows:

Engine/powertrain Control—
    spark timing and duration control
    combustion control (A/F ratio, EGR)
    cruise control
    engine RPM limiting
    emission controls

Chassis and Suspension Control

Exterior Lighting Control

Driver Assistance and Convenience—
    temperature control
    diagnostic readouts
    power seat positioning
    fuel economy/drive radius readout
    routing display

Safety—
    headway control
    obstacle detection
    automatic highway controls
    antitheft system
    driver condition prestart check
    antiskid braking

The modern automobile has a number of different pneumatic/electromechanical control systems, which usually independently measure the required variables. Computers can exercise the desired control action and drive an actuator. To demonstrate the integration of functions in a single general-purpose computer, one experimental system used a DEC PDP-11

quality control. The implications of such developments are of paramount importance to our two industries and to the U.S. economy." He discussed a number of areas, including diagnostics as a response to consumarism: on-board computers in cars and their relationship to energy conservation and emission control; future dual mode highway systems controlling speeds and distances between cars—all dependent on computer controls; and quality control for processes and products. He also stressed new computerized production: ". . . machine for machine jobs and people for people jobs." (News Release: 1973 National Computer Conference and Exposition, New York, May 11, 1973.

minicomputer to control spark timing with an essentially standard distrib-uter used to route the high voltage to the spark plugs. Exhaust gas recircu-lation (EGR—for NOX emissions reduction) was controlled with a simple stepper-motor driven butterfly-valve; and fuel delivery, with an eight-chan-nel fuel injection system that injected into the intake manifold. The engine variables sensed were crankshaft position and speed, ambient and engine coolant. Various other systems controls were developed successfully. Com-puter control was very flexible. The goal of the current work is to develop and demonstrate a digital control system that maximizes fuel economy and drivability for a given level (federal government regulation) of emissions and that could be manufactured in production quantities cost-effectively. Some present systems use a microprocessor and a small number of other custom LSI devices to control the spark ignition timing and EGR valve position based on a number of input engine variables. All these systems are currently being tested on the road in several vehicles.[3]

Ignition computer for automobiles: an example

Integrated circuits are likely soon to be a normal part of an automobile according to Emihus Microcomponents in Surrey, England. The company is now in the advanced stages of developing a microcircuit chip containing some 4,000 transistors, which is capable of controlling the ignition timing of an automobile engine to a quarter of a degree. The chip measures only 4-mm square and, when packaged, will still be small enough to fit into the bottom of a distributor.

The chip amounts to a small computer that is able to accept information about the engine condition—load, acceleration, and engine revolutions —and, according to a program fed into it, adjust the engine timing accu-rately. One of the outcomes of this, says Emihus, is a reduction of exhaust emission by 5 percent to 10 percent. There is also likely to be an improve-ment of gas consumption of 3 percent to 5 percent. Emihus, working with a major automobile manufacturer, which, at the moment, it refuses to name, is working toward a chip that will contain an optical sensor capable of measuring engine revs directly from the distributor shaft. The chip has a partial random access memory and so can be programmed to suit any engine.[4]

---

[3] A yellow flashing light, activated by a monolithic IC to warn following drivers that a front car is slowing down, could be the next safety product to be added to new cars. Called Cyberlites, they were installed on 250 San Francisco taxis in a test June 1973 and helped reduce rear-end collisions by 60 percent. The California Highway Patrol granted approval, on condition that brightness be reduced by a factor of three. That accomplished, the developer went after the U.S. Department of Transportation to adopt the California standard.

[4] *Industrial Research*, June 1973, p. 21.

Microprocessor chips for industrial camera systems

It is a rare engineer today who has not at least considered the possibility of designing a microprocessor into his company's products. One of the latest results of such thinking is an industrial camera system dubbed the "smart camera" by its manufacturer, Reticon Corp. of Mt. View, California. The *smart*, of course, comes from the inclusion of a microprocessor—in this case, the Intel MCS-4. Traditional industrial camera systems are used for noncontact inspection, process control, and size and position measurements. Although they are quite versatile in the types of applications they can be used for, they have a limited measurement and control capability in any particular application because of their hard-wired controllers. Use of a microprocessor-based controller, with its inherent software programmability, removes most of these limitations. It also adds a high degree of computational capability, as well as the ability to store the results of many measurements and read them out at an appropriate time.

In its simplest form, the Reticon camera system will inspect parts passing through the camera's field of view and display their dimensions in engineering units (inches, mils, and so on). It can be programmed to segregate measured parts into ten different categories and provide relay closures for their automatic binning. The system also compares its measurements to desired tolerances that are programmable and gives pass/fail indications. This "smart camera" system keeps records of measurements taken and the distribution of parts and tolerances. On command, it can provide a printout of a day's production on a standard teletypewriter.

Microprocessors for fuel saving

Microcomputer manufacturers have begun to see consumer applications comprising the largest area of use for their products. Even a decade ago, this prediction sounded reasonable. Control of household heating and cooling, computation, inventory, timekeeping and cooking now offer pragmatic useful potential applications of computer technology. Prices of electronics have dropped rapidly. Microcomputers are expected to soon constitute a growing fraction of home costs. This optimistic scenario is now being borne out by reality.

Until 1975 one of the main problems was that peripheral and software costs did not decline with processor costs. I/O devices formerly cost more than central processors. Memory costs (especially those of bulk memory) remained high. Software costs often exceeded hardware costs and often still do.

Now today's high energy prices provide a new impetus to develop computerized housing control. All plans to assure adequate energy supplies postulate reduced demand growth. But employing alternative energy sources will not reduce the need to use energy more efficiently. Some choices, such as solar heating, require efficient implementation to benefit from relatively low temperature supplies. Because residential use accounts for about 15 percent of national fuel consumption, consumers will definitely experience higher energy costs and develop an interest in more efficient energy use.

Where does computerized housing control stand today? Components for inexpensive CPUs exist now, and memory prices, considering volume discounts, lie in acceptable price ranges. Developing low cost peripherals for I/O transfer and transducers for measurement and control now comprises the chief obstacle to tapping a major market area. A low-cost, reliable, and low-performance I/O writer could be the key to this huge market. Fuel burners and heat sources of almost every kind operate optimally over a small range of conditions. Controlling their energy usually wastes energy. Controlling energy storage and use, on the other hand, can match a load to a generator with minimal losses. Although especially important with solar heat, this factor is not negligible with other sources. End use control saves energy.

Using energy derived from low-temperature processes requires utilizing sophisticated regulators to wrest maximum benefit from each BTU. Simple (and thus low-cost) mechanisms can provide this control when backed with sufficient computing power and adequate transducers. Automatically adjusting an energy converter to allow for varying environmental conditions saves energy by continually optimizing performance. Only adequate computing capability can fill this need.[5]

CONCLUSION

A "distributed processing revolution" is occurring owing primarily to very large sales of microprocessor-controlled intelligent terminals of thousands of types at the low-cost/high-performance end of the scale. Recent developments of tiny components used in intelligent terminals and the prodigious programmable calculators have provided mass distribution of computing tools to the ordinary citizen. With these tools, users can directly program their simple problems in various computer languages, which they can learn in a week or so. Expansion of available "free" software and further development of the new simple programming techniques, coupled with the mass production of microcomputers, have the potential of also reducing many of the complications of life and government drastically. Radical changes in the active component technologies produced these LSI circuits. And mass (that

[5] Paraphrased from *Digital Design*, October 1974, p. 84.

is, batch) production of all sorts of electronic devices became a reality in 1974.

Much easier system design even by persons not comfortable in circuit design caused the production volume of circuits to go up beyond all previous expectations. This caused the drastic and continuing fall in prices of components and control instruments. Other important effects, however, were also taking place: (1) As integration levels went up, the interconnections, which were normally masses of external wires, were attached inside. (Hand-held personal calculators are good examples of the elimination of "wires" and interconnections in a complex computing element.) (2) The faster switching speeds of logic circuits were going up, as the access time of main memories came down at a rapid rate, and all this resulted in many more computing operations in the same time period. (3) This was also coupled with reduced peripheral hardware costs. Initially, the increases in speeds and the reduction in prices had occurred in main memories and in integrated circuits for processors. Similar advances and cost reductions occurred in tapes, disks, and other forms of mass memory. Thus all suppliers offered much, much more computing power for a given amount of capital investment.

Formerly, many poorly written systems have occupied so much storage and have had such complex software control of the machine elements that they were almost ridiculous. Micropower is so flexible and yet so straightforward now that hardware designers may economically convert most, or a great many, algorithms to firmware to reduce software costs, control complexity, and main storage space occupancy. And generally, microprogramming that is the hard wiring of software procedures permits the creation of new machine instruction sets by controlling elementary switching paths. It also generates higher level "macro" instructions, so that less user programming, less storage, and less instruction execution are required. Inexpensive and fast ROMs and PROMs have emerged from the new component technology and have advanced to create a dramatic boost to microprogramming technology and use. Dedication of many micros or stacked micros to single, large processing jobs also reduces significantly the software overhead related to complex operating systems and massive time-sharing systems, thus reducing costs to customers of computer service company network offerings.

The minicomputer, in contrast to the micro, has the same basic architecture as the conventional, larger systems. It still takes professional programmers to get them up and running and requires some training and knowledge for a user who occasionally runs a problem. In general or dedicated minicomputer systems, the cost of writing specific software sometimes exceed hardware costs to the user by a considerable amount.

Several distinct events that occurred in the early 1970s were real breaks with the traditional hardware/software systems approach to solving problems. The SYMBOL system developed by Fairchild Camera Co. directly executes a high-level language with all memory management, compiling, time sharing, and most of the other normal software "operating systems" functions directly and as hard-wired. This medium-sized, high-performance, research system is now in operation and demonstrates complete feasibility of hard-wiring software "system" controls at any level desired. The system manages all virtual memory access automatically in a direct, symbolically addressed manner. Furthermore, it allows "dynamic" changes in data field size, data group size, and data file size as the program execution progresses. Hewlett-Packard combined various philosophies that allow the user to directly work in his or her own familiar language on a decimal machine with low-cost, mass-produced, hand-held calculators.

These machines and their successors started a new trend in computing where each user can have his or her own private calculator. It is now profitable to mass-produce even specialized personal calculators. Some systems are specifically directed at software programmers who convert back and forth between decimal, octal, and hexidecimal number systems. Programmable desk-top calculators emerged with user application programs in near natural languages. They are stored on magnetic cards, cassettes, and so on, so that repetitions of the program may be computed without keying the instruction routine again. This speeds computation and, quite drastically, reduces keying errors. Wide ranges of peripherals are available for printing, plotting, storage, and interfacing and so on. The prices for these major calculator systems range from a few hundred to a few thousand dollars.

Single-chip microprocessors, as noted, are, in effect, little computers when coupled with memory and interface circuits. They allow users to apply computing power directly in point of sale terminals, control systems, and innumerable other places. The low prices for these very useful systems range from less than $100 to under $1,000, depending upon the amount of memory, and so on. They provide conventional computer power that may be "distributed" into almost any requirement. Mass production of standard types has provided the low cost needed. Intel Corp. kicked off this revolution. As in the case of hand-held calculators, many new companies have entered this microcomputer arena, too. We are also now seeing many types of processors in autos, homes, and so on.

Why have price changes occurred? Transistor costs dropped from $5.00 to $.001. Memory bit costs dropped from $.20 per bit to less than $.01 per bit. TTL circuits dropped from $5.00 to $.20. MOS/LSI package costs dropped from $100 to $10. Interconnection wires and hardware disappeared into the LSI. Relative cost of software has plummeted through the use of ROMs. Hardware has become a relatively minor cost, depending upon system size and complexity. Standard computers are designed to control very large commercial systems, and their problems have expanded many hundredfold through the forced use of very complex software "operating systems" and quite terrible and costly one-of-a-kind "application" packages. Many of these very expensive and troublesome software components are now finally being hard-wired very cheaply, modularly, and "alterably" in relatively simple ROMs and PROMs for standard machines, changing their architectural designs also.

In consequence, the mass production of LSI silicon component microprocessors has reduced hardware and software costs to the point where "calculating power" can be distributed to all of us and these instruments are purchasable in department stores and practically everywhere else.

MOS/LSI "calculator" and "memory" technology can be coupled and expanded with "macro" functional and control algorithms in PROM/ROM hardware or in RAM (magnetic memory) combinations. Incorporated in them are a great many programmable option features. Microcomputers and calculator-based systems provide hard-copy output to remote calculators or micro-controlled terminals. Tiny circuit boards provide the communication link interfaces for a hundred peripheral devices. Thus per transaction costs have fallen so much that users must reexamine the traditional ideas of centralizing processing or paying the expenses of time sharing over large communications networks. Paradoxically, manufacturers and other large users can now economically "waste" computer power in many applications by dedicating cheap microcomputers to specific tasks and by permitting micropower or calculator power to be idle and to use it only when needed. Mass-produced microcomputers are now multifaceted, very cheap appliances. The distributed processing revolution has started—without focus or knowledge as to either its direction or impact on our current or future lives.

APPENDIX A

MICROCOMPUTER PRODUCT ANALYSIS

Sixteen-bit microprocessors are the real powerhouses. The newest 16-bit single-chip processing units are designed for the high-performance end of the wide-ranging microcomputer market, especially for those applications that require high precision arithmetic and very large memories. As early as 1973, National Semiconductor led the others with its IMP-16; it is now being redesigned with bipolar technology to improve its speed by a factor of ten. The CPU had required five chips, and the company quickly introduced the single-chip version of IMP, the one-chip 16-bit PACE. Competitors in the 16-bit race, as noted below, are Texas Instruments, Inc.'s 9900, General Instrument Corp.'s CP1600, Western Digital's MCP 1600 which was designed originally for and used by Digital Equipment Corp. in their LSI-11 micro and in other systems as indicated in summaries and tables on pages ahead. Most of these are available on a microcomputer board or as one-chip systems, although Western's is a three-chip system interconnected by an 18-bit microinstruction bus that provides bidirectional communications between them for address and instructions. The General Automation, Inc. GA-16/110 and GA-16/220 are full-fledged 16-bit microcomputers, the former designed for dedicated applications while the latter combines a second board with the basic GA-16/110 microcomputer, adding more I/O ports, additional operator controls and displays, expanded remote monitor and control capability, expanded diagnostic capability and optional system console interface and autoload capability. The Data General Corp. microNOVA (mN601) microprocessor is a single 40-pin ceramic package. It is available as a single chip, a chip set, a board, and a fully packaged MOS minicomputer.

The early history of microcomputers, considered to be the "first wave"—1973–1975—found half a dozen manufacturers introducing basic products and seeking domination in specific areas for their machines. The National Semiconductor early machines fought against the early Intel 4004 and 8008 and the Rockwell PPS devices. Most of these, like the Texas Instruments TMS1000, were considered calculator types. But, also quite early in the competition the two most popular microprocessors were introduced, notably the Intel 8080 and the Motorola 6800. Our comparison discussion begins with these early units and lays the foundation for the massive new wave of product introduction of "enhanced models" beginning in late 1975 and continuing through 1976. An analysis of all of the early and most fundamental machines would be general matters of fact, and the comparisons, contrasts, and relationships do fall quite neatly into place. But, such a study would be "historical" and not strictly germane to the current dynamism of the industry. New techniques, new components, capabilities and capacities so dominate current product design and applications that a tremendous amount of competence is required to encompass it all. The examination of the facts alone would not do justice to the true product lines progress, to the rapidly accelerating applications pace, current and coming breakthroughs in ever-increasing speeds, continuing reduction in physical size, and steadily improving cost-performance realities. These can only be described as astonishing even to the most traditional and conservative engineers, purchasing agents, and industrial and institutional executives and leaders. The design and system complexities are challenging. But analyses must also concern the examination of trends, projections, acceptances, new applications and markets that the raw power of these microprocessors, microcomputers, and microcontrollers portend.

The reader should not, however, become dismayed that the range of product and versatility of applications are becoming too complex and far-reaching. The latter section of this appendix clearly demonstrates that the understanding of microprocessor engineering and utilization is not a mystique or a special science controlled by cliques of "high priests." The skills of "inventing" new system design, operating tricks and efficiencies, and exotic applications can be achieved by practically anyone. Hundreds of computer clubs have members that range from grade schoolers to Ph.D.s, with new joiners that include medical doctors, accountants, auto mechanics, "ham" radio members, and every trade and profession. All begin as amateurs and none as masters because each day the literature (dozens of microcomputer magazines, newspapers; hundreds of club newsletters; tons of company product literature; and scores of new books) emphasizes the significance of "worlds" of the exploding microcomputer universe. Practically anyone can become a true specialist in several of the unbounded specific fields of interest now almost too numerous to define. Neighborhood computer stores began multiplying in late 1976, and new stores were computed by closely interested parties (publications, suppliers, market analysts) and companies to be greater than one retailer opening per day. Many of these stores (more than 400 American stores were listed in early 1977, 80 in California alone) conduct continuing beginners classes, offer house-call "doctor" service for ailing machines and practically "baby-sit" with the hundreds of very small business customers who are beginning to flood these stores looking for the $2,000 (outright purchase) systems that will do their payroll, inventory control, and tax accounting. It is a lot easier (and safer) for these individuals to go to a computer store offering low prices like these than to hear standard computer salesmen quote small systems costs to them at $2,000-a-month lease or $30,000-to-$50,000 purchase—as has been the case until now.

The first few years of microprocessor progress were startling. Even the experts were overwhelmed by the specter of their power and versatility. It was difficult to believe that all of these units provide very cheap computing and information processing that is delivered from a very tiny data signal manipulating machine. The microprocessor became a designer's dream. Any owner can place it practically anywhere or have it connect to or become a control part of any device to produce programmable action or intelligence. Microprocessors greatly reduce not only electronic components needed, but they also often substitute for many electromechanical, mechanical, pneumatic, hydraulic, and other parts of old or new machines, devices and appliances. And those engineers who design microprocessors into new products find engineering turnaround time is cut drastically while they incorporate decision-making capability into applications never before considered: in games, test equipment, all ranges of communications devices, industrial machines, medical diagnostic and monitoring gear, and home and environmental appliances. Though micros at first seem complex, they are mass produced very cheaply, are easy to troubleshoot, and expand modularly in capability and capacity with hardware, firmware, or software. The applications chapters of this book demonstrate that many end users find little need to bother with complex software such as assemblers, compilers, etc., but instead program with simple languages as BASIC, FORTRAN, and APL. Others, more software-oriented, will delight in challenging detail work using gates, flip-flops, firmware coding, and special diagnostics.

It is impossible to provide a complete roundup of all the devices and machines that qualify for the title of microprocessor, microcomputer, and/or microcontroller. Hundreds of companies can accurately call themselves microcomputer manufacturers, and the last section of this appendix briefly describes the products of some of the larger and more aggressive ones. However, only a dozen or so manufacturers actually manufacture the microprocessor chip itself. The others use the chip to build many classes and ranges of microcomputers with individual imaginations the only constraining factor. We will stress later the specific architecture and performance of the various specific chips and chip families that comprise the basis for the great majority of all microcomputers. The previous chapters related to the assemblers, compilers, simulators, prototyping devices, exerciser equipment and so on that are fundamental to the designer and applications engineers as well as the hobbyists who use the systems for product development and device or information control. The systems range from 4-bit, 8-bit, 12-bit, and 16-bit sizes and types and add-on or component "slices" of any of these, which can build to machines that handle 32-bit and larger "words." We have also analyzed the active exploration and application of "stacked" processors or multimicrocomputers.

Although it is not necessary to dwell at length on the origins of modern microprocessors, the discussion of specific models began with some pioneering types: the experimental NUBLU, the original Intel 8080, Motorola 6800, Texas Instruments TMS 1000, the National Semiconductor IMPs, the first PACE, the Signetics PIP, the first Intel Bipolar Family, and a few others. Out of this initial race came the domination, at least for user popularity, of the 8080A and the 6800D, both enhanced versions of the original models. The jump ahead that these two models received is confirmed by the number of competing companies that decided, because of the versatility advantages, to make deals (pay royalties, exchange technology developments, etc.) to franchise the manufacture or become a second source to customers for these same 8080 or 6800 family units or devices based on them but improved, enhanced or singly dedicated for various system designs or products. Among the competing manufacturers that offer (manufacture or second source) the original or enhanced Intel 8080 chip are Texas Instruments, Inc., Advanced Micro Devices Inc., National Semiconductor Inc., NEC Microcomputers (Japan), Siemens AG (West Germany), and others. Competing with the 8080, Hitachi Ltd. (Japan), Thomson-CSF (France), American Microsystems, Inc., Fairchild Camera and Instrument Inc., and others are second sources for the Motorola M6800. Other second source arrangements are: Fairchild's F-8 is second sourced by Mostek Corp. as a single-chip CPU, and Motorola has the manufacturing rights also; National Semiconductor second sources the Intel 4040, Rockwell PPS-4, and PPS-8; Hughes second sources RCA's CDP 1802; Harris second sources Intersil's 6100 CMOS 4K processor; Signetics second sources Intel's 3002 2-bit slice TTL unit, and there are many other such cross-licensing manufacturing to provide extra depth of manufacturing sources for the more popular machines. Also, massive cross-purchasing between computer manufacturers takes place; for example, Hewlett-Packard uses hundreds of thousands of chips; many are Motorola M6800s used in its desk-top calculator products; Westinghouse signed a contract with Intel for the purchase of

100,000 units of the 8080 family over a one year period; NCR has purchased large quantities of Intel 8080s for their terminals and other uses; General Instrument has a large cooperative industrial control device venture with Honeywell, and so on.

Microcomputer capacity and lower costs (down to the $5 to $20 ranges in large quantities) continued to characterize the industry as 1976 closed. New orders of performance refinements emerged as most microprocessor family capabilities were enhanced with faster throughput, larger instruction sets and so on, due to new MOS processing techniques and improved CPU architecture, I/O was rapidly improved with new types of programmable I/O chips and better interrupt and interfacing techniques. One-chip controllers with CPU and control ROMs on the same chip provided for program storage, random-access memory (data), and I/O registers for special system manipulation. As will be noted, 8-bit systems predominate, but 4-bit systems sell in huge quantities for dedicated purposes, and 16-bit units are rising in purchasing popularity. Many 8-bit units can handle 16-bit word data and instructions, thus developing an ease for users to upgrade their 8-bit units to a 16-bit program design. Fairchild's F-8, National's SC/MP, and Electronic Array's 9002 handle many miscellaneous jobs with very low chip numbers and thus low costs. But, first some basics and a review of some of the pioneer devices.

Competing bit slice systems

The Intel bit slice systems were quickly followed by several important competitive systems from major manufacturers. Bipolar processors using slices generally are designed for the larger process-control and high-speed controller tasks often handled by minicomputers. They use a "vertical" organization combining on one integrated chip several different functional blocks that operate on the same data. Thus, they are not meant for applications that can be served by or compete with low-cost MOS microprocessors. Some typical applications are signal processing, sophisticated peripherals, industrial control, and so on that formerly required hundreds of TTL or Schottky-TTL, Small or Medium Scale Integrated ICs (SSI and MSI), and many memory packages. A bipolar bit slice is only a section of the CPE (CPU); it is not designed to operate alone. A 16-bit computer, for example, requires eight 2-bit or four 4-bit slices for the CPU plus many peripheral I/O packages, with emphasis on memory devices. In almost all cases standard memories are used, often up to 64 kilobytes and more, but the choice between only a few conflicting constraints is simple. Standard memories permit large arrays with a limited number of pin connections and an efficient use of silicon. And memories, in late 1976, achieved greater functional densities, higher speed, and better versatility at continuously decreasing prices providing huge markets that are ideal for semiconductor manufacturers. The analysis of new efficient ROM and RAM technologies has been provided in previous chapters.

A primary asset of bipolar LSI families relates to their strong processing power, often far greater than what is available from most MOS microprocessors. Because processing power is packaged on several matched chips which can provide 16-bit, even 32-bit word lengths, such systems can be microprogrammed to handle the most powerful high-level instruction sets. Furthermore, because bit slice systems provide for relatively few data inputs and outputs per chip, they contain many levels of logic, thus improving the gate-to-pin ratio and the delay-power-product. Significant numbers of control inputs thus insure maximum flexibility for the user. Control signals are generated by a microprogram stored in fast ROMs or PROMs at low costs. The third essential element, in addition to the data path bit slices and microprogram, is a controller. The controller steps through a sequence of microcodes, performs conditional jumps and allows subroutine nesting. A primary advantage is that microprograms can be changed by substitution of ROM codes without any PC board changes, permitting design modification and error correction in hours instead of weeks as with older fixed logic. As noted below, there are a growing number of bipolar-circuit manufacturers, including Fairchild, Monolithic Memories, Inc. (MMI), Advanced Micro Devices, Inc. (AMD), Raytheon, Intel, and others. Motorola uses highest-performing emitter-coupled-logic (MECL) processor slices for controlling big mainframe memories and has a 4-bit ECL slice set. Texas Instruments has its pioneering SBP0400, a 4-bit I^2L system. Practically all of these bipolar families have processing power that is far greater than that presently available from MOS microprocessors. Though these competing units appear to be quite different from each other, certain circuit blocks are common to all, such as generally running at a microinstruction rate of 5 to 10 MHz. They all have data path circuits, Arithmetic-Logic Units (ALUs), accumulators, shifters, etc. that are expandable to any practical word length and use carry-look-ahead for arithmetic functions. Also, besides the processor slice itself, there are functions of control registers, timing, slice-memory interface, and the control registers always contain the logic necessary for microprogrammable control. The two- or 4-bit (or wider) data path plus enough storage and logic in the control register to address and control the memory circuits, can handle status, branching, and interrupt functions. In essence, then, all families contain one microprogram control or sequencer circuit to address the microinstruction store (ROM or PROM), and various test flag bits to execute conditional branching, allow nesting of subroutines, and so on. In the ALU block the computational logic is, in effect, side-by-side with data routing paths and the I/O ports that handle control-register inputs and memory outputs. Clock phases needed to drive all parts of the system are provided by timing function ties. With these capabilities, flexible instruction sets can be used to optimize performance or to emulate other machines to develop software compatibility. Also, the many benefits of stored-program architecture are achieved because the hardware is independent of software and both can therefore be developed simultaneously. They microprogram quickly, cheaply, and efficiently, without undue complication. To most users, choosing from among the fixed-instruction MOS microprocessors is a tough job; choosing from among the bit-slice machines is even more difficult. Considerable time and effort (knowledge and design skill) is required to select the best-suited family to achieve lowest cost and highest efficiency.

Bit-slice system product summaries

We have already noted Intel's 1974 introduction of its 3000 series of microprogrammable 2-bit slices consisting of two basic circuits and five support chips. The basic units are the 300 Microprogram Control unit in a 40-pin package and the 3002 Central Processing Element in a 28-pin package. The CPE contains the ALU, accumulator, 11 general purpose registers and a memory address register. The 3001 can directly address 512 words of microprogram store and perform tests and branching.

The Advanced Microprocessor 2900 device is a 4-bit slice, the ALU being fed from a 16-word dual port RAM or accumulator array. It has a 1-bit shifter, a separate Q-register, and the other usual auxiliary signals to allow carry-look-ahead expansion. With seventeen working ALU registers and two address operations, it operates twice as fast on less power than the MMI5700/6700 systems of its competitor, Monolithic Memories, Inc., as noted below. It has a 9-bit microinstruction word-decode block that is used to select all ALU source operands and other required ALU functions and destination registers. This permits the microcontroller to be cascaded either with full look-ahead logic capability or with ripple carry. With three-stage outputs, it can provide various status flag outputs directly from the ALU. Its 2-port RAM and ALU are fast enough to handle concurrent input sequences in turn without slowing the system. Any of the 16 words of the RAM can be read from one of its ports under control of the address field input selector; data from the other port can be read with the same code, both data groups then appearing simultaneously at the RAM port for ALU processing. The 2909 Microprogram Control Unit (or sequencer) allows four-deep nesting of subroutines. Only eleven AMD chips are generally required to implement a typical CPU; the four principal data processing functions are microprocessor slice, I/O bus interface transceivers, microprogram control, and CPU control, including priority interrupt and the designed main memory. These eleven principal chips replace about 200

TTL packages, but the Fairchild "Macrologic" bipolar microprocessor family literature suggests it can beat this. Note the comparison table below. (AMD's 2900 is second sourced by Raytheon and Motorola.)

Fairchild claims its Macrologic Bipolar family is faster and cheaper than others. In late 1976, it had eight 200-gate-plus devices and four more about to be announced, this plus more than thirty memory devices. Fairchild also listed many coming products based on its process background in Isoplanar, Injection Logic, Schottky, and Subnanosecond ECL. In the following two tables, Fairchild compares its 9405A 4-bit slice with AMD's 2901 and offers a further comparison saving of its parts as replacement over the former use of Medium Scale Integration (MSI) parts, as regards specific function.

Fairchild's Macrologic differs significantly from other bit slice competitors in logic technology and partitioning. The 9400 family uses Schottky TTL, and the 4700 family uses CMOS, which achieves very low power consumption and high noise immunity. Although the CMOS parts are considerably slower, the functions, pinouts, and timing relationships are identical for the two technologies. Macrologic 4-bit data path slices are less complex and smaller but generally require more parts. Some features are: the 9405/4705 Arithmetic Register Stack combines an 8-word register (multi-accumulator file) with an 8-function ALU and an edge-triggered output register, the 9404/4704 Data Path Switch provides bus selection, complementing byte masking and shifting, the 9406/4706 Program Stack combines the function of a 16-deep address register LIFO stack for subroutine nesting with a program counter (incrementer), the 9407/4707 Data Access Register performs memory address arithmetic for RAM-resident stack operation, the 9410/4710 16 x 4 RAM with edge-triggered output registers that can be used as a bus-oriented scratchpad, the 9408/4708 Microprogram Sequencer controls up to 1024 words of microprogram store directly, performing unrestricted branching and allowing four-deep nesting of subroutines. (Signetics is a second source.)

Fairchild 4-bit slice vs 2901

	9405A Fairchild	2901 AMD
Cost (100-Piece Plastic)	$12.00	$21.00
Speed (Minimum Clock Period)	75 ns	105 ns
Package Size	24-Lead 0.4-Inch Wide	40-Lead 0.6 Inch Wide
Die Size	10,000 MIL^2	30,000 MIL^2
LSI Devices in Family (200 or More Gates)	8	3

Function vs Function (LSI only)

Device	Replaces this many SSI/MSI parts	Function
Fairchild		
9405A	17	4-Bit Slice. ALU/Registers
9408	24	Microprogram Sequencer
9404	22	Data Patch Switch. Byte Masking, Sign Extension, Shifting
9406	12	Program Counter and LIFO Stack
9407	12	Address Arithmetic
9401	12	Cyclic Redundancy Checker
9403	16	FIFO

Monolithic Memory, Inc. (MMI) offers the 5701/6701 microprocessor slice 4-bit ALU with sixteen 2-port registers, separate scratchpad, and a 1-bit shifter. It can address 512 words of microprogram, execute conditional branches, perform single-level subroutine nesting, and contains a loop counter. Additional support circuits were scheduled for early 1977. These and others must compete with Motorola's M10800 very fast 4-bit slice family of ECL LSI circuits. First available was the 4-bit ALU slice with shift capability and a single accumulator. It is a 48-pin device featuring many ALU functions (logic, binary, and BCD) but less storage than competing circuits. The CPU chip design is sliced parallel to the data flow to accomplish fully expandable capability. It can be extended both laterally to any bit length in increments of 4 bits and also vertically. It is a kind of ECL pipeline design that achieves very high data throughput. The slice contains a mask-programmable latch network, including a shift network, input/output bus controls, and associated interconnections. In all of the above architecture, flexibility and adaptability are traded for applications support. But, this is expected to grow rapidly. For example, not content with its progress and spurred on to meet and beat competition, Texas Instruments, Inc. announced a new family of microcomputer components with two new versions of a 4-bit slice. They are the SN54/74S481, that has a microinstruction cycle time of 100 nanoseconds for a maximum program throughput, including implementation of macroinstructions, and an upgraded SBP 0400 4-bit integrated-injection-logic (I^2L) slice that has a wide range of speed/power tradeoff and full military-temperature performance. In late 1976, both 4-bit slices were in prototype production. Other Schottky members of the family were program memory, control elements, and microcontrol memories. Thus the speed, low-cost, low-power competitive battles have barely begun, and more new technologies, new techniques, and new designs will continue to dominate the scene.

The battle of the one-board computers

The two minicomputer manufacturers noted in Chapter 5 (Microdata Inc. and Digital Equipment Corp.) started a major war among mini and micro makers and among the micro suppliers themselves. Obviously, existing software tools greatly ease and accelerate the writing of programs for microprocessor-based systems. Massive amounts and great varieties of software products, tested and field-proven, exist for all major minicomputers. Most microprocessor-based systems produced by the mini makers are compatible with mini mainframes and peripherals and use the same software. These firms' products therefore receive a very major advantage. Other advantages of one-board computers are that the supplier performs much of the testing, and the existing software is usually very cheap or even in the public domain. The LSI microcomputer from Digital Equipment Corp. (DEC) can handle most PDP-11 software and is delivered virtually bug-free. Boards are automatically exhaustively tested for logic faults, temperature-cycling, and so on. Users can save time by avoiding this testing in-house, and they do not require a capital investment in expensive testing equipment. The DEC LSI-11 microcomputer system is a 16-bit unit with 8 kilobytes of memory on an 8.5-by-10-inch board. It is an N-channel MOS CPU with a 4096 (4K)-word RAM, vectored automatic priority interrupt logic, real-time clock input, power failure/auto restart logic, and buffered parallel 16-bit I/O port. Thus, on one board the user has CPU, memory, I/O bus port, and so on that is micro in size and price, but mini in performance. It is expandable with any of 8 memory and I/O modules—RAM, PROM/ROM or core memory, serial and parallel I/O interfaces, DMA interface, bus foundation module (for custom interfaces), printed-circuit backplane/card guide assemblies—all interfaced to the LSI-11 bus. It is a member of the PDP-11 family (more than 20,000 in use), and users profit from that field experience, many software products and techniques, and so on. The summary follows:

A large, flexible instruction repertoire, including the 400-plus instructions of the basic PDP-11/40.

A simplified, application-oriented bus structure for maximum ease in handling I/O and memory operations.

Software and hardware training classes.

Complete documentation, including user's programming, and maintenance manuals, product and option bulletins, configuration and installation guides.

Off-the-shelf, plug-in expansion interfaces.

Off-the-shelf, plug-in core, RAM, and/or PROM/ROM expansion memories.

Resident firmware debugging techniques and ASCII console routines.

Operating system development on standard PDP-11/35, 11/40 or LSI-11.

The resources of the DECUS users' library for PDP-11 application programs.

These tools give users flexibility in developing hardware and software. Users get the LSI-11 in its final, dedicated environment to optimize their system design under actual operating conditions or take advantage of the power, flexibility, and high-level programming languages available with large PDP-11/40 computers to reduce the time to develop their operating system.

The LSI-11 is designated as the PDP-11/03 when it is packaged (power supplies, fans, box, and so on). And the family steps up to the PDP-11V03, 11/04, and 11/34 as minis. Thus, the upward compatibility ranges all the way to the most popular PDP-11s.

The challenge to the other mini makers and the micro manufacturers was formidable, especially because of the low prices—in quantities of 50, $653 for the LSI-11, and $1,697 for the PDP-11/03. (Digital has total volume in the $800 million annual sales range.)

The aggressive Data General Corp. took up the challenge with its microNOVA CPU m1601 16-bit family. The chip itself has all the NOVA minicomputer registers, internal data paths and computational elements, multifunction instruction sets, multiple addressing modes, and hardware stacking . . . plus items that formerly were NOVA options, such as multiply/divide, real-time clock, power fail/auto restart, and so on, all standard at no additional cost. The chip is tiny, measuring 225 mils by 244 mils. The chip system expands to the microNOVA on a board, making it a fully buffered microcomputer that comes with 2K or 4K words of RAM on a single 7½ by 9½ inch board. RAM can be added in either 4K or 8K increments, or PROM boards with up to 4K words. Also available are terminal interfaces, general purpose interfacing boards, card frame, power supply, and PROM burner. The system also is available as a fully packaged 4K-word MOS micro NOVAmini, in 9 and 18 slot versions into which users may place as many as 32K words of RAM or PROM, with plenty of room left for I/O. A program development system is available as well as dual diskette drives, terminals, and Data General's RDOS compatible Disk Operating System, or users may employ the NOVA 3 system with RDOS, one of the best available.

The next big mini manufacturer to plunge into the microprocessor foray under present discussion is General Automation, Inc., Anaheim, CA. The GA-16/110 is also a full-fledged 16-bit computer on a single plug-in board specifically designed for dedicated computer applications, such as remote data collection and control, terminals, and communications concentrators. It is fast, flexible, and low cost with full software support and dozens of off-the-shelf available I/O controllers. It has a repertoire of 120 basic instructions, memory expansion from 512 words to 64K words, sharing "load and go" and other software and I/O capability with all other General Automation Solution Series family members up to and including the GA/440 super mini with 2 mega-bytes of memory. The price in late 1976 in lots of 200 was $474 for a fully operational 512-word computer, to $1,692 for a complete 8K packaged system. More I/O capability can be added and more interactive controls, displays, and so on. The extensive software includes batch operating systems, foreground/background real-time operating systems, indexed file management systems, FORTRAN IV, COBOL, multi-user BASIC, macro assembler, and more as off-the-shelf software currently in the field meeting mini user requirements. The GA-16/220 combines a second board with the basic GA-16/110 microcomputer, adding more I/O ports, additional operator controls and displays, expanded remote monitor and control capability, expanded diagnostic capability, and optional system console interface and autoload capability.

Other mini manufacturers that offer micros are Interdata Inc., Oceanport, N.J., with its 6/16 and 5/16 computers that use the 2900 family of microprocessor chips from Advanced Micro Devices, Inc. (AMD), Sunnyvale, CA.; the Harris Corp. computer systems division, Fort Lauderdale, Fla., offers its Slash/6 system that uses the same AMD parts; Hughes Aircraft Co., Microelectronics Products division, Newport Beach, CA., offers a military computer, the UYK-30, that uses Intel's 3000 series of 2-bit slices. Of special note is Honeywell, Inc., Minneapolis, MI., which has its series 60 low-level minicomputers that use the 5700 family of 4-bit devices from Monolithic Memories, Inc., Sunnyvale, CA. The Honeywell effort is being increased considerably, as noted below, with its arrangements with the large-volume chip maker, General Instrument, Inc.

The General Instruments Corp. products
and the Honeywell design cooperation

The Honeywell Process Control Division and the General Instrument Corporation's Microelectronics Group developed the CP 1600 single-chip 16-bit microprocessor to handle 65K (65,536) words in any combination.

The architecture for the chip was developed and benchmarked by Honeywell. The detailed circuit design and manufacturing was performed by General Instrument Corp. It is a low-cost, high-performance device with a versatile and comprehensive instruction set, upward compatible to other coming units. Its primary design purpose is real-time and process control system applications. Its other applications range from desk calculators, peripheral controllers, production controllers, communication concentrators, POS (point of sale) terminals, and general purpose systems. It is fabricated with N-channel Ion-Implant GIANT II processes. The processor architecture utilizes eight 16-bit general purpose registers, all program accessible and usable as accumulators or address registers. The internal micro-control maintains one register as the Program Counter and as the Memory Stack Pointer, providing last in-first out storage in main memory. The general registers and the high-speed pipelined ALU and its Statis Register form the data processing logic for the CP 1600. The unit easily integrates into a versatile high throughput microcomputer system. The 16-bit word enables fast and efficient processing of numeric- or byte-oriented data. The 16-bit address permits accessing 65K words in any combination of program memory, data memory, or peripheral devices. This single Address Space concept permits full instruction power to operate on memory and peripheral devices.

Some of the CP 1600's general characteristics include:

Sixteen-bit, two's complement, fixed point binary arithmetic

Full sixteen-bit address and data exchange with external devices

Eight general purpose 16-bit registers

Capability for DMA channels for high speed data transfers

Sixteen external sense lines for simple digital state testing

Two interrupt request lines with priority resolution capability and self-identifying vectors

Simple bus structure.

It was also reported in late 1976 that General Instruments and Honeywell were ready to announce a "big brother" to the CP 1600, a new N-channel MOS unit designed with higher speed and a more powerful and easier to use instruction set with improved I/O interfacing.

NCR Corp. moves into microprocessor-based systems

NCR moved swiftly with large orders to Intel for 8080A chips to develop competing machines to IBM's desk-top 5100 terminal computer. One of its models is designed for use in schools and colleges but also is applicable to many small business functions. It is the NCR 7200 Model VI with

24K bytes of RAM, of which 4K bytes can be used for student programming. The unit features a 9-inch visual display screen, alphanumeric and numeric keyboards, and a magnetic-cassette tape recorder for storage and retrieval of programs and data. A second cassette recorder is available as an option. The system is programmed in a special version of NCR BASIC, designed for the microprocessing environment, i.e., learnable in a few hours, conversationally easy to enter, debug, and run programs with guidance from the system itself. The unit can accommodate a variety of off-the-shelf programs which help solve problems in a number of disciplines. Included are more than 100 preprogrammed applications in the NCR BASIC library, plus those developed by users of the system. Aids such as reference manuals, operator's handbooks, BASIC Library Catalog, and so on are supplied. The price in early 1977 was less than $7,000, including a one-time software license charge. The BASIC interpreter occupies 20K of the furnished 24K bytes of memory. The memory uses 4K-bit chips. The optional extra cassette recorder was priced at $1,275, both being housed in the same cabinet. The 100 included programs are gaming programs, math programs, such as tables of sines, cosines, linear regression and probability distributions, scientific programs, financial/statistical, investment, equipment amortization, frequency distributions, and so on. A companion system, the 8200 system with Scholars software for on-line operation, can drive up to 7 CRT terminals, but this system is priced above $50,000 with up to 128K bytes of memory, interactive multiprogramming operating systems, etc.

The original innovators of microprocessor systems, the semiconductor manufacturers, were ready for the invading minicomputer makers of single-board high performance micros. Heaviest competition came from the leader, Intel Corp., already reaping big returns with its most popular of all 8080A CPU chip, by bringing out several one-board models, most notably its SBC 80/10 and 80/20 models. Texas Instruments' 16-bit 990/4 based on its 9900 is a strong competitor, as is Zilog's Z-80, the Super-PACE, and several others. These and others are analyzed below, as are the popular, very low priced Fairchild F-8, National's SC-MP, Rockwell International units, and other big sellers now available.

National Semiconductor's Super-PACE and Texas Instruments' 9900 powerful chip sets

National's PACE is software-compatible with the old standby IMP-16 5-chip CPU set providing 16-bit instruction and address processing and offering a choice of either 8-bit or 16-bit data processing. The PACE, however, includes on its 40-pin chip, for instance, status and control registers, instruction branching, interrupt logic, and so on. The pioneering 6-chip PACE system included a ROM for program control and four 1,024-bit RAMs with on-chip latches for data storage. It becomes a powerful data processing terminal containing 16-kilobits of program storage and 4-kilobits of data RAM. Like other 16-bit machines, PACE can supply fast throughput for many designs, considerably faster than most 8-bit micros. Also, 16-bit systems can work with much shorter programs and thus use less memory. Significantly, if double-precision is required, 8-bit designs require multiple registers and more cost. Also, if 16-bit memory addresses and multiple accesses to memory are used to fetch multibyte instructions, 8-bit units are generally inefficient. System-matched components, together with external ROM and RAM, form the PACE 16-bit system; no TTL parts are needed for most operating systems.

Super-PACE, a recently offered 16-bit bipolar machine, is claimed by National to be more than fifteen times faster than the standard PACE described above. It is offered either mounted on a 8 1/2" by 11" card or as a chip set. Available with the CPU is a wide range of ROM memory cards, 8K and 16K RAM cards, and a card cage. Floppy disk hardware and a floppy-resident operating system for program development are also available, but not a real-time operating system. Various cross assemblers that will accept FORTRAN statements and convert them to assembly code via these prototyping systems are on the market. National also claims the Super-PACE has a 40% greater power base than a NOVA 1200, can handle tasks such as a fully signed 16 by 16 multiply in as few as 13 microseconds, and that its system is 2 to 2 1/2 times faster than the microNOVA. Super-PACE is designed to handle dedicated controller applications, data communications, laboratory equipment, and to serve as a controller element in intelligent terminals. In essence, it is an emulation of PACE built around a five-level priority, vectored interrupt structure. The super-PACE chip set was offered at a price below $85 in early 1977.

Texas Instruments, Inc. has sold minicomputers for years and is now also in the microcomputer business wholeheartedly, as previously noted.

Importance of the new peripheral and support chips

These and other main suppliers from the semiconductor industry are moving in several directions to improve speed, memory density, interfacing, ease of use, and to lower costs. One of the primary achievements relates to the great new capabilities and capacities of ROM/RAM memory (analyzed in chapter 7), and they are an integral component of the surprising new power and performance characteristics of all systems. Also of great importance is that, component manufacturers are adding peripheral chips to their various families that include a great many new circuit blocks needed in designing high-power systems. We have already noticed the competition between MOS and bipolar devices and now find variations and new technologies such as Fairchild's introduction to commercial units of Isoplanar versions of I^2L (thus, I^3L) proving to be twice as fast as N-MOS

4,096-bit dynamic designs but requiring a chip less than 14,000 mils square, so that it fits into the same 0.3 inch-wide dual in-line package (DIP) that's used in most high-density-board MOS designs. But, new MOS static designs are already offering competition to bipolar performance by having access times of under 100 nanoseconds (ns.) (without refresh clocking) and full TTL I/O compatibility. It is the use of peripheral chips with general-purpose 8-bit and 16-bit families that is extending the former into more high-capability systems and the latter into true minicomputer performance. These subsystems formerly required many TTL packages. Now at least a score of peripheral chips are out or on their way from Intel, Rockwell, and others. The most common are interface and communications controllers, interval timers, direct memory access chips, and interrupt controllers. Others (Intel's 70 series) include synchronous data-link controllers as well as controller chips for floppy disks, CRTs, keyboards, and so on. These are very impressive high-level subsystems requiring even more complexity than the CPU chips themselves, and they all plug into the main system bus and are thereby controlled by the signals from the CPU. They are treated by it as I/O and are in effect controlled directly by program data residing in RAM. A designer, therefore, need only increase his or her RAM capacity and add the appropriate instructions. No hardware interfacing or special program implementations are required. We have noted that the Texas Instruments 9900 chip, a 16-bit N-channel micro with peripheral chip support is powerful enough to replace minicomputers in many real-time control and data processing systems. National's Super-PACE and the other 16-bitters are other examples of big power but small chip systems. In the 8-bit group, the high-performance Z-80 from Zilog, Inc., Los Altos, CA., takes the Intel 8080 instruction repertoire and expands it to about 158, and RCA's 1802 single-chip version of its COSMAC C-MOS system moves with enhanced power, as does Intel's newest 8085 chip, promising to be five times faster (throughput) than the 8080. This is to be followed with a 16-bit brother, the 8016. Motorola is expected to upgrade its M6800 to a new chip with about ten times the performance of the original. And the very fast bipolar bit-slice machines are now in many commercial markets. We will next examine the enhancements of the Intel product line, an innovation leader that most others follow.

Intel Corporation again asserts its leadership

Intel offers the SBC 80/20, an 8-bit unit using its 8080A MOS chip to bring out a 6 3/4-by-12-inch board that holds 2 kilobytes of RAM and 4 kilobytes of ROM and has programmable I/O lines. By adding a package (power supply, front panel, and so on) to these units, they become one-board computers. The SBC 80/10 is pictured in Figure A.1, and the SBC 80/20 in Figure A.2. Schematics of these are not shown, but brief discus-

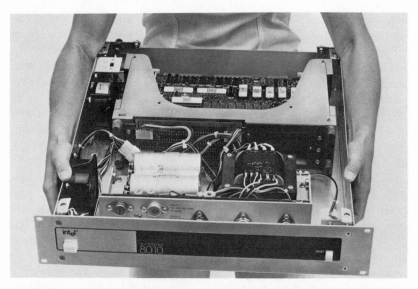

FIGURE A. 1 Intel's new System 80/10 is a completely packaged microcomputer system for OEM applications. Based on the popular SBC 80/10 Single Board Computer, the system also includes a power supply, cooling and OEM front panel. Up to three memory and I/O expansion boards can also be used in the system.

FIGURE A.2 SBC 80/20 System. Intel's second generation Single Board Computer is a complete computer system on a 6.75 by 12 inch printed circuit card. The card contains the central processor, system clock, read/write memory, non-volatile program memory, I/O ports, serial communications interface, multi-master bus arbitration logic, priority interrupt logic, two programmable timers, and expansion drivers. Multiple SBC 80/20's can be interconnected as a multi-processor or distributed processing system.

sions relating to their capabilities follow. The importance of these units cannot be underestimated, and a deep analysis is required. Intel has achieved some extraordinary densities on its basic microprocessor component groups and a very strong line of peripheral chips. It manufactures all the key components on the SBC 80 family and supports the line with development systems, emulators, resident, relocatable and linkable compilers, macro assemblers, text editors, operating systems, and utility programs (see chapter 6). INSITE is the Intel software index and technical user exchange with over 200 contributed programs (in mid-1976), in-depth training courses, an international staff of field application engineers, and so on.

Generally, before the popularity of the new single-board microcomputers, original equipment manufacturers purchased "unpackaged" minicomputer board systems or "start from scratch" components to develop their own dedicated systems. Some packaged minicomputers were sold to solve OEM control problems or to develop information processing systems. However, they were generally expensive, at least for specific purposes, or represented "overkill" by not matching task to machine. The absence of LSI components to implement parallel I/O, serial I/O and bus control functions, and a host of other peripheral, timing, and communication capabilities resulted in the use of relatively complex, expensive, and sometimes unreliable multi-board systems for the most basic OEM requirements. The "start from scratch" alternative, causing the OEM to design and manufacture his own system using effective, low-cost components, is extremely beneficial when those products are manufactured in very large quantities. In this instance the OEM can take advantage of the economies of scale associated with companies that build thousands and hundreds of thousands of systems and subsystems each year, such as those used in games, appliances, calculators, and so on. Although this is attractive for high-volume OEM firms, it is not the solution for low- and medium-volume users. The one-board microcomputers have come to the rescue of these many millions of customers. Like the other one-board complete computer manufacturers, Intel, on its single 6 3/4" x 12" printed circuit boards, offers the SBC 80s that contain all critical computer system functions—the CPU, read/write memory, read-only memory, parallel I/O, and so on, including interrupt networks and bus control functions. This eliminates, for the small and medium OEM, the need to design, develop, debug, and test the total system or subsystem. When volume increases, companies like Intel make the printed circuit board artwork available to them for a minimal license fee and offer attractive volume discounts on all LSI components. The SBC 80/20, the Computer Automation LSI-3/05, General Automation 16/110, Digital Equipment LSI-11, Data General microNOVA, and others all competed with prices well below $1,000 even in single quantity orders, and all offered very heavy discounts for 100 and up.

The Intel 8080A CPU

As previously noted, a computer system's processing and control functions are handled by the central processing unit (CPU). The Intel Single Board Computers use the 8-bit, N-Channel MOS 8080A CPU, which is fabricated on a single LSI chip. The three basic function units of the 8080A—or any CPU—are registers, an arithmetic/logic unit (ALU) and control circuitry.

The 8080A contains six 8-bit general purpose registers and an accumulator. The six registers may be individually addressed or addressed in pairs, providing both single and double precision operators. A 16-bit program counter, which is a special purpose register, allows the 8080A to address up to 65,536 bytes of memory. Another special purpose register is the 16-bit stack pointer which enables the CPU to address any portion of RAM memory as a last-in/first-out stack to store or retrieve the contents of the program counter, flags, the accumulator and any of the six general purpose registers. Use of the stack pointer in conjunction with RAM memory provides subroutine nesting capability which is bounded only by memory size.

The Arithmetic/Logic Unit (ALU) on the 8080A performs arithmetic, logical and shift/rotate operations. Arithmetic and logical instructions set and reset four testable flags, while a fifth flag provides binary coded decimal arithmetic capability. These flags are used to identify the resulting status (e.g., carry, zero, sign, parity) after an arithmetic, logical or shift/rotate operation is concluded. Subsequent program instructions can interrogate the flags and jump to a specified section of the program, depending on the condition of the flags.

Also, in brief review, we have noted that a computer system must have memory capacity for storing the system programs. Non-volatile program storage is usually a necessity, since it eliminates the need to continually reload the program each time the system is "powered up." The SBC 80 Single Board Computers contain sockets for up to 4K bytes of non-volatile read-only memory (ROM) for program storage. The OEM may select either Intel erasable and electrically reprogrammable 8708 EPROMs or masked 8308 ROMs.

Intel 8708 EPROMs provide the capability of altering system program contents during program development. EPROMs may be erased in a matter of minutes by ultraviolet light and reprogrammed. Then, when program development is completed, masked Intel 8308 ROMs may be substituted for volume production. Non-volatile memory may be added to the SBC 80 computers in 1K byte increments up to a total of 4K bytes.

Most computer systems have a requirement for read/write memory to store system data, variable parameters and subroutines that are subject to dynamic change. The SBC 80/20 provides this storage with 2K bytes of read/write (RAM) memory, and the SBC 80/10 provides 1K bytes of RAM memory storage—both using Intel static LSI random/access memories. Power for on-board RAM memory on the SBC 80/20 is provided on an auxiliary power bus, and memory protect logic is included, for battery back-up RAM requirements.

While most OEM applications are resolved with single one-board computers, Intel, like some of its competitors, has developed a variety of peripheral expansion boards designed to help increase memory, I/O requirements, and so on. Originally, six boards were available, two combination boards for read/write memory, ROM/EPROM memory and I/O, a 16K Read-Write memoryboard, and others. To further facilitate the loading, execution and debugging of programs, the System 80/10 includes a comprehensive System Monitor, which resides in two ROMs. Monitor commands include the ability to read and write hexadecimal paper tapes, execute predefined program segments, display and alter memory contents, and display and alter 8080A CPU register contents. Monitor commands and resulting information may be initiated and displayed on a CRT terminal or a teletypewriter. A full description of the SBC 80/10 is presented at this point. It is followed by notes related to the SBC 80/20 with emphasis on the versatility accomplished by adding many on-board Intel LSI peripheral circuits. For example, as is noted ahead, sixteen 80/20s can share system resources. The 80/20 has an eight-level interrupt system while the 80/10 has a single-level interrupt system. Other comparisons are noted later.

The SBC 80/10 is an efficient OEM computer system that uses LSI technology to provide all the essential computer elements—microprocessor, memory and programmable I/O—on one board. All the key components on the SBC 80/10 board are manufactured by Intel. These include the 8080A CPU and its support circuitry, 8111 static LSI RAMs, 8708 EPROMs (erasable and reprogrammable read-only memories), metal-masked 8308 ROMs, an 8251 USART (Universal Synchronous/Asynchronous Receiver/Transmitter) for serial communications interface, and Intel 8255s for parallel peripheral interfaces. Use of these volume-produced Intel LSI components on the SBC 80/10 boards (which are also produced in volume as standard, off-the-shelf computer subsystems) make possible the low unit cost of the Single Board Computers. While individual boards were available from Intel distributors at $495, SBC 80/10 prices reduced to $295 each in quantities of 100 in early 1976 (packaging extra).

Intel has used high-density LSI technology for all computer functions, including I/O and bus control. This eliminates the need for costly additional boards, normally required in computer subsystems to provide non-volatile memory capability, parallel I/O and serial I/O. Expansion is easily accomplished for those applications requiring additional memory or input-output capability. The majority of OEM applications will be solved with a single SBC 80/10 board, but five peripheral expansion boards and a standard modular backplane/card cage assembly are also available. Programs may be written using Intel's high-level language, PL/M®, or 8080 assembly language. In addition, the SBC 80/10 is fully supported with a comprehensive line of hardware and software development aids, which include the Intellec® MDS Microcomputer Development System and its unique ICE-80 In-Circuit Emulator.

Processing power of the SBC 80/10 is sufficient for most OEM products, including industrial process control systems, subsystems of large distributed intelligence control systems, numerically controlled machine tools, automated test instruments, data communications equipment, business machines, desk-top computers, and a variety of commercial equipment. To complement the popular 8080A CPU, which is an 8-bit N-Channel MOS device on a single LSI chip, the central processor subsystem on the SBC 80/10 includes a crystal-stabilized system clock, control buffers for the one-board computer's 16-bit three-state address bus and bi-directional 8-bit three-state data bus, and high-current drivers for expanding memory and I/O via the system bus.

For storing system data, the SBC 80/10 includes eight Intel 8111 static LSI random access (read/write) memory chips. The 8111s provide 1K bytes of RAM memory. Onboard sockets are provided for non-volatile memory of up to 4K bytes. During program development, Intel 8708 EPROMs will generally be selected by the OEM. The EPROMs may be erased by ultra-violet (UV) light in minutes and then reprogrammed. When the OEM system program is firm, masked Intel 8308 ROMs may be substituted for the EPROMs to further economize for high volume production runs. The EPROM or ROM memory may be added in 1K byte increments.

SBC 80/20 single-board micro

What surprised most of the industry and thousands of customers in late 1976 was the Intel 80/20 offering with what was then considered to be "massive" power and capability—and all for about $500 in quantities of 100. Multi-processing, eight-level vectored interrupt capabilities and a host of on-board peripheral chips, with many more now in development, set a target for all others to achieve. It is the "big brother" to the SBC 80/10 that is hard to beat. We have noted that while the 80/10 has a single-level interrupt that may originate from six sources, the 80/20 provides full programmable control for up to eight levels of vectored interrupt—originating from programmable parallel I/O with a USART—or it may be received via the system bus and I/O edge connector. On the 80/20, interrupts can also originate from either of the programmable interval timers. A closer look at some of the timer and bus capabilities is in order.

The Multi-master Bus Control logic provides bus arbitration which allows up to four SBC 80/20's to share the system bus in serial (daisy chain) fashion, and up to 16 SBC 80/20's or high speed controllers may share the system bus with the addition of an external priority network. The bus controller provides its own clock which is derived independently from the processor clock. The bus clock provides a timing reference for resolving bus contention among multiple bus requests. Controllers of different speeds may share resources on the same bus, and transfers via the bus proceed asynchronously. Thus, the transfer speed is dependent on the transmitting and receiving devices only. This design prevents slow master modules from being handicapped in their attempts to gain control of the bus, but does not restrict the speed at which faster modules can transfer data via the same bus. The most obvious applications for the master-slave capabilities of the bus are multi-processor configurations and high-speed Direct Memory Access (DMA) operations, but are by no means limited to these two.

The 8253 programmable interval timer. These timers/counters solve one of the most common problems encountered in OEM computer systems, the generation of accurate time intervals under software control. The usual problems associated with efficient monitoring of external asynchronous events and timing have been virtually eliminated. A fully programmable interval timer, the new 8253 consists of three independent BCD and binary 16-bit counters programmed as I/O peripheral ports. Each of the three counters in the 8253 is initialized via software with the mode and length of the timing desired. On command—the timer counts out the interval and interrupts the CPU when it has completed its task. By assigning interrupt levels to different counters, real time clocks are easily implemented. The third clock serves as the software-selectable baud rate generator. The Programmable Interval Timer is treated by the system software as an array of I/O ports—three serving as counters and a fourth used as a control register for programming. All operational modes are programmable by the systems software.

The 8259 programmable interrupt controller. Another on-board feature of the SBC 80/20 is the new Intel 8259 Programmable Interrupt Controller. This vectored interrupt capability is extremely useful when interrupt service speed is critical. The 8259 can handle up to eight levels of interrupt requests. Programmed by system software as an I/O peripheral, the 8259 allows the user to define interrupt priorities via the system software, so that the manner in which requests are processed by the controller can be configured to match OEM system requirements. The priority assignments and algorithms can be changed or reconfigured dynamically at any time during the main program. This allows the OEM to define his complete interrupt structure as required, based on the total system environment.

The battle of the high-performance
8-bit microcomputers

The several leading 16-bit micros from the minicomputer makers such as Digital Equipment Corporation, General Automation, Computer Automation, Data General, and others were competing with Texas Instruments' 9900, General Instruments' 1600, National Semiconductor's super-PACE, and others. But, the makers of 8-bit micros, a much larger group, were moving swiftly to fight against these more powerful units by upgrading their lower-cost systems with peripheral chips. As previously noted, Intel blasted out with many chip family varities, as did Texas Instruments, Inc., and others. Interface and communications controllers, interval timers, direct-memory access chips, interrupt controllers, and more offered customers unusual power and versatility with a handful of these very tiny but powerful and complex chips. As noted, even higher-level subsystem chips as data-link controllers and controllers for floppy disks, cathode-ray tubes, keyboards, and so on are included in the Intel 70 series, and many of these are becoming available from younger, smaller, independent firms as well. Rockwell International has equipped its PPS-8 microprocessor family with programmable peripheral and communications controllers on chips, and also is beginning to provide floppy-disk and synchronous data-link chips. Most plug into the main stream of the processing unit, the CPU treating them as I/O. Designers, as noted with the TI group, have great expansion opportunity with these peripherals by adding new RAMs and appropriate instructions without hardware interfacing.

One of the first very successful high-performance units is the Z-80 from Zilog, Inc., a subsidiary of EXXON, Inc. Their designers took the 8080 instruction repertoire and expanded it to about 158 instructions. This beat Intel to its own expected augmented 8-bit 8080. The higher performance 8085 chip became available in 1977 with a promised five times greater throughput. The Zilog company likes to call its single-chip N-channel LSI component set "third generation" (it's not) because of its enhanced features which do indeed lord over the older 8080 and other 8-bit sets. The 158 instructions that include the original 78 of the 8080A are included, using the same OP codes; thus, the Z-80 can execute 8080 or 8080A programs stored in existing ROMs. The new instructions include 4-, 8- and 16-bit operations, meaning less programming time, less program storage, and less end costs for many users. Memory-to-memory or memory-to-I/O block transfers, nine types of rotates and shifts, bit manipulation, eleven addressing modes, and a standard instruction speed of 1.6 microseconds are impressive. A quick look at some of the details and the special capabilities is in order here.

The major components in the Z-80 product line are an extremely high performance central processing unit (CPU), a programmable parallel input/output controller (PIO), a programmable serial input/output controller (SIO), a versatile counter timer circuit (CTC) and a high speed direct memory access controller (DMA). All of the Z-80 components utilize the industry standard N-channel silicon gate technology to provide the highest density at the lowest cost. Depletion load technology is also used to provide high performance with a single 5V power supply. The CPU, PIO, SIO and DMA are packaged in standard 40-pin DIPs; the CTC comes in a standard 28-pin DIP. All require only a single 5V power supply plus the Z-80 single-phase TTL level clock.

The Z-80 CPU is an extremely powerful, third generation CPU which incorporates a number of major features over the standard 8080A CPU while retaining total software compatibility. Major improvements include:

More than twice as many registers on the CPU chip, including two real index registers

Many more addressing modes

More than twice as many instructions

Three modes of extremely fast interrupt response

A separate non-maskable interrupt to a fixed location.

Another unique feature of the Z-80 CPU is its ability to generate all of the control signals for standard memory circuits. Static memories can be interfaced using only an external address decoder for chip selects. In addition the Z-80 CPU provides all of the refresh control for dynamic memories, and the Z-80 control bus timing signals are directly compatible with all widely used, standard speed, 18- and 22-pin 4K RAMs (16-pin 4K RAMs require only an external address multiplexer). Thus dynamic RAMs can be interfaced with virtually no additional external logic. This provides the user with the ability to easily interface to the lowest cost dynamic memories without reducing CPU operational speed. By selecting the best standard memory for a given application, the user can reduce his product manufacturing costs, and the product development expenses will also be much lower.

The Z-80 CPU is designed to be totally software compatible with the standard 8080A microprocessor to facilitate the user's transition to the Z-80. By using the Z-80 component set and the most economical memory for the particular application, the user need only re-layout any 8080 based design and use any existing software programs to obtain an immediate and very significant reduction in system hardware costs. A major advantage is that the same ROMs that are used in the 8080 system can be used in the Z-80 system. At a later date the software programs can be upgraded, taking advantage of the powerful Z-80 instruction set and the full capability of the Z-80 component set to obtain increased performance and even further cost reductions for memory components.

Parallel Input/Output (PIO). The Z-80 PIO circuit uses an advanced interrupt driven, program controlled I/O transfer technique for easy handling of virtually any peripheral with a parallel interface. Without other logic, the PIO can interface most line printers, paper tape readers or punches, card readers, keyboards, electronic typewriters and other similar devices. The PIO contains all of the interrupt control logic necessary for nested priority interrupt handling with very fast response time. Thus additional interrupt control circuits are not needed and servicing time is minimized. The parallel I/O can handle two high speed I/O ports, and it interrupts the CPU after each I/O transfer is complete. The PIO circuit includes two independent ports, each with eight I/O lines and two handshake lines which are programmed by the CPU to operate in one of four modes:

Byte output with interrupt driven handshake

Byte input with interrupt driven handshake

Bidirectional byte bus with interrupt driven handshake

Control mode wherein any bit can be programmed as an input or output.

A major feature of the PIO is its ability to generate an interrupt on any bit pattern at the I/O pins, thus eliminating the need for the processor to constantly test I/O lines for a particular peripheral status condition. This feature greatly enhanced the ability of the processor to easily handle peripherals, while also reducing software overhead.

Serial Input/Output (SIO). The SIO circuit is a programmable I/O device similar in concept to the PIO, except that it is designed to handle peripherals with a serial data interface such as floppy disks, CRTs and communication terminals. Each SIO circuit can handle a full duplex serial I/O channel. The device will handle data that is asynchronous with 5- to 8-bit characters and with 1-, 1 1/2- or 2- stop-bits. The SIO will handle 5- to 8-bit synchronous data including IBM BiSync and SDL communication channels. CRC generation and parity checking are also included.

Counter Timer Circuit (CTC). The CTC circuit contains four versatile clocks, each with its own nested priority interrupt control. All clocks have a minimum resolution of 8 μs and can generate interrupts in the range of 8 μs to 32 ms. The circuit may also be used in a mode in which it counts external events. Another major feature is that an interrupt can be programmed to occur after the occurrence of an external event. The four timing circuits greatly ease the CPU software handling requirements for many real-time control applications. For example, the CTC allows the implementation of a very low-cost TTY or CRT I/O port, and simple sector control of floppy disk subsystems.

Direct Memory Access Controller (DMA). The DMA circuit is provided for those applications in which data must be transferred directly into memory at a very high rate rather than going through the central processor unit. This circuit is not needed for most applications due to the fast interrupt response and block transfer capabilities of the Z-80 CPU. However, in large systems applications with many high speed peripherals, such as floppy disks, communications channels, etc., the DMA circuit can greatly improve system performance by totally controlling block transfers between I/O circuits and the system memory.

The DMA circuit contains all control for four I/O circuits including a block length counter and a memory address pointer. The circuits also have a ripple priority chain so that virtually any number of DMA channels can be implemented. The DMA circuit communicates directly between the I/O circuits and the system memory after obtaining a DMA acknowledge signal from the CPU. The Z-80 board is very small, 7.7 x 7.5 inches with a standard 122-pin edge connector. (The Z-80 system is second sourced by Mostek Corporation, a major chip-maker from Carrollton, Texas.)

Software support. The Z-80 component set is supported by as complete a software environment as is available today. Resident microcomputer software, time sharing programs, libraries and high-level languages are all combined to form a totally integrated system. The resident software package operates stand-alone on the Z-80 Development System and has no dependence on external hardware. The package primarily consists of an advanced macro assembler, text editor, disk operating system, file maintenance system and a real-time debugging procedure. The editor, assembler, and file maintenance system are stored on a diskette when they are not in use and can be loaded into the Z-80 System within one second. The System Executive is resident in ROM and automatically starts at power on. The Executive includes a program loader.

Software drivers are also provided to interface the System to floppy disks, CRT or printing terminals, electronic typewriters, line printers, and paper tape peripherals. Additional drivers will be developed and made available for other peripherals that will be interfaced to the System in the future.

Major features of the resident software package include:

macro assembler—Converts sequences of logical operations directly into the machine code. The macro assembler resides in RAM and is written in assembly language for efficiency.

text editor—Permits the user to enter and easily revise programs directly on the System. This character string oriented text editor resides in RAM in the basic system and the work space may be expanded up to 48K bytes. The editor also has the ability to select (and print out) only error statements to simplify and speed up the editing process.

disk file maintenance system—Calls all operating software including the assembler, editor and user's programs from storage diskettes into the

System by simple commands. The file maintenance system stores, organizes and retrieves information efficiently to permit manipulation of large files. Named files of varying lengths can be created, modified and moved easily and efficiently. Data can be transferred to and from any input or output device, and blocks of data in memory can be stored on diskettes and reloaded and executed with a single command.

real-time debugging package—Enables the user to implement Z-80 hardware and software in a particular environment expeditiously and efficiently. A full range of sophisticated software features automatically support the user's design evaluation process to significantly reduce system development time. This package allows the user to stop a program on a wide variety of system transactions and to display on a terminal a clear summary of previous system transactions that took place in real time before the breakpoint.

Offline software. The Z-80 software support package includes a Z-80 CPU simulator and macro cross assembler for use on either time share or in-house computer systems. The cross assembler creates machine language programs that can be read directly into the Zilog development system or loaded into any Z-80 based system. The offline software package includes utility routines such as auxiliary editors, paper tape and disk file loaders. Zilog also provides a translator that will convert simulator output results directly into text patterns that can be loaded into the most popular types of commercial testers.

Zilog is fully committed to the development of high-level languages specifically adapted for microcomputers. PL/Z is available for offline use to support the Z-80 products. Other languages including resident compilers were being developed in 1976 with BASIC being the second offering. These languages are built by the application of the latest techniques of metacompiling and structured programming, so that new languages and new hardware configurations can be easily adapted to existing facilities.

Pertinent here, and as we noted in chapter 6, the exploding hobbyist industry is spawning thousands of innovative fabricated microcomputer systems. One development which is most interesting at this point relates to a company called Ohio Scientific Instruments, Inc. Other items from some companies are covered later, but this one concerns the Zilog-80. The company offers a board which incorporates the new Zilog-80 and Intersil-6100 chips, plus one other microprocessor which the user may designate. The three processors then operate under the executive of a high-speed 6502 on a regular OSI CPU board, allowing use of any 8080, Z-80, PDP-8 or 6502 program, without program modifications.

"Incompatibilities" between program and system I/O and absolute memory references are corrected by the executive, eliminating the need for tedious and exacting rewrite and debugging. With the OSI-460Z CPU

Expander board, the user has options of either accepting the simplicity of picking up software from a wide variety of sources, or of programming, using any of the instructions on any of the CPUs in the system. A person could use a Z-80 instruction, then a PDP-8 instruction, then a 6502 instruction, for example. The third microprocessor on the 460-Z board can be one that hasn't been invented yet, thus protecting System-400 owners from having their machines made obsolete by the availability of new processors.

In October 1976 the company claimed, "While all other Z-80 boards have been priced at $250 or above, the OSI 460-Z board costs only $125, including Z-80 and 6100 processors and manual. Or just $88 without the PDP-8 emulator. That's less than half the single-piece price of the processors!"

Intel's MCS-85

The three key elements in Intel's MCS-85 microcomputer family are:

The 8085 central processor that replaces the 8080 central processing unit, the 8224 system clock generator, the 8228 system controller and in many cases, a serial input/output device.

The 8155, a 2,048-bit random-access memory with on-chip I/O and timer that replaces two 1,024-bit static RAMs, a programmable I/O unit (or three I/O parts), and, often, an interval timer/event counter.

The 16,384-bit 8355 read-only memory or 8755 ultraviolet-erasable programmable ROM with on-chip I/O, which replaces either a 16-K ROM, two to eight smaller ROMs, or two 2708 UV-erasable PROMs, and either two I/O ports or a programmable I/O unit.

In addition, the three power supplies required for the CPU and most ROMs and EPROMs are replaced by a single + 5-volt supply. And since each component sources up to 400 microamperes (versus only 100 μA for the 8080A), the system can be expanded without using TTL buffers.

National's low cost SC/MP (Scamp)

The low cost and wide versatility of microcomputers provide the real basis and reason why the number of possible applications is almost infinite. Originally, designers used them to replace springs, gears, levers, and so on. Next, they began to be number crunchers, controllers of timing, sequencing, testing, communicating, and data processing. For most of the low-cost controller types the basic problem is to sense an event and initiate a response. One of the simplest applications is to sense heat and flash a light or cause an alarm to sound. Hobbyists are especially fond of sense/response activities because of the ease of applying a microprocessor to these devices. Usually, a very simple 12- to 20-step program is all that is required integrated with a very elementary schematic. But, to keep the cost of a microcomputer system low—really low—problems arise regarding input/output devices and their costs. National has found at least one solution to this problem with its Keyboard Kit for SC/MP users.

Many ways have been found to communicate with microcomputers such as Teletype units, CRT terminals, paper tape readers and punched cards, and so on. The basic types have mostly been control panels with discrete switches and LED lights. One of the simplest, lowest cost, and most common is the hexadecimal keyboard/display combination, since the majority of 8-bit microprocessors use hexadecimal numbering instead of octal because octal does not divide evenly into 8 bits. National has been one of the leaders in calculator production and came up with a low-cost calculator type of terminal, one especially designed for its popular SC/MP microprocessor set. A brief description of the device is appropriate here because it is certain to be the forerunner of many similar devices. Calculators are excellent I/O devices.

National's Keyboard Kit gives SC/MP Kit users a low-cost input/output capability. The kit replaces the Teletype normally required by the SC/MP Kit and allows users to evaluate the SC/MP CPU and to develop a variety of application software. The heart of SC/MP Keyboard Kit is a ROM firmware package (512 bytes) called SCMPKB. The SCMPKB ROM replaces the "Kit Bug" ROM originally supplied with the SC/MP Kit and allows the effective use of the hexadecimal keyboard to execute programs, to examine or modify the contents of memory and the SC/MP registers, and to monitor program performance. There is a hole pattern for additional integrated circuits on the SC/MP Kit PC card. By following the simple instructions in the SC/MP Keyboard Kit users manual, one can add buffers, decoders, drivers, multiplexers, etc. They simply replace the Kit Bug ROM (supplied in the SC/MP Kit) with the new SCMPKB ROM, connect the preassembled Keyboard cable connector to the kit card, and are ready to go!

National's Keyboard Kit comes complete with manual, all required integrated circuits resistors, keyboard display cable connector assembly, wire wrap connectors, precut wires—even a hand-held wire wrap tool. This is a great kit for engineers and companies who don't have access to a Teletype. It is a low-cost teaching, learning, and developing tool for hobbyists, professors, students, and electronics entrepreneurs of all levels.

In essence, the "Kitbug" ROM of the SC/MP kit is replaced with new programmed ROM containing "SCMPKB" for keyboard and display routine.

An LCDS (Low Cost Development System) at $499 is now also available.

Upon initialization, all registers are saved in RAM and the SC/MP scans the keyboard and displays "dashes" in the address and data fields. This is called the wait loop. The SC/MP waits for a command—either a go or mem —any other key is ignored. If the go key is pushed, the last referenced address is displayed and the data field is set to "dashes." Only hex numbers or the term command will be accepted. A portion of an article entitled, "National's New Portable Terminal," is quoted below to explain some attributes of the unit.*

The cost of computer/microprocessing has been reduced considerably over the last few years due to the advancement in semiconductor technology. The cost of peripherals or input/output devices has not kept pace with the lower prices. As a result, applications have not been fully explored by the technologists of tomorrow who are working on a shoestring budget.

National Semiconductor has recognized this and, along with the real low cost SC/MP CPU, SC/MP Low Cost Development System, has introduced an SC/MP Keyboard Kit, which will give users of SC/MP Kit a teletype compatible capability simply with hex keyboard and display packaged in low cost calculator case.

The SC/MP Kit includes all the integrated circuits and discrete components required to build a small and complete microprocessor system. The key allows both the microprocessor veteran and the newcomer to build a viable aid to understanding the functions and capabilities of the SC/MP microprocessor. Using the kit, small programs can be developed and entered into memory using a Teletype (TM) (TTY) keyboard. The programs can be executed and their operation monitored by the Kitbug program. Thus, the kit provides a simple and effective way of familiarizing the user with the characteristics of the SC/MP instruction set.

In addition, the SC/MP kit is ideally suited for quickly implementing a variety of simple "real life" applications and demonstrations because no special integrated circuit support chips are needed. The input/output of SC/MP is directly TTL compatible with any memory TTL or MSI device used to implement the users system.

A basic microprocessor system consists of a central processing unit (CPU), Read only memory (ROM), Read/Write memory (RAM) and some peripheral. The peripheral device is used to communicate with the "real world." The SC/MP kit uses a teletype to perform the communications with the "real world." The kit takes advantage of the flag and the sense input to do the interfacing to the TTY. All timing is done in the software to produce the proper timing for the TTY by using the delay instruction which is a feature of SC/MP. The programmable delay instruction range can be programmed from 13 micro cycles to 131,593 micro cycles.

Although the teletype (TTY) is the most commonly used input/output device for the majority of computing systems, its cost often prohibits its use by many hobbyists, schools, universities and entrepreneurs. It is bulky and not portable. These factors led to the development of the Kitbug, a low cost teletype replacement for the SC/MP kit.

A calculator type keyboard was chosen to interface with the SC/MP kit because this type of peripheral is readily available and its cost is not prohibitive.

* Patel, Hash, Hordos, and Barney. *Interface Age*, October 1976, pp. 14–19.

FIGURE A.3.

The calculator type keyboard provides manual input commands to the SC/MP and a 6-digit hex display provides visual output. The keyboard for the SC/MP kit is arranged as an 8 x 4 matrix array, but only twenty of the possible thirty-two keys are used. The functions for each of twenty keys are defined as follows (see Figure A.3):

16 keys for hex command values 0 thru F

Abort Command

Memory Command

Go Command

Terminate Command

Power on/off switch is used for initializing SC/MP

Sixteen keys for hexadecimal number input values range from 0 thru F

Abort key: Terminate current command and return to wait loop

Mem key: Read next memory location. If pressed while in wait loop, will display last referenced address and the data at that address. If pressed while in mem mode, will increment memory address and display data at that address. If in go mode, will display error.

Go key: Display last referenced address. If term key is pushed execution will begin at this address. If a hex key is entered, this will be the address that is first executed when the term key is pushed.

Term key: This key is used to end the present mode of operations. If in the memory mode, the first push of the term key will terminate the input of address and allow input of data. The next push of the term key will write the data entered at the address specified. If in the go mode, pushing the term key will cause execution to begin at the specified address after the registers are restored.

The SC/MP, unlike the F-8, centralizes its computing capabilities in the CPU much like the 8080 and 6800 families; systems can thus be configured directly with standard memories. The CPU chip can use up to 4 kilobytes of memory without additional logic or interface packages. A 5-chip system can handle up to 65 kilobytes of RAM by using the CPU, a 2-chip bidirectional transceiver, address latch, and a buffer. SC/MP is a programmable 8-bit parallel processor with one 8-bit accumulator, four 16-bit pointer registers; one is dedicated to the function of the program counter, another is an 8-bit status register, and another is an 8-bit extension register. Timing circuits are on-chip and eliminate the need for external clocks. TTL compatibility allows easy interfacing with other system components. The system uses a unified bus system connecting the CPU, memory, and peripheral devices. The common data bus thus enables memory-reference instructions to reference peripheral devices, and the SC/MP architecture provides serial data and control streamlining under software control with built-in programmable delay. The bus configuration allows many SC/MPs to be tied to the bus for daisy-chain operation. When one CPU stops transmitting or receiving, it notifies the next SC/MP in line that it may take over.

The 1977 SC/MP II has all the features of the original but operates at twice the speed and dissipates less than 200 milliwatts of power—about 25% as much as the first SC/MP. Working on a single 5-volt power supply, the SC/MP II combines 8-bit data-handling with 16-bit addressing and has serial input/output ports for each interfacing. It also provides an on-chip clock, built-in flags and jump conditions, and three bus-access signals, as well as an interrupt structure that responds quickly to asynchronous events. A delay instruction simplifies timer operations, and there are 46 control-oriented instructions. The SC/MP II is completely pin- and software-compatible with the SC/MP with minor modifications to the crystal frequencies. The quantity price per unit in a plastic package is less than that of the first SC/MP price.

Competing microprocessors

The use of CMOS by both RCA in its 8-bit 1801 and 1802 families and Intersil (and Harris) in the 12-bit 6100 family has brought these companies fast, efficient, and flexible systems. The 6100 was introduced in 1975 and offered three advantages: static CMOS circuitry, 12-bit word lengths, and the use of a large existing base of software products. Because it can emulate the Digital Equipment PDP-8/E, the software developed by tens of thousands of users of this popular mini can often be used by owners of the 6100. It is a single-chip microprocessor that can operate at any speed between dc and the maximum operating frequency (8 MHz). Only one supply, from 4 V to 11 V, is required, and the on-chip oscillator needs only an external crystal. Full MIL temperature range performance and low power consumption are other advantages. All on-chip input/output buffers permit simple interfaces to all TTL logic families. The 40-pin package can access 32K bytes of external memory and can control 64 I/O ports. The 6100's timing and state control lines provide all external signals needed to communicate with memory and peripheral devices. Its 12-bit data word offers significant advantages because many systems use 10- or 12-bit analog-to-digital converters to prepare signals for digital storage. Users of 8-bit systems need at least two data words and some extra control circuitry and instructions to get the data. With the 6100, users require only one instruction and only one memory location to store data. Many direct support circuits are available including a CMOS universal asychronous receiver transmitter (UART), a parallel interface element (PIE), 256 x 4 field programmable CMOS PROMs, a 1024 x 12 mask-programmable ROM for program storage, and a wide selection of CMOS RAMs. A complete system can be built in a straightforward manner from a 6100 microprocessor, a ROM, a RAM, and a PIE.

RCA's CMOS 8-bit 1802 system also offers the full temperature range ($-55°C$ to $+125°C$), wide choice of power supply levels (from 3 V to 12 V), and low power consumption (50 mW for the CPU running at 6.4 MHz). CMOS also means excellent noise immunity, static operation so the clock can be stopped to facilitate debugging, and high speed (2.5 to 3.75 microseconds) instruction times (with 6.4 MHz clock). All this plus a flexible I/O interface with a clean architecture that's easy to learn and use is the theme of the RCA COSMAC family of 1800 systems, the 1802 being the fast singel-chip unit.

RCA is a major supplier of CMOS ICs with capacity in excess of six million units per month. A distinguishing characteristic of the 1802 CPU is its separate instruction and address registers. The address data is placed in an array of sixteen 16-bit scratch-pad registers, each of which can point to either data or program. Thus, the user is not forced to provide an address with each memory reference instruction. Also, individual scratch-pad registers, as address pointers, are selected by any one of three 4-bit registers, the contents of any address being directed to any one of three destinations. When using the scratch-pad memories as data pointers, they can be used to indicate a location in memory or as pointers to support a built-in DMA function. Small programs can be designed in hexadecimal machine code, and the COSMAC language (discussed in chapter 7) offers a convenient way to think out problems.

American microprocessor scoreboard—1976

Type no.	Technology	Address capacity (bytes)	Manufacturers *
4-bit			
4004	p-MOS	4-k	Intel
4040	p-MOS	4-k	Intel (National)
7150	n-MOS	—	ITT
PPS-4	p-MOS	4-k	Rockwell (National)
MM76	p-MOS	4-k	Rockwell
MM77	p-MOS	4-k	Rockwell
PPS-4/2	p-MOS	8-k	Rockwell
PPS-4/1	p-MOS	—	Rockwell
TMS-1000	p-MOS	8-k	Texas Instruments
8-bit			
EA 9002	n-MOS	65-k	Electronic Arrays
F-8	n-MOS	65-k	Fairchild (Mostek, Motorola)
8008-1	p-MOS	16-k	Intel
8080 A	n-MOS	65-k	Intel (AMD, TI, NEC, Siemens)
8048	n-MOS	2-k	Intel
* 8748	n-MOS	4-k	Intel
* 8041	—	—	Intel
* 8741	n-MOS	—	Intel
* 8078	—	—	Intel
* 8085	n-MOS	—	Intel
6502	n-MOS	65-k	MOS Technology—other versions are available with lower address capacity
5065	p-MOS	32-k	Mostek
6800	n-MOS	65-k	Motorola (AMI, Fairchild)
6802	n-MOS	—	Motorola
SCAMP	p-MOS	65-k	National
1801	C-MOS	65-k	RCA: 2-chip CPU
1802	C-MOS	65-k	RCA
PPS-8	p-MOS	32-k	Rockwell (National)
PPS-8/2	p-MOS	32-k	Rockwell
2650	n-MOS	32-k	Signetics
8X300	TTL-S	8-k	Signetics
300	TTL-S	8-k	Scientific Micro Systems
TMS9980	n-MOS	—	Texas Instruments
Z-80	n-MOS	65-k	Zilog (Mostek)
12-bit			
6100	C-MOS	4-k	Intersil (Harris)
TLCS-12	n-MOS	4-k	Toshiba
16-bit			
CP1600	n-MOS	65-k	General Instruments
* 8016	n-MOS	—	Intel

Type no.	Technology	Address capacity (bytes)	Manufacturers *
MCP-1600	n-MOS	65-k	Western Digital
IMP-16	p-MOS	65-k	National
PACE	p-MOS	65-k	National
PFL-1600A	n-MOS	65-k	PanaFacom
SBP9900	I²L	—	Texas Instruments
TMS-9900	n-MOS	65-k	Texas Instruments
Bit slices			
2901	TTL	65-k	Advanced Micro Devices (Motorola, Raytheon)
9400	TTL	65-k	Fairchild
3002	TTL	512	Intel (Signetics)
6701	TTL	65-k	Monolithic Memories
10800	ECL	65-k	Motorola
SRP0400	I²L	65-k	Texas Instruments
Others: (minicomputer manufacturers)			
LSI-11	MOS	4-k	Digital Equipment Corp.
LSI 3/05	TTL-5	—	Computer Automation, Inc.
M1601	MOS	4-k	Data General Corp.
GA-16/110	MOS	65-k	General Automation
6/16-5/16	MOS	65-k	Interdata, Inc.

* New processors announced in press interviews

The last three systems to be reviewed at this point are the Signetics Corp. 2650, the Electronic Arrays, Inc., EA9002, and the MOS Technology, Inc., 6502. All are families of N-channel 8-bit microprocessors. Like the RCA products, the 2650 is designed to be easy to use, operate, learn, and program—and easy to debug. It is totally static so users can single step the clock or turn it off, the clock being single-phased. The 2650 requires interface only to its single 5 V power supply for data bus buffering, and all I/O levels are TTL compatible and all outputs are three state. A teletype can be directly hooked up, for example, because the 2650 features serial I/O operations are separated from the data bus—a UART type; thus, for simple functions no separate chips are required. It has 75 instructions, seven general purpose registers on-chip, vectored rather than polled interrupt (for direct-in flexibility), and variable length instructions. Thus, 8-, 16-, and 24-bit instructions control program memory waste and require fewer chips and less RAM. The series of I/O devices are designed to make use of the 2650 simplicity and include Programmable Communications Interface (PCI),

Synchronous Data Link Control (SDLC) for IBM line protocol, Programmable Peripheral Interface (PPI), System Memory Interface (SMI), and Direct Memory Access (DMA), among others. Signetics is owned by Phillips and is also second sourced by Advanced Memory Systems.

The 40-pin MOS Technology 6502 can handle 65K bytes of memory and a growing number of real-time interrupts; for smaller systems, 28-pin 6503, 6504, and 6505 CPUs are available.

The EA9002 has several distinct characteristics that make it a popular system, perhaps because it has design emphasis as a controller. As such, it is relatively easy to understand, program, and interface. It connects directly to standard ROMs, PROMs, RAMs, I/Os, and MSI circuits from most manufacturers. In essence, it is a stand-alone digital process controller using an 8-bit parallel TTL-compatible bus with timing and control signals that allow users to bring the chip together with a great many bus-oriented devices of their own particular choosing. It is used primarily for small to medium data and process control applications, such as data collection terminals, "smart" instruments, peripheral controllers, POS terminals, elevator controls, video games, machine tool controls, electronic scales, bottling machines, and practically any application that is essentially a logic processing and control operation. It has a 512-bit RAM on the microprocessor chip (users of some control devices may not need external RAM), a single +5v supply, a single-phase clock, a 2-microsecond fetch and execution time all on a 28-pin package. The 9002 combines a 64-byte scratch-pad RAM with a push-pop subroutine stack, simplified timing, standard addressing techniques, and general-purpose registers. Users have available to them a seven-level subroutine stack for multiple interrupt capability and eight 12-bit general-purpose data registers, a 64-byte scratch-pad memory, an internal flag that allows the user to perform either 8-bit binary arithmetic or packed binary-coded decimal (BCD) arithmetic (dual 4-bit operands). And with built-in automatic decimal correction, the flag being set in either state. This is very useful for peripheral controllers where CRT displays need BCD data.

The EA9002 EASE 1001 microcontroller prototype board

Users may plug programmed PROMs or one 16K ROM into the EASE 1001 board to make an operational microcontroller, either for prototypes— or the final product in many cases. Preconnected on the board are an EA 9002 microprocessor (with an on-chip 512-bit RAM), a clock, I/O circuits, and sockets for eight 1702A 2K PROMs plus one EA 4600 16K ROM. The board interfaces directly to standard TTL circuits. Requires only +5v and −10v supplies.

Users thus have a breadboard for their system already complete except for programming. It can save weeks of development time and expenses.

Many use the EASE 1001 primarily for prototyping. The design is so generalized that it works well in a great variety of applications, and many low-volume users find it economical to incorporate this board into their final system.

If users load the board with eight 1702 erasable PROMs, they get 2048 8-bit bytes of program memory. Anytime they're ready, this memory can be replaced with a single economical EA 4600 mask-programmed ROM. There are two 8-bit TTL input ports (16 terminals) and three 8-bit TTL output ports with latches (24 terminals). The board has a crystal-controlled oscillator allowing an instruction execution time of either 3.2 or 6.4 μsecs for 1-byte instructions. The EA 1001 board helps realize the full potential of the EA 9002 microprocessor and helps build complete μP systems, quickly, simply and economically.

APPENDIX B

ANALYSIS OF DESIGN AND TESTING TOOLS:
SOFTWARE SUPPORT SYSTEMS

There are a very large number of applications of microprocessors where only a few identical systems need be produced, such as for specific machine control, and so on. This is in contrast to the very large number of totally identical systems required for, say, "intelligent" games, microwave ovens, etc. In the first group, the more unique systems, the non-recurring software costs generally are the largest costs, often larger than all other costs combined. It is for these systems that the power of the instruction set becomes a more important feature of the particular type or brand of microprocessor used. The usual rule is that the time it takes to produce an operational software program is inversely proportional to the power of the instruction set, i.e., generally microprocessors possessing larger instruction code words, 16 bits vs. 8 bits, for example, will have a more powerful language advantage. Larger words also means using fewer bits of ROM to store shorter programs, and good software support and memory designs for systems have become absolutely essential. The fundamental functions of software support systems are to check each instruction line of the source program for coding errors and to flag them; after correction of errors, to cause execution of the object program in the same manner that the microprocessor would originally execute. Such systems must be designed to also perform many other purposes. A great variety of "software design and test" systems are available, usually from the microprocessor vendor, but also from a wide range of independent equipment and instrument suppliers.

Also, a great many of these software test, design, and support systems can be accessed through remote computer terminals tied to national timesharing commercial networks and at a surprisingly wide range of costs, as noted below. Because millions of microprocessors had been sold from 1974 through 1976, large microprocessor software libraries began to be built very early in the product sales race by both middleman suppliers and manufacturers. As these libraries continue to grow (also through further offerings by users, clubs, schools, and others), the cost effective use of each specific microprocessor family grows in much the same manner but many times faster than mini and standard computer families grew. In order to realize the full potential of microprocessors, company executives, section managers, all engineers, and computer people must learn to express their ideas, designs, and applications desires in software or computer application language rather than in hardware or logic diagrams; they must also learn the hardware and software capabilities and compatibilities to depths commensurate with their responsibility levels. The rewards for becoming expert in microcontrol increase quickly for those who learn fast and well.

There is little need to discuss or analyze any particular vendor's software test or system design products in detail because most are structurally similar. Another reason is that many of the systems first offered in 1974 became obsolete within the first two years. Like other LSI products, the prices of microprocessor development systems (MDS) came crashing down while the utility and capabilities increased tenfold and more. The original development and design systems offered by most of the vendors were complete but expensive. They offered development software programs that included editors, simulators, monitors, assemblers, debuggers, compilers, and so on. They were originally available in three forms: (1) as combined with the manufacturer's microprocessor hardware, with software on punched cards, magnetic tape, or other media for entry on a user-owned large computer (cross-computer programs); (2) from time-sharing companies that were supplied the specific programs (above) by the vendors, and (3) later in special lower-cost user-purchased instruments in a growing variety. Some of these systems and pieces are analyzed below. A brief review of some of the chief software aids precedes the equipment discussion.

Assemblers are programs developed by vendors for customers to aid in writing user programs by permitting the use of mnemonic abbreviations rather than machine program numerics for instruction names. Assembly language is less error prone, makes reading easier, defines registers, locations, and so on. Inserting instructions and moving parts of programs around are easier. In effect, the assembler translates the mnemonic source programs to binary object programs, that is, the actual patterns of bits that are interpreted by the computer. Assemblers also often cause printing of program listings that display, side-by-side, the source and object versions while also giving error messages and other types of diagnostic information useful to programmers. Assemblers can make necessary changes automatically, allowing users to add comments at will.

Editors are programs to help users create their own programs and then to make changes in them such as adding, deleting characters, words, or lines. Also, most editors take the source program, written in assembly or high-level languages, such as BASIC, that are entered through the keyboard, tapes, and so on, and transfer such programs to a file in the computer's auxiliary memory, such as disks, cassettes, tapes, and so on.

Loaders transfer the object programs from an external medium, such as paper tape, to the microcomputer's RAM. Some also convert relocatable versions of the object program to a loadable version. Often the programmer can specify to the loader the program's new base address and the loader will modify all addresses accordingly in the object program or through linkage editing to establish the linkage between different object programs that made reference to one another. Some loaders are designed with editors to work interactively at the user terminal, taking old files and generating new, corrected ones.

Simulators are cross-computer programs that permit the user to test the object program by simulating the specific action of the microcomputer system when the actual circuitry is not available or to simulate an application on specific equipment before purchase. They generally provide specific types of diagnostic information unavailable with the various debugger programs and can warn of an overflow of a processor stack, an attempt by the program to write into a location in ROM, and so on. Most permit manipulation and display of simulated microcomputer memory and CPU registers, setting break points (stopping of processing), tracing, timing informations, counting the number of instructions or machine cycles executed from program start to stop, and so on. Simulator capabilities vary from vendor to vendor, but none can completely replace program testing on the microcomputer itself because simulation cannot cover everything, especially external environmental conditions.

Debuggers are programs that facilitate the testing of object programs and I/O devices by accepting commands from the user to perform such functions as displaying or printing out contents of memories and of registers of CPUs, modifying RAM, starting execution of object programs from specific memory locations, setting break points, and stopping execution of the program at specific memory locations or when specific conditions are met.

Many first users began by programming directly in machine language—the actual pattern of bits designed to be interpreted by the CPU—often using hexadecimal codes. But, they soon graduated to assembly language with mnemonics for easier code association. For assembly programming, many new hardware devices are now on the market. They include keyboards, CRTs, printers, mag tapes, and disks to help programmers edit programs, debug them, and so on. Macroinstruction use is particularly important, i.e., the use of a sequence of instructions, with the assembler substituting the sequence of instructions every time the programmer writes a statement with this name.

Requirements for a good assembler

Assemblers should be able to handle arithmetic and logic expressions and evaluate them; their formats should be easy to use, read, understand, and be easy for programmers to set up. Assemblers should be able to accept symbols for variable data quantities and addresses and translate data constants provided and in the form most meaningful to the programmer; they should be able to provide an alphabetical listing of symbols and their numerical values (in hex) and a sorted cross-reference listing for each symbol in the program; they should flag any source-program statements that violate its syntax rules, the error statement indicating the specific statement or field containing the error, and they should provide a macroinstruction facility in which variable parameters can be included in the macro statement and automatically inserted in proper places.

Design system software

For greater convenience in designing software, RCA offers the CDP 18S801 floppy disc system. It contains two disc drives, each capable of addressing up to 250K bytes of stored files on removable diskettes. The floppy disc system is delivered with an interface card which plugs directly into the system, and with an assembler, an editor, and basic utility programs. A higher-level operating system for the floppy disc was made available recently.

RCA offers three basic options for doing software development:

Stand-alone . . . using the resident assembler and editor on the system, or

In-house timeshare or minicomputer, or

GE Timeshare System.

In the latter two cases, users have a system of programs called the COSMAC Software Development Package (referred to here as CSDP). CSDP includes the COSMAC assembler and an interactive simulator. The assembler can be used with programs written in COSMAC Assembly Language, or alternatively, with the more powerful Level 2 COSMAC Assembly Language. Level 2 allows use of the basic Level 1 Assembly Language statements and, in addition, provides a higher-level capability of representing data movements and manipulations. The CSDP simulator is a form of "software oscilloscope." It gives all the capabilities of the CDS Monitor, and more. Users can start simulated execution anywhere, and stop it under a variety of preset conditions, including read or write access to specified memory locations or execution of specific instructions. Users can look at register and memory locations and modify them. They can dump the entire state of the simulated machine into a file for later recovery. As often as they want, they can load programs directly from simulated memory down into the system by a single command. And, best of all, they operate interactively at their terminal, using the mnemonics of assembly language program rather than their numeric equivalents. To put this powerful system up on an in-house computer, they buy from RCA a FORTRAN IV source program for CSDP, with an installation guide. The program is extremely "portable," and has been successfully installed on a wide variety of computers. Users need provide only a simple logic function routine and the basic I/O routines. To operate in GE Timeshare (the General Electric Information Services International Network), all users need is to open an account with GE and obtain a manual from RCA.

Typical development cycle for microprocessor software products

A typical development cycle diagram and assembler and simulator capabilities are shown and discussed below. To further clarify the differences between these more common software design and development aids, a summary table is provided below with very brief statements of Function, Input(s), Output(s), and Objective. The analysis of higher-level languages and more extensive use of PROM programmers is developed in chapter 7, Microcomputer Software. A typical example is the MAX-11 system.

The MAX-11 system features:

general-purpose minicomputer

dual floppy disk as system device

monitor with general-purpose file system

high-speed (300 bd) typewriter for control and listing

powerful macro assembler

versatile simulator

on-line prom programmer

interlocked prom eraser.

The MACRO-N family of assemblers. The MACRO-N family has a member for every commonly used microprocessor on the market today: MACRO-4 for the INTEL 4000 series, MACRO-80 for the INTEL 8000 series, MACRO-86 for the MOTOROLA 8600, etc.

All MACRO-N assemblers have the following features:

program and command string control of assembly functions

device and file name specification for input and output files

error listings on the command typewriter

alphabetized, formatted symbol table listing

conditional assembly directives

user-defined macros

user-defined system macro library

extensive listing control

symbolic cross-reference listing

off-page reference detection

page boundary control

Ascii string directives

local symbols

block repeats.

The SIMUL-4 family of simulators. Like the MACRO-N family, the SIMUL-N family has a separate member for each commonly used microprocessor.

SIMUL-N executes the object code produced by the corresponding MACRO-N assembler. Execution is done in the same way as the simulated microprocessor, except the SIMUL-N simulators can alter the contents of the simulated read-only memories, thereby allowing interactive debugging. In addition, various status and condition signals, inaccessable to the user in the microprocessor, are available for examination and alteration in the simulator.

All SIMUL-N simulators have the following features:

Examine/change every ROM/RAM location of the simulated microprocessor

Examine/change all simulated registers

Examine/change all simulated status/condition bits

Examine/change up to eight break points

Proceed N steps from the current simulated location

Proceed from the current simulated location in N step mode

Proceed from the current simulated location in N step Mode, typing the contents of any registers that have changed in the process

Reset all simulated registers and changeable data locations

Simulate interrupts on a command basis.

Housekeeping and systems programs summary

Systems program

Name	Function	Input(s)	Output(s)	Objective
Compiler	Translates high-level program to machine language program	High-level source program	Computer usable machine language object program	Compiler and/or object program may be stored on tape, cassette or loaded into memory
Assembler	Translates assembly language program to machine language program	Assembly language source program	Computer usable machine language object program	Machine (binary) object program may be stored on tape, cassette or loaded into memory
Interpreter	"Executes" high-level program	High-level source program (BASIC)	Designed problem solution from program usable by computer	Limited execution. Output is only what the source program produces. Interactively used.
Loader	Loads high-level or machine language programs	High-level or machine language object program(s)	Specific machine language programs ready to be executed	Loaded into memory for each specific operation
Text Editor	Creates, or edits, or adapts files and records	Source programs, data, etc.	Corrected listing or copies of files when requested	Interactive operation between user and output
Debug Program	Facilitates isolation of program bugs; causes signal	Special commands to debug program	Specific responses to commands, e.g. register contents, memory contents, etc.	Runs in conjunction with user's object program to be debugged
Operating System	Overall control of computer system and its resources as input/output, internal transfers	High-level or job control language or equivalent. All other inputs to computer	Automatic responses to commands. Log of system status, error messages to operator, etc.	I/O and communication. Schedules jobs, allocates memory, etc., to minimize need for operator

The Series M9200 PROM Duplicator and Programmer consists of an MM9200 Master Control Unit and the appropriate plug-in Personality Modules. It can be used as a stand alone PROM duplicator. Its single push-button operation makes it ideal as a production duplicator. It can also be used to receive data directly from the MAX-11 host PDP-11. As a peripheral programmer, it can be used to List, Program, Duplicate, and verify PROMs. It can use many Personality Modules available from major vendors. The Series MM9200 Master Control Unit includes Duplicate control key, two LED indicators, 9102-2 TTY control and TTY interface with mating cable, parallel interface connector, connectors for Personality Modules and is housed in an attaché case. (Courtesy of Aivex, Inc., 6 Preston Court, Bedford, Mass. 01730)

Another typical development cycle

First the source code is typed in using the editor. Changes to the source code may be made before the recursive assembly/correction cycles. After each assembly additional corrections to the source code are made, and the cycle repeated until all assembly errors are eliminated.

Simulation then begins, using the object code generated by the assembler. As simulation proceeds, changes to the object code may be made directly thru the simulator without reassembling the sources. When the user is satisfied that the program is operating properly, a final assembly is made incorporating all the changes inserted in the object code during the simulations.

The final object code is next used to program the PROMs, which are inserted in the programmer. The data is transferred directly from the system floppy disk to the programmer without the use of paper tapes.

Both the object code and the source code are usually saved off-line; the source code is saved for documentation purposes, and for future changes and developments; the object code is saved for programming additional PROMs.

The Aivex, Inc. MAX-11 is a complete, integrated, turn-key system for the development of microprocessor programs. With MAX-11 the techniques of large-scale computer systems are applied to microprocessor development. MAX-11 software is available in versions for all major microprocessor systems currently in use.

During 1975, Intel announced its Intellec Microcomputer Development System (MDS) with in-circuit emulation (ICE), as previously noted. The Intellec's operation is typical of most systems. The designer can write, edit, and partially debug his program and, using in-circuit emulation, can run the program in his actual prototype hardware. The Intellec replaces the 8080A microprocessor in the prototype. Many development systems from other manufacturers have come out with in-circuit emulation. Motorola, for example, added the feature to its Exorciser, which is used to develop 6800-based systems, and called it USE, for user system evaluator. An independent, Millenium Information Systems Inc., Santa Clara, CA., designed the development system for 2650 microprocessor from Signetics Corp., Sunnyvale, CA. Then it announced its own version, calling it the Universal One, with two processors, master and slave. It can be used for any processor type for which Millenium has developed the slave unit, as noted below.

The simple modularity of the Z-80 Development System

We have previously noted that the Z-80 microprocessor from Zilog, Inc. and second sourced by Mostek was one of the fastest rising of the popular chip sets in late 1976 and early 1977. Zilog and Mostek both advertise the system as being "third generation" and one that dramatically increases system performance over the Intel 8080A while reducing total system costs. The claims made are that the Z-80 outperforms the 8080A by providing more than 50% additional processor throughput with 25% to 50% less program storage space by using the expanded Z-80 instruction set that includes all of the 78 instructions of the 8080A plus 80 additional instructions. Also, the system has 9 additional internal registers (including two 16-bit index registers) and special control circuitry for extremely fast interrupt servicing. The Z-80 CPU provides all refresh and timing signals to directly drive dynamic memories so that the Z-80 LSI components can interface to most standard 4K dynamic RAM with minimum external logic. The component set includes four general-purpose programmable I/O circuits containing all of the logic required to implement fast I/O transfers with minimal CPU overhead. All control signals are directly compatible with I/O and memory devices so that system control circuits are not required. External interrupt control and prioritization circuits are unnecessary since these are included in each Z-80 I/O circuit. And, often DMA circuits are not required due to the extremely fast interrupt response and powerful I/O block transfer capability of the CPU.

The Z-80 Development System is a turn-key unit designed to support all activities associated with the creation of microprocessor hardware and software. The system includes two floppy disks with a sophisticated file maintenance system. With this capability, the user can quickly retrieve, manipulate and store large files of data to minimize software development time. The system also includes an advanced real-time debug module that connects directly to the user's system, thus providing a simultaneous hardware and software debug capability. System features are:

Turn-key system including:

Z80-CPU with 4K bytes dedicated ROM memory

RS-232 or current-loop serial interface

16K bytes of read/write memory expandable to 60K bytes

Programmable hardware breakpoint module

Programmable real-time event storage module

In-circuit emulation bus to connect system to user's equipment

2 floppy disk drives and controller

Full software including:
    ROM based operating system
    ROM based debug package
    Editor
    Assembler
    File maintenance

Optional Universal Parallal I/O card for interface to printers, PROM programmers, etc.

The heart of the development system is the powerful Z-80 single-chip microprocessor which is ideally suited to the multitask operational requirements of a development system. A single Z80-CPU is shared between both the user's hardware (User Mode) and the System resident monitor (Monitor Mode). In the Monitor Mode the System performs as a stand-alone development tool allowing software programs to be entered into RAM memory, edited, assembled, filed on disk for future use and loaded for execution. This entire process is quickly performed through simple commands from the user's terminal. In the User Mode, the system memory and peripheral elements are dedicated to the user's own system. The system peripherals use I/O port numbers $E0_H$ through FF_H; these port numbers are reserved for the system. In User Mode, a Ram resident user's program is executed in real time.

The use of RAM memory for the program eliminates costly and time-consuming PROM programming in the early phases of software development. The in-circuit emulation bus allows the user to connect his own peripheral devices or memory to the system and use them in conjunction with the system elements. A major feature of the Z-80 is its powerful debug module. This module allows selected User Mode system transactions to be stored in real-time into a special memory. The user can also specify that various types of system transactions can suspend user operation and cause the system to reenter the Monitor Mode. A complete record of the 256 transactions that were recorded in the independent memory just prior to suspension can then be conveniently displayed on the system terminal or listed on a line printer. This ability to preserve real-time event sequences and then review selected events in detail, permits the user to accomplish product design and hardware/software debugging in the shortest time possible.

The National Semiconductor SC/MP
low cost development system

The popular "Scamp" system that offers its microprocessor chip for less than $10 (in quantity) also attempts to lead the pack with a very low cost development system. In late 1976 it had one for less than $500. Its low cost development system (LCDS) is not a kit or an evaluation tool, but is instead a fully assembled and tested system with all the features necessary for development and testing of SC/MP hardware and software designs for a very broad range of applications. Software debug is easy because the system offers a built-in keyboard and display, and expansion is easy with a wide range of standard application cards including readymade RAM and ROM/PROM cards. Some other features of the system follow.

LCDS features easy interfacing and expansion. Four prewired edge connectors, for example, provide a plug-in interface for SC/MP family cards, and also let users interconnect additional SC/MP applications hardware. (There's room for a fifth connector, too, if users wish to add it.) They can also add a flat cable connector for coupling the LCDS to an external card cage. Built-in control and monitor functions permit transfer of control between the LCDS resident firmware—subroutines that let users enter software debug commands via the control and display panel, or an optional Teletype®—and their own application programs.

Expansion is easy because of the cards offered for use with the LCDS. The $2K \times 8$ read/write memory and $4K \times 8$ ROM/PROM cards, for example, provide additional memory: users plug them into the card bus. The minimum LCDS comprises a SC/MP CPU card, scratchpad memory, ROM-based firmware, and control logic. Also included are a 16-key dual-function hexadecimal keyboard, all necessary function keys and control switches, and a six-digit hexadecimal display. With the basic LCDS configuration alone, users can examine and alter the SC/MP registers and memory locations, run SC/MP programs in continuous or single instruction mode, and operate with an optional Teletype using SC/MP debug.

Programmer's control and display panel provides the following software debug capabilities:

Display contents of SC/MP program counter, registers, and accumulator in hexadecimal format.

Alter contents of SC/MP program counter, registers and accumulator.

Display contents of any memory location in hexadecimal format.

Alter contents of any memory location.

Initiate execution of user-generated application program at any memory address.

Select single instruction or normal execution of user-generated application program.

Interrupt execution of user-generated application program at any point.

Teletype interface provides standard 20-milliampere interface for interconnection of optional Teletype. Expanded software debug capabilities associated with Teletype option include:

Print contents of SC/MP program counter, registers, and accumulator

Alter contents of SC/MP program counter, registers, and accumulator

Print contents of any single memory location or selected range of memory locations

Alter contents of any memory location or selected range of memory locations

Set a breakpoint halt in RAM for user-generated application program

Initiate execution of user-generated application program at any memory address

Save application program by punching selected memory range to paper tape

Load development system generated paper tape into memory

Load IMP-16 or FORTRAN Cross Assembler generated paper tape into memory.

The importance of microcomputer compilers

All microcomputer enthusiasts realize that proper software is vital to good systems. The advances in hardware capability and tremendous reductions in size and price have not yet been equalled with software "miracles." But, within a very short time the industry has made very commendable progress, at a rate about five times faster than the predecessor standard computer industry. Perhaps 1976 was the turnaround year because so many firms developed efficient compilers at low prices, and even those low prices were certain to fall fast. Many high-level-language compilers were introduced for versions of PL/1, BASIC, and FORTRAN. Such high-level languages can substantially ease programming, compared with the more detailed assembly-language statements. Intel's PL/M was the first language based on PL/1, and many others are now available. Motorola has its MPL for the 6800; Signetics has PLμS for the 2650; National Semiconductor Corp., Santa Clara, CA., has SMPL for the IMP-16, PACE, and other devices; Zilog Inc., Los Altos, CA., has PL/Z for the Z-80, and many independent software houses introduced compilers for the PL/1 derivatives.

Most of the compilers, however, are cross-compilers, which means that they must be run on a large computer. The big push was to develop computers that can be resident in the semiconductor firm's own microprocessor-development system. Intel recently announced PL/M as resident in the Intellec, and Motorola has installed a resident version of FORTRAN in the Exorciser.

Intel's first resident compiler
and modular programming system

The system, which is resident on the Intellec® Microcomputer Development System, provides the first comprehensive software package for design with a high-level language and resident compiler along with support software to automatically link program modules together to form an applications program. The system supports programming of Intel® 8080 microcomputers, SBC 80 Single Board Computer Systems, and other products based on the 8080A Central Processor Unit. The system represents a major

FIGURE B.1 PL/M goes resident—Intel's 8080 microcomputer system now has the first microcomputer-resident PL/M compiler. The compiler is part of a modular programming system added to the resident software of the Intellec ® Microcomputer Development System, shown here.

advance in microcomputer programming efficiency, flexibility, and reliability. It is comparable to the software library systems sometimes used to prepare applications programs for larger computers. However, it runs entirely on the Intellec Microcomputer Development System, whose central processor is an Intel 8080A.

The system consists of two software packages: an advanced version of the PLM-80 Compiler for the 8080A, and ISIS-II, a new Diskette Operating System. PL/M, originated by Intel in 1973, is now the industry standard high-level programming language for many microcomputers. ISIS-II is a new version of the Intel Systems Implementation Supervisor first released in 1975. Intel introduced the system at the Western Electronics Show and Convention, Sept. 1976. The two packages are supplied on diskettes. ISIS-II is included with the diskette system hardware.

The new PL/M Compiler fully supports modular software design by generating linkable and relocatable object code modules. These modules can be automatically joined to each other, or with object code modules produced by a new relocating Macro Assembler contained in the ISIS-II package. Previous PL/M compilers lacked this capability, making the new high-level language a significant software product. In addition, the previous 8080A PL/M compiler was a cross compiler, written in FORTRAN to run on other large computers such as the IBM 360 or 370. The new compiler runs right on the 8080A itself. The PL/M language is widely used because it typically reduces by 50–80 percent the time and cost required to program microcomputer software over the time required for programming in assembly language. The Intellec resident compiler provides additional cost savings because the designer no longer needs access to a large computer system or expensive timesharing system. The compiler also provides microcomputer designers access to a tried and proven software design technique, modular programming, not heretofore available on microcomputers. That is, it will facilitate the independent development of program modules by different software designers. The designers can use either PL/M or the 8080 system's assembly language for the individual modules.

Previously, microprocessor designers had to develop large monolithic (non-modular) programs, or merge programs at the source language level, or link object code manually. All three techniques are very time-consuming compared with the automatic linking methods provided by the new system. As programs became more complex, these techniques provided generally unreliable programs which were difficult to document and enhance. In addition, the compiler has several other major features. It allows the programmer to define data structures and also gives him access to absolute addresses. The user can request the compiler to generate reentrant code for any procedure. The compiler will also produce a cross-reference listing on request and optionally print an "innerlist" of generated assembly language after each PL/M statement. The simulators usually used with cross compilers are no longer required. They are replaced by the Intellec system's ICE-80™ In-Circuit Emulator module, a powerful debugging tool which allows software to be debugged right in the user's prototype system. In addition, with the ICE-80™ the designer can debug at a high level, referencing PL/M variable names and PL/M statements by line number during the debugging process.

New diskette operating system

ISIS-II includes all other subsystems required for modular programming. These are a new Macro Assembler, Linker, Locater, and Library Manager. ISIS-II also contains a Text Editor with string search, substitution, insertion, and deletion commands. In addition, it provides access to the System Monitor, which contains diagnostic aids and drives all peripherals. The Macro Assembler differs from previous 8080 Macro Assemblers primarily in its ability to generate linkable and relocatable code. The designer uses inter-module references similar to those used by the compiler. Also, the assembler provides full macro capability, expanded from the previous version. The new assembler will also produce a cross-reference listing. With the Library Manager, the system user can create and utilize a library of subroutines or other program modules prepared by the Compiler and Macro Assembler. These are stored in linkable and relocatable form on diskettes, and retrieved automatically by the linker when referenced by a program. The Linker uses the inter-module references to combine several object code modules into a single object module. After linking, the Locater is used to locate the program at a user specified memory address. Separate addresses can be specified for code, data, and stack. The program can then be executed by the Intellec system, or it can be used to operate prototype designs via an ICE-80 In-Circuit Emulator. The first method provides for execution in the resident 8080 system and the second allows the program to be checked out in conjunction with prototype hardware in the actual operating environment.

The new system's main benefits, compared with previous microcomputer programming systems, are:

Software design time can be drastically reduced and lowered in cost by using PL/M. Now that PL/M is resident on the Intellec instead of a cross compiler on a large computer or time-shared computer network, the cost reduction is even greater.

Designers can use different source languages for different modules with assurance that object code will merge properly and easily.

Proven modular programming techniques can be used with the knowledge that all program linking can be done automatically.

Field proven subroutines such as standard peripheral drivers and arithmetic packages can simply be retrieved from the library instead of being manually included in each application.

Software documentation can be substantially enhanced through the use of PL/M and the modular approach to software development greatly aids software maintenance and eases system enhancement.

Program reliability can be greatly improved, since the use of PL/M aids the designer in producing reliable software. In addition, the use of proven library routines also improves software reliability.

Microprocessor design and development system summary

The many types of new tools and techniques on hand and those coming to assist microcomputer designers and users are deeply appreciated by all in the industry and by the many thousands of hobbyists, small shop owners, tradesmen, and so on. These exercisers, trainers, prototypers, and software test and development systems greatly simplify and reduce the time and cost of the design and development tasks. Users can test their systems and software at computer stores, distributor outlets, etc. The pre-assembled prototype boards, the tutorial and training devices, and the low cost peripherals make for continuing rapid increases in the rate of expansion of new utilization of all microprocessor product advances. Printers, keyboards, and visual displays have now become integral components of practically all microcomputer systems so that users can enter programs in assembly or high-level languages, edit them, perform the assembly or compile and then run, debug, and apply the programs. File managers, easier interactive procedures, and so on are being developed rapidly due to the new low costs and convenience of cassettes, cartridges, floppy disks, and their operating systems. Every major semiconductor manufacturer that offers any type of microprocessor system now also offers development systems and tools and special hardware and software to train users to adapt these microcontrol devices to pragmatic utilization. Some of the leading systems, as we have found, are the Intellec from Intel, the Exorciser from Motorola, Formulator from Fairchild, and TWIN from Signetics. Others are Rockwell's Assemulator, the Millenium One, MCSIM from Scientific Micro Systems, and there are many more to be marketed. All have similar systems objectives, equipment design, and assistance software as assemblers, editors, compilers, debuggers, monitors, and so on. Differences relate to the types of peripherals that can be handled on the various systems and the sizes and types of storage capacities.

Designers and users can develop their systems by using these various development and design systems, or use their own in-house mini or standard computers, or use time-sharing services from the many service companies that now cater to micro users. Debugging and prototyping are made easier by the use of several of the many low cost, single-unit microprocessor analyzers. Not only are "universal" (any type of microprocessor) development systems becoming commonplace but electronic distributors, colleges, computer stores, manufacturer branch offices, and other outlets are offering training in the use of these popular development systems and devices either free or at very low cost.

In-circuit emulation, resident compilers, and assemblers are also becoming common, following the lead of Intel Corporation. With in-circuit emulation, designers can build and check prototype systems in stages and run software on whatever parts have been assembled, using the development system to substitute for the facilities not yet included in the prototype. As noted, the Intellec MDS first provides memory and I/O lines and when satisfied, the designer can switch over and use the actual hardware—and these devices come in either two-processor systems, as the Intellec and others, or one as the Exorcisor and Z-80 systems. The most popular are Motorola's USE (User System Evaluator) which is competing favorably with Intel's ICE. These are very practical.

These and other popular development systems are complete system microcomputers in themselves and can be used in a great many standard and even unusual applications. We have stressed PL/M, and have previously mentioned, BASIC, FORTRAN, and APL are becoming very popular and easy to use microprocessor system languages, and Texas Instruments and a few others have also added COBOL.

Some major development systems not fully covered in this book should also be examined by potential purchasers or users. They include Ramtek's MM80, for the Intel 8080 families, Rockwell's PPS-MP Assemulator that executes many debugging commands from a front-panel hexadecimal keyboard and instruction keys, The Tranti Systems, Inc. μScope that is an integral desk-top unit containing an alphabetic keyboard, a 10-key pad, control keys, a CRT, an alpha printer, mag tape cartridge, etc. In this system, the software essentially assembles the program as it is entered, rather than in a later off-line pass-through. The Microkit-8/16 from Microkit, Inc. is also an important development system based on the 6800 and 8080 microprocessors. It includes in-circuit emulation, has a CRT, keyboard, two 2,000-bit-per-second cassette tape units, an editor that can run at 20,000 characters-per-second I/O rate, and so on. As time passes and more and more schools, businesses, professionals, and other potential users of microprocessor systems discover how quickly they can develop not only their systems but also their proficiency and propensity to absorb more and more microcomputer know-how, the society in which we live will change relatively abruptly and hopefully for the betterment of human relations between all peoples as these systems assist in providing more of the needs to more of the needy people.

DEFINITIONS INDEX

accumulator (AC) 109
ACIA (asynchronous communications interface adapter) 216
A/D analog-digital converter 162
address 110
addressing capacity, microprocessor 162
addressing modes, microprocessor 295
address path, microprocessor 295
alarm systems, microprocessor 349
ALU (arithmetic-logic unit) 162
arithmetic registers, microprocessors 216
assembler 110
assembler advantages 216
assembler development systems 254
assembler error messages 296
assembler, hardware 296
assembly testing 296
asynchronous computer 110
automatic interrupt 110
automatic loader 110
auxiliary processor 110

background processing 67
background processing interrupt 111

backplane, microcomputer 162
batch processing 67
battery pack 254
BCD (binary coded decimal) 111
benchmark 254
bidirectional bus 111
bipolar 126
bipolar microcomputer 216
bipolar microprocessor slice, 4-bit 163
Boolean operator 163
bootstrap 111
branch 111
breadboard 254
breadboard, I/O interface 254
breadboard kit 255
bucket 296
buffer storage device 111
bug patches 111
bus 112
bus driver 216
bus priority structure 216
byte manipulation 112

card cage 255
channel 112
chassis assembly 255

checking, automatic 112
check problem 296
check register 297
chip 126
chip architecture 163
chip testing 255
chips, I/O 217
circuit, integrated (IC) 112
circuit, printed 112
clock 163
clock rate 217
CMOS 126
CMOS applications 217
CMOS logic 255
command 163
common programs 297
communications control device 112
compatibility 67
computer circuits 112
computer run 113
conditional jump 113
control circuits 163
controller 113
control panel 113
control read-only memory (CROM) 113
control section 163
control sequence 113
conversational language 113
core memory 113
counter 114
CPE (central processing element) 217
CPU chip 163
CPU chip circuit 164
crippled leapfrog test 297
CROM instruction set 164
cross assembler 255
CRT storage 114
cycle shift 114

data bus components 164
data paths and I/O capability 217
debugging, microprogrammed system 256
debug, microinstructions 256
debug program 256
debug program, assembly 256

diagnostic test 256
diagnostic trace routine 257
DIP (dual in-line package) 127, 164
direct memory access (DMA) 114
diskette operating systems 217
dumping 114
duplexed system 115
dynamic MOS circuits 218

EAROM (electrically alterable ROM) 257
ECL (emitter-coupled logic) advantages 257
ECL microprocessor 218
editor, microcomputer 297
EEROM programmer 257
EPROM erasure 257
error detecting code 257
evaluation module 258
executive control system 115
executive programs 115

feedback control action 115
feedback control loop 115
fetch instruction 115
fetch phase, microprogram 297
FIFO stack operation 115
firmware 115
flexibility 67
floppy disk systems 116
foreground 116
FPLA vs PROM 218

gate 164
general registers 164

handshaking 116
hangup 116
hardware priority interrupts 116
HASP 116
HELP program 116
Hertz 117
hexadecimal 117

housekeeping operation 117
hybrids 127

IC 127
ICE 258
index register 117
indirect address, microprocessor 297
industrial microcomputer 349
industrial microcomputer applications 349
industrial microcomputer, peripherals 349
initial program loading (IPL) 117
input-output bus 117
input-output channels, automatic 165
input-output module exorciser 258
input-output port 165
inserted subroutine 297
instruction control unit 297
instruction cycles 297
instruction groups, microprocessor 298
instruction, microprocessor 298
instruction modification 298
instruction path, microprocessor 165
instruction register, current 218
instruction sets, microprocessor 298
instructions, microprogrammable 299
instructions, variable-length 299
instruction words, location 299
interface 117
interface debugging 258
interface, I/O 165
integrated circuits, basic procedures 165
Integrated Injection Logic (I²L) 218
interleaving 299
interpreter operation 299
interpreters 299
interpret program 300
interrupt capabilities 218
interrupt, external 259
interrupt priorities 166
interrupt types 166
interrupt vectoring 219
I/O interface software 300
I/O memory addresses 300

I/O section, microprocessor 166
IPL (initial program loader) 166
Isoplanar Oxide-Isolation 259
I²L 219
I²L advantages 258
I²L microprocessor 219

job control language JCL 118
JUMP INDEXED 351

kit assemblers 259
kit processor cards 259
kit reliability 259

link 300
linking loader 300
literal 300
load and go 118
loader, bootstrap (microprocessor) 166
loaders, microcomputer 166
logic 167
logic analyzers 260
logic card 260
logic tester, field 260
logic tester, production 260
look ahead 300
loop 118
LSI 127
LSI board tester 260
LSI board tester components 260
LSI board testing 301
LSI circuitry 118
LSI technologies 167

macroassembler 301
macroassembler, resident 301
macrocoding 301
macro cross assembler 261
macro facility 261
macroinstruction 118
macroinstruction design 301
mail box 167
major cycle 118

map 301
mask 219
masking 219
master control routine 167
master scheduler 167
master/slave configuration 167
memory board 168
memory-device access times 118
memory fill 119
memory map list 119
memory protect 119
memory, scratch pad 119
memory sharing, cache 119
memory, virtual (pointer) 119
Metal Oxide Semiconductor (MOS) 168
microcoding 301
microcomputer box 261
microcomputer control panel functions 219
microcomputer CPU 168
microcomputer data base system 168
microcomputer development peripherals 219
microcomputer development system advantages 220
microcomputer disk operating systems (DOS) 168
microcomputer prototyping system 220
microcomputer software 168
microcomputer word processing 350
microcontrolled modems 350
microcontrolled terminals 350
microcontroller 351
microcontroller applications 351
microcontroller control program 351
microcontroller design system 351
microprogramming 68
microprogramming techniques 302
microprogram principles 302
modem, communications 120
modularity 69
modular programming 69
monitor, operating system 302
monitor system, time-sharing 120
MOS (Metal Oxide Semiconductor) 169, 261
MOS microcomputer development systems 261

MSI (Medium Scale Integration) 127
multiprocessing 69, 120
multiprogramming executive 120
multitasking 120

nesting 302
nesting loop 302
NMOS 127
NMOS development 220
NMOS technology applications 262
nondestructive readout 169
nonvolatile PROM 220

OEM (original equipment manufacturer) 120
Oersted 121
one-step operation 262
on-line systems 69
operating console, microcomputer 169
operating system 302
operator interrupt 262
option boards 169
overlay 303
overlay tree 303

package, ceramic 262
package, plastic 262
page addressing 303
panel, removable 262
parity check 121
PC board diagnostic test systems 262
PC testing, personality board 262
peripheral interface adapter (PIA) configuration 263
peripheral interface adapter functions 169
personality cards 263
PLA (programmed logic array) 127, 169
PLA instruction fetch 303
PLA vs ROM 303
PL/M compiler language 303
PL/M Plus 303
plugboard 263
PMOS 127, 169, 263

pointer 303
polling 304
polling list 304
power supply kit 263
program documentation 69
PROM 127
PROM programmer 169
PROM programming 170
protocol 121
prototype printed circuit board kit 263
pseudocode 304
pushdown list 220
pushdown nesting 304

queue, automatic 304
queued telecommunications access
    method (QTAM) 121
queuing list 121
quoted string 304

rack 263
RALU (register, arithmetic, and logic
    unit) 220
RAM (Random Access Memory) 127,
    170
RAM alarm functions and options 352
RAM capability 170
RAM card systems 170
RAM operation 170
RAM testing (IC) 263
read-only memory programmer 220
read-only memory (ROM) programs
    170
real-time computing 70
real-time executive 121
real-time executive systems (RTE) 121
recursion 121
reenterable 305
register complement, microprocessor
    221
register, memory-address (MAR) 305
registers, general purpose 170
remote batch, off-line 121
report generator 305
report program generator 305

ROM (read only memory) 127, 171
ROM emulator 221
ROM loader 171
ROM simulator 221
ROM testing 264

satellite computer 122
schematic diagram, electrical 264
Schottky bipolar LSI microcomputer
    set 221
Schottky bipolar multimodel latch
    buffer 264
semantic error 305
semiconductor 122
semiconductor technologies 171
sensor-based computer 171
service routine 171
servomechanism 352
servo valve control, hydraulic 353
shift 172
shift instructions 305
silicon, processing 172
simulation 264
simulator, cross 305
simultaneity 70
slice architecture 172
slices, bipolar 172
smart terminal capabilities 122
software cross assembler 306
software development system, in-
    circuit emulator 306
software stack 306
SOS 127

three-D process 265
thumbwheel switches 265
time-shared computer utility 173
time sharing 70
time-sharing attributes 71
traffic control, microcomputer 353
transducer devices 353
transistor logic circuit families 221
transistor, MOSFET operation 173
transistor power supplies 265

translators 306
TTL 127

vector, interface 222
Venn diagrams 173
virtual machine techniques 307
virtual memory and virtual machines 72
virtual memory, user-coded 307
visual terminal types 122

VTAM (Vortex Telecommunications
   Method) 122

wire wrap 265
wire-wrap advantages 265
wire-wrap tool 265
word length 122
worst case design 266

SUBJECT INDEX

(ABA) American Bankers Association 323
accumulator 193
accumulator registers 227
A/D converter 230
A/D and D/A converters 252
address and data memory 193
address buffer 193
addressing 63
addressing, extended 63
addressing, indexed 63
addressing, indirect 63
address lines 193
address signals 203
Advanced Micro Devices, Inc. 382, 390
Advanced Research Projects Agency
    (ARPA) 101
ALGOL 45
Allen-Bradley Co. 333
alphanumeric keyboard 230
Altair models 237, 238
ALU 126, 193, 202, 203, 205, 224
American Microsystems, Inc. 130, 382
AMF, Inc. 323
APL 33, 91, 100, 282, 285
application notes 211
Applied Computing Technology, Inc.
    276

APT I,III 44, 277
A-register 60
arithmetic/logic unit
    see also ALU 205, 227, 291, 384, 387,
    397
artificial intelligence 152
ASCII (American Standard Code for
    Information Interchange) 105, 106,
    156, 330
ASCII code 345
ASCII coded data 239
ASR interface 152
ASR 33 Teletype 152
assembler 146, 273, 418
assembler programs 229
assembler requirements 420
assembler, resident 145
assembly languages 34, 82, 273
assembly run 48
assemulator 276, 432
asynchronous communication 328
asynchronous I/O 138
asynchronous receiver transmitter
    (UART) circuit 187
AUTOCODER 45
automated bank teller systems 325
automated clearinghouses (ACH) 323

automated highways 14
automated processing quality control 340
automated warehousing 338
automobile on-board processing systems 370
automotive quality control and production 336

backplane 234
Banknet 324
Bank of America 326
BASIC 18, 21, 33, 40, 44, 78, 91, 100, 129, 143, 151, 229, 246, 282, 284
BASIC compilers 236
BASIC interpreter 392
BASIC language 40, 390
basic logic unit (BLU) 188
baud 330
Baudot 330
BCD arithmetic 193
BCD data 414
benchmark 29
Bendix Corp. 333
bidirectional data bus 192
binary 26
binary-coded decimal (BCD) arithmetic 414
binary codes 279
bipolar 9, 225
bipolar family 198, 384
bipolar LSI 183
bipolar LSI circuits 185
bipolar microcomputer 244
bipolar processors 183
bipolar RAMs 183
bits 26
bit-slice devices 185
bit-slice microprocessors 186
bit-slice processors 186
bit-slice system 385
black box 90
bootstrap loader 275
bootstrap programming 366
branch 29
breadboarding 197
breakpoints 248

breaks 59
B register 139
bubble memories 182
buffers 26, 226
bugs 46
Bunker Ramo, Co. 318, 323
Burroughs Corp. 130, 175, 277
bus 126, 224
bus, DMA 214
business BASIC 21
business communications 339
business data processing 312
bus, I/O 52
bus switch, I/O 95
byte 29
byte processing 52

CAI 89, 277
calculators 376
calculators, preprogrammed 10
calculators, programmable 12
calculator type keyboard 408
calculator, wristwatch-size 161
CAM 310
Canadian Anik Satellite System 328
card readers 42
cartridge 366
cashless transactions 322
cassettes 17, 82
CATV head-end controllers 91
CCD-charge coupled devices 182, 184, 225
CCTV sets 340
centralized data processing 313
central processing unit: see CPU
central processor element: see CPE
ceramic package 380
channel cards 144
channel input 273
channel priorities 331
chassis 145
chip 5, 129
chip computers 363
chip memories 182
chip, readable 14
chip sets 144
chip, silicon-based 5

Chromerics, Inc. 161
CICS-customer information control
    system 89
Cincinnati Milacron Co. 333
circuits, testing and analysis 337
clocks 65, 134
clock and cycle time 211
clock generator 132
clock period 226
clock phases 384
clock, real-time 52
clock, relative time 142
closed circuit TV 94
CMOS 175, 185, 225
CMOS microprocessor 236
CMOS-on-SAPPHIRE processors 132
CMOS parts 386
CMOS RAMs 184
CMOS technology 186
CNC 341
COBOL 18, 21, 33, 44, 89, 285
COBOL compiler 48
coders 100
coding 45
COGO 277
communication network 97
communications 29
communications adapter 82
communications applications 338
compiler 28, 275
compiler, PL/M 275
compiler writers 100
complementary-MOS 183, 212 (See
    CMOS)
components 5
computer-aided design 102
computer-aided instruction (CAI) 77,
    102
computer-aided manufacturing (CAM)
    310
Computer Automation, Inc. 157, 401
computer calculators 158
computer clock 129
computers, education 13
computer development cycle 10
computers, energy conservation 16
computers, "home-built" 79
computer industrial processes 15

computer industry 9
computerized control 344
computerized credit verification 15
computers, medicine 14
computer numerical control (CNC) 104,
    333, 340, 368
computer-on-a-chip 156, 368
computer, one-chip 367
computer output microfilm (COM) sys-
    tems 43
computer, personalized 10
computer, satellite 95
computer system function 18
computer words 225
Comstar Corp. 332, 366
concentrators, communication 105
console, operator's 44
console, operator's video 44
control, data 187
Control Data Corp. (CDC) 207
control device 187
control intelligence 5
controllers 333
controller, data entry 98
control memory 228
control panel 51
control, process 188
control programs 212
control registers 54
control section 29
control signals 384
control unit 224
COSMAC assembly language 420
COSMAC CMOS 394
COSMAC language 411
COSMAC software development pack-
    age 420
CPE (Central Processing Element) 199,
    245, 383
CPU 5, 26, 28, 129, 131, 132, 224, 228
CPU card 143
CPU chip 192, 196
CPU 8-bit, parallel 206
CPU kit 239
CPU nucleus 38
CPU on-a-chip 149
CPU register 28
credit card 326

CROMs 179, 227
CROM triggers 199
cross assembler software 147
CRT 10, 106
CRT displays 17, 177, 226
CRT I/O port 403
cycle time 214

data bases 20
DATABUS 80, 82
data bus, 8-bit 193
data bus signals 203
data capture, local 98
data communications 313, 328
data concentrators 244
data control 36
data entry controller 98
data entry, direct 41
data entry facility 42
Data General Inc. 84, 323, 379, 389,
    396, 403
Datapoint Corporation 86, 268
Datapoint 2200 80
data preparation 36
Datashare 75, 84
Datashare III 85
data words 46, 61
DDS (direct digital service) 330
debut editors 361
debuggers 419
debugging 148, 433
debugging language 82
debugging tools 34
DEC (Digital Equipment Corp.) 186
DEC kit 230
decentralized computer systems 66
decision making 28
decision tables 46
DEC LSI-11 microcomputer system
    388
DEC PDP-11 371
DECUS (Digital Equipment Corp.
    User's Society) 287
DEMON 239
depletion load technology 402
design automation 189

design system software 420
development cycle 424
development systems 248
diagnostics 92
diagnostic messages 46
dictionaries 280
Digi-Log Microterm 106
Digi-Log Systems, Inc. 107, 364
Digital Computer Controls, Inc. 323
Digital Equipment Corp. 78, 102, 157,
    204, 230, 246, 314, 401
direct digital systems (DDS) 270
direct memory access (DMA) 58, 400
direct memory access controller (DMA)
    132, 402, 403
direct numerical control (DNC) 368
disk 130
disk drives 20
diskette drives 389
diskette operating system 238, 248,
    249, 430, 431
disks, floppy 20
disks, magnetic 148
disk memories 41
disk packs 38
disk storage 20
disk storage facility 43
dispersed business data processing
    312, 315
displays 197
display drivers 106
display systems 340
display terminal, video 17, 74
display terminal, TV 17, 74
distributable intelligence 348
distributed intelligence 362
distributed processing revolution 374
distributive information networks 181
DMA 225, 391
DMA bus 214
DMA circuit 405, 425
DMC 59
documentation 21, 35, 156, 211
documentation costs 282
document flow 20
DOS (Disk Operating System) 89
DP personnel 36
drivers 404

drum plotter 43
dual in-line package (DIP) 394

EAROMs 236
EASE 1001 415
EBCDIC 105, 239, 330
ECAP (Electronic Circuit Analysis
    Program) 285
ECL (Emitter-coupled logic) 185, 225,
    387
ECL slice 200, 384
editor 82, 414, 419
editor, resident 239
editor, text 146
EDP systems 159
EFTS 310, 322, 323
EIA standard 240
electronics, applications 16
Electronic Arrays, Inc. 413
electronic distributors 234
electronic funds transfer systems
    (EFTS) 310, 323
electronic systems, consumer 16
emulation 330
emulators 185, 186
ENIAC 361
entry stations 20
entry, source data 21
EPROMs 397, 398
erasable PROMs 415
error parity 64
exception reporting 356
Exorciser 286, 433
EXXON, Inc. 401

Fabri-tek Inc. 203
facsimile 346
Fairchild Camera and Instrument Co.
    136, 143, 157, 175, 190, 241, 376,
    382
Fairchild F-8 382, 383, 392
Fairchild Macrologic bipolar micro-
    processor 286
fatigue testing 337
F-8 system 241, 410
fields 50
field-programmable ROM 213

field programmable read only memory
    (PROM) 291
FIFO 226
file, indexed 39
file, linked sequential 38
file management 38, 177, 205
file managers 432
files, system 19
firmware 294, 360
firmware coding 381
fixed-word-length 51
flag 274
flagged errors 274
flip-flop 28, 226
floppy disks 17, 19, 20, 105, 404
floppy disk drive 43
floppy disk hardware 393
floppy disk system 420
flowchart 249
flowcharting 31
flowchart system 46
FOCAL 79
formulator 432
FORTRAN 18, 21, 33, 44, 78, 91, 100,
    143, 151, 282, 284, 285
FORTRAN assemblers 273
FORTRAN Compiler 48
FORTRAN cross assembler 206
FORTRAN E 89
FORTRAN IV 146, 147, 148, 246
FORTRAN programs 268, 274
Fortune 128

GA-16/110 microcomputer 379
GE (General Electric Co.) 101, 175,
    286, 333
General Automation, Inc. 84, 130, 135,
    157, 186, 390, 396, 401
General Instrument Corp. 323, 379,
    390
graphics 370
graphic answers 92
graphic displays 208
graphic display terminal 246
grid charts 46
grid network 94
Grosch's First Law 73

handshaking 226, 273, 280
hardware features 41
Harris Corp. 390
Hewlett-Packard, Inc. 84, 175, 360, 361, 376, 382
hexadecimal format 145, 239
hex numbers 408
high-level languages 92, 281
higher-level languages 269
Hitachi Ltd. (Japan) 382
hobbyists 382, 406
Honeywell, Inc. 175, 188, 390
Hughes Aircraft Co. 161, 390

IBM Corp. 8, 99, 100, 101, 131, 175, 239, 277, 314, 319, 323
IBM BiSync 403
IBM 5100 Terminal computer 391
IBM SHARE 287
IBM STS/MTS equipment 311
IBM System 360/370 76
IC 130
ICE 248, 277, 424
ICE-80 In-circuit Emulator 399
iCom, Inc. 369
IC packages 130
I²L 175, 225
I²L chips 183
I²L circuits 185
I²L system 384
imagers 13
IMP-16 379
IMP-16P 249
IMSAI BASIC 238
IMSAI 8080 computer 238
IMP-16 A/521D 199
IMS Associates, Inc. 238
In-circuit Emulator (ICE) 249, 424
industrial testing systems 336
information 29
information utilities 280, 330
input-output channels 106
input-output control system 29
input-output system 52, 57
instructions 46
instructions, computer 45
instruction cycle 226

instruction decoder control 193
instruction, macro 47
instruction register 193, 224
instruction repertoire 47
instruction segments 47
instruction storage formats 62
integrated circuits (ICs) 250
integrated circuit devices 182
integrated circuit suppliers 157
integrated circuitry 44
integrated injection logic (I²L) 183
integrated injection logic slice 387
Ingel Corp. 129, 130, 143, 145, 155, 157, 175, 180, 186, 191, 192, 193, 198, 231, 232, 241, 244, 248, 334, 365, 366, 367, 368, 369, 392, 394, 398, 429
Intel bipolar family 382
Intel bit slice systems 383
Intel 3000 series 390
Intel 8008 421
Intel 8080 197
Intel 4000 421
Intel 4004 380
Intel 4040 382
Intel 4004 chip 333
Intel 8080A chip family 237
Intel 8085 central processor 406
Intel MCS 406
Intel MCS-85 microcomputer family 407
Intel single board computers 397
Intellec MDS-Microcomputer Development System 399, 424, 433
intelligence, decentralized 9
intelligent factory 152
intelligent terminal 3, 97, 105, 150, 363
interactive procedures 432
interactive systems 274
Interdata Inc. 390
interfaces 214
interface cards 144
interface chips 228
interface devices 234
Interplex System I 23
interpreters 362
interrupt capability 213

interrupt, controlled 60
interrupt, disabled 138
interrupt program 60
interrupt, stack overflow/underflow 51
interrupts 60, 138
interrupts, priority 58
Intersil, Corp. 130
Intersil 6100 CMOS processor 382,
    405, 410
I/O 134
I/O board 229
I/O bus 129, 137, 144
I/O bus switch 244
I/O channels 225
I/O chips 196
I/O devices 212
I/O device control logic 190
I/O drivers 143
I/O edge connector 399
I/O facilities 126
I/O functions 98
I/O management 38
I/O operations 203, 212
I/O operations, programmed 138
I/O packages 156
I/O pins 403
I/O port 106, 225, 228, 384, 411
I/O programmed 58
I/O registers 383
I/O slots 232
I/O system 57, 137
Isoplanar versions I²L 393
ISIS-II 430

job management 38
JOLT 239
jump 29

keyboard 82
keypunch 26
key to disk direct data 42
key to disk system 98
KIM-1 240
kigbug ROM, SC/MP 407
kit components 234
kit, do it yourself program 108

kit operations diagram 235
kit selection criteria 229
kit size 231

language commonality 283
language, higher-order 47
language, high-level 21
languages, symbolic 45
large-scale integrated LSI technology
    128
large-scale integration LSI 5
laser scanners 319
lasers, microsystem-controlled 148
last-in/first-out stack 397
LCDS features 427
LCDS resident firmware 427
LED (light-emitting diode) 226
LED display 241
LED indicators 424
LED lights 407
LED readouts 239
library manager 431
LIFO 199, 226
LIFO stack 386
light pen 26
linear devices 183
line printers 42
liquid-crystal display 162
loaders 419
loader program 238
logic, hard-wired 88
low cost development system (LCDS)
    427
LSI 126, 132
LSI bipolar-processor technology 185
LSI chips 134, 184, 188, 205, 225, 362
LSI circuits 190
LSI CPU 194
LSI components 396
LSI device 194
LSI digital technology 182
LSI elements 199
LSI-11 bus 388
LSI-11 microcomputer 379, 389
LSI machine 228
LSI microprocessor 149

LSI processor 160, 183
LSI technology 398
LSI testers 248
LISP 44

machine cycles 194
machine language 47
machine operations 36
machine programs 48
machine-readable tags 316
MACROS 279
macro assembler 404, 431
macro assembly language 246
macroinstructions 228, 360
MACRO-N 422
management by objectives MBO 357
magnetic disk 82
magnetic tape 82
magnetic tape system 43
main memory 59, 97
management information system (MIS) 280
Martin Research Co. MIKE 3 247
master control 424
master ROM 294
MAX-11 421, 424
maxi computer 3
MCA 97
MCSIM 432
MDS 248
medium scale integrated ICS (MSI) 383
memories 183
memory cards 143
memory, intermediate storage 28
memory management 38
memory protect 38
memory stack pointer 391
metal oxide silicon (MOS) 315
micro 5, 129
micro chips 364
microcircuits 109
microcomputer advantages 6
microcomputer controller 1
microcomputer, development 10
microcomputer development systems (MDS) 247
microcomputerization 8

microcomputer kits 11, 223
microcomputer, time-sharing 246
microcomputer uses 7
Microdata Corporation 204, 388
Microdata 800/1600 computer 204
microelectronic chip 109
microfiche 14
micro front-ends 75
microinstruction sets 269
microkit hardware 236
microNova CPU 389
Micro-one 205
microperipherals 368, 369
microprocessor 5, 29, 105, 134
microprocessor, advent 4
microprocessor development systems 418
microprocessor, distinction 5
microprocessor software 211
microprocessor software products 421
microprocessor support 215
microprocessors, fuel consumption 17
microprocessors, home entertainment 17
microprocessors, NMOS 239
microprocessors, power stations 16
microprocessors 16-bit 182, 379
microprocessors, stacked 207
microprogram sequencer 386
microprograms 360
microprogrammable micros 357
microprogramming 44, 126, 207, 214, 228, 275, 360
microsystem chip 128
microsystems 8, 182
microterm 364
Millennium Information Systems 249, 425
minicomputer 51, 73
minicomputer development cycle 10
minicomputer front end 28
minicomputer systems 73
minimultiprocessing 237
minis, multiple 94
MIS-Management Information System 89
MITS 237, 238
mnemonics 34, 65

modem packages 328
money cards 15
monitor 420
monitor commands 398
monitor mode 426
Monolithic Memory, Inc. 387, 390
MOS capabilities, linear 182
MOS chip 144, 225
MOS circuits 131
MOSFET 225
MOS logic 9
MOS-LSI (Metal Oxide Semiconductor
    Large Scale Integration) 129
MOS/LSI calculator technology 377
MOS/LSI chip sets 143
MOS/LSI microcomputers 160
MOS/LSI microprocessors 271
MOS/LSI packages 190
MOS/LSI package costs 376
MOS/LSI programmable chips 133
MOS micros 141
MOS processing techniques 182
MOS PROMs 214
MOS Technology, Inc. 239, 413
Mostek, Inc. 175, 382, 404, 425
Motorola emitter-coupled logic
    (MECL) 384
Motorola Exorciser 248
Motorola, Inc. 130, 143, 157, 175, 180,
    195, 235, 394, 428
Motorola M6800 197, 235, 286, 322,
    382
Motorola 6800 chip family 237
Motorola n-channel 8-bit M6800 195
MPL 428
MP-12 204
multimicros 125, 144, 270
multimini 78
multimini processor (MMP) 78
multiplex 52
multiplexer 98
multiprocessing 29, 106, 207
multiprocessing advantages 242
multiprocessor communications adapt-
    ers 95, 97
multiprogramming 42, 207
multiprom 92
Mylar 162

National keyboard SC/MP kit 407
National Semiconductor, Inc. 130, 143,
    157, 158, 186, 199, 241, 249, 318,
    323, 379, 382, 428
National Semiconductor IMP-16 334
National Semiconductor Inc. PACE
    200, 392
National's SC/MP 392, 406, 427
National's Super PACE 401
n-channel designs 184
n-channel Ion Implant GIANT II pro-
    cess 391
n-channel micro 394
n-channel MOS 196, 212
n-channel MOS devices 192
n-channel MOS RAM 140
NCR Corp. 99, 100, 109, 277, 317, 318,
    323, 383, 391
NCR BASIC 392
NCR 770 325
NC tape editing 152
NEC microcomputers (Japan) 382
networks 12, 14
Nippon Electric Co. (NEC) 130, 206
NMOS 132, 185, 225
NMOS 8-bit processors 186, 192
NOVA (mN601) microprocessor 379
NUBLU 188, 382
number pad 82
numerical control 154

OCR (optical character recognition) 310
OEMs (original equipment manufac-
    turers) 131, 132, 151, 153, 369,
    396, 398
OEM building blocks 359
Ohio Scientific Instruments, Inc. 405
Olympia Werke AC (W. Germany) 205
offline software 405
on-line 19, 28
on-line interpreters 283
on-line productivity 19
operand 47, 65
operating systems (OS) 21, 29, 82, 88,
    207, 284
optical scanners 26, 99OSI-16OZ CPU
    405

output control 36
output devices 28

PACE 202, 249, 379, 393, 428
packet switching 327
page 226
page counter register 226
parallel input/output (PIO) 403
parallel I/O system 139
parallel interface element (PIE) 411
parity 64
parity, main memory 52
password 20
PC board 175, 236, 384
PC board production 337
PC board tester 250, 252
PC card 143, 144, 252, 367
PDP-11 424
peripheral equipment 92
peripheral interface adapters 234, 355
peripheral support chips 192
personal computing 237
personal data structures 280
PERT 42
phototypesetting 205
PIA 234, 236, 355
PIO 402, 403
PIP chip 202, 203
PLAs 227
plastic money 15
Plessey, Inc. 130
PL/M 192, 432
PL/M compiler 146, 430
PL/M language 248
PL/M plus 155
PL/M resident 429
PL/1 33, 147, 275, 428
pluggable media 294
PL/Z 405, 428
PMOS 185, 225
PMOS 4-bit slice 186
PMOS/LSI circuits 199
point of sale (POS) 104
point of sale advantages 319
point of sale systems 316
point of sale terminals 150, 177, 321
point of transaction 316

Popular Electronics 237
POS 322, 323, 391
Porta-verter terminal 368
power dissipation 184
power failure interrupt 51
power supplies 235
pre-processing function 133
preprocessors 103
preprogrammed computer 108
printed circuit cards 194
printed circuit (PC) boards 128
printers 82
problem-oriented languages 281
process computer 344
process-control industries 104
process-control microcomputers 331
processor 5, 26
processor, central 5, 41, 52
processor, 8-bit 185
processor operation 54
processor, single-chip 131
processors, 4-bit 185
processors, front-end 98
program assembly 48
program counter (PC) 227
program debugging 273
program, pluggable 180
program, source 48
program, utility 49
programmability 212
programmable calculators 6, 10, 12
programmable communications inter-
    face (PCI) 413
programmable integrated processor
    (PIP) 202
programmable interrupt controller 400
programmable interval timer 400
programmable LSI circuits 194
programmable peripheral interface
    (PPI) 414
programmed processor system 190
programmers 37
programming 33, 37, 293
programming, high-level 284
programming, low-level 281
programs applications 50
programs, packaged 100
Pro-Log Corp. 272

PROM 30, 74, 102, 135, 139, 145, 157, 179, 192, 215, 247, 250, 375, 384
PROM duplicator 424
PROM patch memory 142
PROM programmer kit 236
PROM programmers 289
PROM programming 231
PROM/ROM 388
prototyper 202
prototyping procedures 214
prototyping system 201, 433
pseudocodes 279
PRT, personal rapid transit 14
punched card 27
punched paper tape 27

RALU 199
RAM 4, 11, 105, 129, 130, 132, 134, 135, 145, 148, 160, 176, 179, 180, 182, 184, 192, 194, 198, 204, 213, 224, 227, 230, 234, 247, 250
Ramtek MM80 433
Raytheon, Inc. 186
RCA, Inc. 130, 143, 175, 186, 236, 413, 420
RCA CDP 1802 382
RCA COSMAC 411
RCA 8-bit 180, 410
reader 39
Read Only Memory (ROM) 52, 63
real-time clock 65
real-time processing 39, 284
register 55
registers, arithmetic 56
register, general 63
registers, processing 55
report generators 83
report program generators 49
reprogramming 348
resident compiler 429
Reticon camera 373
robot factory 11
Rockwell International, Inc. 130, 143, 157, 175
Rockwell PPS devices 380
Rockwell PPS-4 382
ROM 4, 11, 17, 30, 63, 99, 101, 105, 106, 129, 130, 132, 134, 160, 176, 179, 180, 182, 188, 194, 197, 198, 204, 224, 227, 229, 234, 250, 268, 367, 375
ROM chip set 206
ROM, customized 287
ROM/EPROM 398
ROM errors 142
ROM family 228
ROM, filed operable 236
ROM firmware 160, 407
ROM patch 140
ROM, piggyback 142
ROM/PROM 200
ROM/PROM cards 427
ROM/RAM 393, 422
ROM stacking 271
routines, conversion 50
routines, library 49
routines, utility 82
RPG 42, 49
RPG II 76
RS232 138
RTOS (Real-time Operating System) 89

satellite operation 44
satellite stations 344
SBC 80/10 394, 396, 398
SBC 80/20 394, 397, 400
scales, electronic 316
Scamp 427
scanners 317, 318
scanning systems 319
Scholars software 392
Schottky TTL 183, 225, 383
scientific data processing 312
SC/MP 241, 410
SC/MP applications 427
SC/MP CPU 407
SC/MP hardware 427
SC/MP keyboard kit 407
SC/MP Kit PC card 407
SC/MP low cost development system 408
SC/MP program counter 428
SC/MP registers 407
SC/MP II 410
Scope Data, Inc. 106

semiconductors 16
sensing 51
sensors 13
sensor system 344
serial input/output (SIO) 403
service companies 278
shared system resources 208
shop floor data control 336
shop management information system
    342
Siemens AC (W. Germany) 344, 382
Signetics, Inc. 130, 175, 202, 425
Signetics 2650 413
Signetics PIP 382
silicon 129
silicon on sapphire 212, 315
Sim One 12
simulating 197
simulator 12, 146, 419
SIMUL-N 422
single board computer 395
single-chip 16-bit microprocessors 200,
    376
single-chip processors 135
SIO 403
situation center 280
SLASH/6 system 390
slave computers 29
smart camera 373
smart CRT terminals 180
software 49
software, applications 42
software companies 278
software, custom 74, 236
software documentation 432
software packages 84
software, peripherals 39
software support, Z-80 404
software supports 343
software systems 160
software users groups 286
soft-wired control 341
SOS (Silicon on Sapphire-LSI) wafers
    129
SOS substrates 184
Southwest Technical Products Corp.
    (SwTPC) 238

Sperry Univac 319
spooler 39
SPS 45
stacked micros 208, 237, 359
stack register 55
standard logic 183
static CMOS-on Sapphire RAM 184
storage devices 28
stored-charge MOS 292
STRESS 277
strings 46
stripe, plastic card 326
STRUDL 277
subnonosecond ECL 386
subroutines 83
subsystems 39
supercomputers 3
Super-PACE 392, 393
supervisory programs 29
SWAP 287
Sweda International, Inc. 318, 323
SwTPC 6800 239
SYMBOL system 376
symbolic codes 279
symbolic coding 278
symbolic language 47
synchronous Data Link Control (SDLC)
    414
syntax 152
systems analysis 37
systems analyst 25, 31
system monitor 145

tabular languages 280
tape, punched 19
task management 38
Technitrol, Inc. 254
Tektronix, Inc. 175
telecommunications 34
telecommunication links 330
Teledyne Corp. 130, 186
Teletype 197, 239, 276, 408
Teletype interface board 247
teletypewriter 54
television, educational 13
terminals, advantages 20

terminal, desk-top 23
terminals, electronic cash 316
terminals, intelligent 12
terminal, interactive 39
terminal, keyboard 98
terminal, manager's 17
terminal, multilingual 365
terminal-oriented computer system 105
terminal, user 85
test programs 250
Texas Instruments, Inc. 130, 143, 175, 198, 379, 382, 393, 401
Texas Instruments' 16-bit 990/4 392
Texas Instruments' TMS 1000 380
text editing 177
text editors 152, 404
Thomson-CSF (France) 382
throughput 208
time-share 92
time-sharing network 290
TMS 1000 microprocessor 198
TMS 6011 universal asynchronous receiver/transmitter 198
Touchtone telephones 15
Trans Canada Dataroute Satellite System 324
transistor-transistor logic packages (TTL) 198, 225
Tranti Systems, Inc. 433
TTL buffers 406
TTL-compatible 141
TTL-compatible bus 414
TTL-compatible microcomputer 191
TTL I/O compatibility 394
TTL logic families 411·
TTL LSI processors 183
TTL packages 394
TTY keyboard 408
trace interrupts 51
TRW Systems, Inc. 84, 130, 150, 323, 333
turnkey approach 108
turnkey data-processing systems 107
TV-like display 82
TWIN 432
two-way TV 359

two-way TV systems 355
TWX 293

UARTs 330, 413
ultraviolet-erasable programmable ROM 406
United Computing Systems 192
UNIVAC 175, 323
universal asynchronous receivers and transmitters 330, 411
universal standard product code (UPC) 316
UPC symbol-printing equipment 317
UPC tags 319
USART (Universal Synchronous/Asynchronous Receiver/Transmitter) 398, 399
user interface 285
user libraries 156
users manuals 234
UV-erasable PROMs 406

value added networks (VANs) 327
vectored interrupt 229
videofax 346
video games 414
visual control systems 356
visual display units 41, 42
voice-transmitted terminal 370

wand reader 317
Wang applications and programs 287
Wang Laboratories, Inc. 84
Wang System 2200S 40
Western Digital, Inc. 130
Western Digital MCP 1600 379
word length requirements 213
word processing (WP) 229, 311, 345
word processing computer systems 102
word processors 7
words 29, 50
words, computer 50
WP system 345

Xerox Corp. 90, 175

Zilog, Inc. 401, 405, 425, 428
Zilog Z-80 392, 394, 401, 405

Z-80 394, 405, 428
Z-80 development system 425
Z-80 LSI components 425
Z-80 microprocessor 425
Z-80 systems 433